Praise for BORDERLANDS

"Supremely enjoyable ... umina-
tion. . . . Lundy— ly self-
deprecating—provide  ighout,
reminding us of what

..ver Sun

"The book is part travelogue and part lesson on the continent's history. But mostly, it's a fascinating look at U.S. national security post–9/11 and the human consequences."

The Georgia Straight

"Lundy employs a wry sense of humour that keeps the pages turning as the miles fly by. . . . In the borderlands between politics and memoir a fine history lesson exists, and Lundy is an excellent teacher."

Quill & Quire (starred review)

"Intrepid adventure traveller, daring investigative reporter and rigorous historian, Derek Lundy rode his motorcycle on 'the edge' in more than one way—the borders of the United States with Mexico and Canada, yes, but he also often rode the edge of survival, against wind, rain, heat, cold, gravel, mud and homicidal logging trucks. . . . *Borderlands* is entertaining, enlightening and important. I hope it will be widely read."

Neil Peart, author of *Ghost Rider* and *Roadshow*

"Informative, entertaining, disturbing. . . . [Derek Lundy is] one adventurous, fearless dude. . . . A masterpiece."

Oscar J. Martinez, author of *Troublesome Border*

ALSO BY DEREK LUNDY

Scott Turow: Meeting the Enemy

Godforsaken Sea: Racing the World's Most Dangerous Waters

The Way of a Ship: A Square-Rigger Voyage in the Last Days of Sail

The Bloody Red Hand: A Journey Through Truth, Myth and Terror in Northern Ireland

BORDERLANDS
RIDING THE EDGE OF AMERICA

DEREK LUNDY

VINTAGE CANADA

VINTAGE CANADA EDITION, 2011

Published in Canada by Vintage Canada, a division of Random House of Canada
Limited, Toronto, in 2011. Originally published in hardcover in Canada by Alfred
A. Knopf Canada, a division of Random House of Canada Limited, in 2010.
Distributed by Random House of Canada Limited.

Vintage Canada with colophon is a registered trademark.

www.randomhouse.ca

Pages 420 to 421 constitute a continuation of the copyright page.

LIBRARY AND ARCHIVES CANADA CATALOGUING IN PUBLICATION

Lundy, Derek
Borderlands : riding the edge of America / Derek Lundy.

Includes bibliographical references.

ISBN 978-0-307-39863-5

1. Lundy, Derek—Travel—North America. 2. United States—Boundaries—
Canada. 3. Canada—Boundaries—United States. 4. United States—Boundaries—
Mexico. 5. Mexico—Boundaries—United States. 6. Mexican-American Border
Region—Description and travel. 7. Motorcycle touring—North America. 8. North
America—Description and travel. I. Title.

GV1059.52.L85 2011   917.04'54   C2010-903824-X

Text and cover design by Jennifer Lum
Maps: Erin Cooper
Cover photograph: Serdar S. Unal

Printed and bound in the United States of America

2 4 6 8 9 7 5 3 1

In memory of Will Walker,
Mike Fitz-James, and Chris Burke

TABLE OF CONTENTS

AUTHOR'S NOTE

Miles or kilometres? A minor, but pesky, problem when one is writing about the United States and the metric countries Canada and Mexico. It seemed artificial to use metric distances in the U.S., and wrong to use miles anywhere else. Therefore, the description of distances in this book follows road map convention. I use miles and yards when I'm in the United States, and kilometres and metres when I'm in Mexico or Canada. Likewise with temperatures: I use Fahrenheit in the United States and Celsius in Canada and Mexico.

PROLOGUE

AND WE AMERICANS ARE THE PECULIAR,
CHOSEN PEOPLE . . . WE BEAR THE ARK OF THE
LIBERTIES OF THE WORLD.
—HERMAN MELVILLE, *White-Jacket*

ABOUT TWO WEEKS INTO MY MOTORCYCLE RIDE along the United States–Mexico border, fifty miles southeast of El Paso, I turn off Ranch Road 192 onto Ranch Road 34. I'm looking for the ruins of Fort Quitman, which my map shows as being at the end of the line. As always, I'm also looking for the Rio Grande—the River—the imperfect, ambiguous southern edge of this part of America. The road is paved, mostly flat and a little twisty, and I move fast through the gentle curves. It's good riding except for the usual treacherous patches of wind-blown sand along the edges of the tarmac, and the occasional wedge of sand and debris marking an intersecting arroyo. I've been riding for long enough now that I feel calm and sure in the saddle.

The road goes on and on, much farther than the map discloses. At first, there are a few scruffy ranch buildings and trailers, then nothing. And no traffic at all. The Chihuahuan desert surrounds me in all directions, a desert-sea stretching out towards the mountain-islands. After fifteen minutes or so, I notice a vehicle in my rear-view mirror. It's an SUV, and that makes me nervous. I'm moving fast, but it gains on me, and that makes me nervous too. Then I see that it has lights on top; it's the Border Patrol. They close to within fifty yards and hold there. In another ten minutes, I reach the long-promised end of the road. I turn the bike in a short circle and stop. The SUV halts twenty yards ahead of me, but the two agents don't move. I flip up my helmet's chin bar and visor, so they can see my face and read its innocence. I ride up and they look at me without expression, saying nothing. They are Hispanic. Two assault rifles nestle in a rack between their seats.

"Hi," I say in a sprightly manner—the harmless tourist. "My map says Fort Quitman's around here somewhere, but I can't find it."

"It's not down here," the driver says. "It's back near 192."

"I must have missed it," I say.

"It's only some adobe walls about a hundred yards off the road," he says. "It's hard to see from the road."

The other agent, the shotgun, says, "You shouldn't be on this road."

"Why not?"

"It's dangerous."

"Why? In what way?"

"Lots of illegal activity."

"What kind of illegal activity?" I ask.

"All kinds," says the driver.

"Drugs and illegals?"

"Both."

"I noticed there was no one around," I say.

"There was plenty around a few days ago," says the driver. "There was a firefight right over there."

He points towards the river. I can't see it, but it must be about two hundred yards away.

"Some SUVs came across with drugs. The sheriff's deputies got a tipoff and they stopped them, but the guys in the SUVs opened fire and headed back to the river. On the other side, there was guys dressed like Mexican army and they fired at the deputies. So there was a lot of shooting for a while."

"Shit," I say. "The Mexican army was shooting at American cops?"

"Yeah," says the shotgun agent. "The cartels pay 'em off. See over there." He points to the ground towards the river. I catch the gleam of shell casings scattered around on the sand among the mesquite and cactus.

"Well, I'll head back towards the fort," I say.

"We'll follow you," says the driver. "It's not safe here."

"How far isn't it safe?" I ask.

"All the way back to 192. This isn't a good road."

"Did you think I was carrying on any illegal activity?" I ask.

"Nah," says the shotgun. "We just thought you were lost."

I ride back towards the 192, with the SUV following me, until I see what I think is Fort Quitman's adobe walls. I pull over, and the SUV stops twenty-five yards behind me. I get off the bike and take a photograph. I intend walking over to the walls, but I'm very hot in my armoured riding gear, and, besides, I don't want to keep my escort waiting. I mount up and ride on. The Border Patrol stays on my tail until I get to the 192; I turn left towards Esperanza, but they turn right towards the freeway. A few minutes later, there's some traffic and a few irrigated fields. Beyond them, I see the line of tamarisks marking the course of the river, and, just beyond it, the sere mountains of Mexico.

Since 9/11, most Americans have come to believe that their country is a fortress under siege, and that its borders must become walls to keep out the barbarians. This renewal of the ancient idea that borders must be guarded and secured is at odds with the contemporary view that they are supposedly much less important because of trade agreements, prosperity and globalization.

Now, in a strange irony, it is the drug cartels and the desperate migrants from the south who treat the border as a modern construct: a permeable membrane that allows the passage of economically necessary goods and services. The U.S. government is using physical barriers, electronic listeners and watchers, and a saturated militarization by the Border Patrol and the National Guard, to turn the Mexican border into a twenty-first century Berlin Wall or Great Wall. It is a barrier—although a porous one at best—designed to keep at bay the poor, the desperate and the bad. At the same time, Americans watch their more tranquil, and certainly more open, northern border with apprehension. Muslims live in Canada (and not in Mexico). Perhaps that is where the next terror strike will come from.

You might say that, for Americans, the Mexican border represents a social and economic threat, in the form of illegal immigrants and drugs. However, in the current American view, the Canadian border is by far the more problematic. Canadian police have arrested putative "homegrown" Islamist terrorists there. If not for being a stupid, greenhorn terrorist, easily caught by a U.S. border guard, Ahmed Ressam, the "Millennium Bomber," would have crossed into the United States from Canada and may even have succeeded in his goal of blowing up the Los Angeles airport. If Mexico equals *indocumentados* and dope, Canada equals the unknown: the subway attack, the dirty bomb in the suitcase—terror and bloody murder, the continuing erosion of the safe isolation of the American heartland.

The United States has had violent or appropriative encounters with both Mexico and Canada. It went to war and seized (or bought cheap) half of Mexico's territory in the middle of the nineteenth century, turning two adjoining countries roughly equal in territory and population into asymmetrical ones. From then on, America was the superior state in every way—it had always been more stable, integrated, single-minded and aggressive. From one perspective, however, the movement of Hispanic migrants north might be seen as a kind of recon-quest—by demographic means—of Mexico's lost territory. Until the 1940s, Mexican school maps showed this huge area as "temporarily" in America. The United States invaded British North America in 1812, and threatened to do so again after the end of the Civil War in 1865, thus consolidating the idea of the confederation of the Canadian colonies of the British Empire as, among other things, a self-defence mea-sure. Canada became a country in 1867.

The residue of this violent history, and the current situation along the borders, forms the context of the three main border problems: drugs, illegal migrants and terrorism. The resulting tensions play out in the ill-defined, ambiguous zones along each line: the borderlands.

Borderlands anywhere are often like a third country, dis-tinct in many ways from the two countries the border defines. The borderlands are far from the centre, sometimes remote, and often disorderly and rebellious, operating according to their own ad hoc system of rules and conventions rather than those of the states to which they belong. "Heaven is high, and the Emperor is far away," goes the old Chinese saying.

This is certainly true of the U.S.-Mexico border. I believe it can only really be understood in these terms. The Canadian border may be a complicated and subtle exception to the typical borderlands scenario, and that, too, requires explanation. In fact, both borders have unique aspects: the Canadian is the longest undefended ("non-militarized" would be a better description) frontier in the world, although that's changing fast. In fact, it may already be a misnomer. It was also the only such border outside some form of economic or political union (Europe, for example). The Mexican is the only land border in the western hemisphere separating a very rich country from a poor one. Hence the flow north of desperate people. And it separates two very disparate societies and cultures: an Anglo-European from an Indian-mestizo-Spanish—although Hispanic movement across the border is diluting the distinction.

I come from "British" Northern Ireland whose border with the independent Republic of Ireland remains contentious, and was a cause of sectarian warfare until almost the end of the twentieth century. Borders have therefore fascinated me for a long time, and I wanted to see these North American borderlands for myself. I had many questions: What do the borders look like on the ground? What do the Americans who live in the borderlands think about the national boundaries and the changes overtaking them? Is it possible to secure thousands of miles of desert, mountain, forest, prairie? What are the risks for the United States along each line? Should Americans be afraid? If so, what should they be afraid of? What does their fear look, sound and smell like? What are its consequences for the subordinate nations lying to the north and south of America? What are the implications for the United States, for the idea it has held of its borders, and for the the old, flawed, weird, ever-living, contradictory dream of America itself: the exceptional nation, the new Jerusalem, the city upon a hill?

To find answers to these questions, I rode a motorcycle the length of the U.S.-Mexico border—from the beach at La Boca Chica on the Gulf of Mexico to the beach at San Ysidro on the Pacific Ocean, just south of San Diego. Later, I rode the Canadian border from Quoddy Head in Maine, on the Grand Manaan Channel of the Bay of Fundy, west to Cape Flattery, Washington, on the Pacific. My rule of engagement was to stick as closely as I could to the border on its U.S. side. Wherever possible, therefore, my route avoided freeways and main highways. I wound up mostly on the small county, farm and ranch roads, some paved, some not, that parallel the border, or dead-end at it. And I tried to look at every official border crossing point, even if it meant a lot of diversions from my east-to-west route. Often, I found myself at the unofficial, ad hoc, illegal border crossings where, it seemed, anything might happen.

I chose to travel by motorcycle for many reasons. First, because it's not travelling by car. On a bike, the rider is completely visible, unprotected from everything around him. The world intrudes on his space in an unstoppable deluge: people; sound, smells, weather (the rider is as exposed to wind, rain, heat and cold as a sailor on a small boat at sea); unheeding, and often threatening, traffic; hostility, ridicule, admiration. The experience of travel on a motorcycle is primitive, harsh, hard, raw—but the rider sees the country and its inhabitants with immediacy, and they see him the same way. It's an unavoidably intense interaction. The rider, necessarily vigilant and focused, learns things about his surroundings to which the passive, distracted occupant of a car remains oblivious.

Second, riding a motorcycle twenty thousand kilometres is inherently dangerous; it's an adventure. The rider experiences the normal perils of the road—any motorcycle ride in traffic is a combat mission—but faces the unique hazards of the borderlands, too. Merely getting from place to place is a tale in itself.

Third, a motorcyclist heading west is the old western motif revived: I was a lone rider, recapitulating the movement of the American frontier. The bike was my horse. In the south, I rode through what used to be Mexican country, Yuma and Apache country, across three thousand miles of desert-sea, and over the endless chains of mountain-islands. I camped at four thousand feet in the Animas Range—the mythic country of Cormac McCarthy's Border Trilogy. Coyotes howled, and the water in my bottle froze. Everything I needed I strapped onto the bike. I rode switchback dirt roads and trails over mountains; I forded streams; there were times I didn't see another vehicle or human for hours at a time. When I came to a small town, I rode through it filthy and sweaty, or filthy and frozen. I was simply riding through, or searching for a restaurant or a motel, but the townspeople looked at me as if I was an armed nomad, a reminder of the old days along the border, which are gone but not quite forgotten.

There is one more reason I had to ride the borders: I wanted adventure and fast, exhilarating movement to shake off a despondent lethargy. Three close friends had died during the previous year. I needed to get away, to see new things. To move. I thought I had to make a vivid declaration to myself that my own life would continue, for its contingent remainder.

Mike died of Lou Gehrig's disease, his end long prefigured, of course. But it is perhaps the worst way to go: the lucid mind able to observe the body's slow, inexorable petrification. He was fifty-four. Chris succumbed to a mixture of prescription drugs and alcohol. He was also profoundly depressed and alcoholic, and so perhaps he committed suicide. He was fifty-two. Will's liver cancer killed him within a few months of diagnosis. When I said goodbye to him, and kissed his forehead and held him, he felt as light and fragile as a flower. He was fifty-four.

Does it make any sense to remember absent friends by riding twenty thousand kilometres alone on a motorcycle? Who cares if it doesn't. It's as good a way as any. And it's not unreasonable to hope for balm and succour as a temporary nomad. It's our ancient nature, after all, to wander on open savannahs. Under the stress of mortality, why not revive the comfort of our old true human selves? In the face of death, movement is life. "In motion a man has a chance," writes Norman Mailer.

I wanted my long rides to be a remembrance of my friends. When I rode for hours into cold wind on the west Texas tableland, or through the astringent, boiling heat of the Sonoran desert; as I swept along deserted roads through the brown, barren mountains of Arizona, or the evergreened, snowy mountains of Montana; as I ploughed through the claustro-phobic New England woods or slogged along the endless, flat-land perimeter of the Great Lakes, I would say to myself: this is for you boys; this is hard as hell, but I'm alive and kicking, and thinking of you. I may be right behind you, following your dire path—but not yet. Or on those few days when it all went right—when the sun shone warm enough, the wind abated, the road wound with kindness and in beauty through desert, woods or mountains, the radius of its curves perfect for the bike's rhythmic, leaning progress—I would say: you'd love this too, my dear friends, these brief quickening moments of life on the edge.

A border, whether it's walled, fenced or open, represents a limit and a limitation. At this arbitrary line, we must stop and ask permission to cross; we must explain and justify our desire to go farther. How strange to live on the U.S. side of the line and to look into the alien blankness of Mexico on the other side—*el otro lado*. For 150 years or more, Anglo-Americans have been impressing their own ideas, caprices and miscon-ceptions upon the odd, insular, shadowed aspect of Mexico. Or to be an American looking north past the 49th parallel or across the Great Lakes, and see . . . What? A remote, cold country whose inhabitants are just like themselves, surely. But, with its odd, inexplicable, slippery distinctions, perhaps it's another cipher. And the unknown is dangerous—or it feels that way.

Borderlands is about the borders America has drawn, and continues to draw, around itself. The periphery of a place can tell us a great deal about its heartland. Along the edge of a nation's territory, its real prejudices, fears and obsessions—but also its virtues—irrepressibly bubble up as its people confront the "other" whom they admire, or fear, or hold in contempt, and know little about. September 11, 2001, changed the United States utterly. And nothing more so than the physical reality, the perception—and the meaning—of its borders.

U.S.-MEXICO BORDER

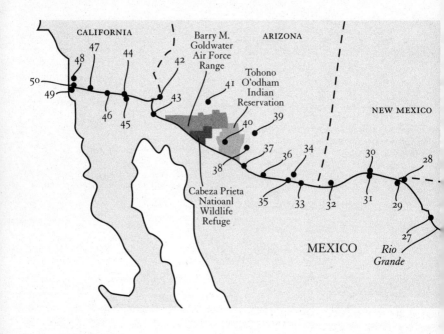

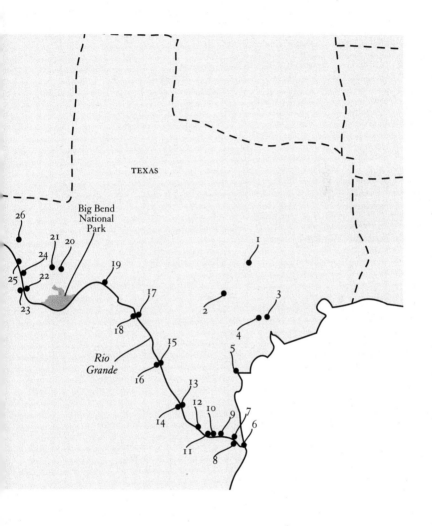

TEXAS

Big Bend
National
Park

Rio
Grande

26

21
20
24
25 22
23

19

17

18

15

16

13
12
10
14 9 7
6
11
8

1

2

3

4

5

PART I

SOUTH

THERE AINT SHIT DOWN THERE.

—CORMAC MᶜCARTHY, *All the Pretty Horses*

THE MEXICAN LINE IS A BORDER LIKE ANY OTHER, but it has its own intimations and meanings. If we think of that border, what disordered, yet vivid, fragments might tumble through the mind?

The South: Dope. Marijuana, coke, heroin, meth, ecstasy. Shoeshine kids and kids with beer and postcards and sisters for sale. Twelve-year-old whores. Paid-off cops and federales. Mafias: Who has the plaza? (nothing to do with the town square or a strip mall, this means: Who runs the dope here?). In Nuevo Laredo, four border guards machine-gunned; grenades tossed into a newspaper office, two dead; a silver dagger in a politician's neck; an Army general, supposed to clean up a city, disappears, never heard of again. Greasy thugs carrying M-16s, M4s, AKs, Glocks, Colts, TECs, Uzis, zip guns, and weapons you've never heard of coming across the River or through the wire, running dope and illegals; MS-13 gangbangers—punks who make the Bloods and Crips look like old tía Manuela shoplifting.

The illegals cluster at the wire every night. A barbarian horde, armed only with desperation, they are bought and sold like things, humped over the border and driven north to where the work is. Along the way, they suffer and some die. When they get there, they toil for the gringos for sweet fuck all.

The Mexican government does nothing. Maybe it's too corrupt to do anything. Or maybe the government is doing exactly what it wants to do: let them cross over; let them flood the land; speak Spanish and procreate mightily. La Reconquista!

CHAPTER 1

A HOLY ALTAR

THIS LAND IS YOUR LAND, THIS LAND IS MY LAND . . .
THIS LAND WAS MADE FOR YOU AND ME.
—WOODY GUTHRIE

REMEMBER THE ALAMO? Part of America was forged there.
Almost all the elements of America's story of itself were
present during the thirteen-day-long battle in 1836 at a small,
remote, old Spanish mission deep in the heart of Texas. I intend
to ride the border from east to west, but the Alamo, in the
centre of San Antonio, is a necessary place to start. It is about
three hundred miles north of Brownsville at the present border's eastern end, but it's as much a part of the history of the
borderlands as if it was right on the Rio Grande—the River—
or in some nearby dusty border town.

Americans remember the story of the Alamo because it
seems to represent everything they hold dear in the United
States: courage and sacrifice in the name of freedom; like-
minded citizens coming together under arms to resist tyranny;
a laconic and offhand heroism; an absorption with democracy
and the rights of man; a demonstration of America's destiny
to grow west and south, and maybe north, too (perhaps only
the ocean could limit this God-sanctioned expansion and

dominion). And military prowess: like the soldiers of the War of Independence, the few men at the Alamo fought for a long time against a superior enemy.

The battle at the Alamo was a siege, and it is the sieges of history that catch the imagination: Masada, Constantinople, Londonderry, Leningrad, the Battle of Britain. The besieged almost always have the choice of surrender, a way out of their fear and suffering. They must keep their guts and hearts strong to resist the threat and press of the encircling enemy over a stretch of time. This is far more than the momentary heroism of battle, which rides on a surge of fear and adrenaline, and is over and done with quickly. At four in the morning, in the dark, with time to think about death, how easy and appealing it must seem to get things over with, to give up.

That's what another group of Americans did a few weeks after the Alamo fell. Between 400 and 450 men under Colonel James Walker Fannin surrendered to the Mexican army under General Antonio López de Santa Anna after the Battle of Coleto Creek, near Goliad, about a hundred miles south of San Antonio. The Americans had been assured of good treatment and they were briefly held prisoner. But on March 27, 1836—Palm Sunday—their guards, under Santa Anna's orders, and over the objections of less bloody-minded officers, divided them into three groups, marched them off in different directions and massacred them. Three hundred and forty-one men were killed, in an atrocity that mobilized support for the Texan cause across the territory, and within the United States, as well.

Coleto Creek made it clear that this was to be a war to the finish, but somehow it did not trigger a popular emotional response, as did the Alamo. Far more men were killed at Goliad, but unlike the massacre there, the Alamo was a fair fight in the sense that the defenders chose to keep resisting. Killing them was not, therefore, a crime, but merely cruel war.

The account of the Alamo in U.S. mythology is dramatic and colourful. Two hundred men fought to the death against an army of five thousand. It was to be a victory for Protestants over Catholics and for free white men over degenerate mestizos. The American commander, Colonel William B. Travis, traced a line in the sand and said: "Those of you who are willing to stay with me and die with me, cross this line." All but one man did so. The defenders knew from the beginning that their position was hopeless, but they fought on. Their battle cry was "Victory or Death!" They died to a man on the mission walls and in the shadowy niches of its stone buildings. Davy Crockett was one of them, and his blood, wrote one historian, was shed upon "a holy altar."

The story has become a part of the mythology of the United States: how it was founded; how it grew and prospered; how it was a beacon for the world it eventually came to dominate. Every nation tells a story of itself to explain and justify how it arrived at where it is now, and to provide guidance and comfort to its people in the present. The myth is the version of itself the nation would like, and in fact needs, to be true.

Historians and other academics revise or debunk myths. They question the story of the Alamo. How can we know what really happened, they churlishly ask, if every man there died? And the fight for Texan independence from Mexico (in 1836, Texas was part of the Mexican state of Coahuila y Tejas) was hardly a battle of cultures. When the Texas Declaration of Independence was signed, David G. Burnet was the president of the new republic, but its vice-president was Lorenzo de Zavala. In those days, a "Texian" was as likely to mean a Spanish-speaking, brown-skinned Catholic whose family had lived in Texas for a hundred years or more, as a white, Protestant Anglo whose parents had recently come from England, Ireland or Germany. But none of these historical nuances or cautions means much to a nation and the story it tells about itself. Historians may quibble, but the people keep the faith.

The chain of events from the Alamo to the border is straightforward. The fight to the death there, and the massacre at Goliad, drew volunteers and aid from the United States. Texas (or the eastern third of the present state north of the Nueces River) won its independence from Mexico with a decisive victory at San Jacinto, later in 1836. Whereas a Texas that was part of a Mexican state could become part of the United States only through invasion and war, an independent Texian republic could join the United States voluntarily. After several unsuccessful attempts (because of disagreements in Congress), the United States annexed a willing Texas in 1845, ignoring Mexico's loud objections.

For all these reasons of history, I must look at the Alamo if I want to understand the border. I'll ride to Goliad, too, to find there the antithesis of remembered glory.

Here's how my motorcycle ride along the two thousand–mile-long U.S.-Mexico border begins: I almost kill myself three, maybe four, times in the first sixty seconds.

In retrospect, this shouldn't really surprise me. I bought this bike new a few months ago, and I've ridden it for about nine hundred miles, none of those in the last six weeks. Before that, I have to go back exactly twenty-five years to the last time I sat on a motorcycle. Now, I'm carrying about ninety pounds of gear on a Kawasaki KLR 650 cc, single-cylinder "thumper," and it's the first time I've ridden with a heavy load of any sort. I'm wearing my brand new armoured riding jacket, pants and boots—the first time I've worn them all together—and their padded bulk distracts me. Protecting my precious skull is a new helmet, different in design from the one I'm somewhat used to. It's a "full coverage" helmet with a chin guard as well as a plastic visor, and it feels claustrophobic.

I have to pull out of a motel parking lot onto the service road of Interstate 10 on the fringe of San Antonio, Texas; the traffic, even on this road, is moving at forty or fifty miles an hour. I must turn into the fast-moving stream, accelerate hard, crunch my way through the gears, and, as I'm doing that, merge left across three lanes to get onto the highway itself. If I wanted to attempt suicide on a motorcycle, this would be a pretty good way to do it.

I wait for a hole in the rush of heavy metal, turn out of the driveway, and twist the throttle. Right away, it's time to change into second. I have to slide my left foot under the shift lever, but I can't do it. The armoured pads in my pants make it difficult to bend my knee, which also butts up against the pannier bag hanging down over the gas tank in front of me. I can't manoeuvre my leg to get my foot into position. It just never occurred to me to check beforehand that I could do this. Cars scream and screech around me, braking hard, swerving; I'm going way too slowly. In my rear-view mirror, I see a jagged wall of vehicles bearing down on me; they look like squadrons of tanks. In a few seconds, I pass from worry to fear to sweaty terror. I've already begun to change lanes; now I reef the bike back to the right, trying to avoid getting sucked onto the highway at twenty miles an hour. The bike's engine is screaming in first gear; if I were in fifth, I'd be hammering along at fifty miles an hour. Then . . . there . . . did it—into second gear. I twist the throttle. I throttle it. I signal left again, but then, the same problem: I can't get into third. I slide back to the right again.

In all these changes of direction, I'm aware of large metal masses flashing by me on both sides, very close. Horns honk in a weird doppler rise and fall—a reflection of how fast the other vehicles are, how slow I am. Someone shouts at me: "Asshole!" He's right. I feel what I'm sure is the slight "thlip" of a car's outside mirror flicking the arm of my jacket as it zips by—another two inches and it could have ripped off my goddamn arm. Holy fucking shit! Dear God, nearer to thee: I renounce atheism. This is madness; I'm going to die. I feel the deep sorrow the prematurely dying feel for the people they're about to leave behind; for my wife, and for my daughter and her teenage orphanhood.

But then a side road appears on the right. I slam the bike into it too fast, and the rear wheel slides; I wobble, unused to the feel of the luggage-loaded machine. Just managing to stay upright, I pull over to the road's quiet edge. I put my boots down, and sit in the saddle. I shake, I almost puke, in the aftershock of my barely avoided death.

Thoughts pass at random through my alleged mind: I'm so stupid . . . no, I'm a colossal idiot; I'm too old for this; I'll never make it to the goddamn border, never mind ride its long length, on bad roads, with bad guys all around; what in the name of sweet Jesus do I think I'm doing? Why the hell didn't I check that I could actually ride this bike with a big load and my unfamiliar riding gear, before inserting myself into heavy traffic? I damn near joined you then, boys, I say to Will, Chris and Mike.

I prop the bike on its side stand and dismount. My legs feel fragile, not quite attached to my torso. I wonder vaguely what my blood pressure was a few minutes ago out there on the road. High, very high. It won't be the last time it red-lines on this trip, I'm sure of that. I'm old enough that this is something I think about.

I reposition the tank panniers so that I have more knee room, but it's not a perfect adjustment for my long legs and feet. Sitting in the saddle again, I can get my toe under the shift lever only if I bend my leg out from the bike at an odd angle. I ride up and down the quiet, dead-end side road trying out my technique. It works most of the time, although I often miss the gear, and sometimes I have to look down to make sure my foot is in the right position before I flip up the lever. Taking your eyes off the road's variegated surface, and away from the close surround of traffic is not at all a safe practice on a two-wheeler. But my adaptation will have to do, and I hope I'll get used to it.

The second beginning of my border ride works well enough. I reach the highway in jerky, knees-akimbo manoeuvres. I'm glad there are no veteran bikers around judging my green-horn style as I jam the lever into top gear and reach a cruising speed of sixty or sixty-five miles an hour—without risking my life more than is usual for a ride in foreign, city-expressway traffic. At least I planned ahead enough to avoid rush hour; it's around eleven o'clock and there's a medium amount of traffic about. I must have made an even distribution of my load because, once I settle down in my lane, in the flow of vehicles, the bike feels balanced and, even with the added weight, there's no lessening of power I'm aware of.

In spite of my very bad start, my discomfort is displaced right away by a surge of pure motorcycle happiness. It's an emotional summary of all the constituents of riding fast: in the open, in the rush of wind, under the wide sky, with the road sweeping by below, everything around brought into insistent and immediate focus. It's the happiness of adrenaline and the abandonment of constraints—with an edge of danger. When you're sitting around and talking about riding, it's easy to acknowledge the possibilities of disaster, but once on the bike, on the road, all those intimations of mortality are swept full away by joy.

I begin my first day by riding away from the Alamo, north and east towards Austin to meet a friend. Jane was a business associate, ex-campaign manager and old friend of Ann Richards, the Democratic governor of Texas whom George W. Bush defeated in his stroll to the presidency. By some unlikely coincidence, Jane lives part of the year on Salt Spring Island, my own small, remote home off the coast of British Columbia.

I head north out of San Antonio, away from the traffic and congestion, and into the low hills, sandy plains and trees—cottonwood, willow and acacia—of this eastern edge of the Texas Hill Country. On this less-travelled road, there are few small towns—Twin Sisters, Blanco, Dripping Springs—and, therefore, only a few gear changes. This is nice, but I'm not getting much practice. As I ride, the weather grows cooler and cloudier. It looks like rain, which is just what I don't need on my first traumatic day, but it holds off. The wind is a problem, though. It blows across my path or dead against me, depending on the road's curves. It's confirmation that this bike doesn't do well in a crosswind; even a gust at twenty miles an hour blows me around my lane. I'm beginning my battle with the wind, which will continue, most days, for the next four weeks. Twice, it will come close to killing me.

I sit on the curb outside a gas-station store eating a ready-made ham and cheese sandwich on white and a Snickers bar, drinking a coffee. While I eat, I admire my motorcycle. Or rather, I try, once again, to justify—and to appreciate—its ungainliness. The KLR 650's tall, somewhat broken-backed profile, high fenders and hand guards make the bike look like a large, steroid-pumped dirt bike. It is to other motorcycles as the head-hunched stork is to birds, the humpback to whales, the hyena to land mammals. With the stock nubby tires (I've changed to more street-kindly rubber for this trip), it can go off-road under a skilled rider, but it's too heavy a machine to do much of that.

The KLR's real appeal is not that it's born to do one thing well, but that it can do several disparate things reasonably well. For example, a sleek, chromed Harley-Davidson can hum along a good road, at speed, in comfort, but it gets into trouble when the road surface turns bad. The KLR can bash over ugly, rocky gravel and dirt roads, and, if necessary, go where there isn't a road; pound along the freeway all day at seventy or seventy-five miles an hour—not in real comfort, but it can do it; carry more fuel than most other motorcycles—a little over five gallons (veteran riders call it the "tanker"); pack a heavy load; and keep going forever. It's a supremely utilitarian machine with a twenty-year record of getting riders across countries, and around the world, too.

It began as a Kawasaki military design for the United States Marine Corps—a bike that could endure rough conditions and offhand treatment. From the beginning, it was clear that the KLR was one of those machines with a soul; that is to say, that for whatever reasons of luck or human ingenuity, all of its intricate constituent parts worked, and held together, with persistent efficiency. It did what it was supposed to do, and it did so for a long time. The company brought out a civilian version in 1987, and didn't make a substantial change to the KLR until the 2008 model. Why tinker with the success of such a subtle and rare amalgam as a superb machine? In fact, it's become something of an icon, and its riders are cultish and devoted. A lot has changed in motorcycle engineering in the last twenty years, but the KLR remains determinedly old-fashioned. You can buy a part now that will fit any year's model back into the 1980s. That's the reason I can climb aboard one now, and have everything about the bike look and feel just the same as the last time I rode bikes, back in 1980.

However, the one thing the Kawasaki designers and engineers didn't spend much time on was looks. Part of the problem is the KLR's dirt-bike heritage, and its original purpose of lugging Marines from the halls of Montezuma to the shores of Tripoli. The best you can say about the KLR is that it has a kind of robust handsomeness. If you can't bear to go that far, perhaps you can admit that it evinces the modest, functional aspect of an unpretentious, purposeful machine. Mostly though, you have to admit it's just butt-ugly.

In Austin, Jane rifles through files, Rolodexes and memories to get me some contacts. She even makes phone calls on the spot to let people know who I am, and that I'll be calling. I leave with a long list.

Before I have a chance to ride southwest, back towards San Antonio and the Alamo, I get a call from Linda, one of the contacts on Jane's list. Linda and her husband, Bob, invite me to join them for lunch. We meet at a Mexican restaurant where they eat so often that one of the house salsas has been named after Bob. The recipe is his: cheese, meat, hot sauce and spices. Bob is in his seventies, friendly, folksy, retired. He was in politics for a while, and acted as Bill Clinton's deputy secretary of the interior. He was the main proponent of converting a huge ranch in the Big Bend country of West Texas into Big Bend Ranch State Park—I'll ride through it in a few weeks. Bob knows British Columbia; he and a partner, together with Linda and their then-young son, once panned for gold in the province's northern interior. The government shut them down, Bob says, to make a park. He sued and won $3.5 million, but the amount was knocked down to $70,000 on appeal, he doesn't know why. He's not fond of Canadian so-called damn justice. I want to know more, but Linda takes over.

She used to be an attorney, and ran the government's antitrust office in Washington. She's energetic, firm and precise, holds definite opinions and does most of the talking. I get the impression she keeps amiable Bob sorted out and organized. We talk about immigration.

The United States, says Linda forcefully, is the only country in the world where, when immigrants arrive, they're immediately considered Americans. Well, I say, Canada does that, too. She looks blank, doesn't respond. There's a silence. Canada doesn't seem to enter into any equation she's aware of; perhaps nothing outside the United States does, even for this educated, intelligent American. And Australia, I say. I think it takes that attitude too. No, she says. There's prejudice there; they hate immigrants. A friend was just there, and she told her that.

Bob and Linda don't like the idea of my border ride. They insist I should call the people on Jane's list along the way and let them know when I plan to arrive. If something happens to me and I don't check in with them, they can call the police. Linda is especially concerned. Many parts of the border on the U.S. side are poor and isolated, she says. A lot of the people there have nothing. I have a big bike with lots of new, shiny things on it. Maybe some guys will decide they'd like to have it; perhaps I'll stumble into a drug deal, or some plain bad or crazy guy. I should just ride through the border counties like Starr, Zapata and Webb as fast as possible. McAllen and Rio Grande City are drug-importing centres; they're very dangerous places.

I tell them I intend to cross into Mexico at Laredo and ride on the other side of the river for a couple of hundred miles— in Mexico, the road follows the river, while on the U.S. side there's a long dogleg inland. Bob and Linda look at me in incredulous silence. Bob shakes his head. No, Linda says. Don't do that. Nuevo Laredo is far too dangerous. Drug wars are being fought out there. And the border road is suicide. But I'll ride through Nuevo Laredo by day, in the morning, I say—drug guys don't get up early. And I'll make a fast non-stop trip. Maybe I'll cross back into the U.S. sooner, at Piedras Negras, instead of riding all the way to Ciudad Acuña. No, no, no, they say. If I were travelling with someone, maybe; but, alone? No, no, no. Don't do it!

I tell them I'll reconsider my plan. I say to myself: Bob and Linda are getting on in years (although they're not that much older than me), and older people always exaggerate the dangers of crime and violence. I've printed out Internet maps of a route through Nuevo Laredo and along Mexico's Highway 2. My intent has always been to stay on the American side—that's the border perspective I want—and to cross into Mexico only when the route is shorter there. I assumed I'd be safe in Mexico if I rode by day and was careful. But maybe I'm wrong.

Riding slowly to get out of Austin, I broil and sweat in the muggy heat, maybe ninety-five degrees. In my riding jacket, gloves and helmet (just jeans on my legs), I can bear the temperature at highway speeds. At stoplights, I feel as if my head and upper body are in a furnace. On Interstate 35, the traffic is very heavy; a Harley-Davidson passes me, gets slowed down, and then I pass him. We alternate for a while. Its rider is fat, and wearing a sleeveless vest and jeans. His arms are tattooed, and on his head is a soft hat—no helmet (if you're over twenty-one in Texas, you don't have to wear one)—whose brim stands up in the wind like a cavalryman's. This rider is certainly more comfortable than me, and he can feel the hot wind on his bare skin, but I shudder when I think of what would happen if he went down. He'd probably die; if he survived, he'd lose a good amount of his body's largest organ, his skin. When denim or other fabric gets embedded in skin after a long slide on tarmac, nurses or doctors must scrub with a stiff brush to get the cloth fibres out. Even morphine won't take care of the pain. Of course, that possibility is part of the motorcycle's traditional mystique: if you ride, you take your chances. Getting togged up in pads and armour like mine defeats the whole idea of a bike. To the fat rider with the hat and tattoos, I'm beneath contempt.

That's also the reason he doesn't wave at me, or nod. It's motorcycle etiquette to do so, thus acknowledging the brotherhood of the road and its shared danger, the making of a mutual promise that the riders will look out for each other in the constant battle to stay upright and alive. The wave or the nod is the non-verbal equivalent of "Be safe," or "Be careful out there." But the practice has exceptions; the apparent democracy of the motorcycle has its hierarchy. Outlaw bikers or *Easy Rider* wannabes don't wave to civilians like me, not even to civilians on Harleys. Harley riders will sometimes wave to non-Harley riders, but often they don't. I'll discover that they hardly ever acknowledge the existence of someone on a jumped-up dirt bike. I give this guy on the I-35 a wave, but he shows no sign that I exist.

A short way out of Austin, the traffic slows to stop-and-go. I'm dutifully shuffling along in my lane, changing gear awkwardly, sweating again, when another rider zooms by me between lanes. A little way ahead, he swerves over to the shoulder and rides nimbly along it. I remember that lane splitting is legal in some states, and tolerated in many. Texas must be one of them. I've never done this before, and I feel a Canadian hesitation about breaking the rules. But I'm hot and the jam stretches ahead as far as I can see. I swing over to the shoulder and accelerate until I'm bowling along, passing the shuffling cars at twenty-five miles an hour. When the shoulder surface gets narrow and bad, I swing right and bump across hard-packed grass, through a dry, shallow ditch, and up onto the service road, on which the traffic is moving well. The KLR can do this cross-country shift so easily, and I'm happy with its versatility and my own ability to ride over the rough ground. After a while, I see the overturned tractor-trailer that's causing the jam. I swing back, triumphantly, onto the highway again.

After all my trepidation, getting to the Alamo next morning isn't bad at all: a few wrong turns, a little heavy traffic, and some missed gear changes. Many of the Texans I've spoken to have told me to be very careful on my bike in Texas because the driving is fast and aggressive. But, so far, the drivers have been courteous, almost solicitous. They give me space, and they don't tailgate—although I'm riding in the most cautious and defensive manner possible.

Soon I'm in downtown San Antonio following the signs to the mission. I give a parking lot attendant a $5 tip above the $10 fee, to look after my bike and gear. He's happy to do it, carefully stowing my helmet and hanging up my jacket inside his shack. Then he comprehensively parses a four-letter word: "I'll look after your bike," he says, "but not that one—Fuck it!" He jerks his thumb at a big, tricked-out Harley parked nearby. "That fucker wouldn't give me no fuckin' tip, man."

The pleasant, grassy, tree-shaded compound of the Alamo is just across the road. It faces the Guinness World Records Museum and Davy Crockett's Tall Tales Ride.

The Alamo is a shrine—its main extant building is the old mission church—and also a place of secular veneration and devotion. Its care and maintenance were assigned by legislation in 1905 to the Daughters of the Republic of Texas. They must preserve it, says the law, "as a sacred memorial to the heroes who immolated themselves upon that hallowed ground."

The Daughters have produced brochures about the history of the place that are surprisingly well balanced; they recount the Alamo's exciting legend, while also gently mentioning that that might not have been exactly the way things happened. They implicitly acknowledge that myth and history are seldom the same thing. I'm impressed by this sophistication. Nevertheless, the Daughters make themselves very clear: the fight in 1836 was a desperate and heroic struggle against overwhelming odds by men who were willing to make "the ultimate sacrifice for freedom." The Alamo is the "Shrine of Texas Liberty."

It's cool in the shade of the old trees, but I stroll about the grounds in a welter of tourists. It's still the March school break, and this is obviously one of the places families go for entertainment, and for patriotic edification. Two and a half million visitors a year make the pilgrimage to the Alamo—almost seven thousand every day. There's a small museum, a theatre, a library (which is closed) and the usual gift shop.

I must line up for an hour to enter the shrine itself. The people wait in the hot sun and humidity with quiet patience. There are as many Hispanics as Anglos; as much Spanish is spoken around me as English. I wonder if the Hispanics have mixed feelings about this place. How, exactly, do they remember the Alamo?

Just outside the door is a sign that says: "Quiet, No Smoking, Gentlemen Remove Hats, No Photos." An attendant reinforces these messages as we shuffle forward: "This is the shrine. Treat it as one, please. Keep your voices down. Please respect the memory of these brave Texans."

Inside, I see many flags: the ubiquitous Revolutionary War's Gadsden flag with a rattlesnake on it and the slogan "Don't Tread on Me"; a Texas banner with the words "Come and Take It." A line of flags represent where the defenders came from: almost all the states within the then-United States, as well as other nations—mostly England, Scotland and Ireland, but there is one each of Wales, Germany and Denmark. There are statues of St. Anthony, and a mission bell. Davy Crockett's rifle and vest hang in the sacristy, like the relics of a saint. In display cases lie books about Crockett, a pocket watch belonging to the last courier who left the Alamo to plead for help, a silver spoon with the name "Bowie" engraved on it, a document written by Crockett to resolve a lawsuit between two litigants.

At the back of the shrine is the altar. Here, during the siege, were constructed earthworks upon which the defenders set up several cannons. On the sacred and consecrated ground, the Texans loaded and fired, loaded and fired. In the end, either Mexican soldiers overran their position and killed them all, or the Texans surrendered and were executed.

Near the shrine is the "Wall of History," a line of panels that tell the legendary story of the battle with gusto, and without the Daughters' qualifications. In front of the wall, a guide shouts out a lurid, blow-by-blow account of the fighting. Although he must have given his spiel many times, he appears, at crucial moments, to be overcome by his own emotion. When all but one man steps across Travis's line in the sand, and when Davy Crockett goes down in a hand-to-hand melee, the guide must pause to stop his tears and steady his voice. The crowd catches the mood; they listen with care, in silence. I see a few nearby women, and a man, wipe their eyes. I feel the emotion myself. This story of men giving up their lives for an idea has a power that rivets us all. We're in the brief, intense, universal thrall of martyrdom.

CHAPTER 2

A LARGER EMPIRE

WE ARE THE PIONEERS OF THE WORLD;
THE ADVANCE-GUARD, SENT ON THROUGH THE
WILDERNESS OF UNTRIED THINGS, TO BREAK A NEW
PATH IN THE NEW WORLD THAT IS OURS.
—HERMAN MELVILLE, *White-Jacket*

WHEN I RIDE INTO GOLIAD, it's as if I've left behind highway
hell. There are a few small motels in the little town, which has
a museum-like centre—a square surrounded by restored
buildings. During the eight years of Texas independence, one
of Goliad's residents described it as "a wild, recky, Indiany
looking place . . . full of lawless men who would throw the
rawhide on to [anyone] in a way that was a pity and a caution."
But the town is sedate and quiet these days, with few signs of
tourists or their accompanying kitsch, and no immediate indication of an epochal historic site nearby.

I check into the Antler Motel. It has two storeys, but the
place is almost empty, and I get a room on the ground floor.
In busy San Antonio and in Austin, I was given second-floor
rooms far from my bike, and it took a long time to load and
unload my gear. Now, I luxuriate in the ease of stripping my
six separate pannier and duffle bags off the machine and

heaving them into the room with a few steps back and forth. And if I see anyone tampering with the KLR during the night, I won't have to run down two halls, three flights of stairs and across a parking lot to tackle the bastard. This is more like it.

The next morning, I oil the chain and give the bike a look over. All its nuts and bolts are tight; its levers display the correct tolerance; its turn signals and brake light—a bright, flashing LED I installed myself, and which must irritate drivers behind me—come alive as they should. Most important, the tire pressure is just right. When your contact with the road on a curve is no more than a couple of inches wide, back and front, you'd better make sure the rubber is good. On a motorcycle, traction is your only friend.

With rain showers threatening, I ride into a strong headwind nine miles east of Goliad to the little town of Fannin, named after the commander of the Goliad Texans who surrendered more than four hundred of his men to the Mexicans. Fannin gave up unconditionally, although he didn't tell his soldiers that. They thought they would be treated as prisoners of war.

I follow the signs to the battlefield through the town's unpretentious roads and its few modest houses. The memorial is a small column in a large, unkempt, grassy field crisscrossed by concrete paths. There's a small shelter with some information panels and a washroom. Even on this Saturday of the March break, there is only one parked car containing three elderly tourists, and a pickup belonging to a maintenance man who's trying to fix a light in the washroom. He can't get something to work and he's grumpy, outright refusing to talk to me. "I'm busy right now, if you can't see that," he says, when I ask him how many people usually come to visit the site. I read the panels, walk over to the memorial, write in my journal, take pictures and use the washroom. I wait out a rain shower that sweeps across the flat fields and woods. A cow bawls nearby. In the course of an hour, no one else arrives to visit the scene of defeat and mendacious surrender. I hear the surly maintenance guy cursing; he still hasn't succeeded in whatever he's trying to do, and he turns to glare at me as though I'd caused his problem in the first place.

Things aren't much different at Presidio La Bahia, the old Spanish frontier fort situated a couple of miles to the south of Goliad. There are half a dozen parked cars, and their few occupants wander around the museum, the restored ramparts, the huge parade ground and the chapel of Our Lady of Loreto, in which Fannin and some of his men were held before they were slaughtered. The elderly lady in the gift shop says that, yes, it's busy sometimes, on holidays and with school trips. But she agrees that it's nothing like the Alamo.

"Everyone wants to see that," she says. Here, at La Bahia, "everything is so sad, because all the men were killed."

"Everyone was killed at the Alamo, too," I say.

"Yes, that's true," she says, "but what they did was so inspiring."

"And Fannin and Coleto Creek, and the massacre—I guess that's not inspiring?"

"No, that's right," she says. "Santa Anna was a murderer; he promised to spare Colonel Fannin and his men if they surrendered, and then he just killed them. It was just like the way things are today: murders and massacres and all those terrible things."

James Fannin had been a slave trader and he had lied about, and libelled, his political opponents in Texas. He was also an incompetent commander. He lost at Coleto Creek because he underestimated the Mexicans' strength and abilities, and because he committed serious strategic and tactical errors. For example, he made his stand on the open prairie, where his men were pounded by enemy cannon, instead of retreating into the solid defensible position of nearby woods.

More insidious were the reasons for Fannin's misjudgments of Mexican competence. Like most Texans and Anglo-Americans of the time, he regarded Mexicans as inferior, degenerate, racially mongrelized, benightedly Catholic, lazy, lying, thieving and slovenly. He never really accepted that an army of such men could defeat him, although he was considerably outnumbered. Even the defenders of the Alamo held the view that they had a pretty good chance: two hundred Americans (and Texans) against fifteen hundred Mexicans (not the five thousand of legend) seemed like reasonable odds to them—especially if they could be reinforced with a few hundred additional volunteers. Until close to the end, they expected to win.

Fannin's view of Mexicans was a widely held stereotype in the border regions where the two disparate cultures abraded one another. During a visit to Mexico City in 1822, Stephen Austin (the "Father of Texas" who organized the first successful Anglo settlement there) wrote: "To be candid the majority of the people of the whole nation as far as I have seen them want nothing but tails to be more brutes than the apes." An American traveller in Mexico in 1822 remarked that the Mexicans' principal occupation consisted "in removing fleas and lice from each other, drinking pulque (a fermented drink), smoking cigars, when they can, and sleeping."

Part of this prejudice was the assumption of white racial superiority usual for the time. Americans were "pure" white, whereas Mexicans were swarthy mestizos. White Americans considered mixed race to be worse than pure black or brown. Anglos thought that the mix of Spanish and Indian combined only the vile qualities of each "race." The belief that Mexicans were lazy may have been, in part, a reflection of the ferocious work ethic of Anglo-Americans—a heritage of Puritanism, Protestantism, and a code of civic responsibility and self-reliance. The fact that the Mexicans along their frontier were as industrious as the Anglo settlers in the same region didn't prevent the stereotype from settling in. Observation of facts on the ground is seldom an antidote to prejudice. A stereotype can abort even the most basic rational assessment .

Historian David J. Weber argues that there may be another reason for American disgust with Mexicans: the "Black Legend," a term coined by Spanish historians to describe the raft of biases towards the Catholic Spanish held by the Protestant English prior to, and during, the American colonial period. The Thirteen-Colonies English believed that the Spanish government was "authoritarian, corrupt, and decadent, and that Spaniards were bigoted, cruel, greedy, tyrannical, fanatical, treacherous and lazy." The Spanish proved all this in the New World. The conquistadors were adventurers who came for gold, rather than settlers who sought freedom and land to work. The Spanish enslaved the Indians for labour and set up a despotic government in the Americas to match the original in Spain.

For nineteenth-century Americans living in the borderlands during the fight for Texan independence, what was happening nearby confirmed all these old preconceptions and assumptions. Santa Anna waged a vicious war whose aim was unconditional surrender. He ordered that no prisoners be taken; if Texans did surrender, they were to be treated as rebels and traitors, and they would be executed. Thus the fight to the finish at the Alamo; thus the massacre at Goliad.

To remember the Alamo is also to remember who you suppose the Mexicans were then, and may still be. Americans must acknowledge that some things have changed in present-day Mexico: the political system is more or less democratic, and prosperity is more widely dispersed. But it could also seem to Americans that other things remain as they were a century and a half ago: political corruption; civil disorder descending, at times, into incipient revolution; poverty and destitution; criminals, police and the army all equally violent and crooked. Drugs come from Mexico, with their attendant evil; illegals swarm across the line because their own country has failed them. Perhaps terrorists will come across the border, too—if they haven't already. And the Mexicans are still brown-skinned, Catholic mestizos.

The American conservative, nativist reaction to illegal immigrants is based in part on the strain that immigration puts on schools and hospitals, and on its implications for the English-speaking, mostly European and Protestant nature of American society. But the reaction is augmented by the old cultural and racist prejudices against Mexico and Mexicans. Conservative writers and politicians call Mexican immigration an "invasion." To such people—who feel insecure, resentful, fearful, and, perhaps, guilty, as well—the movement of illegals across the border can easily look like a reconquest of the land of New Spain, bequeathed to the troubled state of Mexico. After all, Mexicans see that territory as having been lost through the unrelenting aggression of the gringos and their unprovoked war. America's so-called "manifest destiny," to dominate the continent, is nothing but the justification to take from despised, inferior peoples—the mestizos and the Indian savages—the vast southern and western land of America.

From Goliad, I head south on the 183 to Refugio and take Highway 77 towards Corpus Christi, Brownsville and the border. By the time I join the 77, the land has become so flat it's actually interesting. This is obviously the now-exposed floor of a larger, ancient sea. It is mostly scrubby country with herds of floppy-eared and longhorn cattle scattered about the vast fields. Sometimes, there's cultivation—various green vegetable crops.

Now that I'm heading south, the easterly wind is a cross-wind. The Gulf of Mexico is about twenty-five miles to the east, and the wind blows off the gulf strong and gusty across the flat land. It's coming at me from my left side, a sustained 20 or 25 miles an hour, with gusts that must be 35 or 40. When an eighteen-wheeler passes me, the bike flutters and wobbles like a leaf in the turbulence of the truck's passage through this wind. On overpasses, I can barely keep the bike on the road. I try to maintain a speed of 65 miles an hour; almost every other vehicle is running faster. I sit forward on the saddle and countersteer to force the machine to lean into the gusts. I must fight the wind, second by second. But often, I throttle back to 55 or 50 to maintain control. I've been riding for only an hour or so, but my arms, shoulders and neck ache with the strain. I think about turning back to Goliad, but there's no guarantee it won't blow as strong tomorrow.

When I was planning this trip, I contemplated the effects of rain, heat and cold, but for some reason I hadn't thought of wind as a problem. My vulnerability makes me think again of the similarities between motorcycling and sailing small boats. I proceed on nature's sufferance, feeling the same subjection to wind and weather in general; and the exposure is similar— I can get miserably wet and cold in much the same way. The difference is the rest stops and warm gas-station stores and cafes along the highway; at sea, there are no time outs.

I'm about thirty miles south of Corpus Christi the first time the wind nearly kills me. A sudden, strong gust blasts into my left side. I have no time to react; in a second, I'm driven off the road onto the paved shoulder. I can't hold the bike, and in two seconds I'm off the shoulder, careening across a field at sixty miles an hour. It's planted with a small green crop—a variety of lettuce or spinach, I speculate with surprising detachment, as the bike ploughs through, or bounces over, the furrows at close to right angles.

I have the presence of mind to pull in the clutch, disengaging the engine, and—to my later amazement—the even greater presence of mind not to yank on the brake lever like a frantic greenhorn. I wrestle the handlebars as they lurch and wrench from side to side, and just manage to hold the machine to a more or less straight line as it slows down and comes to a gentle stop. This must take only a few seconds, but I can't be sure of the elapsed time because my brain has reverted to reptilian survival mode. I put my boots down into the soft soil to hold the bike upright. I'm still near the edge of the huge field, the highway a hundred yards to my left.

Then, for the second time in four days, I start to shake—although this time, it's much worse. My legs tremble so much that I can barely keep the bike from falling over; my fingers vibrate on the handlebar grips in an adrenaline glissando. But I feel euphoric too: Damn, I'm good! I just rode this goddamn machine through a field of spinach at 100 clicks and didn't crash! I'm still alive, boys, I say to Will, Chris and Mike. I see that the traffic has slowed right down and that the people inside the vehicles are all staring my way. Obviously, they are in awe of my abrupt detour, and of my current improbable, upright, in-one-piece status. In fact, I think, they should all be lined up giving me some fucking applause. Then it occurs to me that, if there had been a fence or a ditch beside the highway, skill would have had nothing to do with it.

After a while, I turn the bike into the little gully between the rows of plants, and ride, at a sedate five miles an hour, back to Highway 77. The occupants of passing vehicles, who didn't see my liftoff from the road, stare in obvious astonishment and confusion at a muddy, loaded motorcycle trundling across a field like a farm implement. But I'm too high to be embarrassed. I accelerate down the shoulder, blend with the traffic, lean into the crosswind and head on south towards the borderlands.

———

I turn off the highway at Raymondville, about fifty miles from Brownsville. I've been worried about running out of gas, especially after most of a day of riding at highway speed in wind. But I get a demonstration of one of the KLR's virtues: it takes only four gallons, two-thirds of capacity. I could ride for another 130 miles. I call one of the names on Jane's Austin list: Rosemary and her husband, Cleve, run an inn in Los Fresnos, just north of Brownsville. Cleve was born in Los Fresnos and has lived in, or close to, the borderlands all his life. Rosemary says they'll be happy to put me up and to talk to me about the border. She gives me directions that sound vague, but I have confidence in my navigational sense.

I shouldn't have. I can't find the road Rosemary named (it turns out its sign faces the opposite direction). I ride until I see the Gulf of Mexico, which is about a dozen miles too far. I turn back but, for some reason, I don't see the road sign—maybe because I'm sweating, headachy, dehydrated, sore-assed and exhausted. I call Rosemary again. She's patient and calm; she'll come to meet me at San Marcos Road. I can't find that either. I'm losing it altogether. I shouldn't be on the bike now; this is when riders crash.

Then, an SUV coming from the other direction honks at me, slows and turns. Rosemary and I make a brief introduction; I apologize for all this trouble. She's still courteous and patient, and says to follow her, but she takes off fast, driving at sixty and sixty-five miles an hour on this narrow country road on which I should be doing fifty. My helmet visor is spattered and smudged with bugs, and has partially fogged up—I assume with the humid Gulf air. I should have cleaned it, but I'm not thinking straight. And the setting sun is in my eyes. At times, all I can see are shadows surrounded by a penumbra of sunlight. I should not be riding, but I try to keep up. Rosemary has gone to so much trouble already; I don't want to inconvenience her more. I say to myself: Fuck, I am risking my life here.

She makes another quick right turn. I follow her into it much too hot. There's gravel on the road. I start to slide, manage to straighten out, and roll right across the intersecting road in front of a car that makes a quick, skidding halt. I miss it by a few feet, and slip and wobble out into the grassy field for thirty feet before I can stop—upright, but barely. This is the second time today I've found myself in a field, and I'm getting goddamn sick of it.

But I'm almost there. In another few minutes, I follow the SUV into an oasis. Cleve and Rosemary's inn is a cluster of elegant and uncommon buildings, surrounded by trees, water and walkways. Tail-wagging dogs amble towards me; cats lie in the deep shade; multicoloured birds swoop by. The grounds border on a *resaca*, a local name for one of the lakes that are the cut-off remains of Rio Grande oxbows. I prop my motorcycle up on its side stand, apologizing again to Rosemary for the trouble, and for my boneheaded intrusion. It's okay, she says, we'll talk later.

I take my gear into a (ground floor) room in a low annex surrounded by palm trees, and by flowers and plants I've never seen before. The room is luxurious—it must be several hundred dollars a night. But right now, I don't give a damn. I take a shower in the huge, tiled bathroom. Afterwards, I walk around the place. There are signs on the trees and plants: snake-eyes, Mexican wild olive, Jerusalem thorn, Texas ebony, night-blooming cereus. Other signs describe some of the birds: chachalacas (a kind of pheasant), green jays, purple martins, Muscovy ducks. I sit by the *resaca*, and I climb an observation tower that looks out over the trees and water. It's cool and tranquil. After the ride down the 77 in the heat and wind, the near-crashes, and the strain of it all, I feel like Hugh Conway in *Lost Horizon*, stumbling into Shangri-La out of the death zone of the high Himalayas.

There is one anomalous thing about the place: several State Trooper cars are parked outside the main building. It's the last two days of the March break, and the nearby state park of Boca Chica is a popular place for college students to drink and carouse. Extra troops are required, and because Cleve and Rosemary's son, Jesse, is an ex-cop himself (now he mostly runs the inn), they provide food and lodging for these troopers drafted in for the week. What a gig, I think. It must be tough out on the road and the beach herding drunken kids, but what balm to come back to this sanctuary.

Some of the young cops, four men and one woman, Anglo and Hispanic, sit around on the porch looking out towards the *resaca*, drinking beer out of cans and talking about all the assholes out there. I ask them if they get involved with border security. A little, they say, but mostly as backup for the Border Patrol, which has primary jurisdiction along the River for drugs and illegals. "There's nothing you can do, anyway," one of them says. "You can't keep out a million people."

Is that the general view of law enforcement guys along the border? I ask.

"They'd be fuckin' crazy if they thought otherwise," says the trooper.

"Look at me," says one of the Hispanic guys. "My mom and dad were *indocumentados*. I was born here, but they're still illegal—technically. I should turn them in if I followed the rules. But there's lots of guys who are troopers now whose folks came across without documents."

"Lots of Border Patrol, too," says the woman.

"There's troopers I know who came over as illegals themselves, when they were kids," says the Hispanic cop. "The River's just a river. I mean, it's the border, don't get me wrong, but it's easy to come across. And if you got nothing on the other side, you're going to come across, right?"

"I guess I would," I say.

"Fuckin' right."

———

Cleve is tall, lean, and looks like Gary Cooper. Rosemary is blond, fast-talking, and looks scholarly in her owlish glasses. They are thoughtful and smart. They listen attentively to each other, laugh at each other's jokes and touch often. They are what can only be described in the United States these days as out-and-out liberals (although in Canada they would be unremarkably mainstream). I feel as if I've landed among simpaticos. Whatever Rosemary thought of my idiotic inability to read road signs and follow directions, she is completely welcoming. She's part of the network of politically and socially active Texas women—like Jane—who gathered around Ann Richards when she was governor. Cleve was a banker, owning a few banks of his own. The couple built the inn themselves, planted the trees, shrubs and cactus, and made a refuge for the birds, whose migration flyway is right overhead.

They take me out to dinner at a Mexican restaurant in Los Fresnos, and drive me around Brownsville and through the grounds of the University of Texas (Rosemary is a member of its board of governors). The university buildings are mostly new, Spanish-southwestern style, and arranged with elegant care around the *resacas* that dot the campus. Its fast expansion has taken place to accommodate the Mexican students coming across from Matamoros every day, or from the new middle-class Hispanic neighbourhoods and the *colonias* (the poor, often unserviced sections) of Brownsville. About 97 per cent of its students are Hispanic (Brownsville itself is more than 90 per cent.)

Downtown Brownsville is almost deserted on this warm March evening. It has a small-town feel, two-storey businesses lining the streets, houses mingled with stores. There's an air of New Orleans about the buildings, in their wrought-iron balconies and wooden gables. This is not surprising, given the city's historical connections with Louisiana and its proximity to Matamoros, whose well-to-do Hispanic residents, in the mid-nineteenth century, spoke French to each other, did business in both cities and sent their children to school in New Orleans.

Brownsville, like all the towns and cities along the border, is in a hassle with the all-powerful Department of Homeland Security. Farmers, business people, conservationists, civil rights advocates, Indians, the Mexican government itself—all are engaged in objections, discussions and lawsuits. Some border residents approve of the fence, but many express general outrage over the plan to build the Great Wall of America. So far, security trumps everything: trade, family and historical connections, farmland access, irrigation, animal migration, tourism and just plain crossing the border for one reason or another.

Construction of the new border fence was authorized by the Secure Fence Act of 2006. It instructed Homeland Security to secure 700 miles of the border with double-layered fencing, as well as other types of barriers, including cameras and motion detectors, all to be built or installed by December 2008. However, because of local resistance and tough terrain, the department settled for 300 miles of vehicle barriers and 370 miles of pedestrian fence by the end of 2008. And the type of fence has been downgraded. In many sectors—along the Arizona border, for example—the new fence is a makeshift hodgepodge of wire, vehicle barriers, old helicopter landing pads, corrugated steel bars and metal mesh.

On April 1, 2008, the Department of Homeland Security announced that any environmental law or regulation that would prevent, or slow down, the construction of the new fence along the entire southern border would be waived. "Criminal activity at the border does not stop for endless debate or protracted litigation," said then-Homeland Security head, Michael Chertoff. The department had used its waiver powers (given to it under the Real ID Act of 2005) three times before to allow new fencing near San Diego, and in two other border areas of Arizona. But the April 1st waiver was massive; it applied to thirty-six federal laws.

The Homeland Security secretary has powers that not even the president can exercise, even during a national or military crisis. And the department's power affects everyone who lives in the third country of the borderlands. In that zone of conflict and confusion, all constitutional and legal bets are off.

It's not surprising that the most concerted objections to the new fence come from the "Valley," as the northern bank of the River from the Gulf to Rio Grande City 150 miles upstream is called. Some ranches and farms straddle the Rio Grande, and tens of thousands of people cross back and forth every day to work, to go to school and to shop. For Homeland Security, anything is fair game in achieving its goal, from waiving laws and regulations to expropriating private land. For the people of the Valley, the fence is a Berlin Wall that will divide a unique Tex-Mex society that exists on both sides of a narrow river. (The 115 miles of border fence allocated to Texas was completed in January 2011.)

In a March 2008 editorial, the *New York Times* paraphrased Winston Churchill, who once upon a time warned about another barrier on another continent: "From San Diego on the Pacific to Brownsville on the Rio Grande, a steel curtain is descending across the continent."

What is one to make of such a barrier? And of the country that would build it? I have seen other barriers: the Berlin Wall, and the so-called peace lines in Northern Ireland— winding their way through the mean, narrow streets, keeping the two sides apart, still in place even though the long war is over. When I see portions of the fence along the Mexican border, I have the same reaction as when I look at the walls in Belfast. My heart drops. The word "eyesore" does not begin to describe these walls and fences, wherever they are. They are ugly when they're first built. They become disgusting as they rust and rot. The barriers are profoundly dispiriting. They stink of failure and stupidity. They signify the end of dialogue, the freezing of attitudes, the paralysis of hope.

The situation along the U.S.–Mexico border is complicated and unusual. The economic discrepancies on each side are unparalleled elsewhere in the world. A pro-fence advocate could make the argument that it is this incongruity that makes the idea of a wall reasonable and inevitable. No country in the position of the United States can stand, indefinitely, the inflow of millions of unregulated economic refugees. The consequences for the American economy, and for its orderly political existence, would be dire.

The Mexican government pays mere lip service to controlling illegal border crossings. In fact, there are good grounds to suspect that that government covertly favours out-migration as a safety valve for its own economic problems. Mexico is not a failed state, but it has certainly failed spectacularly to look after a large number of its own people. And there is always the suspicion that one of the inchoate underlying motivations of Mexican policy is the vague yet potent idea of revenge, of a kind of reconquest of land that is rightfully Mexico's.

No one knows better than Americans the effect on political arrangements of having people occupying the ground. The United States' own expansion west was always preceded by a movement of Americans—trappers, mountain men, ranchers, farmers, traders, miners, opportunists of all kinds—into territory belonging to Indians, or to Mexico, or to the British North American colonies. People preceded political and social infrastructure.

Once there were sufficient Americans in Texas, the Mexican state became independent, and then part of the great republic. The presence of a critical mass of Americans there may not have been a sufficient cause of the annexation of Texas, but it was a necessary one. When tens of thousands of Americans moved into the Oregon Country west of the Rockies—looking for gold and for land—Great Britain was forced to concede part of it to the jurisdiction of the United States, and it had to bargain hard, and keep its powder dry, to maintain control north of the 49th parallel.

Whatever the political and psychological dynamics in Mexico, the fact remains that almost all responsibility for securing the border has fallen on the United States. In that case, a pro-fence advocate can argue that the logic is infallible: it is necessary to stop, or at least to reduce, as much as possible, the influx of *indocumentados*. Lesser fences and virtual barriers discourage entry and slow it down, so that the Border Patrol has a better chance of interdiction. On this border, however, the necessity is even stronger because it is not only a sieve for illegal workers, it is also a drug-importing conduit and, perhaps, a path for the next terrorist strike. And so there is no choice, they say, but to build elaborate walls and fences.

The Mexican War of 1846–48 began in the Valley of the Rio Grande and was one prong of the American drive to take over the vast western territories of the continent. One man's war is another man's invasion. In Mexico, the war is known as "The North American Intervention," or as "The Defensive War," or as "The United States Invasion." The second prong of the United States' "splendid juggernaut" (as the painter George Catlin described it) was to occupy the vast northwest Oregon Country—composed of Washington, Oregon, Idaho, parts of Wyoming and Montana, and what is now my own province of British Columbia—on the Pacific side of the Rocky Mountains. This aim brought the republic into conflict once again with the British Empire in its Canadian colonies and territories.

In 1812, the United States had invaded the eastern colonies of British North America (although the War of 1812 had complex causes beyond American desire for territorial expansion). The resulting stalemate, when the war ended two years later, reaffirmed the eastern boundary between the United States and Canada, and the 49th parallel was soon settled upon as the border westward to the Rocky Mountains. American attention shifted to the land west of the Rockies— and to the southwest.

An emotional national debate took place over how, and how far (but not if) the U.S. should expand. In December 1845, the editor of the *New York Morning News*, John L. O'Sullivan, wrote that the United States should claim all of the Oregon Country "by the right of our manifest destiny to overspread and to possess the whole of the continent which Providence has given us for the development of the great experiment of liberty and federated self-government entrusted to us." Ironically, the pithy dictum became popular only after it was ridiculed in Congress by an opponent of expansionism. It became part of the philosophical underpinning of the American empire.

O'Sullivan had not been thinking of the southwest when he wrote. He thought that Texas would set the pattern for that region: Anglo-Saxons, emigrating west, would set up democratic governments that would, inevitably, follow the Texian precedent and ask for admission to the United States. Annexation would be voluntary. California would likely be next. Canada, too, would eventually see the light. O'Sullivan's idea reflected with accuracy what was happening on the ground: the penetration of new territory by westward-pushing private American citizens who, soon, sought to organize themselves politically as territories and, eventually, as new states within the union.

Manifest destiny became America's project under the expansionist president, James K. Polk. In practice, it meant: sweep west to occupy and civilize the "wilderness"; displace, or kill, the people who are there now, whether Mexicans or Indians.

In 1846, on various pretexts, none of them legitimate, Polk ordered General Zachary Taylor to march to the Rio Grande.

The acknowledged border between Mexico and independent Texas was the Nueces River, which flows into the Gulf of Mexico at Corpus Christi, about 150 miles to the north of the Rio Grande. Sending American troops south of the Nueces was an invasion into Mexican territory. Taylor began the construction of a rudimentary fort—originally called Fort Texas, it later became Fort Brown, and then Brownsville. Polk hesitated to order Taylor across the Rio Grande. If there were vague, although largely bogus, grounds for disagreeing with the Nueces as the Mexican boundary (contained in the agreements signed in 1836 after the American victory at San Jacinto, leading to Texan independence), there was no doubt about the legitimacy of the Rio Grande.

Polk had to be careful about initiating war with Mexico because many Americans objected strenuously to his expansionist plans. In fact, there was far more Congressional opposition to this war than there would be to most of America's wars to come. Abraham Lincoln was against it. Ohio congressman Joshua Giddings called it "an aggressive, unholy, and unjust war." As always, American soldiers were more honest and clearheaded about the prospect of war than their bellicose civilian leaders. Colonel Ethan Hitchcock wrote: "We do not have a particle of right to be here [on the Rio Grande] . . . it looks as if the government sent a small force on purpose to bring on a war." After the war began, Henry David Thoreau went to jail rather than pay taxes to support it. His essay *Civil Disobedience* was motivated by the Mexican War (as well as by slavery).

Eventually, Mexican troops did attack a small patrol of American soldiers north of the Rio Grande. Polk had his *casus belli*, and he declared war. American troops invaded Mexican territory south of the River; they captured Veracruz and marched to Mexico City and to Monterrey. Another American army took California. Weak, divided and coup-ridden, Mexico had no chance.

The Treaty of Guadalupe Hidalgo in 1848 was one of the harshest ever imposed on a loser of a war by a winner. The United States humiliated Mexico, left it diminished and weakened, and subject to attack by other imperialist powers. (France went so far as to invade and occupy Mexico in 1862, with the support of Britain and Spain. The United States was preoccupied with its Civil War, and in no position to enforce the Monroe doctrine—which specified: if anyone's going to invade Mexico, it's us.) Under the treaty's terms, Mexico ceded almost half its territory to the United States: what is now New Mexico, Arizona, California, Nevada, Utah, Colorado and the remainder of Texas down to the Rio Grande. The present border was set in 1853 with the Gadsden Purchase, the acquisition of a chunk of land that is now the southernmost portions of New Mexico and Arizona.

North of the new border lived many long-established Mexican (and Indian) communities. Overnight, these people became Americans. But where Mexican settlement had been most dense—in southern California, and north and east of the Rio Grande, and especially along its lower reaches towards the Gulf of Mexico—the new United States territories were already Hispanic. The pattern of a Spanish-speaking (or bilingual), largely Hispanic culture on the northern bank of the River, and along parts of the border farther west, is the foundation of Anglo-American insecurity in the borderlands.

Brownsville is almost at the eastern end of the Valley. The first business here was cattle, brought in from the Caribbean islands of the Greater Antilles. The first cowboys in America rode here, although they were Mexicans, and so were really vaqueros. The widespread cowboy culture of the United States began in this part of Texas. Later, Anglos adopted the Mexican technology of lariat, saddle, chaps, pointed-toe boots with spurs, and wide-brimmed hats. Spanish words were incorporated into the language of the west: savvy, calaboose, adobe, hoosegow, lasso. As one historian points out, the Americans added some elements of their own: the revolver, barbed wire and lawyers. The simple vaquero on horseback was transformed into the romantic image of the armed American cowboy. The Mexican cattle and horse culture of the Valley of the Rio Grande became the quintessential American model of the West.

Some of those armed and mounted Anglo-machos came back to haunt Mexico. *Los rinches*—the Texas Rangers— were the hard hammer of American power along the River border for generations. They hunted Mexicans like coyotes, ran long-settled Mexican families off their land, strung up "the greasers" whenever they felt like it, and raided across the River into Mexico in hot pursuits, or in cold-blooded retaliatory raids. Everyone along the River remembers *los rinches*, either as killers or as heroes, depending on the rememberer's skin colour.

In 1859, Juan "Cheno" Cortina attacked Brownsville with between forty and eighty men, in protest against the theft of Mexican land under the Treaty of Guadalupe Hidalgo. He cleared the city of Anglo-Texans, and pillaged and burned all along the border. His family had lived in the area for generations, and it owned a large Spanish land grant that included the surroundings of Brownsville. Cortina was the violent embodiment of Mexican resentment at the loss of territory after the Mexican War and the subsequent expropriation of land by Anglos from Mexicans who didn't know how the American legal system worked. The proverbial last straw: Cortina saw a U.S. marshal roughly arresting one of his old employees. Cortina shot the marshal, and began his campaign.

By the time he was defeated and driven across the Rio Grande into Mexico, Cortina commanded close to four hundred men, and the Americans had put Robert E. Lee in command of the Eighth Military District, in which the area of conflict lay. An army major in the campaign summed up

Cortina's depredations: "The whole country from Brownsville to Rio Grande City, one hundred and twenty miles and back to the Arroyo Colorado, has been laid waste. There is not an American [left] or any property belonging to an American that could be destroyed in this large tract of land . . . There have been fifteen Americans and eighty friendly Mexicans killed."

To Americans, Cortina was a common terrorist-bandido, but he was also a most dangerous political foe. He questioned the very legitimacy of their ownership of the Lower Valley of Texas, and he was a violent man who was quite prepared to wipe them out. Mexicans thought he was a freedom fighter, a hero. He embodied all the bitterness and indignation at the gringo invasion of 1846.

Mexicans sang *corridos* about him. These folk songs, part of the *musica norteña* of the Mexican frontier, deal in booze, women, death by the gun or the knife, and in fighting back against the gringos. Now they are sung about drug runners and *pistoleros* along the border, and about the poor men and women who have no choice but to live outside the law.

Cleve and Rosemary drive up onto the berm bordering the River in Brownsville, and we look across the few yards to the Mexican city of Matamoros. Cleve asks me if I have my passport with me, but I've left it back in the room. In that case, we should get off the berm. The Border Patrol checks along here all the time for drug runners. If you're not a citizen and don't have papers with you, you might find yourself having a long conversation in one of their interrogation rooms.

All this time, and later, over whisky back at the inn, we talk about the borderlands. As I expect, my hosts take a sanguine approach to illegals and immigration. The migrants are essential now; the American economy depends on them. A wall or a fence is just a plain dumb idea. It's impossible to keep people out that way; they'll find a way across. And there's no way you can send back the illegals who are here now, as some conservative Americans would like to do. That's close to eleven and a half million people. You can't deny them social services, either, as many towns and cities are trying to do—that's impractical and inhumane. Furthermore, in many ways, they are ideal immigrants: hardworking, family-oriented, God-fearing, with a low crime rate.

But the huge numbers do create "immense social problems," says Cleve. The immigrants have lots of kids so they put tremendous pressure on schools and on the health system. Cameron County has the lowest per-capita income of any county in the U.S.—a result of its huge growth, unacknowledged by the state or federal governments. You have to have some controls—a guest-worker program, for example, whereby the doors would be opened to individuals for a limited period, after which they would be sent home. And, reluctantly, Cleve and Rosemary suggest that more border security is probably necessary, too. Just to put a lid on things until an enlightened immigration policy can be put into effect. One good thing is that Hispanics have got themselves into political power in the Valley, and farther up the River, too. There's no Anglo ruling class. This is a genuine tribute to the openness and the flexibility of American democracy, they say.

Now I'm drunk as well as dead tired. My notes become incoherent. I leave Cleve and Rosemary's house and lurch back to my snazzy room. I can barely look at my bike propped up outside. I don't want to think about climbing aboard next morning and riding on.

I don't ride on. I wake up at six with a grinding headache— I'm prone to muscle-contraction headaches, although this one is part hangover. And the right side of my neck and right shoulder are sore, too. I'm paying the price for yesterday. I sit, doped up, at breakfast with Cleve and Rosemary, and the troopers (who, after a long week among the partying assholes, look as bummed out as I do). Then, I'm handed the excuse I long for. Don't head for La Boca Chica today, says the trooper whose parents are illegals. "It'll be a zoo. You'd have to be nuts." It's Sunday, the last day of the March break. It simply makes sense to wait for tomorrow, and for the crowds and traffic to disperse, before dipping my hand in the Gulf of Mexico. I tell my hosts that, if they don't mind, I'll stay another night.

To hell with the expense; I need the rest. I spend the day medicating my pain, wiping Highway 77 spinach-field mud off the bike and my riding gear, checking over the bike, reading, writing, walking shaded paths and the banks of the *resaca*, watching birds, patting dogs.

In the afternoon, I talk to Cleve and Rosemary's son, Jesse. Besides being an ex-trooper, he's also a reserve cop, a pilot, a paramedic and a dive master. He's tall, blond and amiable. When I say something he agrees with, he says "Yessir," one of the south's common locutions, with especial emphasis. Without my suggesting the phrase, he volunteers that the way to understand the border is that it's a third country. The Border Patrol and ICE (Immigration and Customs Enforcement) know it, he says. That's why they set up their checkpoints well away from the River—thirty or fifty miles north. The attitude is: you Mexicans can come over, live and work here, get a driver's licence, and live your life—as long as you stay in this area. The Border Patrol won't bother you in this third country, but go north of, say, Kingsville (just south of Corpus Christi), and they'll grab you.

I tell Jesse my plan to cross over into Mexico at Laredo, ride through Nuevo Laredo and up Highway 2. He's a young man, and a cop, and I'm curious about whether he'll agree with Bob and Linda in Austin that this isn't a good plan.

"You want to go through Nuevo Laredo and up the Number 2?" he says, as if he hasn't quite heard right.

"Yeah," I say. "Just ride through fast and up to Piedras Negras or Ciudad Acuña, and then cross back over—just to cut the distance. It's much farther on this side."

"What are you carrying?" Jesse asks.

I'm taken aback. "Carrying?" I say.

"Uh, yeah, carrying" he says. "A weapon?" he adds helpfully.

"Uh, I don't carry a weapon," I say, and laugh. "I'm Canadian."

Jesse looks at me for a moment. Then he laughs, too.

"I don't know," he says. "I wouldn't do it."

The next morning, early, I ride out of the haven of Cleve and Rosemary's inn. There's cloud and a high wind, and an intimation of rain. I have no pains this morning, and most important, desire has returned. I hunger to get on the bike, and on the road. My hosts and I have become friends over the last two days, and they will take no payment for the best room, by a very long shot, that I will stay in during my rides. They remember my simple-minded arrival, and give me step-by-step instructions about how to get to the right road and how to bypass Brownsville on my way back through towards the west.

It's an easy ride on near-empty country roads. I feel pretty damned superior for having waited that extra day. As I near the Gulf of Mexico, the wind grows stronger, blowing alternately from behind me, or across, as my route zigzags south and east. The strong easterly on my ride down from Goliad was an anomaly. In this windy season, the wind normally blows from the west, and it's gone round to that direction today. I ride the straight roads through vast, flat, green fields dotted with palms and palmettos. In this Jurassic landscape, a meandering hadrosaur would not be out of place. I pass a Border Patrol checkpoint that is set up to stop vehicles going the other way. I have to slow down, though, to pass through traffic cones. An agent steps out of a small trailer and waves me on. The fields give way to tidal mud flats, pocked with little palmetto islands. Soon after entering Boca Chica State Park, I can see, in the distance, big surf coming ashore.

I park the bike between high sand dunes. There are only five other vehicles, their occupants sitting watching the waves or strolling the beach. Yesterday, according to my state-trooper informants, there might have been ten thousand drunks here. In the humid heat, I plough through the deep, soft sand, and party garbage, and tippytoe back and forth at the waves' undulating edges to avoid getting salt on my leather riding boots. I scoop up a handful of Gulf water, taste it. I hope the next time I do this, I'll have crossed a wide continental isthmus, and it will be Pacific Ocean salt water I hold in my hands. I climb to the top of a big dune and look south to where the Rio Grande flows into the Gulf. It's a few miles away, and too far to see on this hazy day.

When I get back to the bike, I realize that the wind is driving fine sand everywhere—it has insinuated itself into the folds of my bags and riding jacket, and into every plastic and metal crevice on the bike. The salty wind is sandblasting my paint finish. I brush off as much sand as I can, but it's useless labour. I make a short recording on my digital tape recorder— although when I listen to it later, all I can hear are a few intermittent words, the remainder drowned out by the bops and roars of the near-gale-force wind.

I've parked the bike pointing in the direction I want to go, so I put on my jacket, gloves and helmet, and mount up. I think of my lost friends. "Here we go," I tell them. I idle the engine for a minute, snap down my visor and plunk into first gear. I speed up with care on the sand-greasy road, and I ride west into the wind, and into the third country.

CHAPTER 3

THE THIRD COUNTRY

. . . 1,950 MILE LONG OPEN WOUND
DIVIDING A PUEBLO, A CULTURE,
RUNNING DOWN THE LENGTH OF MY BODY,
STAKING FENCE RODS INTO MY FLESH . . .
—GLORIA ANZALDÚA, *Borderlands/La Frontera*

MY FIRST SOLO CONTACT WITH THE RIO GRANDE BORDER between the United States and Mexico is not a happy one.

I bypass downtown Brownsville to its north, riding through a few-mile stretch of strip malls, gas stations and fast-food joints. On the western edge of the city, I pick up the 281, the old military road, which runs close by the River all the way to McAllen. Along the whole length of the Valley, the Rio Grande meanders and bends, and curls almost back on itself, the permeable, ambiguous southern edge of this part of America. There are a hundred *resacas* in the making. It's a good illustration of why volatile and wilful rivers make bad borders.

The land is flat and cultivated, mostly with irrigated vegetable crops: yellow squash, peppers, zucchini and cucumbers. From the 281, dirt farm roads occasionally cut off towards the river, which is anywhere from a couple of miles to a few hundred yards away, depending on how its course writhes. My plan is to cut down to the river's edge from time to time. I want to see what it looks like, how it's defended and how easy it might be to cross. Just before La Paloma, I turn left down a dirt road towards the river a few hundred yards away.

Almost immediately, a large brownish dog comes pounding—barking and snarling—out of a lot with a dilapidated shack surrounded by junk cars and old appliances. I'm riding slowly on the tricky surface, and the cur catches me easily, clamping its teeth into my right jeans leg and riding boot. The goddamn mongrel is a heavyweight and it almost pulls the bike over. I'm barely able to keep control and upright; I accelerate and the mutt lets go. It pursues me, in professional silence now, for a hundred yards, before breaking off the ambush, its border well defended, honour maintained. Looking down, I can see perforations in my jeans, and teeth marks in my new Triumph leather riding boot.

This shakes me up. I don't want to drop the bike on one of these bad roads, and I certainly don't want to get brought down by a Baskervilles-type hound. I hadn't anticipated that my armoured gear might be useful against dog attacks.

I trundle on down to the river. There's a low dirt berm along the water's edge wide enough for a vehicle. I park below it and climb on top. The river is about fifty yards wide, opaque, caramel-coloured water flowing fast. On this side are the green, tended vegetables. On the Mexican shore—the long northwest finger of the state of Tamaulipas—lies a scrubby sand wasteland with a few small, rundown buildings scattered nearby, although I can see green fields farther upstream. Three men are standing beside the shore on the other side of the river, talking. When they catch sight of me, they stop and stare across. One waves; I wave back. The day is growing very hot. I take off my jacket and sit down to drink some water.

Within three or four minutes, an SUV appears round the curve of the berm to my right—the Border Patrol. The vehicle stops ten yards away. Two agents get out and walk towards me. One of them draws his side arm and holds the weapon down along his leg. They are both short, stocky Hispanics, cropped black hair, muscular arms, wraparound sunglasses, tough.

"Hi," I say. "How are you?"

"What are you doing here?" says the guy with the pistol. They stare at me, and at my bike; the other agent turns and scans back and forth along the berm, over the fields towards a treeline, across the river at the men on the Mexican shore, who stand and watch.

"I'm just taking a look at the river. I'm riding west along the border, and I was just curious about how it looked along here."

"Get up," says the pistolero.

"ID" says the other guy.

"It's on the bike."

"Get it."

They follow me down. I show them my passport.

"You from Canada?" exclaims the other guy. "What the hell are you doin' down here?"

I explain about my book and the research I'm doing.

"Well, this is a restricted area," says the pistol-packer.

"I'm sorry," I say. "I didn't know; I didn't see any signs."

"There ain't no signs. Open your bags."

The other guy pokes through my gear, bag by bag, while the gunman stands by, still holding his pistol along his thigh. They are silent. The wind blows hard, kicking up dust. I'm sweating in the searing sun; it must be ninety-five degrees, and it's humid.

"Okay," says the bag searcher. They relax; the gunsel slips his heat back into its holster.

"Just head on back to the highway," he says. "This is a restricted area."

"Is it dangerous down here?" I ask as I re-stow my duffles.

"It's restricted. Just head on back out of here, now."

"Do you get illegals crossing the river around here, or drug smuggling?" I'm pushing my luck.

"Sir, I am telling you to leave this area right now," says the bag searcher.

"Okay. No problem."

While they stand by and watch, I pull on my jacket and helmet, turn the bike and mount up.

One more try: "I guess this area will be easier to secure when the fence is built," I say.

They stare at me, the disembodied blankness of sunglasses. Unnerving. They stay silent. I give up.

"Okay. So long."

They don't reply. In my rear-view mirror, I see them standing motionless, staring after me.

Before I hit the main road again, and as I expected, the goddamn dog makes another sortie. This time, I kick out at it as hard as I can. I miss, but it stops the big pooch from grabbing hold. It follows me all the way to the main road.

"Get outta here! Fuck off!" I shout at it like a fool.

It stands hacking and snarling as I check for traffic, and pull out into the hot west wind.

Welcome to the Borderlands, I say to myself. So this is what America has come to along its southern border. This is how things are in this third country: suspicion, search and seizure without probable cause, intimidation. A Border Patrol state. I haven't been subject to a nasty search by uniformed men holding (almost) a gun on me since I was in Northern Ireland during the Troubles—and that was a kind of war. Unless my first experience with border security was, by chance, an anomaly. Perhaps they were made especially suspicious by the three men just across the river, thought something might be going down between us. I suppose I'll find out.

The term "borderland" was in use at least as long ago as the early nineteenth century, when it described the English-Scottish border, and, a little later, the Welsh marches. From its beginnings, it had the suggestion of a contested region, of a frontier, of one entity shading into another, and of uncertainty, raffishness and danger.

The term "Spanish Borderlands" was first proposed in 1921 by historian Herbert Eugene Bolton, to describe Florida and the southwestern United States boundary area. Since then, historians of this region have gradually shifted the term west to describe the area from Texas to the Pacific Ocean. These borderlands are, therefore, a region mainly of desert and arid mountains, lying opposite the northern states of Mexico. They are Hispanic and Indian, with an admixture of Anglo settlers. It is a laconic landscape of open range, badlands and long views, and of plants and animals with ingenious modes of survival in a hard place.

Americans moving west along the frontier, out of the woods and hills of the east, did not come up against a wilderness upon which they could impose their civilization. They found an older, established civilization already there, a mixture of Spaniards and Indians. It was a culture of pueblos and missions, of trade, and of racial and religious amalgamation well in place long before Americans had even thought about independence from the British Empire. The mingling of Spaniards and Indians had not been easy or peaceful—it was no melting pot. And the newly arriving Anglos added another dissonant element in a region one historian calls "a forge where cultural collisions cause sparks and heat." These are still the constituents of cultural conflict in the borderlands, made more intense by the fact of the border itself, its violent history, the traffic across it, and the huge disparities it marks.

The southern border is the prototypical borderland, and therefore meets perfectly the defining criteria: despite a political boundary, the people living there share common social characteristics; those characteristics make the people more like each other than they are to the general populations in their respective countries; and the very different cultures of the two adjacent countries blend in various ways within the borderlands.

Borders are paradoxes. They both divide and unite. They are bridges between cultures and societies, and, especially in borderlands, create their distinctive hybrid cultures. The poet Gloria Anzaldúa describes how, in the Tex-Mex borderlands, people might put chili on their borscht, or make tortillas out of whole wheat flour. When I rode along the Rio Grande, waitresses would bring me a Budweiser with a chunk of lime wedged in the mouth *cerveza*-style, and sometimes a salted glass. At breakfast, before I ordered French toast or oatmeal, they brought me bowls of tortilla chips and salsa.

However, a border creates barriers, too, and conflict between the adjoining cultures. It's still a line the traveller must cross. For Anzaldúa, the border still fractures her hybrid self: a "1,950 mile long open wound . . . staking fence rods into my flesh."

The United States' border with Mexico (as with Canada) is also the limit that America's own heroic story of itself—its mythology—butts up against. The border is a kind of reality check. It provides an opportunity for perspective on the United States' solipsistic national narrative: the great, God-sanctioned, manifestly destined expansion of the American frontier westward—and also north and south.

At the border, another version of history takes over. But in the southern borderlands, they are histories with similarities. Mexico, too, had its frontier, although it lay north rather than west. The Spanish and mestizos leaving the settled and fertile regions to the south moved into a landscape that was the same as the one Anglos later found when they headed west. The two groups endured identical hardships and dangers: desert, drought, remoteness, great distances and the fierce people already there. For the Indians, the frontier was simply home, and the Anglo frontiersmen or the Spanish-Mexican *norteños* were all invaders to be fought off.

———

Twenty miles down the 281, after my first contact with the Border Patrol, I turn left towards the border and the Mexican town of Nuevo Progreso. I park in a lot on the American side of the river. I intend to walk across so that I won't have to worry about my bike and bags while I look around. I tip the two attendants—two giggling Hispanic girls—$10 to store my jacket and helmet in their hut, and to keep an eye on the KLR. It is a hot day, and the border is busy with many Americans crossing over, by car and on foot, to buy cheap stuff in Mexico.

Halfway across the bridge, I look down into the muddy river and watch Mexican kids swimming back and forth between the two countries. When they get to the American side, they haul themselves up onto the bank and lie in the sun to rest and banter. For a while, they are illegals, but no one gives them a second look. As the bridge crosses over the adjacent land on the Mexican side, a few dozen women and children cluster underneath. They hold out their hands and shout up at the people above: "Dinero! Dollares!" At the Mexican checkpoint, I look for an official, but the four uniformed men cluster a few yards away, smoking and joking, ignoring the pedestrians and vehicles streaming into their country. Two rifles lean casually up against a wall. You could bring anything you like into Mexico; they don't give a damn.

I realize I've forgotten my camera on the bike. I cross the road and head back across the bridge to the American side. I tell the agent I'm just going back to get my camera. He runs my passport through his computer and waves me through. I retrieve the camera, cross the road and walk back into Mexico. Back and forth twice between the two countries has taken me less than five minutes.

The Valley towns I've been riding through look almost like America, except for the people, who are almost all Hispanic, and the signs, which are mostly in Spanish, and the feel of the place, which is third-countryish. In restaurants and gas stations, employees speak English to me, but often badly, and, if I begin in Spanish, they gratefully continue in Spanish. Or rather, they speak in the border Spanish of this region, English words mixed in, full of slang.

Crossing into Nuevo Progreso, however, there's no doubt that I've entered a much different place: the "third world," rather than the south bank of the third country. I'm surrounded by shoeshine kids, and kids selling cigarettes, carved wooden birds, fans, jewellery. School doesn't seem to be in the cards for these sharp-eyed hawkers. The main street stretching away from the border is a jumble of cheap-goods stores, jammed traffic, sidewalk stalls and stands, a mass of people, mostly Hispanic, but with a fair number of white, sweating, stout gringos in shorts and funny shirts. Loud salsa music blares out from half a dozen boom boxes. People shout and sing and dicker. Everything is loud noise and bright colours.

I walk up and down the street unmolested by pint-sized capitalists. I must look as if I'm not in the market for a statue of Jesus for the dashboard of my car. I'm alone—not waddling along with the dyed-blond missus—and I'm wearing my riding boots and, compared to most of these people, I'm tall and skinny.

Later, I stop at an outdoor bar, away from the shoppers. The bartender is a ten-year-old kid with fifty-year-old eyes. I drink a *cerveza* out of the bottle, and, in the hot sun, I relax and order another. I ask the suave, well-dressed Mexican sitting next to me if he's visiting from somewhere.

"No, señor," he says with dignity. "Vivo aquí en Nuevo Progreso."

He wants to speak English, in which he is fluent, but with a strong accent. He owns a store farther up the main road, selling appliances and furniture to Americans, and to Mexicans who have jobs. He has a wife and five children. His kids are all in school today—not like these little *gitanos* who are all over the place. Canada must be very cold, he says. Sometimes, it is, I say. I buy him a beer, and another one for myself. His family has lived in this area for five generations. This is unusual in Progreso, which, even though it looks like a typical old Mexican town, was created only sixty or so years ago. An American farmer built his own bridge across the river to bring Mexican vegetables across. Tourists came, stores and restaurants were built, and the town grew up around them.

I ask my drinking partner what the border means to him. He shrugs. It is the U.S. over there, he says, but the people on both sides of the river are the same. Like everyone here, he has family and friends on the other side. Now, it takes much longer to visit them and this is making people angry. Only criminals cross the river in boats; it's too dangerous for ordinary citizens to do that now. The Border Patrol will arrest you, or the drug guys will kill you if you get in the way.

I ask about smuggling across the river. He shrugs again. It is the main business here, he says. It's nothing to take migrants or drugs across the river. No one pays any attention to it. I mention my earlier run-in with the Border Patrol. Yes, he admits, they are getting tougher. But it doesn't make any difference; people find a way to get across. What about the fence the Americans will build? He laughs. People will find a way to get across, fence or not. He tells me about a local editorial cartoon: it shows a twenty-foot-high border wall running through town. On the Mexican side of the wall is a store, with a sign that reads, "José's 21-foot Ladders."

Now, he must buy me a beer. Honour demands it. I hadn't intended to get drunk in Mexico, but I'm on my way. Fortunately, after we drink and talk a while longer, he has to get back to work. We shake hands. He bows slightly as he does so. "Cuidado, señor," he says. "Be careful." I walk to the river, cross the bridge, go through the same perfunctory passport check, and tell the Hispanic agent I'm not bringing anything back. "Except some alcohol," he says to me. "Right," I say. We both laugh.

The Treaty of Guadalupe Hidalgo ended the Mexican War in 1848, but the new border remained a violent and unstable place. For the next seventy years or so, there was constant small-scale conflict between Anglos and Mexicans in the annexed territories: a gamut of episodes from harassment to land seizures to lynchings and murders. The victims were usually the Mexicans, who now found themselves to be a marginalized, powerless and despised form of American.

The Mexicans hadn't been happy with the distant and autocratic rule of Mexico City—they were, after all, frontier *norteños*—but the new Anglo overlords were much worse. The gringos came with the baggage of their conviction of racial superiority; they were operating within their own legal and political system, about which the Mexicans knew little. And the Anglos, now living almost like *conquistadores* among a resentful and colonial population, were both condescending of their subordinate neighbours, and wary of Mexican resentment and the possibility of resistance to the new order. Such wariness encouraged harsh treatment and, perhaps, pre-emptive violence to keep the "greasers" in line.

The border remained a tenuous thing. The Anglos, imbued with the spirit of manifest destiny, didn't think the new border was necessarily the last word: perhaps the United States should take over more of the weak, divided, inferior country to the south. Mexico itself was bitter about its loss of territory. And for the Mexicans along the border, the new boundary had little meaning. As one historian writes: "Most of them paid no attention. They and their ancestors had passed and re-passed the river at their pleasure for ten generations, and the idea of a 'boundary' set up by a handful of gringos who had moved in only twenty-five years before was a little comic." Comic, that is, until the gringos ferociously asserted their new boundary— and their dominance within it. That Anglo oppression encour- aged Mexicans in Texas and across the river to maintain and nourish their ties of kinship and culture.

The valley of the lower Rio Grande, with its large Mexican population, had more than its share of racial tension and con- flict. Cheno Cortina's raids, near the beginning of this seventy- year-long time of violence, had demonstrated the volatility of feeling in the region. More large-scale raids took place near the end of the period, in 1915–16, during the tumult and chaos of the Mexican Revolution. And it was in the town of McAllen, just upstream, that the Anglos first discovered the extent of the supposed plot against them.

Authorities there arrested Basilio Ramos Jr. on unspecified charges, on January 24, 1915, and discovered a copy of some- thing called the Plan of San Diego. It was a revolutionary man- ifesto that called for a "liberating army of races and peoples"— made up of Mexican-Americans, African-Americans and, oddly, Japanese (possibly because they had recently defeated the white imperialist czarist Russian empire)—that would liberate the territory taken from Mexico under the Treaty of Guadalupe Hidalgo. The "freed" states would form an inde- pendent republic that might seek annexation with Mexico, although not necessarily—the Mexican frontier had its own ideas about independence. The plan was also a call to race war: all white males over the age of sixteen would be sum- marily executed. The revolution would begin in four weeks' time, on February 20, 1915.

Nothing happened on that date. The plan—which was most likely drafted by inmates of the Monterrey jail and had nothing to do with the town of San Diego in Texas—was delir- ious revolutionary rhetoric common among border Mexicans. Nevertheless, in the context of the lengthy disorder and cross-border stress of the Mexican Revolution—American troops had occupied Veracruz the previous year, and Pancho Villa's incursions were soon to come—the half-baked ideology of the Plan of San Diego soon resulted in violence. Between July 1915 and July 1916, Mexican and Mexican-American guerrillas raided all through the Valley. They killed Anglo farmers, a Texas Ranger and other citizens.

Over that year, while only twenty-one Americans were killed, both civilians and military, the deaths caused hysteria among the suspicious Anglos near the border. As always, the Mexicans in south Texas suffered the most. Anglo vigilantes and Rangers carried out summary executions of as many as three hundred people, and thousands of Mexicans crossed the Rio Grande back to Mexico for safety. Memory of the raids faded, but remembrance of the racial conflict they caused persisted for a long time.

The Plan of San Diego is a foreshadowing of a similar but contemporary plan: the movement among a minority of Hispanic-Americans for the establishment of so-called Aztlán, an independent Hispanic state in North America. Aztlán was the mythic, ancestral home of pre-Columbian Mexicans. One legend has it in the Atlantic Ocean, and populated by an advanced civilization: the Chanes—"people of the snake" in Mayan. Aztlán was a form of utopia, and its modern version is the symbol of various Hispanic-American independence movements.

The vision of Aztlán was first revived in 1969 at the Chicano Youth Liberation Conference in Denver and referred explicitly to the hope of reclaiming the American states taken from Mexico in 1848. The concept is a product of the faux-revolutionary fervour of the 1960s, but it remains an active element in the ideology of Hispanic nationalism within the United States. The old anger and resentment at the punitive terms of the Treaty of Guadalupe Hidalgo smoulders; people do not forget such dramatic and total humiliation.

The Chicano (a term for Mexican-Americans, although implying a self-conscious political-cultural identity) poet Alurista may have originated the current use of the term "Aztlán" when he read a poem at the 1969 conference: "Aztlán, Aztlán of the continent that bears the child / your mother is the redearthcontinent / . . . the seed which our father Quetzalcoatl planted / now germinates / in the womb of our / motherearthcontinent, amerindia."

The Mexican-born, American-raised poet also read the following words to the young Chicanos in Denver: "In the spirit of a new people that is conscious not only of its proud historical heritage but also of the brutal gringo invasion of our territories, we, the Chicano inhabitants and civilizers of the northern land of Aztlán from whence came our forefathers, reclaiming the land of their birth and consecrating the determination of our people of the sun, declare that the call of our blood is our power, our responsibility, and our inevitable destiny." The manifesto became known as the Plan Espiritual de Aztlán.

The radical Chicano movement that advocates the reinvention of Aztlán has remained marginal, but the Chicano civil rights movement is going strong. Its more recent manifestations have included a large role in the marches in support of immigration reform and of amnesty for the approximately twelve million *indocumentados* in the United States.

The movement, and its utopian and retaliatory aspirations, also inflames Anglo-American radicals. American nativists—embodied in small groups like the Minutemen, but including the many more people who support their agenda—fear loss of identity and a cultural takeover by the hordes of Hispanic immigrants. Sometimes Mexicans give them reason to worry. The American writer Luis Alberto Urrea quotes a

Mexican politician as telling him: "We have inserted twelve million workers into the United States—it is already Mexico! We have won the war!"

Perhaps the real vision of Aztlán lies in the minds of the poor and wretched *pollos*—the illegal immigrants (literally, the "chickens") who cross over the river, or who climb the border fence and trek across the desert to find a life in the gringo nation. The mythical homeland never existed, but the *indocumentados* may be able to bequeath to their children a life of equality, dignity and prosperity. Aztlán is the precarious hope of a better existence in the north.

Military conflict between Mexico and the United States is long past. However, violence is still a constant of life along the Rio Grande—as it is along the entire border—but, now, it is almost exclusively a consequence of the drug trade. The killing and mayhem associated with drug running, always notable, have become spectacular over the last few years. The Vicente Fox administration—prodded hard by the United States—took on the drug cartels. The Mexicans, by then, had muscled out the Colombian cartels, and they controlled distribution into the illegal drug motherlode: the United States market—60 per cent of the world's total. Fox formed an elite and corruption-free (at least, initially) police force called the Federal Agency of Investigation, modelled on the FBI. The Fox government oversaw the arrest or killing of fifteen high-ranking cartel members and seized record amounts of drugs. The new administration of Felipe Calderón continued, and greatly intensified, this campaign.

The result has been bloody murder and disorder on a scale not seen in Mexico for a generation. American administrations talk about a "War on Drugs." They mostly mean a figurative, metaphorical war. Mexicans are engaged in a literal war on the cartels. The government has saturated the border states, and other drug-centre states such as Sinaloa, with troops. (Sinaloa is to the Mexican cartels as Sicily is to the Italian Mafia.) There have been large-scale firefights with cartel gunmen, who demonstrate a surprising willingness to stand and fight, often to the death.

Calderón's offensive is a justifiable and genuine effort to reverse Mexico's slide into a form of narco-state—similar, for example, to Colombia. But his interventions—sending in the army, rooting out, disarming or firing corrupt local or federal police—have upset the accommodations reached between the police and the local judicial authorities on the one hand, and the drug cartels on the other. A corrupt and criminal system was in place, but it operated relatively smoothly. Everyone had got to know their slot in a predictable process. The cartels had divvied up their turf; the export routes and methods—from "mules" to large-scale truck and air transport—were established; the routine bribery of police and border guards went on without interruption. Fox's initiative, and Calderón's declaration of war, destabilized a precarious balance. The cartels have fought back against the government, but they have also fallen into a terrible and savage war against each other for control of the plaza.

The stakes, after all, are high. How high is anyone's guess, and there have been many guesses. The United Nations Office on Drugs and Crime put the illegal drug market worldwide for 2003 at approximately $322 billion a year. Another UN agency came up with $400 billion, which, supposedly, was equal to 8 per cent of worldwide trade in that year and was the largest business in the world except for the arms trade at $800 billion. There have been criticisms of the United Nations' figures, which, one academic study alleges, were pulled out of a hat before a 1997 UN press conference. According to an article in the Winter 2005 issue of *Journal of Drug Issues*, the best guess for the world illegal drug market is somewhere between $45 and $280 billion. The range here is so large that these supposedly authoritative figures mean nothing. A study by the Mexican internal security agency suggested that if the illegal drug trade stopped, the Mexican economy would shrink by 63 per cent, and the American by about 20 per cent. Again, it's impossible to say whether these figures are even remotely accurate.

The problem is simple: how can anyone measure the value of an illegal business? By definition, the enterprise is secretive and opaque.

In any event, the truth is equally simple: the drug business is one of the largest in the world, many millions of people desire its products, and the profits are mighty high. The estimate that the United States makes up 60 per cent or so of the worldwide illegal drug market is probably accurate. Such a craving demand screams out for a ready supply. And that's where Mexico comes in: it is both a conduit and a source. Its cartels are now the main runners of cocaine, methamphetamine, marijuana and Mexican heroin.

When the American government irritates Mexico with its demands for action, by its suspicion of Mexican competence and willingness to do anything about drugs (the U.S. withholds intelligence from its Mexican counterparts, fearing it will be leaked to the cartels), Mexico reminds the United States that the trade wouldn't exist without American users. And the cartels' gunmen would be far less deadly without American drug money, as well as weapons and technology, which are run across the border in the other direction.

The drug cartels have large-scale and sophisticated criminal organizations in place in Mexico and in the United States. It makes sense that they branch out into other areas of trade. Indeed, they are becoming more involved in the smuggling of illegal migrants across the border. Cartel employees sometimes traffic in migrants themselves, but, even if they don't work directly as smugglers or guides, the gangs take their cut of operations carried out on their turf. The cartels have set up cells of their own within the United States, and they are also more and more involved with U.S.-based prison and street gangs. The Latin Kings and Mara Salvatrucha—MS-13, the most violent Latin-American gang, formed in San Salvador but with branch plants everywhere in Central and North America (Canadian police recently rounded up MS-13 gang-bangers in three cities)—buy methamphetamine from the Mexican cartels, who generally act as wholesalers, and distribute it across the southwestern United States. The cartels also traffic in stolen goods such as automobiles, and in arms. In fact, it's clear they will slip anything, or anyone, across the border, if it makes them a buck. After 9/11, this eclectic approach to crime does not promote a good night's sleep.

At the moment, I am riding along the Rio Grande beside the Mexican state of Tamaulipas. The state is the headquarters of the Gulf Cartel, whose activities spread across the border into the adjoining counties of Texas—Cameron, Starr, Hidalgo, Zapata and Webb—and on into the deeper American market for its products. Reynosa, across the border from McAllen, and Nuevo Laredo are two of its strongholds—as is Matamoros, across from Brownsville, and Monterrey (to the south). President Calderón sent more than seven thousand troops into Tamaulipas alone.

According to the Mexican government, seven drug cartels are now operating in the country. The situation is fluid, as groups change their allegiance and composition. However, at the time of writing, the four most important cartels are the Gulf, the Sinaloa and the Juárez Cartels, and the group known as *los zetas*. Under the pressure of Calderón's assault on their leaders and operations, and for reasons any business finds consolidation attractive, the cartels, in recent years, have formed alliances, although these shift and change. The Gulf and the smaller Tijuana cartels joined forces when their jailed leaders, with lots of time on their hands, negotiated an agreement. Being in jail didn't stop the bosses—like the Gulf Cartel's Osiel Cárdenas Guillén, imprisoned since 2003—from continuing to run their operations. Their proximity to other leaders, courtesy of the government, opened opportunities for co-operation. The Sinaloa, Juárez, Valencia and Familia Michoacán cartels made up the second main group, the "Federation," but this uneasy alliance has broken down—open warfare has recently erupted between the Sinaloa and Juárez groups, and the latter's power seems to be declining. These organizations are fighting it out for control of the trade, and both are resisting, with determined ferocity, the government's campaign against them. More than thirty-five thousand people have been killed since December 2006.

It is a savage war, fought by men on the fringe of a society that offers them limited hope of upward mobility by legitimate means. Their lives, from their beginnings, are saturated with hunger for the easy, big money, and the intoxicating power that pushing and running drugs can give them. The desire for these things must be like the craving of the user: a person will do anything to get it. The entire drug business grows out of these intense needs. It has no half-life; it is hard and ineradicable. If you begin a war against drugs, you're in for a very long haul. It will be an endless war.

There is the more subtle solution of legalization. Turn the trade into a taxed, regulated business. In this vision of transformation from dystopia to normality, drug lords would become mundane, corpulent CEOs of vast companies. Their crimes would consist of the usual corporate malfeasance of insider trading, or stock manipulation, or perhaps a little bribery and corruption, rather than the bloody craft of murder and intimidation. They could leave their side arms at home and cut loose their *asesinos*. Both Mexico and Canada have tried tentative steps in this direction: the "decriminalization"—not quite legalization—of small amounts of marijuana for personal use. These initiatives always run up against the ideology of U.S. policy: an implacable opposition to the production, importation or use of certain drugs under any circumstances. Canada and Mexico withdraw their small, enlightened efforts under American pressure—or bullying, depending on your politics. The war will go on.

The culture of the drug trade in Mexico (and elsewhere) is embedded in the country's violent and disordered past, and in its corrupt and inflexible present. From the street dealer to the gunman, to the cartel boss, the drug business is a recapitulation of earlier lawlessness in a frontier society. It is also the defiant work of a permanently subdued and despised mestizo underclass in a stratified society where the poor are very poor indeed, and disenfranchised from real political power—and likely to remain so. Mexico has provided such people only two routes to economic well-being: emigration to the United States, or supplying drugs to Americans. (Use of illegal narcotics by Mexicans themselves is increasing exponentially.)

In such a country, drug dealers become Robin Hoods. They raise themselves up out of hovels and slums, and, through their illegal business, they take a lot of people up with them. The outlaws are attractive because they are successful, and also because they thumb their noses at the hostile, snooty establishment that impoverished them and their ancestors in the first place. The fact that the drug business is illegal means nothing in a country where the authorities themselves are mostly corrupt. To people in Neuevo Laredo or Tijuana, efforts by Mexico City to halt the drug business look like hypocrisy, or like kowtowing to the gringos. The people admire the drug men. They are like the *norteños* and the *fronterizos* of the old days, and *corridos* are sung about them.

Pablo Acosta ran the plaza in Ojinaga, southeast of Juárez, in the 1980s. Eventually, helicopter-borne Mexican troops from Juárez attacked and killed Acosta in the tiny village of Santa Elena, across the river from Big Bend National Park. His famous quick-draw ability with his .45 semi-automatic didn't do him any good against heavily armed commandos pouncing from above. Acosta had made Ojinaga and the small and dusty town of Presidio across the river in Texas into one of the main drug routes into the United States. After his assassination—coincidentally or not—the Ojinaga plaza was taken over by Amado Carrillo Fuentes, known as the "Lord of the Skies" because he moved product with a huge airborne fleet, who took the operation to the big city of Juárez. Amado died of complications from plastic surgery he was undergoing to help him stay on the loose. His brother, Vicente, still runs the Juárez Cartel. There is a $5 million price on his head.

The recent killing in Mexico ranges from internecine murders among the cartels to assassinations of senior police and army officers, to large-scale firefights between gunmen and the army or the federal police. Some mundane examples: In Uruapan, Michoacán, gunmen from the La Familia cartel kidnap five street-level meth dealers, and decapitate the men with a bowie knife while they are still alive. They throw the heads onto the dance floor of a crowded bar belonging to their rivals. Gunmen assassinate Omar Ramírez, a high-ranking commander in the AFI, the new, clean investigative agency. The state police commander in Pátzcuaro, Michoacán, is killed by gunmen using AK-47 assault rifles after he arrests two cartel members on weapons charges. He is one of sixteen state and federal police commanders assassinated in Mexico in 2007. In two separate incidents in September 2009, gunmen line twenty-eight people up against walls in drug rehabilitation centres in Juárez and kill them. Bodies are found every day all over the country. The dead have often been tortured. In October 2009, federal police arrest five members of the Sinaloa Cartel believed to have been plotting to kill President Calderón.

The worst are *los zetas*. They have become a mythic force in the drug wars. Popular legend (which is most likely true) says that the original *zetas* were rogue special forces soldiers, trained by the Americans at Fort Benning, Georgia, and that they were sent in to track down and kill cartel members, but the Gulf Cartel's money turned them. They became the organization's private army. Now, there are perhaps two hundred *zetas* operating in Mexico, with a few in the southwestern United States. They are organized along the lines of their original army units. They are equipped with the finest weapons and gear—body armour, night-vision specs, heavy killing ordinance like grenade launchers and fifty-calibre machine guns, state-of-the-art communications and electronic spying equipment, humvees.

Los zetas are thoroughly trained and ruthless. They will kill, torture or kidnap anyone. They have recently evolved into an independent cartel and are engaged in a bloody turf war with their former employer, the Gulf Cartel, which has responded by joining in a "New Federation" with the Sinaloa group and La Familia Michoacán. The *zetas* also have contacts with MS-13, and with other criminal gangs like the Texas Syndicate and Hermanos Pistoleros Latinos. Some reports say that the CIA believes the *zetas* may have made connections with al Qaeda and other terrorist groups.

In the small town of La Joya, just upstream from McAllen, I meet the mayor, Billy Leo. He is one of Ann Richards' connections, having run her gubernatorial campaign in the area. We had arranged previously that I would call him when I got to La Joya, and he would talk to me if he had time. He was abrupt and irascible. I stop at a gas station and cafe on La Joya's strip and, while drinking a coffee on a bench out front, call Billy. He asks where I am, and when I tell him, he laughs loudly. "You're at my place!" he shouts. "You're right out front! I'm in my office at the back! I'll be right there."

Billy bursts out the door, and takes me through the convenience store, its cafe and its kitchen to a big back room containing a desk and chairs, cleaning supplies and utility cupboards, and hung with many photographs. There are photos of Bill and Hillary Clinton, of John F. Kennedy giving his inaugural address, of Billy with Ann Richards, and with various Democratic Party bigwigs.

In person, Billy is energetic and friendly. He jumps about his office pointing out photos and files, and he hops from topic to topic with like ease. He has a daughter who has just graduated from Wellesley. His wife is running for re-election as a school trustee. His family has lived in the Valley for generations. One of his ancestors signed the secession of Texas from the Union in January 1861, which joined it to the Confederate cause. Billy wants to talk about his brother, who works for the State Department and was posted in Moscow. That's where there's a real drug problem, Billy says.

It's hard to get him off the topic of Russia and drugs and onto the subject of the Mexican border and drugs. Of course, there are drugs and illegals all along the border, he says. He doesn't know what the solution is to drugs. There's no way to stop them. Illegals? He tries not to hire any, but several times he has done so without knowing it—they have good phony papers. It all boils down to work, he says. That's why they come. The coyotes bring them over the river in groups in boats every night. If American employers stopped hiring them, they would stop coming. That's going to be hard to do, though. The illegals are perfect employees: they work cheap and they don't look at the clock. Most of the people who work on the farms around here come over the river for a week or a month at a time. The main town in Mexico near here is Díaz Ordaz. It has a population of thirty or forty thousand, but it's empty during the week.

I say that I've been surprised by how Spanish everything is here, by how few gringos there are. There used to be more Anglos, says Billy, but they've moved out. I ask him about crossing the border at Laredo. No, no, he says. Don't do that. You have to stay on this side of the river. Nuevo Laredo is a killing zone. It's okay to cross if you're heading on south into Mexico, but it's not safe right along the river. There are *zetas* and other gunmen everywhere, and crooked cops and *federales*. Especially if you're by yourself, don't go along the border in Mexico.

Billy takes me out front and tells his cook to make me a couple of beef tacos—free, no charge—and a coke, which, oddly, I have to pay for. He bustles back to his office; he's a busy mayor.

I ride on a few miles to Sullivan City and turn left to the ferry at Los Ebanos, a tiny Mexican village on the U.S. side of the river. I pass a sign that says: "America is No. 1. Thanks to Our Veterans." Outside the post office is a large banner: "Apply for passports here." The ferry is the only hand-operated ferry along the river, and it can carry three vehicles at a time and a dozen or so people, while five beefy men haul it back and forth on its cables. Today, however, it's hauled up close to the American shore. A guy in a tiny gift stall tells me that this happens every year: the river's too high and fast. I had wanted to cross over and ride to Ciudad Díaz Ordaz, but that's not possible now. When the ferry isn't running, the Mexicans who need to cross over to shop or visit family must drive a round-trip of sixty miles to the bridge upriver at Rio Grande City.

There are Anglos around: a group of six elderly tourists from Illinois. I've already forgotten what it's like to have a quick, casual conversation—the Hispanics here are gravely reserved and laconic with me. These people are the usual garrulous Americans, and I enjoy their company for a few minutes. It's pleasant in the shade of the big ebony trees the village is named for.

Smuggling has always been a tradition across the river right here. There's a natural ford when the water's lower. During Prohibition, *tequiladores* brought booze across on mules. Long before that, Spanish explorers used the ford (and presumably Indians even earlier), and salt traders crossed to the salt fields forty miles northeast at El Sol del Rey. Mexican troops forded the Rio Grande here to fight Americans in 1846, before they were driven south, and Texas Rangers crossed the other way in punitive raids and hot pursuits into Mexico.

With the ferry not running today, the entry checkpoint is closed; there are no officers around, nor any evidence of the Border Patrol, although four surveillance cameras are buzzing away, their view presumably monitored somewhere. On this side of the river, there is a broken down wire fence with a single strand of barbed wire on top. The new Homeland Security fence will run along here, cutting through the village of Los Ebanos, severing sightlines and all the other ties across the river.

At the post office, I ask the clerk how the new fence will affect people on both sides of the river. She sighs.

"Señor," she says, "it will be a disaster. It will hurt our whole way of life."

"Is there a lot of smuggling around here?" I ask.

Everyone I put this question to laughs, and so does the clerk.

"Ah well, this was called Smuggler's Crossing," she says. "Everyone brings across what they need to make a living. It's the way it's always been along the river here."

"Drugs and illegals?"

"Claro" she says. "Of course. But other things, too. Whatever people need."

———

In high heat and wind, I ride on past Rio Grande City, and the landscape begins to change. Farms and field crops give way to desert and the undulations of low hills. I'm out of the Valley. I begin to see mesquite, prickly pear, Jerusalem thorn, and Mexican wild olive trees—I recognize them after my botanical day at Cleve and Rosemary's. I ride on through small, one-horse towns: Rosita, Garceno, Escobares, Roma, Falcon, Zapata. The settlements stretch out, fewer of them, and nothing but desert in-between. The houses are small and poor, surrounded by junk; occasionally, they are the neat and modest homes of an aspiring bourgeoisie. However, beside the road and on nearby hilltops are the big villas and *estancias* of the drug runners. They are often surrounded by barbed wire and high fences. I catch glimpses of swimming pools glistening in the desert sun, and of parked SUVs. The heat becomes intense.

That night, I stay in Laredo. Now, I do have to decide whether or not to cross over and ride along the Mexican side of the river. It's 125 miles from Nuevo Laredo to the next crossing at Piedras Negras, and a further 80 or so to Ciudad Acuña. The road is remote; there are three small settlements to Piedras Negras, and none on the smaller road beyond. I would be close beside the river almost all the way, deep in the territory of the Gulf Cartel, or *los zetas*.

Laredo, like Brownsville, McAllen and El Paso, is on an interstate highway network running from deep in Mexico into the United States, and all the way to the Canadian border. This transportation infrastructure is vital to the cartels' operations. The Mexican cities across the line from their American counterparts—Nuevo Laredo, Matamoros, Reynosa and Juárez—are battlegrounds.

The violence in Nuevo Laredo has been some of the worst along the border. The city's experience demonstrates that the bad guys are likely to remain in charge, no matter what the government does. Years of what amounts to intermittent, low-level warfare have hollowed the heart out of the city. Thousands are dead; legitimate businesses have decamped across the river to the American side. The small *placitas* all over the city are close to empty. The artisan district near the border is almost defunct. Dental offices and pharmacies that used to serve Americans have gone under. Tourists don't spend any time in Nuevo Laredo anymore. Street violence, sometimes on a military platoon-sized scale, is common-place. Kidnappings are widespread, and American citizens have been taken as well.

Former president Vicente Fox sent in six hundred officers of the Federal Preventive Police (PFP) to take over policing in the city. The day after they arrived, cartel traffickers gunned down four of them in an afternoon attack. Corrupt local police probably set up the hit. The officer in charge of the new PFP force in Nuevo Laredo, General Alvaro Moreno, deserted the city early in his tenure, and was eventually relieved of command. A new police chief, Omar Pimentel, resigned after eight months. His predecessor had been killed the previous year on his first day on the job—almost certainly by *zetas*. Before his resignation, Pimentel fired at least half the local police, but he could not recruit replacements. No one wanted the jobs. Soon, even some of his own PFP officers had been suborned by cartel money.

Felipe Calderón's campaign has been more aggressive. He has used army troops and heavier arms, but many of the city's police and civic administrators and employees still work for the Gulf Cartel, and it simply carries on with busi-ness. The official death counts are in the hundreds each year, but many bodies, perhaps the majority, are never found. The gunmen mince them in factory machines, feed them to ani-mals or burn them. In October 2009, a Tijuana Cartel member admitted to disposing of the remains of three hundred bodies by dissolving them in barrels of lye. Since 2008, violence has exploded in Juárez as the cartels carry on internecine war there for control of the plaza. It's called *la Limpia*, "the cleansing." Authorities in the city describe what's going on as "Nuevo Laredo–style violence." The Tamaulipas city is the gold standard of drug-trade savagery.

It's even difficult to find out exactly what's going on in Nuevo Laredo. The Gulf Cartel has intimidated reporters and newspapers into self-censorship, or into complete silence, about drug trafficking or corruption. The cartel has spies in newsrooms. Some reporters work for it, or for the terrifying *zetas*. Gunmen, armed with grenades and assault rifles, attacked the newsroom of the daily *El Mañana*. One reporter was killed; another was paralyzed for life and lives in hiding. A radio reporter was shot and killed while leaving his home one morning. Another was shot outside her office and died a week later. One reporter said: "The truth is, we have become a narco-democracy. Our country's ruling elite is not its business class or its politicians, but the drug lords."

I stay at the Motel 6 in Laredo. It's a truckers' motel and, apparently, a full-service operation. That evening, in the hundred yards between my room and Danny's Restaurant, I'm propositioned by three female prostitutes and one male teenager. One of the hookers, a large Anglo blond, calls out, "Hey, Abraham." Because of my grey beard. "No, thank you," I say politely—the good, married Canadian—to all four offers. One of the women replies, with equal courtesy, "De nada"—"You're welcome."

That evening, I ride my unloaded bike from the motel down to the border crossing in Laredo. I park the bike beside a Border Patrol SUV, and go up to the single agent sitting inside. I tell the young Hispanic officer what I intend to do, and I ask his advice. Like Jesse in Los Fresnos, he reacts as if he hasn't quite heard right.

"You want to cross into Nuevo Laredo and ride up the river?" he repeats.

"Yes," I say. "Just ride right on through."

"You alone?"

"Just me."

He shakes his head.

"No, no, no, no, no, señor. Do not do that. It is way too dangerous. They're killing each other every day in Laredo. Read the papers. Do not do it."

"Even if I just ride right through Nuevo Laredo in daylight, and keep moving along the river to Piedras Negras?"

"No, no, no, sir. You can't do that. If I could stop you, I would. I don't have any jurisdiction to stop you from doing that ride, but if I did have it, I would stop you."

"Too many bad guys?"

"Yessir. Way too many. Maybe *zetas*, coyotes, maybe *federales*. It doesn't matter, man, they're all bad. The city might be okay if you stay on the main roads, but that road up the river—there's zero there. That's where they bring across the drugs and people. Your bike, man. There's lots of guys would kill you for your bike. Doesn't matter what you're carrying."

"Carrying? You mean like a weapon?"

"Yeah. What do you carry?"

"Nothing, I don't carry. I'm from Canada." It seems like a necessary explanation.

"Canada!" He thinks about that. "Well, man, I'm telling you, just stay on this side. If there was a group of you, okay. But not a guy by himself."

I thank him and say I'll think about it.

Eating breakfast, I read the front-page headline in the *Laredo Morning Times*: "Nuevo Laredo—Violence: Death No. 50." Seventy-eight-year-old businessman Fernando Peña Vidaurri, a "former high-ranking official," was found dead on the floor of his kitchen, "his throat slashed and a silver knife still embedded in his neck." (There will be seven more drug murders in the following three days.)

The restaurant is busy, but contains only one other gringo. We make eye contact, nod and half-smile—a visible white minority in a Texas border town (I hope I've read the situation right). Three plainclothes cops enter and sit at a table next to me. They are Hispanic, although they speak English among themselves. They are wearing T-shirts and jeans, but are carrying radios, badges and side arms. I hear them talking about a shooting across the river in the early morning. Two federal policemen and an American undercover agent were ambushed and killed on the outskirts of Nuevo Laredo. The gunmen had heavy ordinance. One of the cops says: "Same shit, man. Different day."

CHAPTER 4

GOD'S RIGHT TO COME

THE ILLEGAL IMMIGRANT IS THE BRAVEST AMONG US.
THE MOST MODERN AMONG US: THE PROPHET.
—RICHARD RODRIGUEZ

"YESTERDAY," SAYS OFFICER LEAL, public affairs man for the Border Patrol's Del Rio sector, "I could have told you anything you wanted, short of state secrets. Today? Nada. Except, maybe, to agree with you the sky's blue."

Leal is young, articulate and genial. He is also very apologetic, but, he assures me, there is nothing he can do. This is a directive from Washington and it hit his desk earlier this morning. It says that Canadians and Mexicans, who, up until now, have been exempt from United States government security clearance requirements, are no longer exempt. Now, like a journalist or a writer from any other country in the world, I must apply for clearance so that I can interview Border Patrol press and public affairs officers. I am not supposed to be talking to field officers in any event, or rather, they are not supposed to be talking to me.

"They have been," I tell Leal.

"They're not supposed to," he says, "but most of them don't know that, or don't give a shit."

My clearance will take twenty business days, says Officer Leal. He has already prepared the papers for me to fill out and sign, and he will forward them to Washington himself. I thank him, and say I'll submit the application, but tell him that, by the time it's approved (assuming it is—"You're not a member of al Qaeda, are you?" Leal jokes), I'll be pretty much back home. He's sorry again, but there's nothing else he can do. "Of course," he says, and he smiles at me, "even for the guys in the field who read memos, it'll take a while to find out about this. If they ever do."

Del Rio was settled around the copious water flowing from nearby San Felipe Springs. In arid west Texas, water is life and income. The Amistad Dam, twelve miles away, was finished in 1969, creating a large reservoir. It is jointly administered by the United States and Mexico, and its name means "friendship." Del Rio and its companion city across the river in Mexico, Ciudad Acuña, consider themselves essentially one place. The mayor of Del Rio, Efrain Valdez, has said that the twin cities are a "binational community." Both towns are dead set against the proposed fence. Like the people in the Valley, they resent the decision, taken in the far-distant capital city, ignorant of local geography—and sensibilities—to build the barrier. Some asshole up there just drew a line on the map, is how the locals feel.

Homeland Security's heavy-handed tactics have made everyone even angrier. The city councils of Del Rio and of Eagle Pass, sixty miles to the south, had been talking with the Del Rio sector Border Patrol chief and, in early 2008, they reached a local agreement to put up a little more than two miles of fence in Del Rio, and a little less than two miles in Eagle Pass. These were the places the Border Patrol, the guys on the ground, thought were crucial—where illegals could get across the line and then immediately blend into the Hispanic-American towns. However, Homeland Security, without warning or consultation, brought a sudden "condemnation" lawsuit against Eagle Pass, seeking to force the city to surrender a large chunk of its land—233 acres—for the fence. A judge made the surrender order without a hearing. The city believed it had been singled out to "send a message" to the other troublesome communities along the river. Homeland Security's new fence is a monster, stretching eighty-nine miles along the river from five miles north of Del Rio downstream to five miles south of Eagle Pass.

Chad Foster, the former mayor of Eagle Pass, told the Fort Worth *Star-Telegram*: "We were sucker-punched by Chertoff with this lawsuit." Foster called the fence "monumentally stupid." Eagle Pass considers itself and Piedras Negras across the river as virtually one city—"Where Yee-Hah meets Olé," as its website puts it.

The Texas Border Coalition, made up of landowners, business people and politicians along the Rio Grande from Brownsville to El Paso, said that the government's action is neither the Texan nor the American way of justice. "It demonstrates again that we are losing our liberties to a federal government that is without restraint and out of control." One of the coalition's members, Pat Ahumada, the mayor of Brownsville, said: "We shouldn't be building walls. We should be building alliances with Mexico. The wall is not the solution."

"A nation of immigrants": that's the shibboleth about America. The symbols are mythic: Ellis Island and waves of impoverished newcomers finding shelter and prosperity on the American shore; the Statue of Liberty with its invitation to safety and a better life. The poor Irish came in their hundreds of thousands, and the poor Germans, and the poor Italians and Poles and Ukrainians, and even the Chinese—although not too many of them, if we can help it. They all became

Americans in this unique country (leaving aside Canada for the moment), a nation of diverse arrivals melding into the great, unified polity of America. *E pluribus unum.* Their energy, wealth and ideas—the sheer power of them—would dazzle the world as no nation in history had done.

Even radical conservatives, or gun-toting vigilantes patrolling the border, admit the legitimacy of immigration, its essential role in populating America and its continued necessity. How could they not, since, like all other Americans, they themselves are descended, earlier or recently, from immigrants? Immigration is a sacrosanct principle; the difficulty lies with immigrants who have entered the country illegally. All the critics ask is that they get in line and come in as everyone else has done over the centuries. The problem now is that the main source of migrants, legal and otherwise, is across a land border, not an ocean. Controlling the flow of new people through ports is one thing; stopping them from wading across a river or climbing through, or over, a stretch of wire is something else. America must make decisions about who gets to enter the promised land. Immigrants, yes, but not just anyone.

The mythology belies the complicated history. For one thing, the American story more or less ignores the people who were here already, and the people who were brought here in chains. The Indians and the African slaves are footnotes to the main narrative. That narrative considered the Indians to be an uncivilized and savage obstacle to white settlement and progress, and the slaves . . . well, the slaves were a regrettable episode in American history. All nations had slaves, went the argument, and America's only sin was in failing to be unique by not having slaves, as it was exceptional in so many other ways. Eventually, white Americans butchered each other in a Civil War to end slavery. At least, they got things right in the end, goes the standard account—although the terrible residues of prejudice and discrimination linger on.

The story of America as a nation of immigrants is deficient in another aspect, which also involves a footnote. Alexis de Tocqueville spent nine months in the United States in 1831, and published his *Democracy in America* in two volumes, one in 1835 and the second five years later. De Tocqueville and his fellow researcher, Gustave de Beaumont, were commissioned to gather research and write a report for the French government on prisons and penitentiaries in the United States. De Tocqueville also took notes on other aspects of American life, and his book was the first thorough study (still one of the best) of the social behaviours and political institutions of the United States.

De Tocqueville liked what he saw in America. He described a people imbued with the notion of liberty under the rule of law. But it was a very specific kind of society: a fully formed Anglo-American people whose political culture had evolved over generations. Americans at the time shared this view of themselves as a society of Anglo-Saxons continuing, and expanding, the English traditions of freedom and democracy (for adult white males) in the New World. They did not think of themselves then as a nation of immigrants. Immigration took place, but it contributed only a fraction of the nation's robust annual population increase of almost 3 per cent. A very high birth rate took care of the rest.

Immigration (at least on that scale) was not a problem for America, de Tocqueville wrote, because of the continent's abundant land. He shared the view of most Americans of the irrelevance of the Indians and of any prior claims to jurisdiction they might have had. The land was "one great desert." The Indians "occupied without possessing it." Americans moved west into this providential emptiness. In doing so, they left opportunities for new immigrants in the east, "a country that is but half-full." The immigrants easily found industrial jobs and prospered. Their sons moved west, and the self-regulating process continued.

But things changed fast. Even before his book was published, de Tocqueville was having second thoughts about America's prospects, and he included a footnote in a later edition. In it, he noted the flood of new lower-class arrivals into eastern cities like New York and Philadelphia: "a multitude of Europeans whom misfortune and misconduct drive . . . toward the shores of the new world"; and free blacks condemned "to a state of hereditary degradation and misery." The great Anglo-American experiment was in peril.

The problem was that the Irish were coming, and the Germans. Later, it got worse as harvests in Europe failed. More Irish came. Most of them were Catholic and few could even speak English. Native-born Americans were English enough to share the prevailing deep prejudice about the Irish—the "simian race," dangerous and unruly ruffians. Scandinavians, French, Belgians, Dutch and many more Germans came to America. Only a small minority of immigrants from the early 1830s to the 1850s were the Anglo-Saxons de Tocqueville thought necessary for the stability and prosperity of the United States. In 1850, for the first time, the U.S. Census distinguished between native- and foreign-born. In the northeast, 15.5 per cent of the people were foreign; ten years later, 22 per cent were. New York City was 51 per cent foreign-born, a 700 per cent increase since de Tocqueville's visit. In the nine years from 1845 to 1854, two and a half million people entered the United States, causing a 13 per cent increase in the country's white population.

By chance, de Tocqueville was at home in France writing his masterpiece during the beginning of a dramatic demographic change in American society, brought about by the huge increase in immigration. The influx of people, and of people who were different from the original, mostly Anglo, Americans, strained and abraded the American polity as nothing had done since the revolutionary war. A reaction was inevitable.

As early as 1834, de Tocqueville heard reports of the violence breaking out in American cities, and it was these that prompted his pessimistic footnote. At least twenty-four large-scale conflicts occurred in that year, and hostilities continued in subsequent years. Some fights were between newly arrived ethnic groups, but a new form of disorder also began to break out: nativist reaction to the newcomers—native-born Americans clashing with foreign-born immigrants. The conflict was made worse by economic depression.

Americans hadn't seen this sort of civil conflict in a generation, and it was a shock. Theologian William Ellery Channing said, "society was shaken to its foundations, all its joints loosened, all its fixtures about to be swept away." Anti-Catholic feeling grew stronger with the influx of Irish. They were viewed as being as completely beyond the American pale as the Negroes. In fact, their instinctive violence and ineradicable Catholicism made them worse than the Negroes, who were, at least, quiescent. The Irish formed an Irish militia. The American Whig party agitated for all "Native Americans" to keep the foreigners from taking their jobs. Nativist reaction provoked further immigrant violence.

Prejudice against Catholics was reinforced in 1836 by the Battle of the Alamo, the Goliad massacre and the subsequent fighting with Mexico. It seemed to many Americans that they were beset on all sides: the demographic assault of the Catholic Irish in the northeast, and the military attack by the Catholic Mexicans in the southwest.

The so-called Know-Nothings (because they said they knew nothing about the secret societies supposedly working to vote in blocs in elections) were the first organized nativist political movement in the United States. In the 1850s, they railed against the Catholic Irish who, the nativists said, were under the control of the Pope, and intended to destroy Anglo-American society. The Know-Nothings wanted to limit immigration, to "purify" politics by restricting office to native-born Americans, and to make immigrants wait for twenty-one years before they could become citizens and vote. The movement had widespread electoral success, even running Millard Fillmore for president in 1856 (he won 21 per cent of the vote), but it faded away after that—as special- or single-interest parties in the United States tend to do. Nevertheless, Know-Nothing ideology lived on, and persists; it is right at home on the right wing of the Republican Party.

In Del Rio, I check into a sterile, cheap Motel 6, my third in three days. Ten Harleys are parked outside several rooms near mine. Large, pot-bellied, long-haired guys have set up a bar-becue and are incinerating hamburgers and hot dogs, and drinking bottles of Lone Star beer. They watch me ride up and dismount. I nod and say, Hello. Several turn away without a sign. A couple of the blubber-bellies clearly sneer at me—or at my humpbacked bike, it's hard to tell.

This reception makes me feel sorry for myself. Hispanics down here are loath to talk to a gringo; other bikers barely restrain themselves from spitting on my machine (or on me). The only guys who will talk to me are the Border Patrol. I'm getting lonely.

The next day, I feel even lonelier when Officer Leal gives me the news: he can't talk to me, either—except to agree that the sky is, indeed, blue—and the Border Patrol guys in the field aren't supposed to. I have a Beckettian moment. At first, I think: I can't go on like this. Then, I think: I'll go on.

When I come out of the Border Patrol's new, high-security compound in Del Rio, the humidity is building and the wind is blasting out of the west to northwest at twenty-five to thirty miles an hour, gusting much higher. This is the windy season, I remind myself. It won't be any better tomorrow, or for a while. So, off we go.

As I ride over the bridge across the Amistad Reservoir, the wind, blowing free across the long fetch of trapped water, almost forces me sideways into the low guardrail. I have to snap the windward handlebar forward and lean like a racer to keep the bike on the road. It's not a long drop down, but the water looks deep and cold. My reaction time is crucial. All this takes close concentration. I'm still learning on the job, and I feel again the now-familiar ache in my neck and shoulders. I fear I might have to ride into this wind for the next three weeks. But, boys, my friends, that's okay—I'm not complaining.

The flat Chihuahuan desert extends beyond me in all directions. There's some spring-green to it, and flowers bloom here and there. Most of the vegetation on this fenced ranchland seems to be the canny desert and steppe survivors: mesquite, cactus, acacia, Jerusalem thorn, and, occasionally, clumps of straggly, dry grama grass. I have the same sense of amplitude, and of letting loose, that I've felt crossing the Canadian prairie, or, most intensely, at sea.

About ten miles north of Amistad Village, I run into a Border Patrol checkpoint. I flip up the front of my helmet so the agent can see my grey hair, white skin and blue eyes.

"American citizen?" he asks.

"No, Canadian."

"OK."

The marginally unconstitutional abnormal has become the normal in the borderlands. Every road running away from the line has checkpoints, or is under static surveillance by Border Patrol agents. By now, if you live near the Mexican boundary, you are completely habituated to what amounts to arbitrary police action, without reasonable cause to believe a crime has been committed. You can't just get in the car and tool down the road any time you feel like it. Everyone gets either stopped and looked at and then waved on, or stopped and questioned. White people like me get a couple of questions, or a wave through. Brown people are always stopped and extensively examined. Down here, it's called "DWM": Driving while Mexican.

I cross the Pecos River where it flows into the Rio Grande, a mighty confluence of running water in the midst of this barren ground. For the next few miles, I'm close to the river again, and, just before Langtry (where saloon-keeping Judge Roy Bean became a western legend), I take a dirt trail down towards the border. I'm far from any but the smallest of settlements now, and I've seen a handful of other vehicles on the road. But when I bump and skid down to the river, there's a Border Patrol SUV parked right beside it. The Hispanic agent appears to have been dozing, and my arrival wakes him with a jerk. He's disoriented and seems miffed. As I pull up and stop nearby, he climbs out of his vehicle, reaches back inside, and pulls out an M4 carbine. He cradles it and watches me prop up the bike and dismount.

"What are you doin' down here?" he says.

"I'm just looking at the river," I say. "I'm heading west, and just wanted to see the river and rest for a few minutes."

For once, the guy doesn't say I'm in a restricted zone. He's relaxing. He stands down his weapon, letting it drop down along his thigh, but he keeps hold of it. The river is wide here, and the Mexican side is desert, indistinguishable from the United States.

"There's just the river down here," he says. Then: "You have any firearms with you?"

I give my now standard denial with an explanation: "No, I don't carry one. I'm Canadian."

"Y'all all the way from Canada?" He's surprised but plainly comforted.

We talk amiably for a while. This guy hasn't got the word about not chatting to civilians. I'm beginning to find out that the dominant emotion among these ubiquitous guardians is plain, intense boredom. Many of them deeply desire to talk. In my isolation, I'm happy to oblige.

Drugs come across the line here, he says. The previous guy who had this part of the sector was just re-assigned because they thought he was taking money to let the runners come across by boat. There wasn't enough evidence to arrest him. The drug guys would run along the Amistad Reservoir, and maybe up the Pecos, until it was safe to unload. You could hear the boats at night, but by the time a chopper with lights got here from Del Rio, it was too late.

"What about illegals?" I ask.

"Hell, we don't have to worry about them all the way out here. They can just cross around Del Rio without any problem. Anyways, it's the drugs I'm lookin' for, not illegals. No one gives a shit about *pollos*"

"Has your family been in the U.S. a long time?" I'm trying to be circumspect, to not give offense. He takes none.

"Yeah, long time. My granddaddy's granddaddy, or about that long ago. Down around Matamoros. Before it was illegal." He laughs.

"Do you kind of sympathize with the illegals?" I ask.

"Sure," he says. "They're just poor people tryin' to get a better life. I feel like they're kinda my people, too, you know? It could be me tryin' to get across that river there."

"But you wouldn't let them go, you wouldn't give them a break because of that?"

Now, he is a little offended.

"Nosir! I got my job to do. I want to keep this country safe, you know what I mean? Anyone can cross over, not just guys who want to get a job on a farm. How do I know who's who? I gotta stop 'em all. Anyway, I'm an American, and these people are tryin' to get into my country against the law."

———

All afternoon, the road has risen higher and higher. Low, rolling hills and buttes appear, and farther away, I can see mountains: the Glass, Rosillos and Christmas ranges, all northern extensions of Mexico's Sierra Madre Oriental. The desert softens into grasslands. Cattle, sheep and a few Brahma bulls graze on the range. Hawks and kites wheel and glide overhead. I pass small trailers here and there, shelter for the vaqueros who drive the interminable fencelines, keeping them in repair. It's the same duty as always for cowboys: the long hours of boring labour in heat or cold, keeping the cattle in. Except that now it's done in four-by-fours instead of on horseback. I don't see another vehicle for thirty minutes at a time. If it weren't for the goddamn wind, I say to Will, Chris and Mike, I would be enjoying this.

During the last hour and a half of the climb into the high-plains town of Alpine, the temperature drops. I stop every half-hour to pull on more clothes until I'm riding in layers of shirt, sweater, fleece and armoured pants and jacket. I turn on my heated handlebar grips. It's been a long day in wind, heat, and now, cold. I have a muscle-contraction headache on my left side—the parts I'm constantly working, to keep the ornery, slab-sided bike upright. My route has angled slightly north as the border has dropped abruptly away to the south, and Alpine is seventy-five miles away from the line, as a bird might fly. Here, there are many more Anglos. For the first time since I arrived in Brownsville, I feel as if I'm back in a familiar country. Clerks in stores chat to me; the gas-station guy asks about my bike. I hadn't realized how cut off I've been feeling, and I bask in the normal American courteous and open interactions. There are disagreements about the extent of the borderlands third-country, but, whatever its limits, I have certainly crossed out of it.

In the morning, the temperature is twenty-three degrees (Fahrenheit)—fourteen degrees with the wind chill says the local weather channel—and my saddle is slick with frost. I'm heading for Big Bend, the huge national park on the Rio Grande, where, a local guy outside the motel tells me, it will be warmer. I wait until nine o'clock, for the frost to clear off the road. The wind is lighter, although it's straight across my path. I've added long underwear to yesterday's clothes. On the 385 south of Marathon, I hit a Border Patrol checkpoint. I slow down, but the agent waves me on through—I am, after all, heading towards the border. I scare up roadrunners, the first I've seen. I'm surprised when they fly away from my noisy machine. Based on my cartoon research earlier in life, I'd expected them to just run faster.

I turn off onto the 2627, which takes me down to the border over the Sierra Larga through Black Gap Wildlife Management Area. This is a dead end, and I'll have to retrace my path thirty miles, but I want to see the border crossing at La Linda. At the end of the road, I find a concrete bridge in good condition, but it is blocked off with cement vehicle barriers and a high wire fence. The brown river swirls by below. There is a pay phone, with a dial tone. Across the river in Mexico, I can see a few small commercial or ranch buildings of some sort, but no people anywhere. A sign nearby advertises Key Canyon Ranch: "Campin', hikin', fishin', No jokin'." No Border Patrol, either, although I saw two of their vehicles on the road here.

La Linda is one of five border crossings over the river between Del Rio and Presidio, to the west of Big Bend Park. Now, they are all closed and blocked off, like this one—a stretch of 350 miles or so in a straight line, twice that with the river's twists and nascent oxbows. If you want to cross the border, or to immigrate, into this section of Texas from Coahuila, or Chihuahua, you've got a long drive, or a much longer walk.

Americans have always viewed the issue of immigration with ambivalence. On one hand, the new republic needed feet on the ground. It required people to help secure its shaky hold on its new vast independent territory. The more whites there were, the more easily American communities could secure themselves against Indian attack, the more prosperous their economy could become—through numerous producers and consumers—and the more likely it was that the necessary expansion of the United States could take place. Later, the ideology of manifest destiny had, as one of its corollaries, unlimited immigration—or nearly so. To occupy and control the vast new land to the west required soldiers, settlers, workers.

From the beginning of the republic, however, its leaders worried about who should be allowed to come to America, about how different the newcomers could be, and about how many of them it was politic to admit. The political and economic writer Tench Coxe, once a Loyalist during the Revolution, and later a member of the Continental Congress, read a paper to a gathering at Benjamin Franklin's house in 1787. He stated the need for an "influx of people," but added: "It is equally clear that we have a right to restrain that influx, whenever it is found to prove hurtful to us."

Franklin, himself, made it clear that only Anglo-Saxons— the ideal white people not in some way "swarthy" or otherwise suspect—should be allowed into the United States. And he stated the proposition about non-British immigrants that would be repeated down the centuries into our own time: "Those who come hither are generally of the most ignorant Stupid Sort of their own Nation."

The counter-proposition to immigration controls and in favour of open borders was stated, most eloquently, by a novelist. Herman Melville had just finished a stint as a sailor aboard an immigrant ship on its run from Liverpool to the United States east coast. He had seen, first-hand, a few hundreds of the many hundreds of thousands of desperate famine-Irish struggling towards a haven in the new world. He knew that, parlous as their condition was, they were the lucky ones. At least as many others were dying, of hunger, or of disease, in Ireland. Who—what country—could refuse such people?

In *Redburn*, Melville enunciated what has become known as the Melville principle. "Let us waive that agitated national topic, as to whether such multitudes of foreign poor should be landed on our American shores; let us waive it, with the one only thought that if they can get here, they have God's right to come; though they bring all Ireland and her miseries with them. For the whole world is the patrimony of the whole world."

The Melville principle may have been defensible in the case of Ireland and in the context of the limited shipping of the day, which could only transport so many people in a year. However, as one immigration scholar writes: "What are we to do today in the face of a world that consists of a thousand Irelands, and in which there is in effect an infinite number of ships?"

The United States is in the midst of its fourth great wave of immigration (the previous ones occurred in the 1840s and fifties, the 1880s, and the early 1900s). The country always claims to be the recipient of record numbers of immigrants. In fact, Canada has taken the most newcomers, in relation to population size. In 1913, for example, arriving immigrants made up 5 per cent of Canada's population, more than three times the percentage in the United States' busiest year.

Nevertheless, the American numbers are huge. And, if the present trend continues, the Hispanic wave may be the biggest of all. By 2025, the percentage of Americans born elsewhere will break the record set a century ago. According to a recent report by the Center for Immigration Studies in Washington, one in eight people—37.9 million—is an immigrant, the highest percentage since the 1920s. The past seven years saw 10.3 million new immigrants, the highest number for any seven-year period in American history. More than half this number are illegal.

It's easy enough to impose restrictions and conditions on immigrants. The harder problem is what to do about those people who will not stand in line, waiting for some bureaucratic mill to grind fine and slow. The European Union passed legislation in June 2008 allowing illegal migrants to be held in detention for up to eighteen months. If the member country doesn't need them as workers, it can deport them. What should the United States do about its *indocumentados*?

I ride into Big Bend National Park. It's disorienting for me at first. To most Canadians, unless they're up on the northern tundra, the term "national park" means trees. Big Bend is desert valleys and distant, panoramic views, the road sweeping in long curves between mesas and buttes. All around are bare mountains, some rising over seven thousand feet. I ride down to the Rio Grande Village campsite, pay $10 for the night, choose a shady piece of grass and pitch my tent. I've descended enough that it's hot down in this valley, and I strip off my long underwear. The friendly female ranger tells me about the trails winding down along the river, and I hike along one of them. I come to the marshy, reed-lined bank of the Rio Grande. I watch it flow by for a while, and then a man appears on the Mexican shore. He isn't carrying anything, just striding with purpose. He wades into the fast-flowing stream, which appears to be shallow here; he picks his way across, and comes ashore a few yards from me. He's not surprised to see me. We nod.

"Buenas tardes," I say.

"Hola," he replies, and keeps on walking towards the road.

The night is freezing. I wear all my riding gear, except for the armour, and even that I spread over my sleeping bag. The bag is too light for this weather, and I shiver through the night, managing only to doze from time to time. In early morning, as the light is opening up a little to the east and the stars still a million brilliant lights domed above me, I step out into a herd of snuffling javelinas, rotund and stumpy legged, like midget wild hogs. They ignore me and munch their way through the grass eighteen inches from my feet.

The next day is cold and clear, and I ride the park's steep, narrow roads to the closed river crossings at Boquillas del Carmen, and, farther west, over the Chisos Mountains, to Santa Elena. For a hundred years, travellers could cross the river, unsupervised, at Boquillas del Carmen in a flat-bottomed boat to and from the village on the Mexican side. That's finished now, as is the border traffic at Santa Elena. The river has sluiced and worn its way through the soft limestone, and Americans raft or canoe down the Rio Grande, under the thousand-foot-high canyon walls. But no one crosses the line anymore. In this remote section of the river, Homeland Security has simply shut down the border. Tourists, and the Mexicans who depended on them, be damned.

I park the bike at Santa Elena and slog through the burning, soft sand in my riding boots—it's hot at this lower elevation at midday—and watch the border flow by. The incongruity strikes me again of this troublesome, phony boundary imposed on the barren beauty of the innocent river cutting blameless canyons through the ancient mountains.

When I get back to the KLR, there's another bike parked. It's a Harley, but the middle-aged couple aboard are friendly and talkative. They are sitting at a picnic table in the shade of cottonwoods, eating sandwiches and drinking beer. It's a nice scene, except that an automatic pistol is also lying on the table. We chat for a while. They are from Fort Stockton, up north on the I-10, and are riding through Big Bend for a day. They are gratifyingly impressed by my trip—"on such a little-bitty bike," says the woman, glancing, for comparative research purposes, from her shining, wide-bodied, black-and-chrome, iconic machine over towards my filthy, humpbacked tanker.

I tell them about my book, and, right away, the guy becomes a vehement, angry white man about the border problem and its solution: Shut the fuckin' border right down; bring in the army; deport the illegals, all twelve or twenty million of them, it don't fuckin' matter; build a fence ("Out here, too?" I ask. "Goddamn right," he says); keep out the fuckin' wetbacks or the United States is finished as a country; if the peckerwoods in Washington can't or don't want to do it because they're getting paid off by special interests, then we need a strong leader who can do it. "We got to save the country, here, man," he says.

I ask him what he thinks about the northern border. He's not saying anything against me personally, he says, but there's a lot of fuckin' liberals up there in Canada, socialists too, and they are fuckin' dangerous sons of bitches who allow terrorists to just walk into the United States. Those twin towers came down, he says, because the Canadian fuckin' government let the terrorists just walk right into the U.S. and do it.

I'm in polite Canadian mode: I look as neutral as possible, nod slightly from time to time, and say, "Hmm," now and then. However, I feel as if I have to set the record straight about 9/11.

"Well, listen, it's really clear the hijackers didn't come into the U.S. from Canada," I say. "They were all in the U.S. on legal visas; they flew into the States from overseas directly."

The guy and his wife look at each other, and shake their heads.

"Is that what your government told you?" the guy says to me. "That's what they're gonna say, isn't that right? Listen, you can't believe your fuckin' government, man. We sure can't believe our own government."

I'm not about to argue with a ranting Harley rider whose pistol is lying on a picnic table in front of us. It crosses my mind again: the abrupt and astonishingly wide contrasts in this country, the divide between my amiable hosts Cleve and Rosemary in Los Fresnos and this red-faced, seething, furious, fearful man. To change the subject, I ask him what he does for a living. He's an accountant, he says.

They finish eating, and prepare to leave. The woman packs up the food and beer cans. The guy stuffs the pistol into the pocket of his leather jacket and zips it closed. They mount up, say to me: "Be careful out there," (I surely will), wave and ride off.

Reading newspapers, books and blogs in 2008, one has a sense of déjà vu. Instead of violent, dirty, criminal, Catholic Irish subverting the American way of life in 1850, one reads about the dirty, brown, Catholic, criminal, mestizos subverting the American way of life right goddamned now, and, in the case of some writers, Western civilization itself.

The latest nativist reaction to immigration by "the different" no longer takes the form of street warfare. Now, the reaction is expressed in printed or Internet diatribes, or through the election of ultra-conservative politicians, or, more directly, by means of the mostly non-violent "border campaigns" of groups such as the Minutemen.

The titles of a sample of recent books that have set out the conservative, or nativist, point of view sum up the writers' concerns: *In Mortal Danger: The Battle for America's Border and Security* by Colorado Republican congressman Tom Tancredo (who was, briefly, a presidential candidate in the 2008 election, and ran unsuccesfully for governor of Colorado in 2010); *Whatever It Takes: Illegal Immigration, Border Security, and the War on Terror* by former Arizona congressman J. D. Hayworth (he was defeated in the 2006 mid-term elections, and lost to John McCain in the 2010 Arizona State Primary); and, most apocalyptically, *State of Emergency: The Third World Invasion and Conquest of America* by Patrick J. Buchanan (part of whose ancestry includes the Germans and, worse, the Irish, who so inflamed America 150 years ago).

Tancredo, Hayworth and Buchanan—and conservatives generally—continue the traditional American line that immigration is a good thing, so long as it's controlled. But they also agree that the twelve to twenty million illegals they believe are in the United States must be expelled (the Center for Immigration Studies in Washington estimates 11.3 million undocumented workers). They insist that the fence must be built, in one form or another, along the entire length of the southern border (and maybe, eventually, along the northern boundary, too—to keep out those deceptively bland, mysterious and vaguely dangerous Canadians). Finally, say Tancredo, et al., American businesses must be forced to stop hiring illegal workers.

The stakes range from the economic well-being of America, to ensuring the country's security from terrorist infiltration, to—in Buchanan's opinion—defending America, and ultimately, the West, from destruction by an invading third-world horde. For Buchanan, there is a nexus between *indocumentados* picking lettuce and the collapse of Western civilization.

Underlying these arguments are two strands of thought: the real and valid concerns of the effects of unchecked immigration; and a racist, nativist, prejudice rife with guilt and fear.

The real relationship between America and its immigrants—its illegal immigrants in particular—is complex. Undocumented workers do put strains on social and medical services, and on local schools. These are the problems that Cleve and Rosemary pointed out in Brownsville and elsewhere in surrounding Cameron County. There is no doubt that certain categories of American workers—in construction, or in low-paying manufacturing or service jobs—are hurt by illegal migrants who will work for less and keep quiet about job conditions. Hospitals in some areas of the southwest must write off tens of millions of dollars in unpaid medical bills for treating illegals: at least $45 million in 2000. That's not a large number in the health care business, but it hit hospitals hard in places like Pima County, including Tucson, and in Yuma, where other facilities had to be shut down to make up the deficit.

However, almost all Hispanic immigrants, including the illegals, work hard—and risk their lives to get across the border to do so. They pay taxes, they make sure their children go to school, and they fear God. Their cheap labour keeps prices down and the American standard of living up. They work both ends: pick the veggies; flip the burgers. They make sure that the United States will not go the way of Russia or Japan, demographically doomed countries with low birth rates and no immigration. Contrary to the hysterical propaganda, Hispanic immigrants in the United States have crime rates lower than those of native-born Americans, and that statistic includes the illegals.

Apart from that, the illegals pay sales taxes, mortgages, rent, and bank transaction fees on remittances back home to keep the rest of the family alive. And they buy things: Pampers to candy bars, cars to computers. A twenty-first century study by UCLA's North American Integration and Development Center found that undocumented immigrants contributed at least $300 billion a year to the country's gross domestic product. That's a lot of medical care, school costs and welfare.

Americans as a whole experience deeply conflicted emotions and opinions about immigration. The disjunction has sometimes seemed schizophrenic: the Chinese Exclusion Act, the first real legislated immigration restriction in the United States, was passed four years after the Statue of Liberty was erected in New York harbour.

Conservatives like Tancredo and Buchanan talk the talk of economic distortion and hardship for Americans, and of security problems, but what they really dread is racial and cultural dilution, and even annihilation. They think that they, and their Anglo heritage, will be snuffed out in the southwestern

United States. There is also guilt. Everyone knows the history: the unjust aggressive war against Mexico, the punitive Treaty of Guadalupe Hidalgo. Because of their intuition that their cause is not altogether just, nativists shout all the louder and suggest remedies all the more drastic. Perhaps they also remember that each time Americans have singled out a group of immigrants for punishment—the Chinese, the Irish, the Italians, the Japanese—everlasting dishonour and shame are all that have remained.

It is genuinely frightening to see the familiar slip away, wobble and dissolve; any human being feels the strain of cultural dislocation, or, in this case, of cultural displacement. In 2007, for the first time, the list of most common American surnames included two Hispanic names: Garcia and Rodriguez, and Martinez almost edged out Wilson for tenth spot. A Texas journalist once wrote: "Home, in the twentieth century, is less where your heart is, than where you understand the sons of bitches." Behind the brutal "solutions"—the two thousand–mile-long fence; the deportation of twelve million people—lies the terror of loss and extinction.

With the augmented fences, and the economic downturn in the United States, the numbers of illegal migrants dropped in 2009 and 2010. The decline is steepest where the new wall was built to the original elaborate specifications; for example, by 72 per cent on the border near Yuma, Arizona.

However, the fences are like the Maginot Line: they have ends. Like the earlier portions of the barriers built in the mid-1990s—for example, south of San Diego or along the river at El Paso, under "Operation Gatekeeper" and "Operation Hold the Line"—the new fences simply change the border crossing venue, driving migrants farther out into the desert to try to cross where many more dangers await them. They must walk for a long time—sometimes for several days. In the isolation of the desert, they are more at the mercy of the migrant-smugglers—the coyotes—who may abandon them, or rape the women. Each summer, the heat kills hundreds of illegals walking north for their new lives. Between 1994 and 2004, approximately three thousand people died crossing the border, the same number, as Mexican-American activists have pointed out, who died on 9/11. The American Civil Liberties Union estimates more than five thousand dead from 1994 to 2010.

It's ironic, too, that the new security, which makes it harder for migrants to get into the United States, also makes it much more unlikely they'll go back to Mexico. They used to do that all the time when they could simply walk across the border, almost at will. They'd work a while at seasonal farm or construction work, send money home, and then, when that kind of work dried up for a while (half a million workers returned to Mexico during the Great Depression), or they got tired of being goddamn wetbacks, or they longed for home too much, they'd go back. Now, it's a one-time deal: make it over the first time—probably after several, or many, very hazardous tries—and you'd better stay, take steady work, become part of the permanent, underground, illegal-worker population in the United States. If you go home and, later, decide you want to sell your labour and your soul to America after all, you'll have to risk your life all over again. In a sense, the walls and fences and the intensive patrolling of the border have created the permanent resident illegal migrant.

Americans perceive illegal immigration as being out of control, wave after wave of migrants rising higher each year. But that's not the reality. In fact, the number of migrants, in relation to the American population, is the same now as it was in the 1970s and 1980s. The difference is that then, they crossed from, say, Tijuana into San Diego or from Juárez into El Paso, or they took a quick wade, or swim, or boat ride across the Rio Grande. In the United States, they remained almost invisible within the large Hispanic populations of the cities, or of the River's third country. Now that they're forced to cross in the desert, populated sparsely by Anglo ranchers, and dotted with a few small, dusty towns, the migrants stand out. They're an obvious, alien presence.

In fact, poor Mexicans crossing the border for work in the rich United States have been a staple of relations between the two countries since the southwest was settled enough to attract agricultural workers (to tend and pick sugar beets and cotton, for example) and other unskilled labourers. Between 1900 and 1910, as many as 500,000 Mexicans entered the United States. They were called "sojourners," and they came and went, but an unknown, although certainly substantial, number of them settled. The supposedly recent pattern of Hispanic workers spreading throughout the entire country is not new either (although the numbers now are far greater). A 1908 Bureau of Labor analysis noted the marked distribution of Mexican labourers across the country. In the past, they seldom strayed more than a hundred miles from the border, said the report, but now, they are working "as far east as Chicago and as far north as Iowa, Wyoming and San Francisco." The 1908 report added: "The number of different industries dependent upon Mexican labour is increasing."

Two of the organizing principles of the United States have always been capitalism and racial prejudice. In the case of the illegal migrants, one trumps the other: Americans are willing to subordinate racial prejudice to the imperatives of producing and consuming.

If you hire them, they will come. That's always been the nub of the deal between the immigrants and America. As long as American employers hire undocumented workers, illegals will find some way of hauling themselves across the border. They will cut their way through the fence—as they have done already, even with the new, improved version—or they will climb over it with José's twenty-one-foot ladders, or they will drive, or walk, across the most remote desert where there will never be a fence, and where the electronic devices aren't all they're cracked up to be. If the *pollos* truly desire to get across, they'll get across.

CHAPTER 5

HISTORY IS WHAT HURTS

SAY YES, BUT NEVER SAY WHEN.
—BENITO JUÁREZ, ON HOW TO DEAL
WITH THE UNITED STATES

LATER THE NEXT DAY, I stop at the Rio Grande near the town of
Redford. A Border Patrol SUV squats beside the River. The
lone Anglo agent inside looks in my direction through opaque,
wraparound sunglasses as I walk up to him.

"Hi there," I say.

He nods.

"Um, I'm visiting down here, riding my bike along the
river. I'm doing research for a book on the border—I'm a
journalist, a writer."

He nods.

"I was wondering if you could give me an idea of the problems with drugs and illegals along this stretch of the river."

He shakes his head. I can see my reflection in his sunglasses. I wait: ten, fifteen seconds.

"Uh, does that mean you can't talk to me about this?"

He nods.

"Is that kind of standard procedure for Border Patrol agents?

He doesn't move at all. Time goes by. His head points in

my direction, but, for all I know, he could have fallen asleep, or had a stroke.

"Uh, is that standard procedure? You're not allowed to talk to me about your duties here?"

There is a long silence. He is still looking in my direction, but it's as if he has succumbed to a strange and instant paralysis. Maybe, by a really weird coincidence, he died at the very moment I was asking my last question. I look at his chest to see if he's still breathing, and I see a slight rise and fall.

"Well, er, thanks anyway," I say.

I turn, mount up, and get out of there. In that lonely place by the river, he spooked me.

I hurry to Presidio. It is a bigger town, befitting the first border crossing in hundreds of miles, with dirt side roads, and some Mexican-style houses—blank-walled adobe, looking inwards. It looks like small towns I've visited deep in Mexico, or like a frontier town. It is across from Ojinaga, four times the size of Presidio and one of the main plazas in the drug trade.

One of the big battles of the Mexican Revolution took place at Ojinaga between federal soldiers and Villistas. Ambrose Bierce, the writer and epigrammatist who renounced his life in the United States and travelled to Mexico to ride with Pancho Villa, disappeared there. It is where Pablo Acosta, "El Zorro de Ojinaga," ran the plaza for years—just a little way upriver from the town of Santa Elena where he was from, and where the chopper-borne commandos took him out in a fierce firefight. Some of the best-known *norteño* troubadors come from Ojinaga. It is still a violent and busy drug emporium, and it, too, is caught up in the fierce wars between the cartels and government troops, and among the cartels. As with all these settlements along the river, the town has been a smuggling centre since the marauding gringos imposed a new border on broken Mexico.

Before finding a motel in Presidio, I ride down to the river. I stop on a scrubby rise of waste ground and *carrizo* cane along the bank (*carrizo* grows very high, making good cover for illegals travelling on foot). I look down to my right. Twenty feet away, slightly below me, there are a dozen or so men in camouflage uniforms and body armour, carrying assault rifles. They are chatting quietly, and checking their gear and weapons. They look like a grunt patrol heading out to look for contact. They stop and gaze up at me. I flip up my helmet visor so that they can see my face, and I give a short wave; I feel as if I should salute. One of the troopers makes emphatic pointing motions back towards the road. No one speaks or moves. I nod, wave again, turn the bike around and get out of there. Maybe they are BORTAC SWAT troops, members of the secretive Border Patrol tactical unit. Whoever they are, I don't want to disturb them at their work.

Next day, I ride fifty-five miles along the river, to the end of the road. There's not much there: Ruidosa, population 43; Candelaria, 55. The day is hot but I'm comfortable enough in my riding jacket over a shirt. Still north of Presidio, I take several dirt roads towards the Rio Grande, but each one ends at fences around private property and I can't get to the water.

The road to Ruidosa is a series of dips and long curves following the river's meanderings. This is a remote part of the border even now, cut off from the rest of Texas by the Chinati Mountains. Ruidosa began as an outpost—built and manned by a unit of convicts called the "Condemned Regiment"—to guard cattle and horses in northern Chihuahua state against Apaches and Comanches. They were condemned: the Comanches wiped them out. When the Indians were "pacified," there grew to be almost two thousand people here, ranching, growing cotton, running a flour mill. Now, I ride straight on through Ruidosa in about five seconds and I don't encounter a soul.

Between Presidio and Ruidosa, I see two vehicles: a new SUV with Chihuahua plates, and a beat-up station wagon pulling an open trailer with a cow standing tied down onto it. Both vehicles and cow pass me at seventy-five miles an hour. The animal turns its head and looks at me with interest as it cruises by. The road to Candelaria is completely empty. There are no Border Patrol vehicles, which is unusual; I seldom ride more than half an hour without seeing one. The river flows by to my left, visible most of the way, winding muddy and high between lines of trees—tamarisks now, rather than cottonwoods. On the Mexican side, the desert is the same, and the arid, jagged mountains of the Sierra Grande roll away to the west.

I ride slowly through the small cluster of rundown adobe houses, crumbling shacks and rusty trailers. My plan is to eat lunch, maybe in a quiet spot by the river. One crummy house is like all the rest except that it has nine or ten late-model SUVs and sedans parked outside. They gleam in the sun. As far as I can see, all of them bear Chihuahua plates. I ride on another two hundred yards or so to the end of the road. There is no one around. I turn the bike and stop. The shoddy, paint-peeled house and the bright, new vehicles definitely do not go together. Maybe I'll forgo a lunch by the river just here. I'll head back to Ruidosa, where I plan to take a dirt road that the map shows running over the mountains to the town of Marfa.

As I ride past the incongruous house again, I see that a Hispanic man in jeans and a blue shirt has stepped out the front door and is standing on the porch. He is carrying an assault rifle nestled on his forearm. We stare at each other as I cruise by and accelerate away. I watch my rear-view mirror. Within a few minutes, an SUV appears behind me. It closes to within a hundred yards, and then drops to my speed and holds there. I felt unnerved before; now, I feel damned scared. I keep riding towards Ruidosa—nothing else to do on the deserted road. Where the fuck is the Border Patrol when you want them?

The SUV maintains its distance into Ruidosa, where I pull over in front of the tiny general store. There is still no one around. The SUV drives slowly by. Its windows are tinted and I can't see inside. It keeps going, speeds up, and disappears from sight. I'm not sure what I've just seen. I have no idea whether I was in a little, or grave—or, indeed, any—danger. I wait for several minutes, but the SUV doesn't reappear. I take a swig of water, check my map, and turn the bike off Ranch Road 170, through a cattle gate and onto the nearby dirt road, which, I hope, will be passable over the Chinati Mountains.

This is my first long ride on dirt, and, between checking my rear-view mirror for an SUV full of armed gangsters, and climbing the bike over rocky ledges the size of coffee tables, fording streams—one deep enough to submerge my wheel hubs and soak my boots—and struggling to stay upright on the rutted, sandy, stony surface, I'm done in long before I hit pavement again. I sweat and eke my way along the trail for hours at ten or fifteen miles an hour. I very soon regret taking this so-called road, in part because it's much harder to ride than I thought it would be, and in part because, if I'd wanted to put myself in some out-of-the-way place where I could be safely and efficiently murdered by cartel gunmen, I couldn't have found a better one.

No turning back. Nothing around me but the desert rising higher, arroyos and gulches, and rock hills and cactus to the horizon, a distant ranch building. Chinati Peak lies to my right, more than 7,700 feet high. I catch a glimpse of three riders on horseback in single file about two or three miles away to the northwest, but they quickly disappear. I ride on, grimy and soaked with sweat, although it gets cooler as I climb higher. I don't want to take off my armoured jacket because there's such a good chance I'm going to go down. But I don't, and my confidence grows. I stand on my footpegs and let the bike move around under me. I get my speed up a little. Faster is better on these shifting surfaces, the augmented inertia stabilizing the machine. By the time I reach paved Ranch Road 2810, I believe I'm getting the hang of it.

I ride on, across a wide, rolling grassland, dotted with palms and small evergreen trees and cattle herds—Herefords and longhorns. The wind is strong here, in the open, but it's mostly behind me. The joy of a following wind—on sailing vessels and motorcycles—is devoutly to be wished for. By the time I get close to Marfa, I haven't seen another vehicle for almost three hours.

Once again, I'm being forced north in a dogleg away from the border. There are no roads beside the river, which is barricaded for 150 miles—even farther, with the river's vagaries— by chains of mountains: the Sierra Vieja, the Van Horn, the Eagle, and the Quitman. I pass right through Marfa, an incongruous place on the high desert plain. It has a large, elegant town hall, art galleries, fancy coffee shops, stores selling Gucci, and a theatre running a play by Sam Shepard. As I ride on to Van Horn, the strong wind is back to the normal head-on, or crossways. I hunker down for the last slog of the day on the unbending road striking through the desert plain. In a motel in Van Horn that evening, I see that the forecast for tomorrow is for a west wind, thirty to thirty-five miles an hour. Gale force, I say to Will, Mike and Chris; you wouldn't like it here.

I'm on the final approach to El Paso. I ride the I-10 back to the river, and to Ranch Road 34, where I began this book.

I look for the ruins of Fort Quitman, run into a solicitous pair of Border Patrol agents, am shown the site of a firefight between Mexican gunmen and U.S. deputies, am lectured about safety in the deserted area where all kinds of illegal activities take place, and am escorted back to the main road by the kindly cops. I continue up the river road through irrigated crop fields and pecan orchards. It reminds me of the Valley: heavily populated, or it seems so to me after the long empty stretches I've ridden through; it is fertile land, and, once again, adjacent to the Rio Grande.

In Acala, I stop for a Coke at a small store. The owner wears a holstered handgun. Outside, I fall into conversation with two half-drunk Mexicans who want to sell me a watch for $5. They are damp because they have just swum across the river, which is close by—genuine "wetbacks." They are broke and they need money either to travel farther north for work or to buy more beer—they haven't decided yet. Or maybe they'll just swim back to Mexico.

"Did you have any problem crossing the river?"

They are puzzled.

"No, none. We can swim."

"No *migra*?" (Mexican slang for the U.S. Border Patrol or immigration officers).

"No. They drive by. Then, we swim across."

I give them $5, not for the watch, but, as one of them suggests, for "la historia de los dos Mexicanos tristos": the story of two sad Mexicans. They seem embarrassed by the money, but they take it.

I ride on through Alamo Alta, Tornillo, Clint, Socorro, and, with caution and some trepidation, into the big-time traffic of El Paso. Here, I will rest for a couple of days, and the trusty KLR will also receive kindly servicing attention and renewal. Here, too, I'll see, writ large, the dramatic interface of rich America in entangled and intimate proximity to poor and roiling Mexico.

"Oh, poor Mexico, so far from God, so close to the United States." The aphorism (which Canadians could also adopt easily as their own) is attributed to the late-nineteenth-century president-dictator Porfirio Díaz. Mexico is a small nation attached to a huge power, a sleeper next to the elephant (to appropriate a former Canadian prime minister's phrase) whose dreams and twitches it must watch with unremitting attention.

Mexico's profoundly asymmetrical relationship with the United States began early. Mexico was late to achieve independence; it lacked the political and legal culture for organized, stable and relatively honest government; and it bogged down in a confusion of identity. Its people are 90 per cent mestizos, who struggle to accept their *mestizaje*—their essential mixed nature. Unlike the Americans, who, at best, practiced apartheid against the Indians, and, at worst, genocide, the Spanish mated and fused with the indigenous nations. The mestizos are descendants of both Cortés, the Spanish conqueror, and Cuauhtémoc, the vanquished Indian king. With whom should they identify?

Mexico fought for eleven long, bitter years, from 1810 to 1821, to win independence from Spain. The savage struggle impoverished the country and destroyed the colonial political system. It took fifty more years to sort out a new, more-or-less effective government and political structure—although both remained dysfunctional in many ways through corruption, class divisions, and the absence of a tradition of democratic politics and a notion of the rule of law. The conflict and disorder of that half-century did as much damage to Mexico as the War of Independence itself. It was this nation and culture in profound crisis that the United States confronted, invaded and dismembered during the Mexican War (or the United States Invasion). The discrepancy between the fierce and structured Anglo-Protestant United States, with its brutally lucid vision of its own manifest destiny, and the fractious, tractable Catholic Mexico was hugely amplified by Mexico's loss of half its territory.

Seventy years of Mexican turmoil and American development followed, and the pattern of an extraordinarily rich
country adjacent to a poor one had been set. On one side of
the stolen border was the cheap labour—the *pollos*—and dep-
rivation, oppression, no-hope; on the other, were the gringo
employers, and a life of work, stability and progress.

The essence of the asymmetrical relationship between
Mexico and the United States is that the U.S. can, apart from oil
supplies, do without Mexico (albeit with some dislocation and
shortages). Mexico (like Canada) is dependent upon the United
States; a sudden cessation of trade and investment would destroy
Mexico (and impoverish Canada). Mexico depends most specifically on the U.S. for the maquiladoras—the duty- and tariff-
free manufacturing and assembly plants along the Mexican side
of the border—and as the principal market for the drug trade.

Even the maquiladoras are an ambiguous benefit for
Mexicans. Most of them are sweatshops—as these are defined
by the United States government. That is, they violate laws
governing hours, minimum pay, child labour and home work.
The majority of the workers are women, who will toil longer
hours for less and are more compliant about working conditions. The result is high turnover: perhaps 10 per cent a month,
so that a factory might have to hire an entirely new labour
force every ten months. The maquiladoras have drawn hundreds of thousands of poor Mexicans (and Central Americans)
to the border cities, where they live in slums and barely get by,
where they must live with violence, drugs, prostitution and
enormous environmental problems in an arid and unforgiving landscape. Still, it's better there than where they came
from. And it's always better across the border in the United
States—for the maquiladora peons, there is always the chance
of making it to *el otro lado*.

There is more asymmetry: the American counties along
the border—milk and honey to the *pollos*—are among the

poorest in the United States. Even so, the contrast is great. The border, Gloria Anzaldúa writes, is "where the Third World grates against the first and bleeds." Mexican towns and cities along the border have twice the per capita income of those farther south, but about one-fifth the income of comparable cities in the United States, as relatively poor as they are by American standards. A Ford worker in the States averages six times the pay of a Ford worker in Hermosillo, in Sonora, the most prosperous Mexican state.

Perhaps the most notable inequality on the border is what happens when people try to cross it. I could wander into Nuevo Progreso in the Valley without a glance from the men with the uniforms and guns. I could travel anywhere along the Mexican side without a visa or any other authorization so long as I stayed within twenty miles of the border. In some places, there are special zones: for example, sixty miles south of Tijuana to Ensenada, with no permits or visas required. Otherwise, a six-month *visa turista* takes five minutes to get (not counting lineups). Needless to say, coming the other way is somewhat harder: long waits, questions, forms, a green card or a visa obtained in advance, vehicle searches, body searches, suspicion, fear. The Americans don't routinely spray Mexicans for lice at the border any more, but they used to.

I talked to Hispanic-American historian Oscar Martínez in his office at the University of Arizona in Tucson. The son of an illegal immigrant, he took a long and benign view of U.S.-Mexican relations. The process of economic integration is well underway through the North American Free Trade Agreement, he said. Over the next thirty years or so, Mexican demographics and economic development will equalize with the United States. An equilibrium will be established between the two countries. The illegal migrant problem will wither away. That's why the fence won't work, said Martínez: it won't stop *indocumentados* from making it across now; and in the future, it won't be necessary. The wall will stand as a monument to impatient, knee-jerk prejudice and short-sighted politics.

Needless to say, not everyone is as sanguine as Martínez. And in any event, he admits, the problem of illegal immigration may devolve to Central America. Mexico might become prosperous enough to look after its own people, but that won't happen anytime soon with Guatemala, Honduras, El Salvador and the countries farther south. Mexico already has its own porous border problem along its southern frontier, as Central Americans flood into Mexico to work there, or to transit towards the land of milk and honey to the north. These people will keep coming, and, in the future, both Mexico and the United States may have a joint problem controlling illegal and undocumented "OTMs"—"other than Mexicans." The fence, the Border Patrol, and riding herd on American employers may be deemed necessary for a long time to come.

Americans are "an essentially historyless people," writes historian Arthur M. Schlesinger, Jr. He meant that Americans see the past as over and done with, and as having little relevance to current events and problems. "He's history" means: He is no longer relevant in any way, forget him. In the same way, the Mexican War has no meaning for the United States today; it has no effect whatsoever on American decisions made about Mexico, or perspectives held on it. For Mexicans, on the other hand, the Invasion, or the Intervention, remains a distressing and traumatic event. It continues to mould how Mexico thinks about the United States, and the policies it forms towards it. If Americans cannot remember, Mexicans cannot forget. When dealing with the United States, Mexico must always try to cope with the historical vacuum within which American politicians make decisions.

Living as they do alongside the oblivious self-confidence of the United States, Mexicans, like Canadians, struggle to define their identity—to explain to themselves who they are. What is a Mexican? A Canadian? For Canadians, it is a necessarily subtle process: how to differentiate themselves from people who look the same, speak the same language, come from the same places. For many Canadians, the definition of Canadian is simply: not-American.

For Mexicans, the confusion of identity is grounded in the mixed origins of the people, in the blended culture that evolved over centuries, from the time of conquest when Spanish men killed Indian men and procreated with Indian women. On the one hand the white, civilized, Christian conqueror; on the other, the brown, pagan, primitive vanquished. Hernán Cortés, who overthrew the Aztecs, took La Malinche, an Indian, as his courtesan. Was she raped? Did she give herself willingly to the conqueror? Did she collaborate to make an alliance with the Spanish and thus save what was left of her people's power? Or did she act only to save her own skin? No one knows. But from La Malinche came the mestizos: orphaned and confused, forever colonized.

A nation originating in conquest and forced intercourse seldom has a quiet existence. Such a beginning has often been cited as the source for the notion of machismo in Mexico. The wounded and degraded male compensates for his original humiliation through the exaggeration and glorification of male brutality, toughness and apparent self-sufficiency.

The problem of identity in Mexico is exacerbated along the border. In this zone of proximity to the United States, of contact and interpenetration by its overwhelming, fascinating and seductive culture—the "bulldozer culture"—Mexican selfhood is weakened. To the underlying uncertainty of identity are added the problems of remoteness from the national centre to the south, and the correspondingly greater vulnerability to influence from the north. To Mexicans in Mexico City, the border is the land where proximity to the gringos makes the inhabitants suspect. Maybe they are selling out to the Americans—turning into *pochos*, gringo-ized Mexicans.

Mexico was plundered once by the Americans in 1848. One of the ways to make sure that doesn't happen again is to establish a sure sense of *mexicanidad*, of Mexican-ness. This means a stable and consistent culture, language, and set of social and political values throughout the country. The Mexican side of the border benefits Mexico as a whole because, with the maquiladoras, it is a relatively prosperous area. It is also the staging ground for emigration to the United States— both legal and illegal immigration are essential aspects of Mexican economic well-being. But the bastardization of both language and culture in the borderlands (Spanglish and the third-country way of life) threaten this unifying effort and subvert the economic benefits of proximity to the gringos.

In the remote northern deserts, and along the iconic River, far from the metropolitan centre around Mexico City, it may seem to the arbiters of *mexicanidad* that a new and distinct kind of Mexican has come into existence. It's true that millions of Mexican migrants have steadily transformed the southwestern United States into a kind of extension of Mexico, a new mixed version of the ancient Hispanic culture of the Americas. But it's a two-way street. America has a long history of eventually absorbing different newcomers—a nation of immigrants, indeed. It is flexible and adaptable, and the most likely fate of the American Hispanics is, eventually, to become Hispanic-Americans, an ethnic identity within the United States, just like the formerly despised Irish or Italians. Even the strong forces of Hispanic demographics and culture don't stand a chance of forming Aztlán inside the territory of the United States. Yet if Americans do fear the Hispanicization of their country, Mexicans worry about the *agringamiento* of theirs—the gringos, with their energy and wealth, and their unstoppable culture, reaching south across the line into Mexico, into the borderlands, transforming the people there into something other than Mexican. The gringos won't invade—those days are long past—but there are other ways of taking possession.

"History plays itself out here in El Paso," says Gary Williams. "I love that." Williams has lived in the city for thirty-five years. When I spoke to him, he was working for the El Paso Community Foundation, which supports various local social and artistic projects. When he arrived in El Paso, the population was roughly fifty-fifty Anglo and Hispanic, and it had the feel of a small town with a university. Ciudad Juárez was a rooted community, poor, but with a centre and a civic integrity. The border was a sieve. People crossed more or less at will. And drugs as well. Now, Juárez is a conglomeration of maquiladoras, and hundreds of thousands of new people have moved there from farther south in Mexico and from elsewhere in Latin America. Juárez's growth has had an effect on El Paso. The American city (or the American side of the trans-border city made up of El Paso and Juárez) has close to 700,000 people, 85 per cent of whom are Hispanic.

Gary confirms my stupidity in riding blithely down the Fort Quitman road. He tells me his version of the firefight between American lawmen and what looked like Mexican soldiers. "It's a real hot spot," he says. The drugs are never-ending. Americans want them, of course, and Mexicans need the money the trade brings. More insidious is the image the drug runners have within Mexico: the Robin Hood effect. I mention Pablo Acosta, who owned the Ojinaga plaza for so long. Yeah, says Gary; he was a very bad guy, but the Mexicans loved him.

Gary, who is originally from unilingual, monocultural Kansas, remains fascinated by El Paso. The city is, indeed, situated within a kind of third country, he says. It's unique. That bothers a lot of people. They can't understand it, or even come to terms with it. "But I've embraced it. The border is a window." What's happening here is "going north whether people like it or not." He means the migrants. It's a universal phenomenon: Turks in Germany, Arabs in France, Mexicans in the United States, including in northern cities like Chicago.

The fence is impossible, says Gary; it won't work. There are miles of fences along the river in El Paso now. They don't keep people out, and new fences won't either. The demand for labour within the United States is too strong.

I spoke to Gary as Homeland Security's new fence project was getting underway. The plan includes new double-layer steel fencing stretching from just east of downtown El Paso fifty-five miles to Fort Hancock, downstream on the River (a vehicle-barrier fence was completed in 2009). Twelve miles of the new fence are within El Paso city limits. There hasn't been as much resistance to the new barrier here as farther south. People in the city have been living with fourteen miles of fences, towers and floodlights ever since "Operation Hold the Line" got underway. They're used to the inconvenience of the barricade and its ungainly, repellent appearance. They have accepted what it says about the United States, about Mexico and about their third country. They are also used to the fact that it doesn't work.

A recent study supports their opinion. In 2008, the Center for Comparative Immigration Studies at the University of California at San Diego had the original and compelling idea that, if someone actually interviewed *indocumentados*, it might be possible to find out how successful they are at getting over the border. The results confirm what the Texas Border Coalition, landowners, politicians and lawmen along the Rio Grande have been saying for a couple of years. All the fences, electronic sensors, barriers, wire, National Guard and greatly increased numbers of Border Patrol don't mean much. The survey showed that fewer than half of illegals were caught by the Border Patrol. Those who were caught tried over and over again until they succeeded. Through all the operations and beefed-up security measures over the last ten or more years, the average success rate for illegals getting into the United States has remained over 90 per cent, and because of those measures, illegals who get into the U.S. stay there, bring their families over and settle permanently.

The drug wars have hit Juárez hard over the last few years— since presidents Fox and Calderón sent in the army and desta- bilized the cartels, who now fight the government and each other with such savage ferocity. *La Limpia*—the cleansing— is unrelenting.

As in Nuevo Laredo, Juárez reporters have censored them- selves. The editor of *Norte de Ciudad Juárez*, Alfredo Quijano, told his employees to report "dead bodies and not investiga- tions." Two reporters fled to El Paso because of death threats, yet no one doubts that the cartels have a strong presence in the American city. Mexican-Americans have been kidnapped off the streets there. Juárez policemen have taken refuge in El Paso, as have at least three thousand families from the Mexican side, and wounded officers have been treated in the city's R. E. Thomason General Hospital. An injured Commander Fernando Sandoval of the Chihuahua State Investigations Agency was treated at the hospital, and El Paso police put armed guards and metal detectors in place to prevent gunmen from finishing him off.

As an example of the mood in Juárez, consider what hap- pened one May weekend in 2008. An anonymous email circu- lated around the city warning of a bloodbath. It said that gunmen would open fire in malls, restaurants and other public places, and told people to stay home. They did. On Saturday night, the city was a ghost town. As it turned out, the weekend toll was normal: eight homicides, including two policemen machine-gunned as they were getting into their car. However, it's notable that the people of Juárez either believed the email, or weren't prepared to trust that it was a hoax.

On top of everything else that happens in Juárez, there are the women. Over the last ten years, more than 450 have been murdered, their bodies found around the city in garbage dumps or nearby in the desert, mutilated, tortured, sexually assaulted. The violence of the assaults and murders is extreme and horrifying. Many more women are missing. Most are young, and many work in the maquiladoras; few are prostitutes or criminals. No one knows who is doing it, or why, although possibilities include the cartels, "white slavers," pornography rings, police death squads, a loose network of freelancers, some or all of the above.

The campus of the University of Texas at El Paso (UTEP) is built on a bluff overlooking the river and a section of Juárez. The Rio Grande here is a narrow, muddy stream flowing between concrete walls. It looks inconsequential and no one would give it a glance if it weren't an international boundary. UTEP's original campus buildings are bizarrely idiosyncratic. The first ones were built in 1917 to reproduce a small Bhutanese village. The dean's wife liked photographs in *National Geographic* of Bhutan's landscape, and noticed its similarity to El Paso's. Now, says a university brochure, the buildings "resemble a Himalayan kingdom . . . modelled after Bhutanese monasteries, or dzongs." With their sloping high walls and small windows, they are a jarring sight in a U.S.-Mexico borderlands city. Along its perimeter, facing Mexico, the campus looks like a castle on the hill, a fortress of knowledge and privilege.

From UTEP's shadeless promontory, I look across into Juárez. It is a warren of dirt roads running over the bare, stony hills onto which the city has spilled over. I see fires burning on waste ground; jumbled adobe houses and small, dilapidated shacks; junk cars, some of them in motion; the small figures of children everywhere but not in school; and a penumbra of dust hanging over the mean streets. Peering into Juárez from UTEP is like looking down from an outpost of an old, ordered, and opulent civilization into a wretched post-apocalyptic future. Juárez and El Paso may be one city divided by a paltry river boundary, as some of its inhabitants claim, but if that's so, Juárez is certainly on the other side of the tracks.

Nevertheless, the university is one of the bridges over those tracks. Eighteen hundred students cross the border from Juárez each day to go to classes, UTEP's president, Diana Natalicio, tells me. The main problem with the border is the fundamental disparity between the United States and Mexico, she says. And so, the key is to ameliorate the conditions of Mexicans, invest more in America's neighbour, and reduce the pressure on them to move north. Education is one way of doing that, and UTEP is helping—eighteen hundred Mexicans at a time.

Natalicio, like other "doves" on the immigration issue, believes Hispanics are ideal immigrants. "They are kind and gentle and earnest. They just want a better life." She had a tough life herself, she says (Natalicio is a married name—she's from a blue-collar Anglo family). She had a hardscrabble path upwards, and education was the key. She made her way on scholarships and with the encouragement she got in a Jesuit school. "My life was no cakewalk," she says, "but I stand in awe of my Hispanic students here. They bear burdens I never dreamed of." As a community, "they are very hard-working, and they have a wonderfully unselfish attitude to success. These fundamental assets will help integrate them into

American life. As they have moved north out of the border area, people in the rest of the United States have seen their qualities." They are a huge untapped pool of talent, she says. "We can't afford to squander that."

Natalicio sees the marches and demonstrations, beginning in 2006, by Hispanics across the country against punitive immigration legislation as a critical moment in Hispanic history. "They used to be a fearful population," she explains. "Now, the opening of the dialogue has liberated the Hispanic willingness to step out on stage; it has unleashed Hispanic political consciousness."

El Paso itself is almost a unique city, she says. Its centre is just one part of a downtown that includes Juárez. There is one downtown in two different countries. So the two cities need to work together. The border must be "seamless."

One evening, I cross the border from El Paso into Juárez with Mick and Jon. They are descendants of Anglo families that settled here in the nineteenth century. Mick's great-grandfather came to the New World from County Kilkenny in Ireland in the 1890s. He looked for gold in the Klondike, and then travelled south, eventually acquiring sixty-five thousand acres of land in Hudspeth County, just to the east of El Paso County. Hudspeth is three times the size of Rhode Island, but has a population of thirty-five hundred people. Mick and his family still own a good portion of the ranch, although they continue to fight long-standing legal battles over water rights—as in the entire southwest, aquifers in west Texas are dwindling. Jon's ancestors came to this part of the country before Mick's. Both men are very familiar with the border as it once was.

We drive across a bridge into Juárez in Mick's yellow Volkswagen Beetle. As always, there are no controls in this direction; we just drive into Mexico. El Paso and Juárez may be one downtown in theory, but certainly not in practice. El Paso

is quiet and orderly, Juárez noisy and chaotic; it teems, perco-
lates, jumps. It seems to promise all the nighttime pleasures of
a Mexican border town, the sorts of illicit and exotic vices pro-
scribed on the straightlaced and regulated American side. The
word "Juárez"—and, farther west, "Tijuana"—is synonymous
with booze, dope, women, boys, loud music, danger, whatever
your lurid little heart desires. In both cities' names there is an
intimation of a rite of passage, a crossing over to where things
are different, where the rules don't apply, where anything
might happen. It's a kind of liberation, and I feel it run though
me, too, as our yellow Beetle careens through the fast streets of
Ciudad Juárez.

We're looking, prosaically, for food. Mike knows Juárez
well, and he wants to take me to places the turistas don't know.
Not that there are many tourists in Juárez these days. The first
restaurant is a tiny bistro sort of place, but it's closed. The
second one we can't get into because various cars are blocking
the entrance, and there's some sort of commotion. I see cops,
several armed with rifles, walking over to the kerfuffle. We
drive on to a big, elaborate, courtyard restaurant where tourists
might, indeed, go. Mick gives a guy outside, whom he knows,
$10 to watch the Beetle. Inside, in an immense, hollow room
that could seat two hundred, are just two dozen diners—all
Mexicans—and a loud mariachi band and dancers, but the
food is decent nevertheless.

Mick and Jon speak surprisingly bad Spanish. Mine isn't
good but it's better than theirs, even though I studied it in
school for only two years and I've had few and scattered
opportunities to use it in travels in Latin-America. It's as if
they grudgingly speak a little of the majority language of
their city with noblesse oblige, like the privileged Anglo landowners and overseers of the American southwest they are.
Diana Natalicio, the academic, admires the Mexican migrants
who come across the river, and so do Mick and Jon: their hard

work, their family and religious values, their pride in their craft. Jon and his wife run an Internet jewellery business. It's doing all right, but they hope to expand and grow, and, says Jon, smiling, have "lots of little brown hands" make the stuff. He employs a cleaning woman who comes across from Juárez illegally every day. She just says she's "shopping," and—nod and a wink—there are no problems.

I mention Cormac McCarthy's *Border Trilogy*. I have passed through some of the border places in West Texas that he writes about, and I will do the same in New Mexico. Mick tells me that McCarthy wrote the first book of his Border Trilogy, *All the Pretty Horses*, when he was living in an old house just down the street from Mick's. McCarthy lived alone, like a recluse, and he seemed a little crazy. He didn't water anything, and all the grass and plants around his house died in the desert sun. He had an old pickup that made one hell of a noise when he started it up, which he might do at any hour of the day or night. He would sometimes disappear for days at a time, perhaps driving through the country he would write about with such vividness; he was fanatical about getting everything just right. Once in a while, Mick would see McCarthy in a run-down restaurant nearby, sitting alone, listening to the border Spanish spoken around him, writing in his notebook.

Mick and Jon remember with nostalgia the border as it used to be. You went over to Juárez to buy things, or just because you felt like it, without thinking much—or at all—about the fact that you were crossing an international boundary. It was a casual, normal part of life. Now the border is all gridlock and drugs and questions and armed men. Mick is amused when I tell him about my experience on the road to Fort Quitman. The insouciance of the naive traveller. Only an idiot local would drive a road where the Mexican army engages in open firefights with American lawmen, and where drugs come across the river like they're a pizza delivery.

When we head back to El Paso, the border isn't busy at all—about a half-hour lineup. As we're inching forward, a car filled with young, buzz-cut, drunk Anglo and Hispanic men cuts into the line ahead of us and a dozen other vehicles. "It's okay," one of them shouts, leaning his entire upper body out of the car window, "we're Navy. We've been in fuckin' Eye-raq!" When they reach the immigration booth a few cars ahead of us, we hear them yahooing and hollering—rebel yells.

As we're pulling up to the booth a few minutes later, Mick scares the hell out of Jon and me: he gives a loud faux drunken yell himself. It scares the agent, too. He steps back and his hand falls reflexively onto the butt of his side arm. Jon, in the back seat, leans forward and says, soothingly: "Well those guys were yelling. He figured he might as well, too." Mick smiles wolfishly at the agent, who relaxes and asks his few questions. He seems to recognize what he's dealing with: Americans, locals. Except for me; I show him my passport. As we drive off, Jon and I mention to Mick that his gesture was a mite alarming. He is unrepentant. He doesn't give a rat's ass. He'll yell if he wants to. "This is my country," he says. "This is my fucking border!"

CHAPTER 6

LINE IN THE SAND

DON'T LET IT END LIKE THIS.
TELL THEM I SAID SOMETHING.
—PANCHO VILLA'S LAST WORDS

AT BREAKFAST IN A GREASY SPOON near my motel, on my last day in El Paso, an elderly Hispanic man standing behind me, having a conversation in Spanish with the cashier, says the word "gringo" several times. I've never heard a Spanish-speaker along the border use the word, and I'm surprised. I turn to see who's talking. The man doesn't see me, but his wife does. She smiles and shrugs apologetically. She looks ashamed. As they're leaving, she says something to the man. He turns and looks at me, a little bewildered. Then he comes over, and he actually bows.

"I should not have said that word," he says in accented English. "I am sorry, sir."

"It's okay," I say. "I was just curious about who had said it, because I'm visiting and I haven't heard it used down here."

"Well, I should not have used it, sir."

I tell him it really doesn't matter, not to worry, and I thank him for his courtesy. He bows again, and walks out.

——

I pick up the KLR from the Mexican mechanic, who speaks only a little English. The bill is surprisingly low, and I wonder if he's done everything he should have for this servicing. The morning I'm packed up to leave, the bike is very reluctant to start: for the first time, I need a lot of throttle as well as the choke. I return to the dealership. The mechanic starts the bike and says it's okay. I tell him I'm heading west along the border.

"You won't strand me in the mountains, will you?"

"No, no, señor. No te preocupes. Don't worry. They are very good bikes."

Nevertheless, the sudden onset of a starting problem worries me.

As I'm mounting up, another mechanic says: "Be careful out there, amigo."

I ride out of El Paso, across the Rio Grande, out of Texas and into New Mexico. The river curls north, a completely American waterway now. I feel as if I've broken the back of my southern journey, as if I'm much closer to the Pacific than I really am. But it's a reasonable impression. The southern border is really the Texas-Mexico border, along with short sections of New Mexico, Arizona and California. Twelve hundred miles of the two-thousand-mile boundary is in Texas, marked by the River. From here on, I follow a line in the sand.

I follow Highway 9 close to the border, over the Potrillo Mountains, into a very cold and strong wind, on long straightaways through the desert. Three Border Patrol vehicles pass me at about eighty miles an hour on the otherwise almost deserted road. Three times, I turn off and take trails across the stony sand, weaving around mesquite and yucca, towards the border. It's difficult riding on the soft surface. I don't want to leach air out of my tires because I'll be back on pavement soon, and I'm just not skilled enough to ride over this terrain, especially on a bike carrying heavy cargo, and in a gale-force crosswind.

Scattered around me here and there, in small piles and ragged lines, lie discarded plastic bottles, Styrofoam food containers and clothes. They are the markers of the illegals who have tramped these trails. To people who deplore the *indocumentados*, one of the worst things they do is strew garbage over the pristine desert.

Somehow, I make it to a dilapidated fence of three-strand wire, with a top line of razor wire, and my way is blocked. Judging by my map, this is, indeed, the border. The wire sags in places so that I can easily step over it—the old, symbolic border marker. (Now, a new section of the fence authorized by the Safe Borders Act has been thrown up along here, stretching from the other side of Columbus, New Mexico, to El Paso, a distance of roughly seventy-five miles.)

This land is still officially Chihuahuan desert, but here the earth's surface looks volcanic and cindery, with craters and old lava flows. It is also flat enough that I can see the Border Patrol SUV turn off the highway a mile away and lumber over the trail towards me. Here is the aspect, once again, of America at its fringe. I decide I may as well face the music, and turn and ride to meet the men with the guns.

Two agents, one Hispanic, the other Anglo, get out of the SUV, the Hispanic agent with his pistol drawn. I dismount and take off my helmet—my customary exposure of white-skinned, blue-eyed respectability. The ensuing conversation is, by now, wholly predictable. It has been played many times already, and it will be played again with regularity—with variations on the theme—in the coming days. I have come to think of it as: The Script.

The Opening Command: "Stop right there, and keep your hands in view."

The Precautions: The Hispanic agent is holding his side arm in two hands, near his head, elbows cocked, combat-ready.

The Question: "What are you doing here, sir?"

I go through my usual explanation.

The Admonition: "You should not be here. This is a dangerous area."

At least it's not a restricted one.

The Supplementary Question: "Are you carrying any firearms?"

No, I'm not. They relax, and the Hispanic agent holsters his pistol.

The Bonding and Dénouement: We chat about the vastness of the country, the difficulty of patrolling it, the need for a fence (they are in distinct favour of a fence), the suffering the *pollos* experience in their desperation to reach the promised land (they are sympathetic), the fact that anyone who approaches the border around here by himself on a motorcycle is a large pannier bag short of a full load.

The Benediction: "Have a good day," says the Anglo agent as I start the bike to ride back to the highway.

I can see the small cluster of buildings of Columbus across the desert plain twenty minutes before I get there. I ride through the dusty town to a two-storey, flat-roofed adobe building, which used to be known as the Hoover Hotel. It is in the style of Mission, or Spanish Colonial Revival. The exterior has been re-stuccoed so that the bullet holes are no longer visible. The interior has been opened up into a large, airy, high-ceilinged first-floor living room and kitchen. The second floor is a studio where a beautiful artist pursues her obsession with black line on white space, and with shapes that arise from primeval earth.

Outside the adobe house, ninety years ago, American troops set up a Benet-Mercie machine gun. They positioned a second weapon south of the hotel so that they could bring crossfire to bear in the intersection on which the building is located. Americans and Mexicans died on the street outside the adobe house that day. Americans took refuge inside because its thick walls were mostly bulletproof and fireproof. All this happened because Pancho Villa had come to town.

It was yet another time of terror and bloodshed in Mexico. The Revolution had begun in 1910 and was still raging on. The factions and reactions ravaged the country, as armies and bands of raiders marched and fought. Americans were often caught up in the fighting in sorties across the border by Mexican raiders. Stray bullets fired in Juárez would kill or wound people walking the streets of El Paso. But in somnolent and isolated Columbus, New Mexico, the people felt secure enough.

In the early morning darkness of March 9, 1916, however, approximately five hundred Mexican soldiers said to be under the command of Pancho Villa, crossed the border and attacked Columbus from the southwest. An army detachment of 350 men from the 13th Cavalry was stationed in Fort Furlong, just outside Columbus. There had been intimations of trouble—Mexican strangers poking around the town—but the assault was a complete surprise for both the American civilians and the troops. With rational tactics, the Villistas could have destroyed the town completely and slaughtered most of its inhabitants, before the U.S. army had time to respond. But Villa's men mostly engaged themselves in burning down a good part of the town's business section, in robbing civilians and in shooting them if they got in the way.

The 13th Cavalry pulled themselves together, and made an efficient and courageous counterattack. That's when they set up their machine guns outside the Hoover Hotel. By dawn, the action was over. Eighteen Americans were dead, including eight soldiers, but as many as a hundred Villistas died before Villa withdrew his men back into Mexico.

Villa's raid was the last attack by foreigners on mainland United States' soil until September 11, 2001.

———

The Hoover Hotel—the adobe house—was one of several buildings to survive the raid intact. I have ridden to it because it is an historical building in the town, but also because it is now owned by Mick's cousin, Linda, the beautiful artist, and I will stay the night there. Her husband, Paul, a correspondent for the *Chicago Tribune*, is here, too, working on a long story to a short deadline. I enter the adobe house out of the strong desert wind, earlier cold and now hot, into a haven of ease, warmth and kindness. I still feel as if I'm travelling in a strange land; I need the comfort, once in a while, of opinions I agree with, and of people who are not angry, not violent. As in Los Fresnos near the beginning of my ride, I have come upon a home of rationality and moderation in these stark, martial borderlands.

Paul once travelled by mule through six hundred miles of Mexico. He saw whole valleys engaged in intensive drug cultivation. The Mexican government sprayed these areas—to keep the Americans happy—but, more often than not, they used water, or even fertilizer. Then, in a period of less government corruption, the Mexicans got more serious and began spraying with herbicide. Lately, however, with the military and police crackdowns by Fox and Calderón, the brutish cartel warfare has resumed. The drug trade remains as vigorous as ever.

Linda, like Mick, recalls the old days when her family would travel from their ranch and casually cross over into Juárez to buy clothes or bread. It was no big deal. There was a lot of marijuana around then, but no one thought there was a drug problem. Nor did they think of Juárez as a violent place. That has changed. She employs Hispanics to work on the adobe house renovation. The foreman, Jésus, told her just earlier today that his mother-in-law and his sister-in-law were stabbed to death in Juárez two weeks ago. Someone broke into their house to rob it, and killed them.

While Paul and Linda agree that the idea of the borderlands as a third country makes sense, there are complex relationships and local differences to account for. For example, Hispanics who have been in the United States for a long time, perhaps for generations, look down on the new arrivals, and especially the *indocumentados*. This is most emphatically true along the River in Texas, with its long-standing Mexican community that is so different from the New Mexico and Arizona border areas. In Arizona in particular, there are many more recently arrived Anglos, who have a more nativist attitude to Hispanic migrants and to immigration in general.

She often gets so weary of living on the border, Linda says, with all the problems, all the attention.

Later, we drive in cold desert evening air to the border crossing, and park Linda's pickup. We're going to walk into Puerto Palomas to eat at the Pink House restaurant. As we stroll towards the gate to Mexico, a Border Patrol bus pulls up. About twenty young Hispanic men climb out and stand around. Agents point to the border fence walkway, and the young men amble over towards it. Before they get there, however, the agents climb back aboard, and the bus pulls away. The young men watch it leave. They look at each other, and at us, in disbelief, smiling. A couple of them walk into Mexico, but the rest stand around in the United States, still illegal migrants. They don't seem to know what to do. As we walk past, one man says to me in English: "Hello, how are you?"

"Very well," I say, "and you?"

"Very good," he says.

We leave the *indocumentados* in America contemplating their luck, their apparent second chance, and the careless vagaries of the migra.

The new, improved border fence has been erected along the border between Columbus and Palomas. It is strung on close-set, fifteen-foot, cement-filled steel poles driven three feet into the ground. In other sections of the line, the fence will consist of woven-steel panels. Almost immediately, illegals, or the coyotes responsible for their transit, began to cut through the fence with acetylene and plasma torches, or—the old laborious method of breaking out, or in—with hacksaws and axes. Cameras have recorded groups of migrants using tall ladders to scale the fence ("José's 21-foot Ladders"), and bungee lines or rope to drop down onto the gringo side. The fence is already beginning to deteriorate. Posts are settling into the sand, and the gaps between posts have already become, in places, wide enough for a skinny Mexican to slip through.

The Columbus Historical Museum is in the old railway station, which is a symbol of the town's decline from the years when trains used to haul copper from Arizona through Columbus to Texan smelters. When the El Paso and Southwestern Railroad pulled out, the town didn't quite die, but it dwindled down close to it. Linda must be a liberal minority in town, I suggest, a proposition Linda confirms with laughter. She's pretty much a one-person show in a gallery of conservative nativism. In the museum I meet the face of Anglo reaction along the desert border.

Richard Dean's grandmother was one of the civilians killed in the Columbus raid. He is one angry white man. His wife, Betty, isn't far behind. They are bitter about what's happened here over the last twenty years. Mexicans from Palomas are sucking Columbus dry. Kids come over and crowd the school here. Mexicans on the other side get to use Columbus's ambulance and fire services for free. The medics and the firefighters treat people on both sides of the line the same—except the Americans are paying for it all. As more Mexicans arrive, more and more old trailers and *basura* litter the edge of town. It looks like hell.

The government is paying attention to illegals now, says Dean, because they're not just along the border any more. Now, they're in Chicago and Denver—you name it. The New Mexico state government thought the border ran just south of Santa Fe. It ignored the border towns and their people. They might as well have been living in a separate third country, he says. Now, the cities farther north are getting the problems these migrants cause, and so they're doing something; although, Dean goes on, the whole border strategy has gone to hell, too. More money and fences and Border Patrol won't stop these people. The fence? Hell, they're already cutting through it with torches. But what else can be done, he just doesn't know.

After the shock had worn off and the dead had been mourned, Villa's raid was deemed good for Columbus. The attack initiated the town's period of expansion and prosperity, and for a while it became the most populous settlement in the state. It was the staging ground for the Punitive Expedition. President Woodrow Wilson sent General John "Black Jack" Pershing into Mexico to hunt down Pancho Villa. Just five days after the raid, Pershing crossed the border with more than five thousand men, a number that would soon increase to around eleven thousand. Wilson ordered Pershing to capture Villa and disperse his raiders. Pershing was also supposed to co-operate with the Mexican forces loyal to the government of Venustiano Carranza, and, if they were capable of getting Villa, then Pershing was to withdraw.

Earlier in the revolution, Villa had, for a while, taken refuge in the United States. There is an extant photograph of Villa and Pershing posing together at Fort Bliss, in El Paso. Now, "Black Jack" thrashed through, over, and around the deserts and mountains of northern Mexico for close to a year, penetrating three hundred miles into the country, without once sighting Villa or his raiders. However, he did manage to get into fights with Mexican civilians and regular troops, and both sides suffered substantial casualties. The Carranza government had approved limited hot-pursuit across the border by American forces if another raid occurred. But they had not envisioned, nor agreed to, an incursion in response to Villa's raid, let alone the large-scale, and extended, campaign that Pershing was carrying out.

To Mexicans of all political persuasions, the Punitive Expedition looked like a Yankee invasion of their country. Villa, already a hero because of the audacity of his raid on Columbus—you could never go wrong tweaking the noses of the gringos, or even, it seemed, gunning them down in their own streets—became even more revered for his agile slipperiness in the face of Pershing's laborious pursuit.

There were other incidents and cross-border attacks. In January 1916, Villista troops pulled eighteen American mine employees off a train at Santa Ysabel in northern Chihuahua and massacred them. In the chaos of revolutionary warfare, Carranza could not prevent freelance bandidos from making sorties across the border. Bandits made raids on Glenn Springs and Boquillas in the Big Bend country of Texas, and on San Ygnacio, farther south, in which both American soldiers and civilians were killed.

The United States undertook a "second punitive expedition" to hunt down the Glenn Springs attackers, who had taken two American hostages. Both sides of the tense border had become thoroughly militarized. Things were getting dangerous, and there was the possibility of full-scale war. It seemed as if the United States could not give up its habit of telling Hispanic republics, and especially Mexico, handily next door, how to live their lives.

The context of Mexican resentment had two parts. First was the memory of 1846–48: the contrived American invasion, and the dismemberment of the fragile young republic. Any time American soldiers crossed the border, or American politicians told Mexicans how to run their country, or pressured it, or interfered in its governance, or in its revolutionary torment, Mexicans saw the humiliating shadow of the invasion of 1846.

The second element of Mexican fear and resentment was economic. Economic tensions had replaced earlier, more earthy, concerns such as smuggling (although, obviously, that would be a persistent problem), cattle rustling (the Brownsville raider, Juan Cortina, was a notorious rustler), and Indian raids in the wild borderlands. In a pattern familiar to any Canadian, the United States, by the beginning of the revolution in 1910, had penetrated, and taken control over, large parts of the Mexican economy: 78 per cent of mining, for example; 58 per cent of petroleum; 60 per cent of import-export trade. Foreigners, mostly American, controlled one-seventh of the land of Mexico, and the bulk of that was close to, or in, the borderlands, with their ambivalent sensitivities. William Randolph Hearst owned seven million acres in Chihuahua; John D. Rockefeller controlled all the big oil fields in the Yucatán. The Americans might not have any plans to invade Mexico once again, but they were gaining a sort of control, nevertheless. With the diminution of economic autonomy came a loss of political independence.

The Mexican Revolution, which became a civil war, was a long, agonizing nightmare from which Mexicans took decades to fully awaken. The revolution was one of the central acts in the tragic drama of Mexican history, a moulder of the nation's character. The line of formative events stretches from the Spanish conquests to the war of independence from Spain, to the Mexican War and the ruinous Treaty of Guadalupe Hidalgo, to the French invasion and occupation during the time of the American Civil War, and culminating in the Revolution itself. All nations have these benchmarks of violent birth and transformation; they seem to be a necessary condition of human society. In the United States, the War of Independence and the Civil War are the main such events, with Pearl Harbor and 9/11 as more contemporary occurrences.

The Mexican Revolution also had profound effects on the borderlands. Like any war, this one produced refugees. Close to a million Mexicans crossed the line between 1910 and 1920. For many of them, the United States was a temporary haven, but many stayed on. Members of the existing large Mexican community in the southwestern United States were used to coming and going across the essentially open border, but they, too, stayed put during the decade of war. The revolution continued for so long that migrants had children in the United States, got jobs and made connections with their new country. After the revolution, all along the border, especially in Texas, there was a critical mass of Mexican-Americans that would make the United States even more inviting for future migrants.

The revolution exacerbated the disparity between Mexican and American economic strength. When the United States caught a cold, Mexico (like Canada) got pneumonia. Mexico's dislike and resentment of the gringos couldn't stop the surge of investment and control which, like water, flowed irresistibly downhill. Poor Mexicans came out of the revolution even poorer, and especially so in relation to Americans. With its jobs, its peaceful security and its sense of a future, the land across the Rio Grande or on the other side of the line in the sand looked better than ever.

Finally, the revolution confirmed that Mexicans and Americans didn't much like each other. Gringos and greasers had, once again, lived up to their stereotypical reputations. Mexicans had killed Americans in Mexico—at Santa Ysabel and elsewhere—and had destroyed a great deal of their property. Stray shells and bullets had killed and wounded Americans walking their own streets in their own country. The Plan of

San Diego raids, the Columbus raid, and all the other cross-border incursions by bandidos had terrified Americans and taken more than a few of their lives.

And there had been the sheer, brute demonstration, once again, and for ten years, of what Americans thought of as the ineradicable violence of Mexicans, a consequence of their mestizo heritage. To Americans, mostly prejudiced to begin with, the Mexicans seemed to have behaved exactly as one would expect of a Catholic, non-white, "mongrel" race. The American view of the alien culture south of the border was one of contempt. The ethnocentric attitude towards Mexico was a template for America's reactions to the other unfamiliar and exotic cultures it would encounter as an imperial power.

For Mexicans, the revolution emphasized the barely tolerable aspects of the United States: its great wealth, based in part on its seizure of Mexican territory; its sense of racial superiority; its arrogance in foreign policy, the Monroe doctrine as a prime example; American military incursions across the border, Pershing's Punitive Expedition above all. These were the attitudes and actions of an overbearing imperial power—a new Spain—which, it seemed to Mexico, had become dominant over it. Mexico had thrown out one overlord only to suffer penetration by another.

Some Americans died in the course of the revolution, but in meagre numbers compared with the many hundreds of Mexicans, and Mexican-Americans—some of whom had lived in Texas for generations—who were shot or strung up, by gringo vigilantes, or by *los rinches*—the Texas Rangers—in retaliation for raids, or in expressions of hysteria or racial loathing.

If Mexico hadn't been laid out by six years of war, Pershing's campaign alone might have been enough to trigger general war between the neighbouring countries. In the end, Mexico couldn't even have its own revolution in peace (as it were). At every stage, and in every important event, the United States interfered or intervened or affected the outcome in some way, with various and contradictory policies and actions.

Time has not necessarily lessened these emotions. In 1981, Mexico institutionalized its outrage at the long story of American meddling. It opened a National Museum of Interventions in Mexico City. A habitual Mexican feeling of inferiority can produce an exaggerated view of American power. In 1980, for example, Mexican newspapers and officials accused the United States of stealing Mexico's rain by diverting hurricanes away from Mexican territory. Even the director of the national meteorological service of Mexico accepted that Americans could divert a hurricane. (This assumption of superhuman power surfaced in Iraq, where many people believed that the sunglasses American soldiers wore gave them X-ray vision so that they could ogle women with impunity. Belief in American omnipotence, somewhat attenuated these days, is also the glue of conspiracy theories involving the United States—which is to say, most of them.)

American attitudes have not done much to assuage Mexico's sense of grievance. One example, of many: in 1978, a distinguished American historian wrote in a foreword to a respected academic work on the border that America's borders, unlike those in Europe, have been mostly peaceful, and that American expansion has taken place largely through buying land from other powers—the Louisiana Purchase, and Alaska, for instance. Even the Treaty of Guadalupe Hidalgo, writes the scholar, can be seen as a kind of commercial deal, because the United States gave Mexico $15 million for its ceded territory (a larger amount than for the Louisiana Purchase, he points out). There has hardly ever been a threat of warfare in the United States' border experience, he concludes.

Needless to say, this perspective would be laughed (or cried) out of the room by any Mexican. Canadians, too, would be interested to read such an interpretation of a century of American invasion, and the periodic threat of invasion, of Canada—a country originally formed from British colonies in large part because they feared American attack and annexation.

The Mexican Revolution also produced a little good news. Afterwards, things did settle down along the border, at least in relative terms. No more large-scale violence occurred. The hitherto meddling powers of Europe recognized that Mexico, and its border with the United States, was no concern of theirs—a belated acquiescence in the Monroe doctrine. The Indians had been finally suppressed, or exterminated, and there were no more raids. The bandidos hung up their spurs and carbines. Some measure of prosperity began to develop in the north of Mexico, lessening the impulse to violence and armed movements. Both Mexico and the United States realized that, from then on, the mutual problems they had to deal with were those of normal neighbours.

Nevertheless, the old fears, suspicions and prejudices persist in the borderlands on each side of the line. They may lie dormant under the veneer of maquiladora jobs, or of cross-border co-operation on drugs, or as the Mexican state becomes somewhat more democratic and open, and less corrupt. But in a more sombre season—when times are hard, or when *indocumentados* are too numerous and Americans fear for their Anglo identity, or when the drug wars, like the revolution, spill over into the United States, or when an ugly fence is raised along the entire length of the border, or if terrorists strike from the south—then the borderlands become a zone of uncertainty and conflict once again.

CHAPTER 7

RIDING THE DIRT

I LEAVE THE ADOBE HOUSE IN COLUMBUS with reluctance, feeling like a sailor forced out of safe harbour onto a stormy sea. But the sun is warm, not yet hot, and the wind this early is light, and, as always, the joy of the ride overtakes me. Travelling day after day northwest or southwest, but always making my westing, without a consideration of turning around and retracing my path, crossing from one side of the continent to the other, taking what comes with the road and the weather, all of this is still an intoxication. Even when the desert heats up, and the wind rises and becomes strong—from the west as always—I crouch and countersteer, and hang on, and I feel exultant. I say to myself, and to my friends: life is movement, and movement is a crux of life.

I ride west on the narrow, sparse-traffic road over the Cedar Mountains to Hachita, where I turn south on the 81 towards the border crossing at Antelope Wells. The road lies straight through the mesquite, creosote and cactus—now mostly Mexican fire barrel and Arizona rainbow—that I've watched slide by me for ten days. I'm riding through a valley with mountains all around, the Big Hatchet to my left, the Animas of the Continental Divide to my right, and near the border, the Alamo Huecos. In the forty-five miles from Hachita to Antelope Wells, I see three vehicles, two of them Border Patrol. Red-tailed hawks and Aplomado falcons stand sentinel or patrol overhead. A sign on the road says: "Running Water." Someone has scrawled before it: "Pray for."

The strong crosswind kicks up dust devils that sweep across the desert and over the road; sometimes they blast me with sand and grit. A few of the gusts are so sudden and strong that they wrench the bike violently to one side, and I think at first there's a problem with the road surface—a groove or long slash in the tarmac I haven't seen.

From time to time, as I ride, I try to foresee how I'll hit and roll: get clear of the bike, keep my legs up, let the Kevlar and hard armour of the jacket (I could take a bullet and survive if it hit me in the right spot) absorb the impact and the friction of a long slide on tarmac or hard sand. In this windy season, there's sand all over the roads. Sometimes, it's like riding on black-ice surfaces up north. I lean into a curve, holding a conservative angle from the vertical, but I still feel the rear wheel skidding a little on sand I haven't seen, or can't avoid—short sideways skips and bursts of no-traction that make the gut tumble and the heart clutch. All I can do is focus hard and without let-up on the road's surface, scrutinize it for treachery and unsoundness, and try to read its minute topography yard by yard at forty, fifty or sixty miles an hour. And accept that, no matter how careful I am, I still might go down—just a matter of luck, or lack of it. That's why an hour on a motorcycle on these roads takes far more out of you than eight hours lounging in a car.

At Antelope Wells, I discover that the dirt ranch road I

wanted to take along the border is closed. A Border Patrol agent is sitting in an SUV in front of the closed gate.

"There's a drug interdiction action goin' on down the road so we've closed it for a day," he says.

"Who's involved in the operation?" I ask. He's an amiable, middle-aged Anglo with longish hair, unusual in the buzz-cut culture of these coppers, and he doesn't mind chatting, in a rolling, barely comprehensible drawl.

"Our guys," he says, "and Hidalgo deputies. I don't know what the deal is, but there must be fifty guys out there on wheels, ATVs, horseback, trackers. Some big dope deal."

"Is this a big drug-running area?"

He laughs.

"Yessir, it is. Where the hell ain't it?"

"Am I right that there's no new fence planned here?

"Yessir, that's right. That's why the drug guys will come across here instead. We put out cameras and Oscars (the in-ground sensors), but that's all there is in this part of the sector."

I tell him I wanted to ride the ranch road to the small settlement of Cloverdale on the edge of the Coronado National Forest. I don't tell him I want to go there because one of the novelist Cormac McCarthy's young knight errants, in *The Crossing*, part of the *Border Trilogy*, rides through Cloverdale and traverses the border to the south, dragging a lame, pregnant wolf into Mexico to set her free there.

The agent snorts.

"There ain't nothin' to Cloverdale. It's the end of the line. There's all kinds of shit goin' on there these days. The drug guys come over in SUVs and trucks, and pick up the dirt roads hereabouts and then on up the 338 or the 81, and then up to the interstate to Albuquerque or El Paso. I'd stay the hell offa these dirt roads if I was you, son."

Son? I'm older than he is. Does riding a motorcycle make you seem younger? Or infantilize you?

I'm going to get to Cloverdale, no matter what this genial agent says, but it will be the long way around. I ride back to Hachita, and turn west towards Animas.

Along the way, I cross the Continental Divide. That sounds to me like a turning point in my journey. It feels as if, after I'm over the Divide, it will all be downhill to the Pacific Ocean—from now on, that's where the rivers flowing through here will wind up.

It's no good. There's a Border Patrol roadblock at the beginning of the dirt road to Cloverdale off the 338. Two SUVs turn me back.

"We have a lot of troops in this area, sir," says one of the young Hispanic agents. "This whole area is closed to civilians."

Troops? Civilians? This is like a war zone. I say I just want to ride to Cloverdale, look at it and come right back. It'll take me an hour. I explain about the novel and how much it means to me.

"I understand, sir, but I can't let you go down the road." He's sympathetic and polite. And doing the right thing, too. It would not be good for anyone if some dumb Canadian literary tourist got gunned down on his watch.

There's another dirt road, which isn't blocked off, running from the 338 at this intersection. It will take me sixty miles to Douglas, Arizona, and for a while it runs right on top of the border. I tell the agent I'll forget about Cloverdale and just head on down to Douglas. He is a worried man. That road is open, he says, but his advice is to stick to the main roads. It's not safe on the dirt sections; a lot of bad guys use them. I tell him I feel pretty safe because every time I turn a corner or crest a hill, I see the Border Patrol. He laughs. Okay, good luck, he says.

The evil dirt roads I've taken before were too soft. The gravel or sand sucked my wheels into erratic slides and uncontrollable trajectories. This road's sin is the opposite: a hard-packed, rocky washboard surface that shakes the KLR without mercy. I go slow and my teeth rattle; I go fast and my eyeballs oscillate; at three thousand rpms my hair vibrates. I have to clench my teeth so as not to chomp off my tongue. I think about turning back, but I decide: Hell, this bike is made to slog over terrain like this. It's supposed to carry Marines. Now's the time to see what it will do. I let some air out of the tires to soothe the machine a little, and I keep on, seeking out the slicks of the ribbed chop I'm rattling over.

It is a hard ride through the Peloncillo Mountains, with steep grades and switchbacks. The omnipresent west wind blows hard, and it gusts without warning off the higher ground. At some point, I cross the state line into Arizona. Two states down, two to go.

The diversion by the Border Patrol, and the flinty, ragged road, have put me behind schedule. I could just make Douglas before dark—I can ride this trail only in daylight—but I want to camp out in these mountains. They resonate with the feel of the old days. I could turn a corner and come upon a solitary, laconic horseman, or a band of Apaches, raiding or running, or a unit of blue-coated, long-knived cavalry. The Apache Geronimo surrendered at Skeleton Canyon, about fifteen miles north of here. With thirty-eight men, women and children, he had evaded five thousand American troops and a number of Mexican army units for months. The promises made to him were broken. The Old West is a mythology rather than a historical place, but this stark and arid landscape feels true.

I find a level ledge about thirty yards off the road, and set up camp there for the night. I wedge my tent pegs under piles of rock and set up my sleeping gear and my spidery single-burner stove. I heat up a can of stew and eat it with bread, an apple and water. As I eat, I look out to the south, towards Mexico a few miles away. The Sierra Madres, jagged and ribbed, fade away for as far as I can see.

It's not quite Cloverdale, but it's close to where McCarthy's protagonist, Billy Parham, camped his last night in America. I look down on a similar "broad volcanic plain bounded within the rim of hills." The next day, around noon, he will cross "the international boundary line into Mexico, State of Sonora, undifferentiated in its terrain from the country they quit and yet wholly alien and wholly strange." There is no fence, but Billy sees a boundary marker—a concrete obelisk—as he passes by. "In that desert waste it had the look of some monument to a lost expedition." Here, the mountains and the rivers run north and south. Only the border hews to a contrary line.

Night falls fast, and when the light has faded completely, I am in a profound darkness, cold and velvety. I can see no human lights anywhere, nor is there a moon. But the stars reveal themselves in numbers and intensities that always astonish the dweller near cities. I'm up around four thousand feet or more, and the high desert cold comes down sharp and crystalline. By the time I go to bed, I can see my breath. I am so cold, I can't sleep much, but can only doze now and then. The night is filled with rustling and scuttling as the desert nightlife revs up. I make the continual hopeful assumption that none of the noises are made by a member of *Panthera onca*, the American jaguar. Owls hoo-hoo close by, all around me. From time to time, I hear coyotes howling far away to the northwest, an eerie and echoing testament.

In the morning, the water in my bottles is partially frozen. I crawl out of my tent at first light, stiff and tired, the sun still unseen behind the Peloncillo peaks. The mountains and the desert are pastel pink, mauve and red, with long shadows that shorten by the minute as the sun climbs. I'm like a lizard, moving slowly in the cold, pale light, waiting for the sun to appear and juice my metabolism. I boil water on my marvellous one-burner. I drink hot tea and eat a bagel with jam, now and then peeling off another layer of clothes as the day's heat builds. The KLR stands behind me, a filthy and humble machine, a steady iron horse on which to ride this mountainous desert.

It's not far to Douglas; I was no more than twenty miles away when I set up camp. I rattle down the abominable road for a few miles, and through the San Bernardino Wildlife Refuge, until the Border Patrol reappears: an SUV parked by the road, and two agents scanning the country to the south with binoculars. The border is, at most, a few hundred yards away. They wave me over, both of them grasping the butts of their pistols, right elbows akimbo. We go through the Script: I should not be on this road; it's dangerous; there is a lot of illegal activity around here; drugs. The two Hispanic agents are polite, but they want to search my bags. I must be tired: I ask why. Everything sours; they immediately turn nasty and suspicious.

"Driver's licence," one guy demands.

He hasn't a clue where British Columbia is.

"You from Colombia?" he asks. He's completely confused: a blue-eyed, English-speaking gringo from Colombia, where the drugs come from?

"No, British Columbia is a province in Canada."

"Canada!" Back to the Script: "What the hell are you doing all the way down here?" It's not a friendly question.

The other guy begins to try to open one of my pannier bags. Without my permission.

"Wait a minute! Okay, okay, go ahead and look, but I'll open the bags for you," I say. "I am objecting to this search, but go ahead."

"We don't give a fuck what you object to, sir," says the first guy, smiling at me.

The other guy pokes through my bags one by one. The first guy stares at me all the while, hand on pistol butt.

"Okay," says the other guy.

"Go ahead," says the first guy.

I mount up, flip my visor back down, start the bike, and haul my constitutionally violated ass out of there.

Douglas is a substantial town, showing the prosperity of its former glory as a copper-smelting centre for the ore from the nearby Bisbee mines. It is named after Canadian amateur mining engineer and tycoon James Douglas, who opened the Copper Queen Mine in Bisbee. Douglas has wide, tree-lined streets and large, elegant houses. It is the first smaller settlement I've seen since the Valley on the lower Rio Grande, with substantial and distinguished buildings. There may be sagging trailers and ruined shacks in Douglas, but I don't come across them. The Gadsden Hotel is named after James Gadsden, who negotiated the eponymous Purchase, which completed the United States' takeover of its current southern border. The deal was a real purchase, five years after the end of the Mexican War, and not a euphemism for war-prize territory. It cost the Americans $10 million. They thought they were getting a transcontinental railroad route around the mountains, but they also unwittingly acquired some of the world's richest deposits of copper. More good luck for the gringos.

Bisbee is thirty miles up the road from Douglas. I ride past the huge, open pits and the tailings mountains of the closed copper mines, and into the town along Tombstone Canyon Road. The narrow lanes, crooked alleyways and staircases of this eccentric place lead off up the hills surrounding its winding, climbing main street. The makeshift and tumbledown shacks the copper miners once lived in have been remodelled and renovated by Bisbee's artists, artisans and city-escapees into cabins and small houses. They cram the steep slopes and the hill crests, jumbles of endlessly varied wooden structures with complex additions and annexes, a welter of bright colours and decorative flourishes. The main street is filled with galleries, coffee shops, theme pubs and modish, tony restaurants. Bisbee is a liberal, commie-loving enclave in the conservative, redneck border-lands. There is not a firearm around, or, at least, not in sight.

It is Saturday in Bisbee and the roar of the Harleys is heard in the land. The town is choked with shining, chromed, full-dressed choppers and stock machines. The riders are standard Harley issue: big bellies, grey beards, leather chaps, head scarves, cereal-bowl helmets, the chicks tank-topped and tanned, down from Tucson or Phoenix for the weekend, every-one making the scene. These are the first other riders I've seen since El Paso, and I've never seen so many in one place on this trip. I'm so used to being the lone rider, meeting a few other two-wheelers once in a while, that this noisy, roiling crowd of bikers unnerves me. Now, instead of having one, or a few, big-shiny-bike people staring with contempt and bemusement at my ugly, humpbacked—and now filthy—dirt-basher, I have a whole goddamn town of them looking askance at it, and at me. The Harleys, the Japanese Harley clones, and the chopped hogs are beautiful machines, and look, without exception that I can see, as if they just came off the showroom floor. My KLR looks as if it has been wallowing, with some strange, frenzied animate-machine glee, in a desert mud sinkhole.

Nevertheless, and even though I have only ridden a few miles today, I decide to stay in Bisbee for the night. I'm short of sleep and a day of R and R in a benign town sounds good. I revel in the indulgence of speaking English with friendly, open Americans. I understand the Hispanic reserve. I am, after all, a Canadian, and we present our own subtle reticence to the world. But I am originally from Ireland, where free-flowing, superfluous talk is deeply valued, and I feel at ease with informal and voluble Americans.

Living as I do in the Canadian southwest, which is con-tiguous geographically and culturally with the American northwest, I feel at home here in Bisbee, too, with its lattes, fancy food, and salad that has real green things in it. In fact, the feel of Bisbee, and the people I meet, remind me of nothing more than my own artist-musician-writer-hippie-retiree–infested home island of Salt Spring.

In one friendly coffee shop, next to a painter-sculptor studio, I talk to Peyton, the owner, who used to be an actress in New York City, and to her friend, Susan, a massage therapist who lived for years in New Orleans. Peyton has a house a few miles away in Bisbee Junction, close to the border town of Naco. Her property is on an illegal migration route. The coyotes tell the *indocumentados* to use a billboard on her property as a landmark after they cross the line in or around Naco. She helps them whenever she can, she says. She gives them water, and allows them to hide or sleep in her outbuildings. Many people around here do that. The fence doesn't stop the migrants. It peters out on the outskirts of Naco, and they just walk around it. What about the new extended fence in the works? It won't matter, says Susan. Even seven thousand feet up in the Mule and the Patagonia Mountains, you see the abandoned clothes, water bottles and garbage the migrants drop as they hike north. The coyotes tell them Phoenix is close by. That's where they think they're walking—until they give up, or the Border Patrol nails them, or, as sometimes happens, they die.

Later in the day, I interview Cecile Lumer in her house on a lower ridge above Bisbee. Lumer is a founding member of Citizens for Border Solutions, a group, based in the town, which supports migrants and deplores fences. "We do political work: make contact with politicians," she says, "but we help on the ground, as well. We put water out on trails the illegals use." The group also co-operates with the American Civil Liberties Union (ACLU) in its monitoring of Minuteman operations in the area.

The border ranchers used to hire Mexicans all the time, she says, but now they're raising hell about illegals—because there are so many of them. And racism is a big element in the anger. The ranchers hate the Border Patrol, too, because they tear up private land in hot pursuit of illegals or drug runners. And everyone hates what the migrants do to the beautiful areas of the desert: the trash everywhere.

Lumer gives me the usual, tolerant line on the illegal problem and the fence solution: a fence won't change anything; the migrants are desperate, and they will just find a way around, or over, whatever is built. Her group hands out pamphlets to illegals whenever they encounter them. The pamphlets explain to the migrants what their legal rights are, and they contain phone numbers for sympathetic American organizations and for the Mexican consulates in Douglas and Nogales. There is also a warning: the desert is dangerous; a person needs at least a gallon of water a day to survive.

The only reasonable solution, says Lumer, is a visa program so that workers can come and go across the border, their movements not tied to a specific job. The illegals in the United States now should be subject to graduated admission as citizens, she says. There's a fence in Naco right now, but it's bedlam there every night. Thousands of migrants wait for dark each day to climb the fence, or to cut through it, or, for most of them, to just go around it. The barrier dividing the two Nacos is substantial within the town limits. Farther out, there are some lights and cameras and sensors; then nothing—a few strings of wire that disappear out in the desert.

The next day, I ride the few miles to Naco, and through the small dusty American side of town—eight hundred people live on the Arizona side, eight thousand on the Sonoran—to look at the barrier. I watch crowds of young men, and some women and children, on the Mexican side hanging about the streets in front of the hotels and cantinas that have opened up to serve this rush of people from the south. Sometimes, the Border Patrol reports that it picks up more people in the surrounding desert each week than make up the population of the Mexican side of Naco.

The drugs are here, too, of course. This portion of the Arizona border is quiet compared with Nuevo Laredo, Juárez or, nearby, Agua Prieta, but the drug war goes on: Naco has had twelve police chiefs over the three years prior to 2007. One of them, the brother of a murdered Agua Prieta chief, was arrested in March 2007 when he tried to smuggle fifty-nine pounds of marijuana into the United States—a penny-ante operation by border standards.

I bump along the dirt road running beside the fence until its end, where the straggly wire takes over. I stop and look into Mexico, where, even out here, groups of men, and a few women, hang about, eyeing the promised land. In a few minutes, a Border Patrol Jeep arrives. The agent goes through the Script with me, although politely, and I turn away towards the road to the west.

Things are changing fast along the border. Recently I visited the Arizona and New Mexico borderlands again, to see what had happened since my ride. This time, I flew to Tucson and rented an SUV, and I was able to look at portions of the new fence promised in the Secure Fence Act.

The fence has always been a theoretical amalgam of other barriers: the Berlin Wall and the Maginot Line—it is designed to keep people out, but you can go around it. The new fence will certainly keep more people out; it will be a lot harder to get to the end of it.

Around Naco, what used to be about a four-and-a-half-mile-long barrier has extended out into the desert on each side of town, twenty-five miles in all. At night, the blinding sodium lights on the Arizona side snap on. More cameras and, no doubt, more motion-detecting Oscars are scattered about the desert nearby. As in many sections of the border, the fence here (we could think of it as something like version 2.2.1 of Mexican border fences) is a seedy, eclectic construction. There are sections of metal mesh, concrete bollards, corrugated metal, old helicopter landing mats from the Vietnam War, five-foot-high railroad rails, and—the old standby—barbed wire. The work in the area has been carried out by unarmed National Guard units and civilian contractors.

It has been much easier to get the fence up fast in New Mexico and Arizona because the federal government owns most of the land along the line. Homeland Security didn't have to fight outraged landowners and invade private property, the way it did along the Rio Grande, where opposition has stalled construction. Unlike the long-established Mexican-American ranchers and landowners on the river, the Anglos here don't own land on the Mexican side, and the fence doesn't cut off portions of their holdings.

The Border Patrol claims that the patchwork job suits their purposes. Using leftovers is cheaper than the standard purpose-made metal fencing, which costs, on average, between $3 and $4 million, and as much as $9 million, a mile, depending on the topography. The mesh and bollards allow agents to see whatever shit is being planned on the Mexican side. And the variety of styles means that coyotes or drug runners have to use different techniques to breach the barrier. However, people can clearly still get through, or over, or around the fence. Looking at it, I see places where, given a few minutes, I could manage to get my middle-aged body over without too much strain. The fence may stretch farther out, but it does still quit.

From Naco I ride the 92 west to Palominas, and then south towards the border again. I could head north on nice paved roads to Huachuca City, and then west and southwest, in smooth, if windy, comfort through the scenic Coronado National Forest to Nogales. But I'm not yet through eating dust. If my rule of engagement is to keep as close to the border as possible, well, I can choose a dirt road that runs close to, or right along, the line sixty miles to Nogales.

I take to the dirt again, and soon, the road begins to climb, in steep switchbacks, into the Huachuca Mountains. The grassland and scrub are dotted with stands of small oak trees, and, higher up, with ponderosa pine. The surface is hard washboard once more, but not as rock-ribbed as the trail to Douglas. Although I'm getting better at piloting the KLR, with its heavy load, over dubious, gravelly dirt, the 180-degree curves are a problem, as are the sheer drop-offs on my side of the narrow road. Looking down into the canyon below, I decide I would rather not make a single small mistake on the tricky turns. From a lookout at seven thousand feet, I can see the San Pedro River valley where, in 1540, Francisco Vásquez de Coronado led his expedition north, looking, as Spaniards at the time very seriously did, for a reported city of gold on a hill. To the west, is Baboquivari Peak, the home of the Tohono O'odham gods. From there, so it's said, you can see the salt water of the Gulf of California glinting in the sun. To the south I look fifty miles across the San Rafael Valley and deep into Mexico.

The descending switchbacks are bad. I have to gear down, and brake, and I skid around on the slithery surface. My whole body clenches as I come unavoidably close to the drop-offs. The bike, running slowly but at high revs, heats up more than it should. Worse, there is some traffic on this remote road: a few pickups coming the other way. I meet one truck, which is going much too fast, while I'm on a hairpin bend and a steep downgrade. We both must swerve, except that he crowds the cliff side, while I head for the abyss. I catch a quick glimpse of three young Hispanics. The driver yells at me as we barely avoid collision, and he doesn't sound friendly. The son of a bitch almost runs me off the road down into the gorge below.

The settlement of Lochiel is right on the border, twenty-five miles from Nogales. I stop and find the monument to the Franciscan monk Marcos de Niza, who preceded Coronado, and whose supposed report of Cíbola and the seven cities of gold spurred the conquistador's expedition (de Niza probably did not make the preposterous claims attributed to him and doesn't deserve his historical reputation as "the lying priest").

There is not much in Lochiel—a few rundown buildings. In front of a barn, two vaqueros, sitting on their horses, and wearing side arms, watch me ride slowly by. I give them a wave, but they don't return it. I pass two Border Patrol Blazers, but no one challenges me. I take a trail to the border, which turns out to be marked by a clear-cut through the desert shrub and low trees, and a broken-down wire fence. (On my second visit, I drove the SUV to pay Lochiel another visit. The fence had been re-strung with new wire. Iron-rail, Normandy vehicle barriers had been set up beside the wire extending as far as I could see along the freshly cleared border trail. A person on foot could still get across with ease.)

Five miles farther along, I come to the ghost town of Duquesne. Like Lochiel, it had been a mining town, set up with great difficulty in the face of continuous Apache raids, to excavate minerals: turquoise and azurite. Barbed wire rings most of the remaining vandalized buildings in Duquesne. I read somewhere that the whole place has been sold. A decrepit sign reads: "Do not stop for any reason."

However, when I take a sandy trail off the road towards the line, a Border Patrol agent waves me to a halt and that's reason enough for me. The young, lean, balding, sunglassed Hispanic is alone, standing beside his SUV, and cradling an M4 carbine, finger along the trigger guard, butt on forearm, like an infantryman ready for contact. We follow the Script. Soon he relaxes and lowers his weapon, turns and stashes it inside his vehicle.

"The Duquesne road isn't a good road these days," he says.

"Drugs and illegals?" It seems to me I've asked that question many times.

"It's mostly drugs out here. It's too far out for the illegals. They can cross closer to Nogales. The main problem here is guys just driving right through the wire. We're warning tourists to take care along here. Don't stop."

"I noticed it wasn't much of a barrier," I say.

"Huh!" he says. "It's a joke, man."

I ride on over the southern end of the Patagonia Mountains, up more switchback road and down the other side. A few ranch buildings sit on the open grasslands, and I see cattle and deer. I am ten miles from the 82, the paved road into Nogales, when the rough, hard dirt turns to soft, deep sand. This is the worst surface for a two-wheeler, and I stop to further deflate my tires. I come within a hair of crashing time and again as the bike catches in ridges, and slides in the sand that is often hub-deep. Several times, I lose control and stay upright only by ramming the bike into the soft berm lining the road, burying the front wheel and regaining stability.

I'm down in a valley, and the heat has become intense. It's Saturday, and, as I get closer to Nogales, the road becomes crowded with pickups hauling ATVs for some yahooing around the desert bush. I pass several groups of guys on the small machines. The pickup drivers are all Hispanic. They do not slow down and they kick up dense clouds of blinding, choking, sand-dust that coats my KLR and me. I curse at these inconsiderate sons of bitches. They give me no quarter. I keep the bike vertical, with difficulty, and, eventually, soaked with sweat, and with a grinding muscle-tension headache,

I reach pavement. I swat off some of the dust, but we—the bike and I—look like we've ridden cross-country through a sandstorm. I dictate how I feel on my tape recorder. I listen to it now, and I sound like an extremely tired guy who could, nevertheless, find it in himself to summon the energy to commit mass murder. As I'm mounting up again, a group of clean, shiny Harleys thunders by on the paved road, their riders looking serene and comfy on their plush saddles.

I ride through downtown Nogales to look at the border crossing. People stare with surprise, suspicion, disgust, amusement, at a filthy bike and rider, out of place amid the bright stores and clean cars of the city. I feel like a nomad coming off the steppes and into civilization. In a Spanglish-speaking motel on the edge of town, a suspicious and disdainful desk clerk gives me a room. I wash myself and I sluice down my faithful machine with water that I carry outside in the motel's garbage container.

Nogales has escaped the worst of the drug war along the border. Prosperous Sonora as a whole is less violent than the other border states. There have been killings, of course, but nothing on the scale of events along the Rio Grande, or even in the much smaller city of Agua Prieta. However, the drugs keep coming. Nogales used to be one of the main shipment crossings for marijuana. It's on one of the main north-south, cross-border corridors: the I-19 heads north to Tucson, the transshipment point for many kinds of drugs; Mexico's smooth, four-lane Highway 15 leads south through Hermosillo and Ciudad Obregón, and on into Sinaloa, where the drug trade thrives and the cartel runs amok.

Crackdowns on both sides of the border have reduced the amount of marijuana coming through Nogales, but the relative peacefulness of the city is making it more attractive for cocaine and heroin shipments. Mexican heroin is a growth industry.

The U.S. National Drug Intelligence Center reports that 12.7 metric tons of heroin were grown in Mexico in 2006, 95 per cent of which made it into the United States. So-called black tar heroin is powerful, and very cheap compared with coke or meth. In July 2008, U.S. border agents seized forty-seven pounds of black tar heroin in a car at the Nogales downtown crossing, equal to one-tenth of all seizures in Mexico for a whole year.

A fifteen-foot-high steel border fence through downtown Nogales went up in 1995—Tucson sector's "Operation Safeguard," which was part of "Operation Gatekeeper." Ambos Nogales is the same place with two sides. The Arizona city has 20,000 people. Maquiladora-heavy Sonoran Nogales has an official population of 250,000, but, like all the Mexican border cities and towns, the real figure is much higher, perhaps as many as 400,000. It's impossible to build a secondary fence along the downtown border without buying and tearing down numerous buildings that cluster right along the line. Outside the city, however, the new fence stretches out over the bare hills. Waiting to cross back into the United States from Mexico on my later SUV drive, I could see the construction going on to the west, the fence a dark, snaking scar across the landscape.

Today, I'm going to look for the Minutemen, who are engaged in a campaign north of the border crossing of Sasabe, the next port-of-entry west from Nogales. I take the I-19 north thirty miles and turn off onto Arivaca Road. Running on pavement feels luxurious. A few miles along, I go through a Border Patrol checkpoint—a quick, polite look at my passport. The road winds over a rolling plain of Sonoran desert flora, and down to the 286. I turn south to look at the border at Sasabe, which is a tiny, scruffy Mexican village. Just outside the town, half a dozen Border Patrol agents from three vehicles are rounding up and handcuffing four young men—"getting bodies," as the agents like to say. Another SUV is parked near the immigration checkpoint. The lone occupant is an amiable young Hispanic who is busy wiping down the inside of his vehicle with Armor All. His name tag says "López." I ask him if I can take a photograph of the border.

"You can," he says, "but maybe the FBI will come along and arrest you."

Irony and humour are not common attributes on the border. I ask him about the situation around Sasabe; he begins to talk, and he keeps on talking for the next forty-five minutes.

He is from Laredo, and he volunteered for this duty. It's a forty-six-day rotation; he stays in a motel in Tucson and drives to and fro each day. The migrants come in droves through the desert at night, out of sight in the gullies and arroyos. The Patrol doesn't try to stop them there, but rather, sets up blocking patrols on the 286 on the theory that "undocumented entrants"—he uses the Arizona label—have to hit the road eventually.

I ask him the delicate question: when did his family arrive in the United States? He doesn't mind.

"My grandpa came up with work papers into California, into the fields there. But when the time was up, he just stayed in the U.S."

What does he think about the migrants coming over now? Is he sympathetic to them?

"Oh yeah, sure I am. They're just poor people, man. They just want a better life. I mean, it's our job to apprehend them, but we got nothing against them. Some guys do, though. Some guys are mad at them, y'know, Mexican guys who are in the Patrol. They think the illegals make them look bad because they're Mexican, too. So they treat them bad, y'know what I mean? Some guys push them around. You know the word, 'tonk'? That's when they hit these guys on the head with flashlights. That's what the noise is when they do that."

The drugs come through this desert valley all the time, in huge amounts, he says. The other day, they stopped a guy on the 286 with four hundred pounds of marijuana in his car. I ask this open and guileless agent about corruption. There's lots of it, he says. Some guys take bribes. They only catch a few of the agents who do it. One K-9 guy took $1.5 million to make sure his dog didn't sniff a truck coming through. Another agent was paid $6,000 just to let a guy through a checkpoint. He would never do anything like that, he says. It's too dangerous. But there are a lot of agents on the take, and so he avoids socializing with guys he works with. He doesn't want to get dirty. Off duty, he stays at home with his family in Laredo, plays softball sometimes. He doesn't have many friends, but keeps to himself.

I mention the agents who have drawn weapons on me along the border. López is not surprised.

"You were in deserted places, man. They don't know who you are until you get close, and they can see you're not a bad guy."

It is sometimes dangerous, especially for the one-man patrols, which is a lot of the time. The agents often cover each other, one vehicle in sight of another—there's an SUV parked a few hundred yards away from where we're talking now—or they can call in a chopper. Sometimes, though, an agent may be two or three hours away from help, if he's out in the country on dirt roads.

"Like where you were, man, when they pulled weapons on you."

López's stories of corruption are borne out by the facts. Between 2004 and 2010, the Border Patrol doubled the number of its agents to twenty-one thousand—making it the largest federal law enforcement agency. That's a lot of fast hiring, and vetting new employees has been a patchy effort. Homeland Security says it is concerned that the Mexican cartels may deliberately plant people in the Border Patrol or in Customs and Border Protection. Law enforcement officers on the border are much more susceptible to being corrupted because they often work alone, or because people are so desperate to cross that they will do anything to reach the United States. And there is so much money in drugs that the runners can afford to pay huge bribes for relatively quick, easy and insignificant effort, or risk, by the agents. The agency administered lie-detector tests at random to 10 per cent of new hires in 2008, and plans to test all applicants. As of mid-2008, there were two hundred cases pending against border law-enforcement employees charged with smuggling drugs, guns or illegals.

I take a chance the FBI won't arrest me, and take a photograph of the Sasabe border crossing. I turn back up the 286, but I pull over to the side of the road after a couple of miles to record the details of my long conversation with the talkative agent before I forget them.

The sun is high and hot, but the narrow shoulder is soft sand, sloping away from the tarmac like so many of these Arizona back roads. I can't prop the bike up to dismount and take off my riding gear. I'll just sweat it out, make a quick verbal note, and ride on north in the cooling wind. I talk into the machine for less than a minute, and a white Jeep comes into sight. It slows as it approaches, and I see that it belongs to the deputy sheriff. I cover up the Sony between my hand and my jacket. I've discovered that all the coppers of various kinds along the border are suspicious of my tape recorder and my camera. I fear they'll confiscate my precious records—maybe like in the movies: rip the tape out of the recorder and unspool it, chuck the camera into the sand and grind it underboot, evil smile, ride on, boy, and keep riding.

The Jeep sidles by at ten miles an hour. The two deputies inside, a Hispanic and an Anglo, stare at me through their sunglasses, heads slowly swivelling as the vehicle passes. Through their open window, I can see a shotgun on its rack behind their seats. I give them a restrained wave: hand up, palm out, motionless, the old sign of peace in the west. They don't wave back. I stay still, and watch them in my rear-view mirror. They drive on for a hundred yards, then stop, do a three-point turn in the narrow, deserted road, and come back towards me. Again, they cruise by, staring, impassive, heads doing the slow yaw. I wave again. And I also give them a big, reassuring smile, and a nod. Again, they don't respond, but just keep giving me the blank, Ray-Ban, RoboCop survey. Then they speed up, heading north, until the Jeep drops out of sight over a low rise.

It appears to me that they came down this way just to take a look at me. I wonder if the friendly agent radioed in a report about the lone rider. More likely the other one did—my informant's backup, watching us the whole time we talked. Perhaps that looked suspicious: he must have wondered what the hell we could have been talking about all that time? Maybe López is in the shit now.

I watch the road for a while, but the deputies don't come back. So I start recording again.

The motorcycle, which intimidates some ordinary citizens, should reassure the varieties of border lawmen. A car hides how many people are inside, what they're doing, whether or not they're armed—maybe one of them has locked and loaded, and is drawing a bead on the agent even as he walks towards them (illegals and drug runners shot, assaulted or ambushed the Border Patrol 118 times in 2004 along one nearby thirty-mile stretch of the Arizona border). Perhaps there's contraband in the trunk they will kill to keep and deliver. But the bike and I are right out there in the open, with nothing concealed. The agents can see everything about us at a glance—whether or not I have a weapon (although, as part of the Script, they ask me if I'm carrying). And they're the sort of men who like motorcycles. More than one of them has told me he rides, too—a Harley of course, not a butt-ugly, Jap-shit, back-road tanker like mine—and how he'd like to be mounted up right now instead of humping around this goddamn desert scrub catching the same goddamn ragged *pollos* ten times over, and maybe running out of luck one day, stumbling into a Mexican army hummer, or an SUV crammed with dope and hard-ass *vaquetones* making its run north.

I understand. He'd ride alone across the wide open plain, and lean into the twisties through the mountains, the bike's vibrating, roaring power between his legs, running west or north towards the far rim of what he can see, wind and sun leaching away the sweat and stink of the borderlands. Nothing can touch him then; it may be as close to God as he'll get.

I stow my recorder, rearrange my Gore-Tex bandana, zip up my riding jacket, pull on my light gloves, and snap down my helmet chin bar and visor. Then I pull back onto the road and head north to find the Minutemen.

CHAPTER 8

A WELL REGULATED MILITIA . . .

DEREK, LET ME SHOW YOU HOW A VIGILANTE SETS UP
FOR THE NIGHT: MY RADIO, MY THERMOS, MY APPLES,
MY SPECIAL CHAIR, MY SLEEPING BAG AND BLANKET,
MY COFFEE—VIGILANTE ON DUTY!
—RICK LOWELL, MINUTEMAN

THE MINUTEMAN HEADQUARTERS is an old ranch house north of Sasabe, close to Mile 31. It's easy to find because signs, banners and American flags hang off the surrounding wooden fence and the ramshackle building itself. I kick down my side-stand in the dusty lot behind the main white-walled house. There are some outbuildings, a tent for serving food and a single outhouse; in an adjacent field are parked two dozen or so trailers, RVs and a few tents. There's a low flatbed trailer and some pickups parked at odd angles behind the house. Three dogs mooch about. The Minuteman HQ looks like the communal, utilitarian, ad hoc encampment it is. I can see only a handful of people around. I assume most of the volunteers are out in the desert Mexican-spotting.

I stand by the bike for a while peeling off my riding gear—it feels good to get out of my heavy armour—but no one pays any attention to me. As if guys on dirty, ugly motorcycles, with panniers and duffle bags hanging off them, ride in here every day. I take my notebook and pen out of the tank bag and walk over to an older guy in jeans, checked shirt, and stetson, with a pot-belly, and a tanned, seamed face—an old cowboy. He's wearing a holstered pistol on his belt.

"Hello," I say. "I'm a writer and I'm doing research for a book about the border and I wondered if I could ask some questions about your operation here."

"Well, hey," says the old guy. "You riding that bike?"

"Yeah, all the way along the border—Brownsville to San Diego."

"Well, sumbitch," he says. "You're press then, right? Come on into the house; we'll get you signed up."

He leads me around the side of the house towards the front door.

The Minuteman Civil Defense Corps was founded by Chris Simcox, who owns the *Tombstone Tumbleweed* newspaper in the plastic-cowboy tourist town of Tombstone, Arizona. He patterned the group on the minutemen of the War of Independence: the regiments of militia set up in 1774 in Worcester County, Massachusetts, a third of whose members had to be ready to jump to arms at a minute's notice. But the first modern revival of the old revolutionary idea took place in the 1960s, as an offshoot of the John Birch Society, whose members were conspiracy-theory true believers.

The Birchers envisaged a great Communist conspiracy, operating through that most sinister of organizations, the Council on Foreign Relations, together with a cabal of crooked politicians and corporate leaders, to infiltrate the government of the United States, take it over, and set up a new world order under a "one-world socialist government" run by the United Nations (whose sign of evil intent is the iconic "black helicopters"). Even the amiable, golf-playing president Dwight Eisenhower might have been an agent of the dire conspiracy. (The John Birch Society still exists; back issues of its biweekly magazine, *The New American*, were handed out free at the Minuteman encampment in Arizona.)

In the mid-1960s, an even more radical, paranoid offshoot of the John Birch Society constituted itself as the Minutemen. Its members shared the society's views, but thought that the danger was imminent. They armed themselves and prepared to fight the Communist enemy within the infiltrated government, and against the coming invasion by Communist troops. The Birch Minutemen were genuine domestic terrorists, but they didn't last long. In 1967, the FBI broke up their plot to bomb the city hall and power station in Redmond, Washington (pre-Microsoft—why Redmond?). They collapsed under these arrests and their own lunacy.

"I had some trouble finding you," I tell the old cowboy. "I've heard a lot about the Minutemen, but you were hard to find."

He stops short.

"What have you heard about us?" he asks.

He's pleasant, and the question is part genuine curiosity, part challenge. I'm taken aback by this abrupt turning of the tables, the interviewer interviewed.

"Well, quite a lot," I say, stalling. It often takes me a while after I get off the bike to disconnect from it, to switch focus from the road and its perils. The concentration in the desert wind and heat seem to put me in a kind of mute trance, and I need a few moments more to step back down to safe, unremarkable life on foot.

"Do you think we're vigilantes?" he asks. He's smiling, however, still friendly.

"Well, I know a lot of people think you are," I say, weaselling out. "I'm here to find out more about you."

Inside, a pleasant, middle-aged, bleach-blond woman stands behind a table with brochures and forms fanned out on top. She's flustered and doesn't know which ones I should sign, but she's friendly, too—and unarmed. I write my name and address, and so on, on a form. She asks if I'm a "documentary" journalist. I think she means some kind of filmmaker. I tell her, no, I'm a writer, I write books and magazine stories. She sighs, says okay, fills out a press card and hands it to me. Later, I'll find out she should have done much more. We talk about Canada, and how far I've come, and just where the heck is British Columbia anyway.

I go outside through the back door into a little dirt courtyard to one side of the house. To my surprise, it's filled with a dozen men sitting and standing around in a rough circle, talking; I couldn't see them from the parking lot.

They're not just talking about the weather. The discussion is earnest and intense, and it's about the state of the country and how it's going to hell, about the constitution, and about the goddamn government, which ain't doin' a goddamn thing about these goddamn illegals and drug runners. As far as I can tell, only three men, including me, aren't packing some kind of side arm.

The Minutemen are mostly middle-aged or later, dressed in blue jeans and nondescript shirts, with a scattering of fatigue pants or jackets. Grey hair predominates, with a lot of beards, tanned faces and hands—men who spend a lot of time outside. They look like tough ex-cops, or Vietnam-era veterans, as many of them are. I feel a little intimidated. I'm not used to being around openly armed men who aren't in uniform, and who are not necessarily susceptible to discipline and rules of engagement. And, contrary to my non-answer earlier, my preconception of these people—my working hypothesis—is that if they aren't exactly vigilantes, nevertheless they're weird and dangerous.

I listen for a while. They're deep into swapping explanations of why they're there, taking time off from work and, for some of them, travelling a long way, just to do their bit for their country. The month-long operation is only a couple of days old, and these men are still getting to know each other.

For a previous book about the Protestants of Northern Ireland, I spent time with tough, bigoted Prods and paramilitary hard men who had fought for years during the long war there, the so-called Troubles. In my first impression of these Minutemen, they give off something of the same aura of deep frustration and aggrievement, and of barely contained violence. They make me feel I'd better watch what I say.

This is a prime chance to get a lot of Minutemen opinions at once. And I don't want them to say things in front of me assuming I'm a volunteer like them, and then have them find out I have a press card. That could be dicey. When there's a break in the conversation, I jump in.

"Hi, I should introduce myself. I'm a Canadian writer doing some . . ."

That's as far as I get.

The reaction is a kind of verbal, and physical, explosion: shouts, exclamations, knee slaps ricochet around the little dirt yard as if a brawl is breaking out. Every man there jerks and hollers. The stereotypes fly.

"Wha-haaa! Get me some bacon, boy!"

"Canada, shit!"

"That's where the 9/11 hijackers came through from. You fuckin' people just let 'em right in."

"You still can't even have any guns up there."

"Canada—that's as bad as goddamn Mexico!"

"Fuckin' Canada! It's worse'n goddamn Mexico. You're all socialists up there, aren't you?"

"We get things fixed down here, then we'll start on y'all up there."

"At least we got Fox News in there now. The truth'll get out."

"I hate Canada. Those bastards gave me a helluva time when I was up there."

And so on. For a couple of minutes.

"Well," I say, as things die down, "Wow, you guys have strong feelings about Canada." I sound like a therapist; I'm scared. I say to the guy who had a helluva time up there: "What happened when you were there?"

He's tall, lean, bearded, armed, and pissed off. He says, "I was up in Vancouver last year."

"That's near where I live," I say. I'm trying to get a conversation going here, to stop the ranting.

"We were in a taxi," says the tall guy. "The driver was one of them, what are they—with the cloth on his head?"

"A Sikh?" I say helpfully. Things are calming down a little.

"Maybe. We tell this fuckin' guy to take us to a restaurant we've been told about. And he takes us around the city, over bridges, backwards and forwards. He can't find it. He says he can't find it. The fuckin' guy was screwin' us around."

There's a short silence.

"So you ran into a crooked taxi driver?" I say—helpfully once again.

"That's right," he says. He gives me a belligerent stare.

There's more silence. Like me, some of the other men don't appear to think this story qualifies as grounds for hating a whole country.

"You're all liberals up there, aren't you?" says another guy, returning the discussion to more reliable political ground. He looks to be about the youngest there: late-thirties, muscular, wearing a leather vest, a stetson, rawhide boots, a large side arm, and, on his wrist, a wide watch band with inset blue stones and dangling leather strips.

"Well," I say, "in Canada, one of the main political parties is the Liberal Party, so the word means something a lot different up there than down here."

"When I was up there," interrupts another man, "they wouldn't even let me across the border. They wanted ID."

I don't know what to say. How is that a problem, or an insult?

"You need a driver's licence or photo ID," I say. "Everyone needs that to get across the border—either way."

"Shit, I had a driver's licence," he says, "but it wasn't enough. They wouldn't let me through."

I just don't know what the hell he's talking about.

"*Are* you a liberal?" demands the younger guy with the blue-stone watch band.

I'm not getting off to a good start here.

Anger is always the most notable thing about the people (mostly men) who join these fringe, or marginal, political or vigilante organizations. The Minutemen show all the typical signs. They are completely, one hundred per cent, pissed off. They're not sure why, but things are going to hell, and it's someone's fault: the liberals, the government, the smartasses in suits and offices, the Mexicans coming over the border like a plague, all of the above. Besides being angry, they are paranoid, a little or a lot; and they're open to any conspiracy theory you can concoct.

It doesn't seem like a good or sensible idea to get together a group of such people, allow them to carry weapons, and then send them out into the desert, near the most volatile section of the border with Mexico, to intercept desperate illegal migrants and vicious drug runners. It sounds like a recipe for violence and death.

The people who run the Minutemen seem to be aware of this danger. They're also acutely aware of the public's perception of the organization, and of how a few yahoos could derail its self-sought image of an orderly, dignified and restrained unit of "force multipliers" for the Border Patrol. In one version of the Minuteman standard operating procedure, Chris Simcox warns volunteers over and over again: "Your challenge will be, simplistically put, to behave yourself."

His prolix prose returns many times to the theme of self-destruction. "You will adhere to a no-contact policy. . . If one individual puts their selfish desires before the mandate of the mission, we all lose." One "self-serving fool" can ruin years, and thousands of hours, of efforts. And the "mission?" Simcox restates it many times in his confused and repetitive rhetoric. It boils down to: the government has failed, or declined, to act to prevent this Hispanic invasion of America. It has broken its social contract with its citizens. If it won't act, then the citizens must—although strictly within the law—to try to shame the government into doing its duty. "Our efforts will change the course of history," writes Simcox. "Are you with us, Americans? If yes, then 'let's roll'!"

It's obvious that Simcox knows the Minuteman Civil Defense Corps will inevitably attract a certain kind of person. The "Volunteer Training Manual" warns against the "Ninja Turtle Effect." Many volunteers were in the military and law enforcement, and they may see their desert duty as a chance to "relive the glory days." The Minutemen have a "zero-tolerance policy regarding Ninja Turtles," says the twenty-three-page manual (presumably written by Simcox—it's in his style). No full military or "special ops"–type clothing or gear. And absolutely no long guns. You want to be a Rambo weekend warrior, you will be "dismissed from the operation." If you still need the hit of a contact-high, you'll have to find it somewhere else. This ain't the Nam, boys; go yahooing in someone else's desert.

The Minutemen I talked to were a large enough group to be considered a typical sample of the organization's rank and file. They confirmed my assumptions about them. But these angry, confused, fearful white men (and a few women) who don't understand, and who hate, what is happening to their country, aren't quite vigilantes—at least, so long as they adhere to Simcox's rules of engagement. They don't meet the requirements of the word's definition: someone who carries out law enforcement and executes summary justice because he believes that legally constituted law enforcement agencies aren't doing the job. Nor are they paramilitaries, nor, unlike their eighteenth-century–Massachusetts progenitors, a militia. The Minutemen are supposed only to watch for illegals, and to report them to the Border Patrol; their rules say they must not make contact of any kind with migrants. They must not carry long guns, and had better be at death's door before they haul a side arm out of its holster. Perhaps the Minutemen can be described as a kind of self-appointed, non-deputized posse, or as a particularly aggressive neighbourhood watch.

The Border Patrol sends out mixed messages about them. Its agents usually take advantage of Minutemen eyes and ears, and respond quickly to reports of illegals on the move. But agents often complain about these amateurs and their desert stunts because they get in the way. They set off Oscars buried in the sand on illegals' transit routes. They call out the over-stretched Border Patrol on false alarms. Small sheriff's departments complain about the tens of thousands of dollars they have to spend on overtime for deputies to ride herd on the volunteers. The Minutemen make footprints that confuse the Border Patrol's sign cutters; a tracker may spend hours sniffing down a promising trail only to find Minutemen, not migrants, at the end of it.

In the compound, things are settling down. I no longer fear an assault, or getting heaved out onto Highway 286 and told to get the hell back to where I came from. The volunteers seem to have decided that, even if I am a goddamn Canadian and no better than a Mexican, at least I'm there legally, I'm white and blue-eyed, and I have one of their press cards. They unload their beefs as I take notes, as quickly as I can:

"There's all kinds of atrocities going on along this stretch of the border: drugs, coyotes and bandits all over the place . . ."

"It's cocaine alley . . ."

"Just the past night, we found a girl wandering nearby, shaking, separated from her group for a day and a half . . . She'd been gang-raped. That happens all the time . . ."

"There's people dying out here every day and night. Last October, we found four people who'd been lost for four days. The Pima County Sheriff found sixteen bodies in one week. Hundreds each year . . ."

"Just last night—so damn funny—I'm here at the ranch and there's a knock right here at the door. There's five Mexicans there asking for water. Then four more come up. They were hungry so I gave them some ham and cheese sandwiches, and called the Border Patrol. Some losers, huh? Knocking on our door! . . ."

"It's hard to keep the ranches going. The illegals leave garbage all over the desert; the cows eat it and die . . ."

"The U.S. is a generous and giving country. I despair when people abuse it . . ."

"We got to stop the anchor babies. They come here, have a kid, and he's a U.S. citizen. They use hospitals and schools and don't pay fuckin' taxes . . ."

"Bush says illegals do jobs Americans don't want. Bullshit. I know drywallers used to get $22 an hour; now they get $8 to $10 . . ."

"It's all about the goddamn companies and cheap labour. They bribe the politicians . . ."

"We got to secure the goddamn border. Put in a fence; bring troops in. There's only thirty-six thousand Guard and troops and Patrol along the whole southern border now. We got to have thousands more . . ."

"This county—Pima County—is one of the worst. Four hundred thousand illegals, over thirty thousand of 'em have criminal records. Thousands of prostitutes, some of 'em maybe seven to twelve years old. All that would end if we shut down the border . . ."

"The fuckin' Senate bill is unbelievable; it's an amnesty. The House bill? It's bullshit; it's just so they can say in the election coming up: look how I voted . . ."

"How the fuck are we supposed to be racists and right wing? It's the Hispanic groups that are racists. What about the Raza? Brown Berets [radical Chicano organizations]? All our members are checked out; no one with racist leanings is allowed in . . ."

"It's not just Mexicans. The Salvadorean gangs are the worst—MS-13—they're just organized crime. The Bloods and the Crips aren't nothing anymore. Now it's MS-13 that's in charge. I've heard they feed guys' testicles to their dogs. The dogs won't eat anything else . . ."

"Man, that's a lotta balls . . ."

"They said they'd kill Chris if he didn't quit . . ."

"The Mexican army comes across the border all the time. Last year, Chris saw a unit of them five hundred yards into the U.S.—down to the San Pedro River. He got 'em on video. He sent it to Homeland Security but they never fuckin' replied . . ."

"They say they're drug runners dressed up like army, but it's all the same goddamn thing; the army runs the goddamn drugs . . ."

"We don't carry long guns. We're very strict: if you pull out a gun, you're out—unless you're in real bad danger. But we get a bad name because of Freddy Puckett and his Minutemen One. They're down there by the border with long guns tracking down the illegals, chasing them down and apprehending them themselves. They're fuckin' crazy guys . . ." [Fred Puckett founded the rogue Minuteman of

One when he was expelled from the main organization for carrying an assault rifle. "We don't have no bylaws, we don't have nothing," Puckett told a Phoenix television crew. "We go out in two-man teams and we hit them like we did forty years ago in Vietnam."]

—Those bastards hunt the coyotes as well as illegals. They track them and then just open fire . . ."

—Yeah, a while ago, I was down near Naco, and Puckett and some other guys were down there and I told them they were wrong. They wanted to fight. They had guns out. They're nuts . . ."

—Yeah, but it scares the hell out of the Mexicans. They see Minuteman One guys on this side, there's no fuckin' way they're going to come across . . ."

These desert Minutemen are, at heart, yet another species of conspiracy theorists. When they try to analyze the genuine issue of the porous and violent southern border, paranoia, disordered thinking and curious leaps of imagination are never far away. The effect of unrelenting Hispanic settlement in the southwestern United States may look—metaphorically—like a kind of retaking of the huge territory Mexico lost in 1848. But the Minutemen confuse unintended consequence with causation. They assume a plot: *la Reconquista.*

Jim Gilchrist is a California accountant and Marine Corps–Vietnam veteran who, in 2004, founded the Minuteman Project, a group similar to Simcox's organization though less activist. Gilchrist has said: "To me there is a clear and present danger of insurrection, sedition and secession by those who buy into the fact that this really is Mexico's territory and doesn't belong to the United States and should be taken back." It's not just a matter of poor and desperate people trying to stay to make a living; instead, dark, hostile and cunning forces beyond the knowledge of law-abiding, upright

Anglo-Americans are conspiring to displace them and to create a new Mexico in America.

There's been a line of border vigilantism as a kind of political theatre over the last thirty years. It's essentially racist nature as an Anglo-American, nativist reaction to the influx of brown-skinned people was clear from the beginning. In 1977, the Ku Klux Klan began things with its Klan Border Watch at the San Ysidro port of entry south of San Diego. The Klan's Imperial Wizard, David Duke, envisioned thousands of Klansmen patrolling from the Pacific to the Gulf of Mexico. It was part of the battle "to halt the flow of illegal aliens streaming across the border from Mexico," he said. The Klan's aim was to force, or shame, the government into doing something to stop the flow. Only a few dozen Klansmen turned out.

More recently, other groups have formed. In Texas, Ranch Rescue openly says it is "hunting undocumented aliens"; its president, Jack Foote, said his men would open fire on Mexican soldiers on U.S. soil, or on drug runners: "Two in the chest and one in the head."

Members of American Border Patrol (also known as American Patrol) are unarmed, but its founder, Glenn Spencer, writes things like this: "The Mexican culture is based on deceit. Chicanos and Mexicanos lie as a means of survival." He called Mario Obledo, a respected activist who was awarded the Presidential Medal of Freedom in 1998, a "pinche cockroach." Pinche can mean "lousy" or "worthless," but also "fucking." Spencer has connections with neo-Nazis, and he believes that the Mexican government and Mexican-Americans are conspiring to set up the nation of Aztlán in the U.S. southwest.

In June 2009, three members of another Minuteman movement offshoot, the Minutemen American Defense, were arrested in Arizona for allegedly murdering Raul Flores and his nine-year-old daughter in the small town of Arivaca, eleven miles north of the border, because they suspected Flores of drug trafficking. (In February 2011, the group's leader, Shawna Forde, was found guilty of first-degree murder and sentenced to death.)

All these organizations are elements of the so-called patriot movement, an umbrella term for all those Americans on the far-right wing, who are paramilitary militia members, extreme Christian fundamentalists, anti-abortionists, new-world-order-phobes, white supremacists, tax protestors, survivalists, homophobes, excessive Second Amendment enthusiasts—and border watchers. At the violent end of the patriot spectrum are the failed bombers of the 1960s Minutemen, the cultists at Waco, the survivalists of Ruby Ridge, and the most terrible domestic terrorist: the Oklahoma City bomber, Timothy McVeigh.

There's a flurry in the Minuteman compound at Mile 31. Chris Simcox is here. I see a young, lean, almost ascetic-looking man, seeming out of place among these old bellies and grey beards. He's with a fortyish, beefy, blond man who's glad-handing like a politician. If he is one, I say to myself, he's taking a chance with these volunteers, one of whose dearest present wishes in life is to string up a few pols. However, that won't happen here. This man is Don Goldwater, a nephew of the revered 1964 Republican presidential candidate Barry Goldwater. I go over and introduce myself to Simcox. He shakes my hand absently, making only a brief flick of eye contact. I ask him if I can interview him when he has a moment. He ignores me; he's sucking up to Goldwater, basking in the gubernatorial candidate's aura. I ask again, but Simcox can't be diverted. He's smitten.

Goldwater is another matter. He turns around, gives me the old thousand-watt smile and a two-handed shake; he doesn't just make eye contact, he envelops me in it, and, in a sonorous, well-modulated voice, says:

"I'm so pleased to meet you and all these other patriots here today. I'm so pleased with the work you're doing for our state and our country. Can I count on your support for Governor?"

I'm taken aback, and still confused by Simcox's snub.

"Sure, yeah," I say, blown away by the man's sheer Aryan glamour.

"Outstanding," says Goldwater, and turns towards a goofily grinning Minuteman, who looks as star-struck as I probably do, and who will, no doubt, support the candidate.

A slim, blond, middle-aged woman whose name is Carmen asks me if I'd like to go out with one of the night patrols—the four to midnight shift. Yes, I would. Carmen has a German accent; she's wearing tight jeans and a low-cut, clingy sweater; she's got a very nice figure; she lives in Tombstone, like Simcox; she's wearing a pistol in a holster which is tied down low on her thigh, as if she's a gunslinger who might have to quick-draw and plug any guy who pisses her off. This is one sexy Minuteman. I've been on the road a long time.

I wonder vaguely about the public relations aspect of someone with a German accent apparently having a supervisory role in an organization whose raison d'être is to hunt down and round up non-white people, and which shares many views with groups that are openly anti-Semitic. But that's unfair, prejudiced; maybe I've watched too many World War II movies. If Wernher von Braun could run the U.S. space program after using Nazi slave labour to build rockets and fire them indiscriminately at English civilians, Carmen is certainly entitled to ramrod a posse of quasi-vigilantes in the Arizona desert.

Before the patrol begins, we gather in the dusty yard for a briefing. There are about thirty men and a few women. A tall Minuteman named Whitney talks to us. He has a kind face, a wry smile, and a grey ponytail hanging down from under his stetson; he speaks with a slight lisp.

No long guns, he says (this obviously can't bear repeating enough). And yesterday, he saw a guy carrying his pistol
at half-cock. You can't do that; it's dangerous, especially if
you value your own co—Whoa! Sorry, ladies. Absolutely no
contact with the illegals; no Spanish—don't talk to them at
all; if they need water, put some down, and back away.
Remember, they're scared of us. Keep a light on them. Count
the females and kids; see if they're in distress—maybe the
kids need water or the women have been raped. And keep
quiet! Last night, out on the line, sometimes it sounded like
goddamn suppertime at the Taco Bell. Sound carries in the
desert. Do not respond to taunts from outside agitators. The
ACLU is warning Mexicans that the Minutemen are here, but
just ignore them. Keep lights out; disable vehicle lights so they
don't come on when you open a door. Don't smoke; you can
smell it a mile away. If you need to smoke, cut a chew instead.
Watch each other's backs; stand together. No garbage. Don't
wander away from your post—you don't want to be out there
by yourself looking for a place to piss—sorry, ladies—and run
into a large group. The Minuteman One guys are out in the
desert close to Sasabe right now—hunting illegals with long
guns. They're far enough away, they shouldn't be a problem.
But if you see someone out there with a rifle—it could be a
coyote or a drug runner—immediately say, "Code Black" into
your radio. "This is Post . . . whatever." Then, everyone shut
up; sit down. Be quiet; be invisible.

I'm assigned to Minutemen Rick and Hank, and I climb
into the front seat of their pickup. Rick looks to be in his early
seventies, and I'm pleased to see he's the amiable cowboy who
welcomed me earlier in the day and asked me what I thought
about the Minutemen. Hank is a heavy, jowly man, a little bow-
legged, close to seventy, balding, worried, a shift boss of some
kind; he stumps about, trying to organize the line of pickups,
SUVs and sedans. These people, for all their military and police

backgrounds, seem hard to herd and resistant to orders. There's some problem, and Hank loses it, shouting at someone who wants to change the plan. When he climbs into the driver's seat, he's upset at himself for his outburst, and he apologizes. Like Rick, he's seems to be a nice guy, and he's flustered. I feel lucky to have drawn these two, and not someone like the angry man who couldn't get into Canada. Or maybe visitors are always assigned to genial, polite Hank and Rick? No, Hank claims, it's just done at random. Finally, at 4:55, the convoy pulls out of the compound onto the 286 and heads north.

We pass an ACLU picket just across the road—half a dozen young men and women, a couple of parked cars and signs denouncing vigilantes. I hadn't realized who they were when I rode in: I'll talk to them tomorrow. Rick tells me that yesterday they had to kick out one of the ACLU-ers who had "infiltrated" the Minuteman compound and was "collecting intelligence on our operations." I wonder why they're so sure I'm not a spy—the only document I've shown anyone here is my driver's licence. I could be a communist, pedophile-loving, liberal, civil libertarian myself, burrowing into their secrets—whatever they could be. In a few minutes, we pull off the highway onto a sand road, past a small ranch house surrounded by a new wire fence, with barbed wire on top, big spotlights, a watchtower. It looks like a small fort in Indian country. We'll establish our line on the owners' private land. A ranch vaquero sits on horseback beside the road watching us drive by, a rifle resting across his saddle in front of him.

One of the Minutemen is a part-Choctaw, part-Delaware Indian, and an ex-Marine, Hank tells me, and he's the tracker for this operation. He finds the most heavily used of the migrants' trails—each coyote has his own routes—and stakes out where he wants the line set up. We park the pickup just off the dirt trail. We're the twelfth of fourteen posts, and

"Bravo 12" is our radio call sign. The posts average a few hundred yards apart. On the weekends, there may be twenty of them, but fewer volunteers get out on weekdays, especially at night. To me, it seems as if it wouldn't be difficult to just walk around all of us. Several tall transmission towers of some sort rise up about five miles to our north. There are lights on them at night, and they are what the migrants trek towards, their beacons in the desert.

A Fox News truck drives by our position, then three Border Patrol vehicles. The last one stops and an agent leans out the window.

"We couldn't find that last group, but we found some old dope," he says. "I've been on this job nineteen years. I can't say this officially, but I'm glad you guys are here. Thank you for being here. Wish you'd been here nineteen years ago."

Hank and Rick thank him, and say that they're just doing what they can. They're very pleased.

When the Border Patrol leaves, the two Minutemen pull out and arrange their lawn chairs, sleeping bags, blankets, food, coffee and night scopes. They're like fussy old guys setting up the living room for the big game on television. Rick has a book with the title *Diversity: The Invention of a Concept*. I flip through it and I'm surprised to find that it's a serious and literate work with all the scholarly apparatus. (Its author, Peter Wood, has a Ph.D. in anthropology and teaches at King's College in New York City. The college's mission statement begins: "Through its commitment to the truths of Christianity and a biblical worldview . . .") Rick recommends it to me. Hank says you don't need any books. It's all very simple: "One language, one culture, one border." No, says Rick, "Four borders—all around."

Before we left the compound, I pulled out of my pannier bag some sorry-looking fruit, bread and cheese left over from my cold, starry, high-altitude camp in the Peloncillo Mountains.

I also have my two-litre water bottle, a sweater and my riding fleece underjacket. For the first time on my ride, I've left all my gear strapped onto the bike, parked in the Minuteman compound. I suspect these men of many things, but not of being thieves. Rick is solicitous, and insists that I take his special chair while he perches on the bottom of an upturned plastic pail. He also insists I take several of his apples—it's important to eat apples on these night shifts, he says—and tells me to drink lots of water. I will; you get dehydrated fast out in the sand, among the mesquite, ocotillo and cactus, even in the cooling evening, and during the cold desert night.

Nothing much will happen until after dark. Rick and Hank tell me how much they admire Simcox. He often gives speeches at colleges. The students support the liberal line at first, but after his talk, they're lined up to shake his hand. Chris is "a good ole man," says Hank. We look out west towards the Baboquivari Mountains. He and Rick were up at sunrise this morning, says Hank, and "it was drop-dead beautiful." He lights a cigarette. I mention Whitney's no-smoking injunction during the briefing. "Hell with him," says Hank. We listen to the radio chatter, of which there's a lot. It's confused and jumbled, some of the posts doing radio checks and arguing about the call signs they've been given, asking if they can use their own. Hank and Rick shake their heads and laugh: such incompetence. Only one guy can jazz up his call sign: "Pineapple" is the shift boss. A Fox News SUV drives by, then an unidentified pickup. Low overhead, a flight of four warplanes roars across us. I ask about Hank's and Rick's firearms. Rick is carrying his favourite of the nine weapons he owns, a snug .38 Special; Hank has a Springfield 9 mm.

Post 14 reports three illegals coming our way, then amends the number to nine. "Okay," says Hank, "we're going quiet mode." There's still light, although it's fading, the sun breaking though light cloud just above the western mountains. We begin to scan around the nearby desert. It belatedly occurs to me that, of course, I'll have to say nothing if I see anyone. I'm not going to turn in any illegals. If Hank and Rick don't see them, that's fine with me.

There may be migrants close by, but an SUV drives noisily up. It's Carmen. Even though it's getting cold, she's still wearing her scanty getup, and I'm happy to see her again. She and Hank talk about meetings and how to organize them better. For twenty minutes or so, they mostly discuss Minuteman business in normal voices that carry out over the desert. Post 14 calls to cancel its sighting—no more action. No wonder, I think, with all this driving around, and palaver. In her soft German accent, Carmen says: "They're flooding in to beat the deadline, the Senate amnesty bill." She and Rick talk about what's for breakfast—Rick does a lot of the Minuteman cooking. As Carmen gets into her vehicle and drives away, Rick and Hank smile at each other, that knowing, male, what-a-babe smile—they're always happy to see her too.

The Kitt Observatory is visible on one of the nearby peaks. Rick tells me his great-uncle was Percival Lowell. He was the astronomer who inferred the existence of Pluto and thought he saw canals on Mars. I say to Rick that Amy Lowell, the poet, and Percival's sister, must, therefore, have been his great-aunt. He hasn't heard of her. We talk about how peaceful and quiet the desert is. Rick won't hear of my not continuing to sit in his special chair, while he still hunkers on the upturned pail. I'm beginning to like these two gentle, courteous men.

But things change; I bring up politics. What do you think of Bush and the Iraq war, I ask Rick.

That's it for Mister Nice Guy. He fully supports the war. Liberals and democrats are against it, but they are all liars. Kennedy and Kerry, they're both liars. McCain, he's a liar, too. He was last in his class; he dropped a bomb on his own ship. He's a yellow-belly coward. He informed on his fellow prisoners when he was in the "Hanoi Hilton." John Murtha is a piece of shit. John Kerry lied about his record in Vietnam; it's all false. Obama? Don't ask.

Hank isn't really listening, or he wants to change the subject. He interrupts to point out the beautiful light on the mountains. The sun is setting over them now, and shafts of its bright light join the earth and the sky, looking as if, at any moment, angels will descend upon their stream to settle our petty disputes.

Rick ignores the view—to hell with the sunset. He hates the liberal media; they're all liars, too. Abortionists are goddamn murderers who should be murdered themselves. You can't keep church and state apart. A state without the church is a Communist abomination. But the liberals are the worst. They're liars, but they're evil, too, because they're smart people, yet they support killing babies, and they coddle pedophiles, and most of them are Communist sympathizers—like the ACLU, the "American Communist Lawyers Union." They're all indoctrinated by liberal professors in colleges.

I take notes until Rick's diatribe winds down. In silence, we all sit looking west towards the beautiful sky. After a while, Hank asks me what my ride has been like. Before I can reply, Rick, amiable and smiling again, says: "Riding a motorcycle is just like riding a horse. Here's how you do it: keep one leg on each side and your ass in the middle and nothing can go wrong." That's pretty funny; it breaks the tension, and we all laugh. Maybe I'll risk another question.

But, I say, isn't it possible to think of liberals not as evil liars, but as fellow American citizens who happen to hold different views from you on questions of war and politics, or abortion, the border, immigration? Can't they be just as well-intentioned, good and sincere people like you, but with a different world view from yours?

Rick stares at me as if I've suggested that, for example, pedophiles may actually be onto something, or that maybe it is time to hand over the United States government to the United Nations. He's angry again, but more than that, he's uncomprehending. My question makes no sense to him; he doesn't understand its premises. My question implies complexity and ambiguity, the suggestion that morality is relative, or at least, that moral dilemmas may have several contradictory solutions. But his brain—all his instincts—tell him to reject complexity, to embrace simplicity, and to hate the things and people he doesn't understand, and who he thinks are dead wrong. It's a kind of purity of heart. There's no room for compromise. This is the essence of the polarized political culture of the United States. And it works both ways. Rick's incomprehension has its analogue in, say, the northeastern big-city liberal democrat or independent who favours abortion, and amnesty for illegal migrants, and abhors vigilantism, but who sees, say, a Christian, evangelical, right-wing, republican, NRA member as a stupid, uneducated, deluded and dangerous hick.

After he's stared at me for a while, Rick says: "Bullshit."

Darkness falls, and it gets colder. I put on my fleece jacket over my sweater. There's some cloud, but a quarter-moon showing, circled by a moon dog. There may be bad weather tomorrow, which probably means more strong headwind as I ride west. Rick climbs up onto the pickup's bed to get a better look through his night scope—it's a "second generation," like the boys in Iraq use, lights things up like a flare. Hank smokes another cigarette—he's been violating the blackout rule all evening. The dry desert wind flows cold over us. As Rick tries to climb down from the truck, he tumbles off the tailboard hard onto the sand, a heavy fall. I'm afraid he's broken something—he's the right age to smash a hip. But he hauls himself upright and says he's fine, the sand is soft. Hank and I brush him off.

At around 8:45, Post 13 comes on the radio and reports a sighting: twenty people are heading our way along the dirt road; they saw the post's vehicle and started running. The Minutemen have reported the sighting to the Border Patrol. Rick climbs back up onto the pickup, and stares through his night scope. After a minute or two, he says: "I got 'em. Four or five long-hairs; the rest men. More than twenty; I count thirty-two altogether."

Hank climbs up onto the pickup bed beside Rick and gets the big searchlight ready. I can't see anything, but then I hear them: people jogging along the sand trail beside us, heavy panting, fragments of Spanish, a woman sobbing.

Rick whispers to Hank to get the big light ready. But Hank's a little hard of hearing. "What?" he whispers back.

"What?" says Rick, whose ears aren't the best either. This is getting funny.

Hank fumbles with the searchlight, flashes it on and off again. We duck away from the shocking high candlepower. They know we're here.

Rick abandons discretion: "Over there," he hollers, pointing west. "Light 'em up!"

Hank manages to turn on the light again, swings it a little, and picks up the group right away. The figures, burdened with bundles and bags, freeze in a weird tableau of fear and shock. They're blinded by the sudden light, as are we. After a few seconds, they explode in all directions, stumbling over the sand and shouldering noisily through the thorny desert flora. They shout to each other; the woman's sobbing gets louder, frantic. They run like terrified animals. Hank and Rick whoop and shout. I feel sick; I want to run over with water. I want to say: It's all right; I'll help you; if you want to come this badly, I'll help you stay alive.

The migrants run out of the light, and half a minute later it's silent again. Until we hear the whop of the Border Patrol chopper coming up from Sasabe. It hovers overhead, its searchlight sweeping the desert, lighting it up as bright as a phosphorous flare. Two Border Patrol vehicles bump up the dirt track—an SUV and an armoured Jeep. The four agents fan out around us, following the tracks left by the fleeing illegals. Their flashlights bob around us in the darkness for half an hour. The chopper circles around, then clatters off to the east. Through his night scope, Rick sees four more people off to the southwest. I view them, too; they're like dark-haired figures in a fuzzy video game. They're running away to the south, the wrong way for them.

Over the radio, the post down the line reports that one man has surrendered: he put up his hands in their flashlight beams and said, "Agua, agua, por favor."

In all the excitement, Hank falls off the truck too, hitting the sand with a thump louder than Rick's. I'm beginning to wonder if these two will survive the night, and how many casualties there usually are per shift. But Hank gets up right away as well, and seems to be all right. Rick and I brush him off. These may be Keystone Minutemen, but they can certainly take a fall.

Later, we hear that the Patrol rounded up four men who got caught in a cactus thicket. Apprehending around 10 per cent of them is typical, says Rick. The other illegals have escaped, perhaps up towards Three Points and their coyote rendezvous, or back towards Mexico, or maybe they just got lost in the desert.

It's quiet after the Border Patrol leaves. That's when the illegals often pop up again, says Rick. The three of us chat a little as he scans the desert with his scope. Hank says he's buying as much gold as he can—the way things are going, it may soon be the only currency. Rick tells a story of how, against his advice, a friend of his rented a house to some Mexicans. Of course, they trashed the place, and left without paying the rent. Hank tells a story about Mexicans fishing with tacos and wondering why they can't catch anything. The conversation dies away. Hank dozes off. Rick keeps a watch from the pickup. I can see his profile from my spot on the ground; he's wrapped in his sleeping bag and wearing his stetson, and is sitting on the upside-down pail. He still insists that I sit in his special chair—which is pretty comfortable. It's very cold and I'm shivering, waiting out the last hour of our shift. Behind me, to the north, coyotes—animals, not migrant-smugglers—start to yelp and howl. The clear and wild sound echoes across the desert valley like a memento of the past.

I sleep cold, and not much, on a cot in a tent in the Minuteman compound. In the morning, I walk across the road from the ranch house to the small group of pickets set up by the American Civil Liberties Union. Another Minuteman, a new recruit from Massachusetts, saunters across behind me. I introduce myself to the young Hispanic and Anglo pickets. The Minuteman is immediately latched onto by a reporter from the Netherlands who has been interviewing the ACLU people.

They are just riding herd on the Minutemen, says Ray, a Stanford law student, making sure they don't violate anyone's civil rights, or get violent. The ACLU does not, of course, support illegal activity of any sort, and migrants are entering the country illegally. However, once they cross the line, they immediately acquire constitutional and human rights. The United States Supreme Court has made it clear in a hundred-years'–worth of decisions that the constitution's guarantees apply even to aliens whose presence in the country is unlawful.

So: the government can certainly arrest and try, or deport, illegal migrants, but it must do so according to law. It can't, for example, carry out illegal searches and seizures. I tell Ray that

I've been subject to a number of those myself over the previous few weeks. He is not surprised.

The ACLU believes that the Minutemen are vigilantes, pure and simple, usurping the legitimate role of government in ensuring the rule of law. They are extrajudicial nutbars. But, I say—I'm still mindful of kindly Rick and Hank, and their hospitality—the Minutemen say they simply want the law to be applied properly. They agree with you about the law and illegals in theory; they claim it's not being applied in any kind of practice. Ray dismisses my advocacy with a laugh; it is sympathy for the devil.

Once again: the great divide. To the Minutemen, the ACLU is an evil, soul-less, Communist-front organization; to the ACLU pickets, the Minutemen are armed quasi-fascists. Once again: the rigid and contemptuous divide between American liberal and conservative, between left and right; there is no sense of fellow citizens carrying on an intense, but respectfully and mutually engaged, political debate. Instead, the conflict is, for both sides, one of reductive and dismissive good versus evil.

Our conversation is suddenly interrupted by the arrival of Connie, the Minuteman press officer. She is furious. She demands to know what the hell I think I'm doing talking to these people. I signed onto the rules, she says; I agreed not to talk to anyone outside the compound while I had their press badge. I don't know what she's talking about. She demands my press pass back, and says: "Pack up your stuff and get the hell out of our headquarters." Then, she sees the Massachusetts Minuteman blithely yakking away to a foreign reporter. She gives him much more hell than she gave me. I'm a rule breaker; he is an apostate. She does everything but grab the sheepish and cowed man by the ear and drag him back across the road. Obviously, you can't trust these blue-state guys.

I cross back over, too, and begin to load up my bike. I see Rick and say to him:

"I went over and talked to the ACLU, and now I've been kicked out."

Rick says, noncommittally, "Oh well."

He doesn't want to get involved, and I don't blame him. Just as I'm ready to leave, Connie comes back and apologizes, although grudgingly. She says she couldn't find any form I signed attesting that I knew the rules for press. The nice, vague lady I met when I arrived should have given me the sheet, but didn't. Connie invites me to stay on. I thank her, but I was leaving anyway. I have to get riding west.

At the Three Points crossroad, I'm filling my gas tank when Ray of the ACLU drives up. He has a cellphone; a reporter from the *Arizona Republic* wants to interview me about the press pass incident. I realize that Ray has called the newspaper; he is using me for the ACLU's political purposes, but I talk to the reporter anyway. I'm still annoyed by the abrupt and rude treatment I received, and I tell the reporter that the Minuteman rules about not talking to anyone are a violation of my right of free speech, and an unjustified restriction on my freedom of movement and association, and so on. The story is published in the paper the next day, and it includes a statement from the Minuteman Director of Media Liaison, Stacey O'Connell, offering to reinstate my press pass. (O'Connell was subsequently expelled from the organization when he accused Simcox of keeping donated cash for himself.)

Later, my lawyerly instincts kick in (I have a law degree), and I regret my one-sided comments. In fact, the Minutemen have every right to make rules about how the press will behave on their property. If you sign on, they have a right to evict you if you break them.

———

As I finish gassing up the KLR, three Border Patrol vehicles pull in for fuel. An agent comes over smiling and genial, as if I'm an old friend. He noticed my licence plate. Where do I live in British Columbia? He is from Seattle, and he knows Salt Spring Island. He is also an odd sort of Border Patrol agent in these parts. He is pale-skinned, his hair is blond and combed with care, his uniform is fresh and pressed, and he's well-spoken. He just graduated from the Border Patrol academy, and he is looking forward to getting posted back up along the border in the northwest. His girlfriend and his family are there. However, all new recruits must serve a period of time along the southern border before they can apply for duty elsewhere in the country.

This guy is like the people I know back home; he emphasizes for me the mild culture shock I've been going through.

"Well, I'm sure it will be good to get back close to Seattle," I say.

"I can't wait," he says. He looks around to make sure none of his colleagues are nearby. Then he leans close to me, and speaks in a low voice, like a fellow conspirator.

"It's crazy down here," he says, "it is just fucking crazy."

CHAPTER 9

THE THIRD NATION

IT'S ONLY A MATTER OF TIME, INDIAN,
YOU CAN'T SLEEP WITH THE RIVER FOREVER.
—LESLIE MARMON SILKO,
"INDIAN SONG: SURVIVAL," *Storyteller*

THE STORY OF THE BORDER BETWEEN MEXICO and the United States is usually told as if Mexicans and Americans were the only players. For example, the influential American scholar of the borderlands, Américo Paredes, begins an essay on identity and culture along the southern border: "If we view a border not simply as a line on a map but, more fundamentally, as a sensitized area where two cultures or two political systems come face to face . . ." But the Spaniards and Americans made their presumptuous incursions upon land already long occupied by the Indians of the southwestern United States and northern Mexico.

Highway 1 on the Tohono O'odham Indian Reservation ends in a small village that isn't marked on my map, but which is called Menagers Dam. The village is composed of a few small, rundown houses and a community hall. The paved road peters out here, and three dirt trails run south towards the border, which is no more than half a mile away. Two Indian men walk across in front of my bike as I cruise slowly along. They ignore me completely, and I must brake and stop to avoid hitting them. They don't even look in my direction. One of them is carrying a rifle, and the other is wearing a side arm. On the porch of a house, a group of men watch me. One of them waves, and I wave back.

I choose a dirt road to ride down, but a Border Patrol Blazer appears from around a bend ahead of me. The vehicle stops and the lone agent gets out and gestures me to stop. We go through the Script. Except that this time, there were signs on the road down here that this is a restricted area. I saw them, but kept going anyway, I tell the agent, because I need the information for my book. He is polite but adamant that I turn back right away. What a surprise to find out that it is dangerous down here, and that lots of drugs and illegals come across the border and right through where we're standing. I turn and ride back to the main highway.

I make a second attempt to reach the Tohono O'odham border with Mexico on my later trip with the SUV. This time, I drive through the main reservation town of Sells and carry on down Highway 19 through the villages of Topawa and San Miguel, and to the border at Newfield, which is just a few dusty buildings. One of the more than a dozen "gates" through the fence should be close by. Again, the paved road ends and several trails head on towards the border. I pick one and bump my way along the stony-sandy road for a few hundred yards, then stop. I must be close to the line by now, although I can't see any signs of a fence. I'm looking at my map, when I become aware of movement in the scrub and stunted trees to my left. Two men emerge. They are wearing khaki uniforms and body armour, and carrying assault rifles, side arms and radios. They look like combat soldiers—like the men I came upon by the river in Presidio, in Texas. One of them holds his rifle—it looks like an M4—to his shoulder in point-shooting position, and he is scoping me as he moves. I advise myself: keep your hands still and in plain sight on the wheel. I look right and see three more men walking towards me. One is in uniform, and the other two are dressed in blue T-shirts and jeans, but they are carrying rifles and side arms. One of them also has his weapon in firing position. I say to my friends: maybe I've got myself into a real mess now, boys. The men surround my vehicle. The Script is a little different this time.

"What the hell are you doing here?" says one of the uniformed guys. He is angry.

"Er, I'm a writer from Canada, and I'm doing research for a book about the border with Mexico. Um, I just wanted to see what the border looked like down here."

"Well, you should not be here. This is a restricted area. Didn't you see the signs?"

"No, I'm sorry, I didn't notice them," I lie. I'm unnerved by the guy's anger and all these firearms. I'm not even sure I'm still in the United States. Maybe I've blundered across the border. The four other men stand and stare at me with unabashed hostility and irritation, although the two ready shooters have relaxed their rifles. One of the plainclothes steps forward and peers in through the windows at my SUV's empty interior.

"Well, this is a restricted area," says the spokesman. "Just turn your vehicle around and get the hell out of here."

"Okay, sorry, I'll do that right now." I really want to be nice to these guys, to reassure them. "Am I close to the border, by the way?"

"Sir, if you'd driven another fifty yards, you would have been in Mexico," he says. "We don't give a shit about that, but we would have had something to say to you when you turned around and tried to come back in."

"Okay, thanks," I say. "I'll turn around right here and leave you guys to it. Can I ask what you're doing here?"

"Sir, you just drove into a joint-agency interdiction ambush."
He sounds proud of it. "Now turn around right now, and get
out of here."

The heavily armed men back off to give me manoeuvring
room. I three-point turn the SUV, and trundle back along the
trail. I wave as I leave, but I'm hardly surprised that no one
waves back. In my rear-view mirror, I see the five men staring
after me, motionless in the desert heat. Behind them, Mexico
is an indistinguishable continuation of American landscape
across an invisible border.

New fencing has gone up on Tohono O'odham land. (Tohono
O'odham means "people of the desert." It is their own name
for themselves, and it has replaced the vaguely insulting
"Papago"—meaning "beaneater"—which was applied to them
by the Spanish conquistadors.) Until recently, the border was
marked by a rickety three- or five-strand cattle barrier fence
that a person could easily climb over or through, and which a
vehicle could simply knock down. It was perforated by thirteen gates through which the O'odham (and drug runners
and illegal migrants) could pass without any hindrance. The
gates, which are all named, were openings in the wire protected by a cattle grid and nothing else. There were other
unofficial cuts in the fence that didn't have names.

To deal with the O'odham, Homeland Security has used
its sweeping environmental waiver of April 2008, but it must
also waive laws dealing specifically with Indian affairs, such
as the American Indian Religious Freedom Act. The Real ID
Act allows for both; its wording includes "the authority to
waive all legal requirements." A fence prevents the people
from crossing to some of their spiritual sites in Mexico—to
Quitovac for the prayer stick rain ceremony every August, for
example—which are only reasonably accessible from the
American side of the line.

In the case of the border fence, as in so many other areas of presidential, or executive, powers since 9/11, the rule of law—and the mass of cumbersome bureaucratic regulations that are the necessary guarantors of due process—has been abrogated in the overbearing name of security.

The Tohono O'odham Nation claims that any kind of new fence violates not only United States domestic laws, but also international declarations like the United Nations Universal Declaration of Human Rights, and the Declaration on the Rights of Indigenous Peoples.

Furthermore, says Ofelia Rivas, a representative of the Tohono O'odham Nation in Washington, her nation lives in a militarized zone. "We, as original people, are now required to answer to United States armed forces as to our nationality on our own lands." She deals in the ideological language of confrontation. The United States is a government of occupation—throughout North America. The attacks of 9/11 gave the government an excuse to ratchet up "its attacks against the indigenous residents of the United States . . . in the guise of borderlands defence." To justify its new fence, the government is using "the fear of terrorism, as has become common since 9/11, to advance its fascistic imperialist interests."

Rivas herself has been asked, at gunpoint, to prove she had the right to be on land on which she was born, and on which her ancestors have lived for centuries. A Border Patrol agent stopped Vivian Juan-Saunders, a former chairwoman of the Tohono O'odham Nation, when she was driving her Jeep with her eight-year-old son. The agent got out of his vehicle, drew his side arm and pointed it at her as he approached. The Patrol moves at will. For example: Margaret Garcia, who is sixty-eight years old and lives in a two-room shack, woke up one night to find that agents with night-vision goggles and shotguns had set up an observation post in her yard.

The Border Patrol claims it is trying to get along better with the O'odham, by instructing agents in tribal traditions, and by enlisting the tribal police to enter private property. "However," a Patrol spokesman said, "if it's hot pursuit, it's a different story." There is a lot of hot pursuit in O'odham territory. Nothing radicalizes people more than being pushed around on their own land by alien armed men.

The O'odham have the same problem as other tribes in the south—the Kickapoo, Comanche, Kiowa and Apache, for example (and the Mohawk and the Blackfoot in the north). The land they had occupied since time immemorial was split in two by the sudden and arbitrary imposition of a border by the Europeans who claimed their land by right of conquest. However, the O'odham tribe is the only one with a substantial reservation abutting against the southern border; it is the second largest reservation in the United States after the Navajo. The people's lives are integrated and continuous across the border, which splits families and communities, as well as the Tohono O'odham Nation as a whole.

As with indigenous people throughout the Americas, the Apache, Comanche, Kiowa, Ute and Navajo, among other tribes, fought a centuries-long war against the invaders and occupiers. The southern borderlands tribes resisted over as long a period of time as any: the Tepehuán uprising took place in Durango, Mexico, in 1616; the Tarahumara in Chihuahua in the 1640s; and the Pueblo Revolt in New Mexico in 1680. The Apache leader, Geronimo, surrendered more than two hundred years later, in 1886. The Lakota Sioux fought a subsequent battle at Wounded Knee in South Dakota, in 1890, in which hundreds of Sioux men, women and children were massacred by the United States Army.

There was scattered Indian violence in Mexico in the following decades: the Yaquis revolted in the north in the

1890s—prompting a policy of extermination and deportation to forced labour by the dictator Porfirio Díaz—and were still waging small-scale guerrilla resistance in the Sonoran mountains into the 1920s; Chiricahua Apaches made minor raids in Sonora as late as 1926. However, these were the last-ditch actions of a few desperate survivors (although, one could describe the Zapatista revolt in Chiapas state in 1994 as an Indian uprising, since almost all the rebels were ethnic Maya). The long war of the Indians against the whites was, for all of them, a long death.

However, while that war went on in the U.S.-Mexico borderlands, it played a pivotal role in relations between the two countries. The Indians are largely invisible in historical narratives—the lot of all conquered peoples. History is, after all, mostly written by the victors, at least until ambitious, young revisionist historians right the balance a little. But the borderlands Indians (who would not have had any concept of the adjective) were a source of almost obsessive fear for northern Mexicans and, to a lesser extent, for southwestern Americans. The Indians may even have been a decisive arbiter of American victory in the Mexican War of 1846.

While the Spanish controlled Mexico, they did, eventually, manage to build up a system of frontier defence against the tribes who refused to submit to invasion and occupation: the fierce, tough warrior societies of the Apache, Comanche and Navajo. Towards the end of the eighteenth century, a combination of forts, missions, free food rations and liquor—and, as always, the profound debilitation of European diseases—had the desired policy effect of "dependency" on European largesse, and a weakening of indigenous culture.

However, the struggle of Mexico, and other colonies, for independence diverted the attention of the imperial power away from its fractious borders and towards trying to hang onto the colonial centres themselves. By the time Mexico got its independence from Spain, the neglected northern border area was becoming more and more unstable. On the fringe of the new republic, things began to fly apart.

By the early 1830s, Apaches had resumed raiding in five northern Mexican states, including New Mexico (the latter not yet United States territory). By 1840, Comanches and Arapahos had joined in, and the borderlands were under siege as far east as the lower Rio Grande. The fast-moving, mounted Indians were ruthless, and raiding parties often consisted of many hundreds of warriors. They struck far south into Mexican territory into the state of San Luis Potosí. The Indians killed men, and took women and children as slaves, or as new additions to the tribes—as many as five thousand, by one count. Thousands of Mexicans died along their northern frontier. The *norteños* pleaded for help, but the new republic was politically unstable and economically devastated. The *fronterizos* had to look mostly to their own defence against *los indios bárbaros*. Many became refugees, abandoning their hard-won, and hardscrabble, ranches and farms. They relinquished villages, and even small towns.

Anglos began moving into Texas in the 1820s and 1830s with the grudging acceptance of the Mexican government; the state needed more men to fight Indians. The newly arrived Anglos saw a war going on between two despised peoples in Texas and elsewhere in the borderlands: the degenerate mestizo Mexicans and the unregenerate, savage Indians. Surely, they thought, the country could not be left in the possession of either of these combatants, one as uncivilized as the other, each unworthy of ownership of the vast and rich territory; the Mexicans in particular, by their inability to subdue the savage Indians, had abdicated their right to their alluring borderlands.

The Indian wars here became the iconic model for the mythology of the West: buttes and parched gulches, the Sonoran desert of cactus, jackrabbits, antelope, lizards, scattered watering holes, unforgiving sun, and the savage, yet noble, mounted warriors who would not quit. They were fighting John Wayne, but they were defending their land, too—an ambiguous, yet manly and honourable contest. Cowboys and Indians: each a version of the laconic, violent, nomadic man of the frontier.

By the time the United States annexed newly independent Texas and began its moves towards war with Mexico, the Mexican army was deeply distracted, almost exhausted, by internal conflict, but also by its long, defensive war against the Apache and Comanche raiders in the northern third of its country.

To add a perceived insult to injury, Mexicans believed that Texans, and Americans generally, perhaps even the United States government itself, encouraged Indian raids on weak Mexico, and then provided sanctuary for the raiders. "Those infamous North American enemies," fulminated one Mexican editorial, "push the bloody hordes of savages upon us and direct their operations with unparalleled astuteness and ferocity!" But this denied Indian strength and independence. In fact, there is no evidence that either private Americans or their government had much, or any, influence over Comanches and Kiowas. And, up until the early 1840s, Americans had little or no contact with Apaches or Navajos.

When American army columns moved south into Mexican territory in 1846, they found country already blasted by war: abandoned settlements, uncultivated fields, larger towns filled with refugees—and graves: "a perfect forest of crosses, many of them mutilated or thrown down by Indians," in the words of the English traveller, ex-soldier and mountain man, George Ruxton. When General, and President, Santa Anna ordered the northern Mexican states to muster all men between the ages of sixteen and fifty, the states refused, saying they needed them to fight Indians. The shortfall of these tough frontiersmen in the Mexican army could have made the difference at the crucial battle of Buena Vista in 1847, which Santa Anna lost by a hair.

During the Mexican War, the Americans had concerns about their long supply lines and the regular Mexican army, but mostly they feared a guerrilla insurgency—the familiar bane of all unjust and ill-founded wars of invasion. American commanders tried to head off this possibility by convincing the northern Mexicans that they would be better off co-operating with the occupiers. In a refrain that would also become familiar, the Americans said that they were in Mexico to liberate the people from despots. And, also, as General Zachary Taylor put it, "to drive back the savage Cumanches, to prevent the renewal of their assaults, and to compel them to restore to you from captivity your long lost wives and children." The Mexican government couldn't protect its people, but the American army would.

Norteños, long used to neglect and indifference from Mexico City, alienated from the centre on their remote periphery, and almost done in by constant and desperate warfare, were willing to be persuaded. They may have regarded the gringos as hypocrites. Americans had encouraged the Indians to attack Mexico—so the Mexicans believed—and now, they claimed to have invaded the country to protect the *norteños* from the Indians. Still, the more or less disciplined gringo soldiers were preferable to the warriors without mercy.

The Tohono O'odham were mostly "good Indians," a "model tribe." They were farmers. Ingenious on their arid ground, they harvested the fruit of the saguaro, mesquite pods and cholla buds. They coaxed tepary beans, squash and amaranth, or pigweed, out of sandy soil watered by desert sheet flooding when it rained. They had the feast-or-famine metabolism of aboriginal people in hard country everywhere (and which, today, now that there is always more than enough junk food to eat, triggers diabetes in most of them).

It seemed impossible for almost any tribe, no matter how accommodating it was to the heedless, or violently extreme, demands of white miners, hunters and settlers, to avoid resorting to violence at some time or other. Even the peaceful O'odham revolted three times, twice against the Spanish, in 1695 and in 1751, and, for a third time, against the Mexicans in the early 1840s. After that, however, the O'odham gave up resisting. On an O'odham calendar stick, a notation for 1843 reads: "The peace was permanent."

Robert Williams teaches law, and runs the Indigenous Peoples Law and Policy Program, at the University of Arizona in Tucson. He is an advocate for Native-American human and legal rights, and, among many other activities, has acted as a trial judge for the Tohono O'odham Nation. As a result, he knows the O'odham, and their border territory, well. During one talk with Rob, he told me he had just had a conversation with the O'odham Nation chairman, Ned Norris Jr.

"I asked Norris what was happening with the fence. He said he doesn't know a thing about the fence unless he drives down there and looks, and he hasn't had a chance to do that lately."

The government's private contractors just showed up on O'odham land one day—without notifying the tribal government, let alone getting its permission—and started clearing land and hammering new fence posts into the ground, says Rob. "That is unprecedented—not to get O'odham permission to go onto their land. The O'odham are shocked by this. Norris had no communication with Homeland Security. He couldn't get [former Homeland Security chief] Chertoff to talk to him, or communicate in any way."

Not long ago, says Rob, he got an early-morning phone call from the reserve asking him to come down; they needed his help.

"When I got close to Sells, the reservation police met me in cruisers and escorted me to the administration building, which was surrounded by cops. They were in full body armour, with rifles and shotguns. They had uncovered a safe house on the reserve, for the narco gangs, full of drugs and cash, just huge amounts of both, and they needed a judge to arraign the guys they'd arrested. None of the judges on the reserve would do it. They were afraid the gangs would come across the border and kill them. So they called me and didn't tell me what they needed me for. Because I lived some distance away, they thought I should be safe. I went ahead and did the work. But I was very reluctant to go down there again for a long while. I was afraid they might try to retaliate."

The portion of the border running through Tohono O'odham land has been a nightmare for the United States government. As the crackdowns on drugs and illegals in the border towns and cities, and, in particular, as the various walls and fences that were built there, drove illegal migration and drug running out into the desert, the reservation became, more and more, an attractive conduit for people and dope. It is a huge area (the size of Connecticut), and offers numerous trails north from the border to State Highway 86. The reservation has few people (about eleven thousand, with a further fourteen hundred or so on the Mexican side); they are very poor and are prone to disaffection with law enforcement and with official views of the sanctity of the border. They are, therefore, especially open to temptation: the huge amounts of money that smuggling illegal migrants or drugs can bring them. A simple matter of transporting a group of illegals can bring in $3,000 or $4,000 for an O'odham who might be making the reservation average of around $7,000 a year—which is well below even the American Indian average of $13,000.

"It's heartbreaking, what's happening to the O'odham," says Rob. Many of them, the young men, in particular, are getting drawn into drug running, or into bringing migrants across the line. Even some family members of the former chairwoman, Vivian Juan-Saunders, have become involved with drugs. And, says Rob, there is increasing evidence of cartel activity and of Los Angeles gangs operating on O'odham land. This view is confirmed by the tribal police chief. He counts members of twenty-six gangs on the reservation, including the Bloods and the Crips, and maybe, worst of all, MS-13.

In a typical year, authorities seize tons of drugs on O'odham land, mostly marijuana, cocaine and methamphetamine, although, as elsewhere along the border, more Mexican black tar heroin is also coming across. The illegals cause the same problems on O'odham land as they cause everywhere along the border, except that their impact is concentrated and amplified in the seventy-five-mile-long border area of the reserve. Migrants cut new trails through the fragile desert flora, compact soil, accelerate erosion and put endangered species in more danger. A few walkers wouldn't matter, but a thousand or fifteen hundred people each day wounds the earth they cross over. They leave tons of trash—four million pounds a year, by one estimate—and human waste. *Pollos*, or their coyotes, abandoned seven thousand vehicles in the reservation's desert in one recent year.

The *pollos* also leave their bodies in the desert. The O'odham police collect about sixty-five to seventy a year. It is a twenty-five-mile trek from the border at the San Miguel Gate to Sells. Migrants avoid the reservation's roads, and they walk through the rough ground of canyons and foothills, which give them cover. When the 105-degree heat begins to grind them down, there are few houses to crawl to for help, and fewer Border Patrol to whom they can surrender for the life-restoring *agua*. Even the compassionate O'odham have been driven to close their doors against such floods of people.

A few O'odham put out water barrels for the walkers, but the tribe refuses permission for the Humane Borders organization to install water tanks, as it has done elsewhere along the Arizona line. Humane Borders and the O'odham say the same thing: this problem didn't exist until the United States government built its fences, and lined the border with its agents, and drove the yearning *pollos* out into this perilous desert.

The O'odham are the people of the desert. It has always been a refuge for them, clean and uncluttered. It is a mystical place. You went out into the desert to clear your mind, or to meet spirits, or to solve a problem. Like the wilderness of the ocean for other people, the wild desert was dangerous yet nourishing. You respected it, and the animals and plants that could survive there. You knew you must learn all about it in order to survive, but you did not fear it.

Now, all that is over. The desert is contaminated.

I ask Rob: If you don't build a fence, what on earth can you do to stop this carnage? What is the solution?

"Well, the Indians can live with a situation for which there is no solution much better than we can," he says. "There is no solution to border security. The problem is addiction and drugs, but in a second sense, too: United States business is the addict; cheap labour is the drug. You have to crack down on employers."

Doing so is a huge challenge, from the smallest employer— Rob himself hires an Hispanic gardener, and he doesn't check the guy's ID to see if he's legal or not—to the largest industrial or agricultural operations, which have, indeed, become addicted to cheap labour, legal or otherwise. Everywhere in the United States, a long-standing laissez-faire attitude towards enforcement of immigration laws has been replaced by a policy of raids on workplaces. Almost six thousand illegal workers were arrested in 2008. However, arresting six thousand of the almost twelve million illegals over the course of one year is a mere gesture.

Arizona is a kind of laboratory: can a state stop, or reduce, illegal immigration on its own? The Republican-controlled legislature passed a harsh new law, the Legal Arizona Workers Act, which came into effect on January 1, 2008. The law revokes the licences of businesses caught twice with illegal migrants, unless they can show they used the government's E-Verify system to check the validity of Social Security numbers. Arizona business resisted the new impositions, and succeeded in reducing the law's coverage so that it exempted workers hired before 2008.

The Arizona legislation (and similar state laws concerning illegal-migrant employment—more than 175 of them so far) seems to have had an effect. For obvious reasons, it's a difficult trend to measure, but some undocumented workers are heading back to Mexico, although possibly as much because of the economic slowdown as the crackdown. Neighbouring Sonora has complained about the number of returned workers it must deal with. The unwelcoming legislation may, arguably, deter would-be *pollos*. There are reports that some companies have given up their plans to expand in Arizona, but will, instead, do so in other states with less draconian laws. Nevertheless— until the general economic collapse of late 2008—Arizona's economy remained robust, and Maricopa County, which includes Phoenix and three-fifths of the state's population, was the fastest-growing county in the country.

The state's legislation against immigrants may drive illegal migrants back home—or farther underground in America— but it also encourages distrust and paranoia. The nativists, and the simply prejudiced, come out and play.

The sheriff of Maricopa County, Joe Arpaio, has become known across the United States over the last few years for his vigorous (to put it nicely) campaign against illegal migrants.

Arpaio and his deputies, and volunteer posses, make sorties into Hispanic neighbourhoods searching for the slightest cause—usually minor traffic infractions—to stop people. Then they ask the detained about their immigration status. Arpaio makes no bones about it: he uses any excuse to stop and question Hispanics about their status. His aim is not safer driving, but rooting out illegals. Arpaio believes in tough enforcement: "The more who leave the better. They shouldn't be here in the first place."

The sheriff clearly enjoys his notoriety. He is the conservative poster boy for tough American law enforcement, and he has appeared often on television. He has written (with a professional co-author) a book called *Joe's Law: America's Toughest Sheriff Takes on Illegal Immigration, Drugs and Everything Else That Threatens America*—which pretty much covers it all. Just the way it used to be in the old days. The lone sheriff takes on the bad guys his own way, no matter what the lily-livered law says, and runs them out of town.

Not everyone is happy with Sheriff Joe. The FBI investigated him to find out whether he had violated civil rights laws. The mayor of Phoenix said that county deputies and their posses have long made improper stops, searches and seizures, and that they have carried out "discriminatory harassment." Civil rights organizations issued a letter that said the "saturation patrols" in Hispanic neighbourhoods created a "police-state" atmosphere, and that detentions are made "on the basis of a racial profile and dehumanization of innocent people."

"We don't profile," responded the sheriff. The mayor doesn't get the point; he is trying "to get the public against me."

In October 2009, Homeland Security forced Arpaio to sign an agreement to give up his immigration sweeps, but the sheriff promised to find other ways of catching illegals—perhaps, he suggested, through the state's anti–human-smuggling law. If that didn't work, said Arpaio, "I'll take a little trip to the border and turn them over the border."

———

Isabel Garcia is a Tucson civil rights lawyer and Pima County public defender, says Rob Williams. A while ago, she made a piñata of Arpaio for a kids' party. The kids whacked it apart, and Isabel picked up the head—Joe's head. The whole thing got onto YouTube, as these sorts of things tend to.

Then, says Rob, Isabel was threatened, and there was a huge movement started up to fire her. The piñata is just a game; it means nothing, a little fun, he says. But, to him, the incident encapsulates the whole situation. "It symbolizes the craziness down here."

CHAPTER 10

RIDING TO THE SEA

GOODBYE TO MY JUAN, GOODBYE, ROSALITA,
ADIOS MIS AMIGOS, JESUS Y MARIA.
—WOODY GUTHRIE, "PLANE WRECK AT
LOS GATOS (DEPORTEE)"

TIME IS SHORTENING. I have to get back to my family, and to work. I must ride hard and bring this first border passage to an end—it's mid-April and I have another, longer, one in the north still to do. Even when I reach the sea, I am three tough days from home—maybe four, with the rain and wind that has roughed up the west coast for the last few weeks. I'm used to heat, cold and wind, but riding in rain will be something new for me. I am apprehensive of its slick dangers, and of the high mountains farther north, where snow lingers.

I ride another long dogleg away from the border, north fifty miles to Gila Bend, and then west on the Interstate-8 to Yuma. This long way around is necessary because there are no passable roads through the space in-between. It is one of the worst places in the world: the part of the Arizona desert that includes El Camino del Diablo—the "Devil's Highway," where so many desperate illegal migrants perish.

Mountain chains lace their way through the barrens: the Growlers, the Craters, the Sierra Pintas, the Mohawks, the Cabeza Prietas, and the Tinajas Atlas range. Between them lie desolate valleys—rough ground scored with washes, gullies, arroyos, the jaggy, sawtooth rock of old lava flows, spotted with drifting sand dunes, and sprinkled with the sparse plants of the desert that survive through their ingenious parsimony and patience. The whole shebang is the sun's anvil.

The Devil's Highway was named by Melchior Díaz, one of the captains of the conquistador, Francisco Coronado. Díaz was looking for the rumoured conjunction of two big rivers to the west. (The Colorado and Gila Rivers aren't far away.) It was a practical side trip, while the main party continued its chimeric search for the seven golden cities. Like all these early Spaniards from the arid Extremadura region of their homeland, Díaz and his men were hardy. For 120 miles, there is no flowing water. The Indians had watched the bighorned mountain sheep and had learned from them where the *tinajas*—the rocky rain catchments—lay. The Spaniards survived the desert, but they suffered there, and the country they travelled through seemed hot and hellish enough to be memorialized.

The name is apt today. The Devil's Highway is an actual public road, no more than a trail, that runs close to the border on the U.S. side from near Sonoyta, just west of the Tohono O'odham reservation, to the Colorado River near Yuma. However, the name also stands for all the migrant and smuggling trails and paths going north across the desert. The country is the same as in the time of Coronado—and the heat—but the travellers across the satanic domain now are the poor, walking *pollos*.

It is the worst of combinations. On the American side, there is nothing, unless the migrants can make it thirty or forty miles to Ajo, or, even farther away, to one of the towns along the I-8, such as Wellton, Tacna or Mohawk. But on the Mexican side of the line, the migrants have easy access to the border from Highway 2, which runs close by all the way from San Luis Rio Colorado, south of Yuma, to Sonoyta. The *pollos* can get a ride to any place along the border. Then, they begin to walk.

On average, one of them dies each day on the Devil's Highway. Sometimes they die in groups—like the fourteen men who perished over one long weekend in 2001. Their bodies lay, already mummifying, when the Border Patrol found them, sometimes just too late, scattered here and there in the desert. In this region, Border Patrol agents are as much a compassionate search and rescue service as they are hard-assed enforcers. BORSTAR (Border Patrol Search, Trauma, and Rescue) teams sweep the area. Trackers cut trail, and choppers patrol. Agents leave water on well-trodden paths. They want to intercept the "tonks"—and if they have to use their flashlights or weapons on them, they will—but who cannot feel compassion for these walkers going through hell just to come to America?

Homeland Security is throwing up barriers even along this isolated stretch of the line: miles of steel slabs along the southern edge of the Goldwater Air Force Range east from San Luis; a virtual fence, composed of 80- to 200-foot-high towers, in Organ Pipe Cactus National Monument, and in Cabeza Prieta. The towers will support cameras, radar and communications gear.

An earlier version of a virtual fence along the border near Sasabe—where the Minutemen patrolled and Agent López spilled the beans—failed. The government, and Boeing, the manufacturer, promised that the new towers would work. However, they too have been plagued by weather and mechanical problems. In January 2011, Janet Napolitano cancelled the entire virtual fence project which by then had cost $1 billion.

Critics of the robot fence say that it will further threaten already endangered species, in particular, the Sonoran pronghorn antelope in Cabeza Prieta. There are fewer than three hundred of the animals remaining in the United States, as well as two small groups in Sonora. The fence's supporters say that nothing the towers do will even approach the damage to wildlife and plants caused by migrants and drug runners, by their garbage and their vehicles.

The wind has been my constant companion on this ride. If nothing else, I have learned the quick, instinctive reactions that will keep my tall bike upright and on the road in wind. I thought that the sudden, strong gust that drove me off the highway near the start of my ride on the 77, near Corpus Christi, still not quite at the border, was a beginner's fault. However, more than three weeks later, on the I-8 to Yuma, and even though I've become a seasoned and hard-assed rider, the wind almost kills me again.

As I ride between the mountains, through the Mohawk Valley, the wind is at sustained gale force, and must be gusting to forty or forty-five miles an hour from the southwest, mostly a crosswind. If a truck passes me, the slipstream eddies and circles, buffeting me from all sides. In the narrower mountain cuts, the williwaws hit so hard that the bike goes into the beginnings of a high-speed wobble, the front wheel fluttering from side to side. These wobbles occur in bikes that are going fast, creating their own strong wind. Beginning with a slight anomaly—an imbalance or vibration, increasing and pushing the front wheel to one side—the handlebars begin to oscillate from side to side, faster and faster. They may go so far as to slap the sides of the gas tank in quick succession. Long before that, I know with fearful certainty, the rider is as good as down.

I come close to this highly undesirable condition several times. I brake to fifteen or twenty miles an hour, so I'm not driven off the pavement onto the flat, stony sand, and I stay upright. I'm lucky the traffic is light. The combination of a strong gust and a passing truck would do me in. This encourages adrenaline secretion. Three weeks ago, I would have crashed already. My skill level has, undeniably, increased, but I should not be riding in these conditions. I keep going anyway. I have to make time, at least get to Yuma. And, my real rationalization: in this windy season, it may be just as bad tomorrow.

Dust devils race along beside me, and across the highway. Small, local sandstorms dot the flat desert of the Mohawk Valley. Then, several small sand squalls nearby coalesce into a big storm. The horizon, already closed in, disappears around me. Before I understand what's happening, I'm riding at fifty miles an hour inside a gritty, blinding cloud. I can't see more than ten or fifteen feet, and the bike begins to skitter on the suddenly slick surface. The wind drives the dust and sand into my eyes around my visor; it rattles off my helmet, and my jacket's armour. It's a "grey-out"—like a snow whiteout up north when a winter squall shuts down all visibility, in a few seconds, just like that. Sometimes, scores of vehicles pile into one another in a long chain of blind, rear-ended collisions.

That is exactly what I fear now. I slow down, pull off and stop where I can see the shoulder's edge. There was traffic behind me: a few cars and eighteen-wheelers, and a big RV, but I have no idea whether or not they are still coming. I ride off the shoulder over the sandy, pebbly ground, perhaps fifty yards or so into the desert. I dismount and shut down the bike. I can hear engine noise over the gale and blatting sand; something is still underway out there. I prop the bike on its side stand, square to the wind. Then, I sit down behind it on the stony ground, and wait like a Bedouin, sandblasted and sightless, for the storm to blow over. It's okay, my dear friends, only another pause in this ride to the west. We're almost there. The world will reappear, and then we'll move again.

After fifteen minutes, visibility returns, although the wind remains high. I can see a few miles. Some traffic on the I-8 kept going, but cars and tractor-trailers are parked here and there along the shoulder in both directions. They begin to move again, and so do I. However, sand squalls persist, dotted round about, and I surrender. I ride a mile down the highway to the providentially available Exit 37, where I reverse my course, hoping to find a motel in Tacna.

The Chaparral is the only one there, and the owner, a kind grandmother, is just what I need: a sanctuary from the storm and stress. She tells me I look as if I've just crossed the Sahara, that I look tired, that she'll make me a cup of coffee, and that, even though her rooms are already inexpensive at $36, she'll give me one for $25 because I look like I've been through so much.

I am the only customer, and from my clean, quiet room, I watch palm trees writhe in the wind. Road signs shiver and flap like the ones you see in on-the-spot news reports about hurricanes. The motel's neon marquee collapses in a tangled heap. The Weather Channel says that gusts at Yuma are reaching fifty-five miles an hour.

In my journal for that day, I write: "When I get home, I will methodically track down and thrash within an inch of their lives the authors of motorcycle touring books who make no mention of WIND when talking about riding the southwest in March and April."

The next day is moderately windy, although clear and cold. I'm surprised to see that I'm surrounded by mountains that were invisible yesterday. I head west, riding fast. The sea is less than two days away.

I ride the new four-lane highway through huge irrigated fields of cabbages and strawberries—the ones illegal migrants pick—to the border at San Luis. Near the fence, a Border Patrol agent stops me, and we go through the Script. In both directions along the already fenced border, I can see the new, triple-layer barrier along the line, the one that will prove to be very effective in making sure migrants head out into the deep desert in their unstoppable desire to come to America.

Yuma is one of those proverbial gateways of exploration: in this case, to California. The settlement's site was one of the very few places to get over the wide Colorado River with any ease. Melchior Díaz probably made it here, and saw the possibilities. And so the Yuma Crossing became the lynchpin of the Gila Trail over which, earlier, Anglo—and, therefore, acceptable and legal—migrants trekked west. Soldiers, surveyors, farmers, gold-hungry prospectors, sheepherders and cattlemen, all crossed the Colorado here on their way to the last promised land. So did the desperados, outlaws, gunmen and Indian fighters, whose inevitable presence gave the American frontier its dark and murderous resonance. The scalp hunter John Joel Glanton died at the Yuma Crossing, killed by Indians from whom he had stolen the Colorado River ferry. Glanton and his gang's depradations—when they ran out of Apaches to scalp for a Chihuahua state bounty, they killed peaceful Indians, and even Mexicans, to augment their take—were the inspiration for Cormac McCarthy's *Blood Meridian*. The book is the final, and unanswerable, antidote to the romantic lies of the mythology of the frontier, and of the Old West. Conquest is always bloody, and mass-murder is often its corollary.

Now, Yuma remains on a frontier: the strange, ambiguous line between the United States and Mexico, with its mixed messages of approach and avoidance. Yuma has its very own frontier wall; the triple-layer fence (the San Luis fence, to be precise) is state-of-the-art, the Cadillac version, of all of Homeland Security's new barriers. It seems doubly odd: the fence, as impregnable as a barrier can be; and spreading away from it, to the north and east, the immense fields of irrigated crops that

can be picked only by using the migrants the fence keeps out.
Yuma is the whole, confused, conflicted, schizophrenic mess of
American immigration policy laid out, plain and incontrovert-
ible, under the hot desert sun, the clear desert sky.

Back on the I-8, I ride over the Colorado River and into
California. I pass through the southern fringe of the Algodones
Dunes, where drifting sand in the windy season, one of my
constant problems, is much worse. I'm slip-sliding along. Soon,
I cut off the interstate onto Highway 98, which hugs the border.
I ride past the big crossing at Calexico-Mexicali, join the I-8
again near Ocotillo, climb over Mountain Springs pass, and
then turn onto the narrow Highway 80, which takes me to the
small town of Jacumba, right on the international boundary,
and where I spend my last night on the U.S.-Mexico line.

Illegal activities—the Border Patrol catch-all—are as active
along this stretch of the border, right to San Ysidro (the southern,
urban extension of San Diego), as they are anywhere else. The
country from east of San Ysidro, through Tecate, and east
twenty-five miles to Jacumba, and beyond it, is mountainous and
desert-like, but it's nothing compared to the Devil's Highway, or
the Altar Valley around Sasabe in Arizona. When the fancy
fence stops, the migrants and illegals take their chances with the
new, stopgap vehicle barriers and beefed-up miscellaneous steel
slabs and posts, or with the old, broken-down five-strand wire,
where that's still all there is.

From Jacumba, I ride for the sea. Descending towards
Tecate, I come out of the desert and into the dry maritime
zone of the coast. Almost right away, I scent the odours of
fragrant plants, and moist earth—it has rained a lot here
lately. I can't smell the Pacific yet, but it's only twenty-eight
miles away straight along the line.

I detour to the Tecate border crossing—the last one before
San Ysidro-Tijuana—and I have one last conversation with a

Border Patrol agent. It is somewhat one-sided. He is getting ready to ride out on an ATV, and he's all kitted out in body armour and packing an M4. I pull up beside the tall, lean Anglo.

"Hi," I say, "are you heading out on a patrol?"

That's a bit too abrupt. He looks at me as if I might be dangerous, or at least eccentric—maybe one of those uniform-and-gun nerds who get off on the whole cowboy aspect of guys humping the boonies, tracking the little chickens.

"Yeah," he says eventually, reluctantly.

"Is there a lot of illegal activity around here?" I ask (of course there is, dumb-ass).

"Yeah," he says.

"I'm sorry," I say, belatedly, "I'm a writer doing some research for a book about the border, would you mind if I asked you a few questions?"

I should have seen it coming.

"Yeah," he says, as he mounts up. He guns his machine, and without a glance my way, peels off across the road and onto the dirt trail along the slab-sided border fence. I feel cha-grined. Good going, I say to myself. You've really perfected your journalistic skills. Mostly, however, I feel tired, and I'm content enough to turn away and head west again.

Soon, I enter suburbia, and then the heavy traffic of the city freeways. It's a shock to be surrounded by affluent malls and clean, expensive cars. I feel my shabbiness, but here, among west-coasters, perhaps I seem more like an adventurous rider coming out of the desert, and less like an odd and armoured gringo biker.

I turn south on I-5 towards this border for the last time. I feel my way, without a map—it all seems intuitive—to the San Diego-Tijuana fence. It's one of the originals, a product of "Operation Gatekeeper" in the mid-1990s, although it has been continually "improved" since then. I follow it down to the entrance of Border Field State Park, counting eight Border

Patrol vehicles parked within a couple of miles of the waste-land alongside the barrier. It ain't pretty—none of it.

The park occupies the southwestern corner of the United States on the Pacific. It's where the famous, often-photo-graphed, raggedy fence trails down into the ocean and peters out in the surf. A quick swim around—or wriggle through, before it got beefed up—would get you into America.

I meet a last impediment. Not the Border Patrol this time, but a closed gate and a fence around the park entrance. A four-man construction crew is working on a new building inside. I park the bike and enter through a pedestrian gate. Unusually, the men are all Anglos, and they look at me with friendly interest as I clump up in my full riding gear on this cool, cloudy day on the coast. I tell them I've ridden the border from the Gulf of Mexico, and I want to finish it off by dipping my hand in the Pacific Ocean. I know it sounds hokey, I tell them, but I have to round off my trip by doing this.

They understand completely. Yeah, there's a way in: just go along the fence a few hundred yards; I'll find a truck entrance and a gravel road; follow that and I'll pick up the dirt trail out to the beach. Good luck, they say to me. Good riding.

With all the rain over the last few weeks, the dirt trail to the sea is muddy, slippery and dotted with deep potholed puddles. But I can see the Pacific a mile away. I skid and splash my way along until I reach the soft sand of the beach. I park the bike. There is no one in sight, although I can make out two Border Patrol SUVs parked near the fence a few hundred yards away. I want to get to the water fast, before they come down on me. I trudge the sand to the water, and, this time, damn the salt, I wade in and sluice my face and head with the cold, tart sea water.

Two hundred yards or so to the south lies the border fence with its odd, dwindling disappearance into the ocean. Now I regret my exuberant entry into the sea, as my boots squelch, and encrust with sand. The Border Patrol vehicles haven't moved. The beach is completely deserted. I look around for a few minutes and take some photographs. It is ten past one in the afternoon, and it looks like rain. I sit down and look out to sea. I say to Will and to Mike and to Chris: We made it.

My last tape recorder entry says: "So, that's it. Got a shot of the border crossing, and lots of photos of this area round here. Now I just have to retrace my steps and start heading north. That's it. Head north."

Five days later, I have a dream. I'm riding my motorcycle when I'm stopped by the police. They turn me back. "There's a bad guy out there," says one cop. I ride around a fence, and then I see many cops running towards something with their side arms drawn. I stop the bike and say to myself: "Just three more days, but I should stay here longer than that. I have a lot to do."

A phone rings, and I wake up. I lie in bed, and slowly, I realize that I'm home. There's no need to go anywhere. I can spend as much time here—in bed, and at home—as I want. I feel so relieved.

U.S.-CANADIAN BORDER

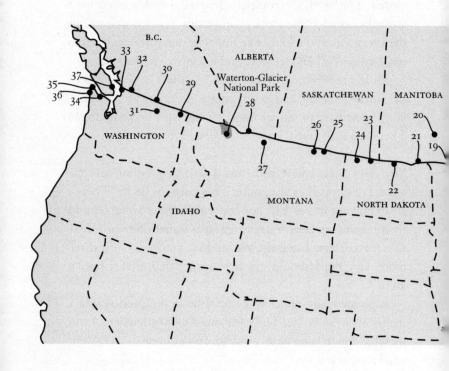

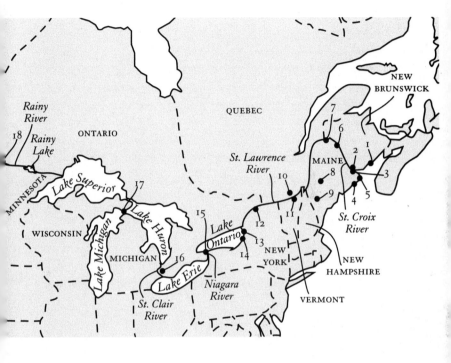

PART II

NORTH

THAT LONG FRONTIER FROM THE ATLANTIC TO THE
PACIFIC OCEANS, GUARDED ONLY BY NEIGHBOURLY
RESPECT AND HONOURABLE OBLIGATIONS, IS AN
EXAMPLE TO EVERY COUNTRY AND A PATTERN
FOR THE FUTURE OF THE WORLD.
—WINSTON CHURCHILL, CANADA CLUB, LONDON,
APRIL 20, 1939

The North: Dope there, too. Canadian potgrowers make more money from marijuana than from hewing subsidized wood to sell to the U.S. cheap. Three-hundred-yard tunnels under the border, with concrete walls, lights and air blowers. Until the northern so-called Border Patrol finds them and stuffs them with concrete, the dope flows both ways—the white powder poppy comes north; the green, fragrant weed goes south. There are no ebbs— just a two-way, continuous tide of money, despair, desperation, body- and soul-destroying devotion.

Apart from that, what the hell's up there? Moose, bear, fish, water they won't share. An army of poor white boys that might, on a good day, be able to take on the women's soccer team of the United States of America. Queers who can marry. Freeloaders who hide behind the greatest military the world has ever seen.

Now their rinky-dink money is reputedly worth as much as real money. That's because the lazy fuckers have a pile of gooey oil, and gold and copper and uranium, and trees and a big country they don't know what to do with; and they don't have to pay a dime for protection because we do all that for them, gratis.

Okay, what the hell else is up there? Some kind of parliament, provinces, not states (provincial, right), and a Queen (makes sense). At least the Canucks who speak white went to war in the two big ones; the Quebecers stayed home, warm and peachy, sucking up wine and scarfing croissants while white men died for them and their freedoms.

Snow, of course: cold, Eskimos, ice, hockey—the good-old honky game. The North Pole is in Canada, which figures, although it's drifting away from them; they're losing it. They want to keep the Northwest Passage for themselves—with what? A few hundred Eskimo "rangers" with World War I rifles, a couple of old icebreakers? Now we hear they're planning to build a few gunboats. It's typical: they want something very big, and they claim it, but they're not willing to put out to take it and hold it.

The worst thing of all: Muslims live in Canada. Mexico may be a corrupt shithole, but at least it isn't crawling with the sons of Allah. The goddamn 9/11 hijackers came through Canada. The border is a sieve. It's worse than that; it strains out fuck all. The next terrorist to come from Canada is a short paddle across a river away, or a nice stroll through the woods away, or a pleasant drive down a dirt road away. The guy with a pile of explosives in his trunk who wanted to blow up the L.A. airport took a ferry. Just dumb luck he was a stupid mother. If he'd had half a brain, he could have rolled into the United States somewhere along the five thousand–mile-long undefended, un-fuck-all border and blown up anything he wanted, courtesy of Canadian security. If there's a next time, it'll be goodbye to the true north strong and free.

CHAPTER 11

A PORTAL FOR TERROR

BEFORE I BUILT A WALL I'D ASK TO KNOW
WHAT I WAS WALLING IN OR WALLING OUT,
AND TO WHOM I WAS LIKE TO GIVE OFFENCE.
—ROBERT FROST, "MENDING WALL"

LIKE ALL DIRT ROADS, this one starts out all right, and then it goes to hell on me. At first, it's rutted and gravelly, but firm, and the bike is comfortable at twenty-five or thirty miles an hour. The front wheel skips and skids once in a while, but I'm a veteran of unpaved roads. I slide my weight forward, mashing my body against the gas tank. In the worst places, I try to rise up and stand with my full weight on the footpegs, to allow the heavy-laden bike to move around under me, as my body hews a straight line through air. But I ripped up my right ankle a while ago and it still can't take the pressure. I flop back down again. I resist the instinct to go slow, and, instead, keep up my speed, trying again for the traction that comes with velocity.

Then I hit the Renville-Burke county line and things fall apart. Sensible Renville ignores its outlying border roads. But Burke is diligent in its road maintenance—and profligate with its gravel. Three or four fresh inches of the stuff are piled on the road, verge to verge. It's groomed smooth with slight ruts, and has the consistency of soft snow or sand. For this northern ride, I have, once again, fitted hard-inflated road tires onto my dual-purpose brute. As always, it is very unhappy on mushy surfaces, and I jerk and skid. The gravel is too heavy to plough through at speed. As I've done so often on these border rides, I slow—avoiding the brakes—make a wobbly stop, and put my feet down. The pain in my ankle makes me sweat as I contemplate this fresh hell.

I was warned. A quarter of an hour earlier, a few miles west of Sherwood, about two miles south of the border, I stopped at a three-way intersection at the end of the paved road to piss, drink water and eat a granola bar. A pickup truck hauling a horse trailer pulled up before turning up to the north towards the only buildings I could see. The driver wore a stetson. Like everyone on this prairie, he was friendly and open. Beside him, a pretty blond woman smiled at me. Both had bright blue eyes.

"Hey," the man said, "you out here to take the gravel?"

I laughed. He asked me where I was from. He had heard of British Columbia.

"Farther west, right?"

"Right," I said.

We talked about the weather. It always came up out here. Farmers and ranchers are like sailors: weather rules their lives. We agreed it would rain later. To the west, I could see the thunderheads beginning to build their mushroom spirals.

"How's the road out ahead?" I asked.

"It's okay. It's a bit bumpy here, but it gets a lot better when you cross the county line. They just put down new gravel."

I should have known.

I start out again, in first gear, searching out the flattened ruts. Right away, I feel the familiar tight muscle pain in my neck and shoulders. I say to Will, and to Mike and Chris: You're missing sweet fuck all today, my friends. This ain't no fun at all; in fact, it's the usual. No choice; it's too far to go back, and, in any case, I want to keep to this road. A little farther on, according to the map, it turns up towards the border and seems to straddle it. As always, I'm trying to get as close as I can to the iconic latitude—the 49th parallel—to try to find the slight, incongruous imprint of its line upon the land.

I'm on the high plateau of North Dakota, just south of the Saskatchewan border, about two-thirds of the way through my northern ride from the Atlantic to the Pacific oceans. The fields, some ploughed, or in new crop, some open range, run out to the far, hazy horizon of land and sky. A building intrudes here and there, farm houses or small silos. It's sunny today, with a light wind. I've been wet more often than not the last three weeks, often very wet—and very cold. I savour the rare dry warmth.

In a while, as the map predicts, the road swings right towards Canada. A few hundred yards farther, it turns west again, and now, I must be very close to the border. I can't look around while I pick my way over and through these tiresome stones. I stop every couple of minutes, ankle throbbing, and look north, searching for signs of the parliamentary constitutional monarchy, distinct from this federal republic.

I come to a gravelly, muddy track going north, and take it. I ride about fifty yards, and stop. Off to my right, and slightly behind me, I glimpse a small stone marker. I've crossed the border; I'm in Canada. I prop the bike on its side stand, dismount and limp back down the track until I'm about level with the marker. This is the border. I can see two buildings far away, and some clumps of trees scattered about, but not a single human being.

I hop from one country to the other, back and forth, laughing and yahooing, but my ankle puts a quick stop to that. North and south, the land looks the same. The border is invisible.

The idea of a border here seems superfluous, ludicrous. I stand in the mild, high-prairie air and bright sun. I don't know which country I'm in.

My sense of the border's incongruity as I straddle the dirt-track line between North Dakota and Saskatchewan has been the same all along the United States' northern perimeter. The border has real manifestations, of course: an untidy clear-cut through woods; the glimpse of a stone pylon; and rivers and lakes—although the country looks the same on both sides of them. More often than not, however, the border feels like an abstraction. I know it's there, but I have trouble believing in it.

With its scant physical presence, it is easy to view America's border with Canada as an example of the new kind of boundary that exists between like-minded nation-states in a globalized world. More like the borders between countries in the European Union: you drive from France into Germany almost as if from Oregon into Idaho, or from Alberta into Saskatchewan. One scholar describes the contemporary border as a "zone of overlapping territoriality." Its adjoining states have mutual interests and necessities—trade, clean air, security—and they have no alternative but to find joint solutions to their common problems. Marshall McLuhan, in his typical style—once considered elliptic, now merely descriptive—long ago defined a border as "a field of negotiated relationships rather than as a line of authoritarian demarcation." A border and its environs, whether or not they constitute borderlands, both create and eliminate differences. They are dualistic, ambiguous places. McLuhan again: a border is an "interval of resonance."

Such a border is still a barrier. Wallace Stegner wrote about his childhood along the western, high-plains frontier: "The 49th parallel ran directly through my childhood, dividing me in two." It was, nevertheless, a permeable, equivocal line: "our lives slopped over the international boundary every summer day."

Where the paved roads breach the line between Canada and the United States, the border checkpoints—with their wooden barriers, concrete pylons, cameras and little kiosks containing bored uniformed people—create a real boundary. But the roads are a few score of skinny corridors that pop up here and there in minuscule incongruity. If you clumped them all together, they would be no more than, maybe, a kilometre wide in all, scattered across nine thousand kilometres of undifferentiated forest, river, lake, prairie and mountain. The continent has its own massive, unarguable logic. Its huge north-south landforms ridicule the feeble, human east-west conceit of the border. It's always been that way: "The meat of the buffalo tastes the same on both sides," said Sitting Bull.

Even the populations on either side of the line or the other seem, at first glance, to be more or less identical people, unaccountably divided into two countries. There are the obvious signs of apparent similarity: Canadians and Americans speak the same language with much the same accent (leaving aside the French of Quebec and the growing Hispanic nation within the United States); they have similar legal systems and forms of federal representative government; they took over their present territories by means of incessant westward movement, and, although the methods of displacement differed a great deal between the two countries, the result was the wholesale displacement of the original, aboriginal inhabitants; Canada and the United States are each one of the other's biggest trading partners (and their bilateral trade volume is, for now, the largest in the world); both peoples were originally blends of British and European immigrants, increasingly mixed with immigrants from everywhere else (although, in the case of the United States, with African-Americans); they share a similar culture. If you disagree, consider this: Canadians are simply the natural, and most seamless, adopters of the universal mass culture of America. When they travel outside North America,

Canadians typically try not to be taken for Americans, and Americans may pose as temporary Canadians. But in Europe and Asia, they are indistinguishable; in Latin America, they're all gringos.

Most Americans agree: if Canada comes to mind at all, it is as a vague continuation of the United States—the cold, empty space to the north, which has remained, unaccountably, separate and independent. Canada is safe but dull, beautiful, placid in a bovine way. It has trees, wheat, water, metals and minerals, and now—lucky lottery winners—oil. It is, as Edmund Wilson thought of it when he was growing up nearby, a "gigantic wildlife reserve situated conveniently next door." If any country can be taken for granted, safely ignored, patted on the head, invested in with comfort, visited from time to time to unwind, it's Canada.

As long as Americans saw Canada in this way, the border didn't matter much. It seemed to be a mere and arbitrary formality. Americans would seldom have agreed with anything Friedrich Engels—the co-author, with Karl Marx, of *The Communist Manifesto*—had to say. But they would not have argued with his view of "this ridiculous boundary line" separating the United States from Canada. He thought it would disappear in time. The border became more like a county line delineating a kind of local sovereignty, or a porous and amicable division between close neighbours.

In fact, "neighbourliness" has been a much-used trope in North American political rhetoric—Churchill's "long frontier . . . guarded only by neighbourly respect," for example. Or Franklin Roosevelt in 1935: "Between Canada and the United States exists a neighborliness, a genuine friendship, which over a century has dispelled every parting rift." Or Lyndon Johnson in 1964: "Canada is such a close neighbor and such a good neighbor . . . Our problems are kind of like problems in a home town." Johnson despised the Canadian prime minister of the time, the scholarly Nobel Peace Prize winner, Lester Pearson, and he was irritated by Canada's reluctance to support American escalation in Vietnam (as he would have been by Canadian unwillingness to join the "coalition of the willing" invading Iraq in 2003). Nevertheless, Johnson could not avoid the clichés of Canadian-American relations.

In the past, many Canadians themselves have been receptive to this vision of cultural and political neighbourliness, although with provisos and reservations. Canada's adolescent dependence on Great Britain—its constitutional mother country, and the centre of the greatest empire since Rome's—was inevitably transferred to the United States. As Britain declined, its geopolitical reach shrank, and America became the world's dominant power.

In the course of the twentieth century, Canadians established their right to declare war independent of Britain, to sign their own treaties and to conduct their own foreign policy. In 1982 came the final and long-delayed step towards independence. The Constitution Act of that year allowed Canada to amend its own constitution without asking the British Parliament's approval.

At the same time, Canada was faced with the overwhelming propinquity of the United States; it was just next door—for almost nine thousand kilometres. It had ten times as many people; it was loud, aggressive, explosive, seductive, impossible to ignore—or to resist. Canadians were ambivalent: fascinated, envious, admiring, smugly contemptuous, childishly awed, half in love with America's relentless energy, but afraid of its power to absorb and assimilate. If Americans and Canadians were neighbours, the neighbourhood was, for Canadians, both alluring and uneasy.

Lately, however, Americans, too, have been having unusual intimations of trouble along the line to their north: a worry about more drugs coming across than usual—not just knockout marijuana, but industrial killers like methampheta-mine; a feeling that North American free trade works in Canada's favour more than it should; a suspicion of slack secu-rity and an untoward toleration of terrorist fundraisers and cover organizations; a fear of Muslim terrorists—the belief by many that the 9/11 murderers came from Canada; a certain Canadian dragging of the feet when it comes to fighting them "over there."

More and more, it seems as if this northern border is as good as its name: it divides and separates. To Americans, it's feeling more and more like the border with Mexico: a line to be watched, patrolled, perhaps fortified, walled and fenced. The cliché of an undefended border from the Bay of Fundy to the Strait of Juan de Fuca—true only intermittently in the past, in any case—must be jettisoned. Fear rules along the northern border now as well as along the southern. America is in jeopardy from all sides, and it must draw in upon itself. It must become a fortress.

There's a spectrum of concern among Americans about the border with Canada. Some are merely apprehensive about security and may advocate nothing more than getting the two countries to work together to create a North America–wide security zone. This view recognizes the facts on the ground: you just can't fence, or guard, or even monitor in any compre-hensive way, a border running the width of the continent.

At the other end of the spectrum, however, the idea of Fortress America prevails. What must be done along the southern border should be duplicated along the northern. Build fences and walls, flood the borderlands with armed men, cameras and motion detectors, patrol the Great Lakes and the river boundaries—the St. Lawrence, the St. Clair, the Niagara, the St. Croix—as if they separated sworn enemies. In February 2009, the first of five U.S. drones, called Predators, otherwise known as unmanned aerial vehicles (UAVs), was deployed along the border where Canada and North Dakota meet. These planes are flown by pilots on the ground via remote control. It almost sounds like fun. And, in fact, the suggestion of strong security measures seems to embody fantasy as well as paranoia.

We can round up the usual suspects. Colorado congressman Tom Tancredo: Terrorists have been bringing explosives into the United States from Canada, as well as from Mexico, for years. The bad guys will soon detonate the stuff simultaneously all around the country. The solution for the Canadian border is the same as for the Mexican: a "high-tech, two-layer" fence backed by many more Border Patrol agents, and by the army, which means amending the Posse Comitatus Act (it prohibits American soldiers from acting like police within the United States). Tancredo claims the fence shouldn't cost more than $1.5 million a mile (but, so far, the southern fence has cost an average of $3.9 million a mile). According to his math, a total of $3 billion would be spent in the south, and $7.5 billion in the north, and that's not counting upkeep and the necessary military backup. (A September 2009 report by the U.S. Government Accountability Office said it would cost $6.5 billion over twenty years to maintain the southern fence.) This is a good investment, says Tancredo, since the U.S. is spending more than $3 billion in Iraq every month. (Yet again, in fact, as of March 2009, it was spending between $8 and $12 billion a month, depending on the estimate.)

Commentator and politician Patrick J. Buchanan points to the arrest in Canada of eighteen young Muslims—almost all were Canadian citizens, and many were born in the country—for allegedly plotting to storm the Parliament buildings in Ottawa, take hostages, behead the prime minister and other politicians, and demand the release of Taliban prisoners in Afghanistan. (Eleven of the arrested men have been convicted and seven have had the charges against them dropped. The guilty include the group's ringleader who, in January 2010, was sentenced to life in prison, although he will be eligible for parole in six years.) These men became putative mass murderers, Buchanan says, because of Canada's policy of multiculturalism and its abandonment, in the 1960s, of its European-centred immigration policy. The threat these sorts of homegrown terrorists pose for the United States is obvious, he says. His solution, not surprisingly, is the same sort of heavily fortified and patrolled fence along the northern border as the one he advocates in the south to keep out Hispanics, and especially Mexicans.

Former Arizona congressman J. D. Hayworth asserts that Canada is a "refuge for terrorists." He cites the case of Ahmed Ressam, the "Millennium Bomber," and those of two other purported Islamist terrorists whom the weak-kneed Canadian government and police failed to arrest. Hayworth says that Canadian police knew about Ressam's plan, yet "did nothing to stop [him]." (The truth is they had simply lost him.) Canada is a "safe haven" for terrorists, he says, and more than fifty terrorist organizations have some sort of presence in the country. Unlike his alarmed colleagues, Hayworth at least uses a Canadian source for his views. He quotes, very briefly, from *Cold Terror: How Canada Nurtures and Exports Terrorism to the World* by the Canadian investigative reporter Stewart Bell. Bell's book contains one-sided, alarmist rants against Canadian politicians who refuse to act against terrorist organizations and fronts in Canada. Like Hayworth, Bell is on the side of gonzo law enforcement and has no time for elected politicians.

In *Illegals: The Imminent Threat Posed by Our Unsecured U.S.-Mexico Border*, author Jon E. Dougherty includes a chapter on Canada: "Way Up North." He describes the big drug busts and the illegal immigrant trafficking, mostly of Chinese "snakeheads" (a minuscule number compared with the illegals crossing the Mexican border), going on "up north." And he notes the vulnerable vastness of the Canadian border, and how simple it would be for a terrorist to land on some quiet Great Lakes beach or cross over on an isolated prairie gravel road. He believes the southern border is the immediate problem, and he advocates the usual extreme measures to deal with it. But he joins the ripening consensus about the northern line. Few Americans know much about it, or about the country north of it; the Canadian border is "up there" somewhere. Yet its unknown remoteness is more and more alarming.

A striking event for Canadians took place in April 2009. In an interview in Washington with a reporter for the Canadian Broadcasting Corporation, Janet Napolitano, the then-newly appointed head of the Department of Homeland Security, clearly implied she believed that all, or some, of the 9/11 hijackers had entered the United States from Canada. (Not so; all had entered the United States from overseas on legal visas.)

"To the extent that terrorists have come into our country or suspected or known terrorists have entered our country across a border, it's been across the Canadian border," she said.

The Canadian interviewer, Neil Macdonald, asked: "Are you talking about the 9/11 perpetrators?"

"Not just those, but others as well," Napolitano replied.

Macdonald gave her another chance. He mentioned the prominent American politicians, including Hillary Clinton when she was a senator, who had accused Canada of harbouring the 9/11 terrorists and of allowing them to enter the United States. Why is this misconception so common in the U.S.? he asked.

Napolitano ignored the opportunity to retract or to amend her statement.

"I'm not privileged to say everything that has occurred. I mean some things have occurred in the past. I can't talk to that. I can talk about the future."

She mentioned more terrorists and implied that other, unnamed, bad guys had tried to attack the United States from Canada, but that her department had headed them off—no thanks to the Canadians, as usual. It was the worst sort of accusation: her suggestion that Canada had put the United States in mortal danger; her refusal, in the name of national-security secrecy, to divulge details. How does one refute such vague, yet devastating, innuendo? Napolitano's office later "explained" her statements by denying she had meant what she said.

It wasn't just the big 9/11 lie that rankled; it was also the lack of any awareness of Canadian sensitivity about it. Napolitano wasn't only saying that Canada was guilty of lax security; she was also speaking as though the country had no substance for her, no reality as a separate, and physically huge, North American presence.

The 9/11 slander is a lie that will not die. Canadian ambassadors in Washington have spent a substantial amount of their time since September 2001 trying to set straight the belief held by the majority of Americans that Canada was somehow complicit in the deaths of more than three thousand innocent civilians, a majority that includes members of Congress and state governors. After Napolitano's interview, the failed presidential candidate, John McCain, stated his view that she was correct, that the 9/11 hijackers had come through Canada. Consider the potential effects on U.S.-Canadian relations of a president who believes that lie. The Canadian cabinet might as well include a Minister for Setting the Damn Record Straight on 9/11; it would be an active portfolio.

In her interview with Macdonald (and subsequently), Napolitano also stated the following proposition: Whatever the

United States does to secure its boundary with Mexico it will also do, sooner or later, along its border with Canada. "The law says the borders are the borders," she said. "[It] does not differentiate between the Mexican border and the Canadian border."

About halfway through my northern border ride, I pull off State Highway 11 between International Falls and Baudette, Minnesota, onto a boat-access road. Half a mile in from the main road, there's a small parking lot overlooking the Rainy River, which runs for about eighty-five miles through the isolated country between Rainy Lake and Lake of the Woods. For this distance, the river is the border.

It's cold but not raining, with a brisk wind and scattered scudding cloud. "Not raining" has long ago become my definition of good weather. I prop the bike up in the parking lot. There are no other vehicles on this early June day. When I turn off the engine, the silence hums in my ears for a while, soon to be replaced by birdsong, and the sigh of wind flowing through pine and spruce. I feel the sun warm my head and shoulders as I limp around taking off my riding gear. I turn the key to restart the engine—to test it. There's a slight click, but nothing more; my reliable thumper is dead. Again.

Yesterday, for the first time, it failed me, refusing to start after I had filled up in a gas station in International Falls. It was a shock. KLRs were supposed to be bulletproof, for the first twenty thousand miles or so, anyway.

It had already been a long day by then—I'd ridden through heavy rain, light rain, mist, thick fog and strong crosswind—and the pain in my ankle had overpowered the painkillers. I suspected a burnt out fuse. I pushed the bike away from the pumps, pulled off the bags, slid out my tool roll, and stripped off the side panels and saddle to expose the fuse case. The fuses were exceedingly whole and unblemished. I put things back together. The gas station was opposite the Northern Lights

Motel. I pushed the bike across the street, and made three more trips for my various bags. My ankle got much worse.

The motel owner was a lean, long-haired guy in his thirties—instead of the usual portly middle-aged grump. His name was Harry, and he rode a bike himself (a Harley), and his dad knew the go-to bike guy in town. While I waited, Harry called his father, and then he left a message for the bike guy. Twenty minutes later, I was lounging on the bed in my room with a wad of ice on my ankle, deciphering the trouble-shooting section of my shop manual when a huge diesel pickup arrived outside. The bike guy was bearish with big, scarred hands and dirty fingernails; he wore a lumberjack jacket, a beard and a Stihl Chainsaw cap. He took off the side panel, tightened the loose connector back into the starter relay, pressed the ignition, and the bike started. It took him three minutes. He was polite, but he looked at me as if he was thinking: What the fuck are you doing out here riding across the goddamn country if you can't find a simple loose connection? I gave him twenty bucks.

Today at the State Park beside the Rainy River, however, it's not the starter relay—male and female parts are still firmly entwined. As I work, the mosquitoes arrive. They are small but efficient. I haul out my smelly, deep-woods, DEET-laced repellent and spray the sticky stuff over my head, neck and hands. I've had a muscle-contraction headache since I woke up this morning, and now it's much worse. I take another Tylenol 3—lots of codeine. I think, Fuck this bike; I've had it. But then I think I might as well do my job, since I may be here a while.

Camera in hand, I shuffle down a stony path to the river. I take some photographs of the river border, and I record my impressions of the tranquil scene, and of my goddamn bike. I'm beside a narrows with gentle rapids calming down to a shallow, smooth stream as the river widens just below me. Both banks are thick-wooded. I take off my right boot and submerge my swollen, bright-shining, blue-black foot and ankle in the cold flowing water.

After a few minutes, two men appear on the other bank— the Canadian side. They're carrying backpacks and toting a rubber boat. They launch the boat, climb in and paddle across to my shore—the American side—landing about a hundred yards downstream from me. They look around but don't appear to see me. They shoulder their packs, haul the boat out of the water and lug it into the woods. A few minutes later, I hear a vehicle start up nearby, and then pull away. The sound of bird-song, wind and running water returns. I don't know what I've seen: smugglers, cops, terrorists, good guys, bad guys?

Back at the bike, I dismantle things to get at the fuses again. They look fine, but I jiggle the attaching wires. The ignition light comes on and the fickle engine starts. The connections seem tight. I shut off to reload my bags; the light stays steady, and I get underway again. But now—the worst thing for a long rider—I don't trust my machine.

When I get to Baudette, I stop at a convenience store to buy a coffee. There's a Border Patrol Jeep parked outside. It's a big coincidence; I hardly ever see them on this northern line—so different from the southern border. The officer is at the register buying a Snickers bar. I go up to him, excuse myself, and tell him what I just saw on the river down the road. He looks at me, standing dishevelled in stained and muddy riding pants and armoured jacket, with wary mistrust.

"What were you doing there?"

"Me?" I say. "I was just looking at the river. And my bike broke down. I had to fix it." My head is sore; my ankle hurts; I'm sticky with bug spray. This guy is suspicious of *me*. He's my height, sandy-haired, buzz cut, stocky turning to fat, wide pale face, pale blue eyes, spreading ass loaded down with the tools of his trade.

"There's nothing along the river," he says. It's an accusation.

I'm not sure what he means. "I know," I say. "I just needed to stop for a while and it seemed like a good spot." I try again. "Do you want to follow up with these guys in the boat?"

As we talk, we go outside. The cop looks at my dirty, laden bike the same way he's looking at me. "Where are you from?" he asks.

"Me?" I say again. Apparently it's all about me. I deeply regret deciding to talk to this asshole. So much for reporting suspicious activity to the appropriate authorities along the Canadian border. Unlike in the south, at least this guy isn't pointing a weapon at me.

"I'm from British Columbia, Canada. I'm riding west, home."

He looks at the bike again, and then back at me.

"Okay," he says, and climbs into his Jeep. He pulls away, heading in the opposite direction from the boat-access road I've described. I can see him through his window taking a bite out of his Snickers bar.

The politicians and writers Tancredo, Hayworth, Buchanan and Dougherty represent the extreme of American opinion on the borders. Their diagnoses of the problem are simplistic; their solutions are unworkable, and they run against the grain of the United States' benevolent founding ideas. These men are examples of the closed, fearful, angry, violent men of America. They also describe, for Canadians, the reverse of historical reality: that men with violent agendas have always crossed the border from south to north; that cross-border terrorism has always been a Canadian, not an American, problem. The invasion of British North America during the War of 1812, the Fenian raids, the pinprick incursions in-between—not to mention the frequent threat of armed action across the border into Canada—these were part of Canada's American problem, rather than the other way around.

Nevertheless, Tancredo and the others have a point.

No one can deny the possibility of terrorist attack across a border over which guys with packs and a rubber boat, or an errant motorcyclist, can paddle, ride, or hop, back and forth without notice or consequences. I could have lugged a Kawasaki-load of explosives or dirty bomb components into the United States with ease. The Canadian border offers lush opportunities for asymmetrical warfare. Even the most reasonable observer has to admit that it could happen. If none of the 9/11 hijackers did, in fact, enter the United States from Canada, there is the notable precedent of Ahmed Ressam with the trunk full of (conventional) explosives and on his way to the Los Angeles airport when he was easily caught by an observant U.S. border guard. He tried to cross on a ferry from British Columbia to Washington State known for its close scrutiny of passengers. He could have breezed over in a thousand remote or unmonitored places to the east. I could point out a few dozen of them myself.

The cranky journalist Stewart Bell quotes the Canadian Senate Subcommittee on Security and Intelligence, which warned in its 1999 report that "most of the major international terrorist organizations have a presence in Canada," which is "a venue of opportunity" for them. In 2003, the Senate's Standing Committee on National Security and Defence wrote: "Never has a combined physical and economic threat to the Canadian homeland been more palpable."

Canada has more active international terrorist groups operating within its borders than any other country in the world—with the exception, ironically, of the United States itself—according to Ward Elcock, a former director of the Canadian Security Intelligence Service (CSIS). These groups are sometimes organized and disciplined cells, writes Bell, and sometimes, just BOGs (intelligence slang for a "bunch of guys"). There is certainly a slew of them: Hezbollah, Sikhs,

Tamil Tigers, Basque ETA, Hamas (no more Irish Republican Army now that the Northern Irish war is over) and, of course, al Qaeda.

The groups other than al Qaeda mostly raise money to kill the other side back home. Although that could change; one can imagine Lebanese Hezbollah, for example, carrying out attacks in North America in retaliation, say, for U.S. support of Israeli actions. And there is one big exception: the worst recent terrorist atrocity in the West prior to 9/11 happened in 1985 when Sikh extremists from British Columbia brought down an Air India flight off the coast of Ireland. It was flying from Montreal to London, and most of the 329 passengers were Canadian citizens, although of South Asian origin—an explanation, perhaps, for why then–prime minister of Canada Brian Mulroney called then–prime minister of India Rajiv Gandhi to commiserate, and for the fact that no government officials contacted grieving family members.

Al Qaeda, of course, is different from other terrorist organizations—not really an organization at all, but rather, a pan-national, multi-ethnic, geographically dispersed, loosely structured collection of groups of Islamist fundamentalists who are informally connected with each other, or who have taken al Qaeda as the name for their local organization ("Al Qaeda in Iraq"), or who are inspired by it—such as the homegrown BOGs of the London bombings, and, allegedly, the Canadian plotters. Thus, al Qaeda, and its offshoots, are supple and slippery, charismatically inspired by Osama bin Laden—the contemporary Pimpernel—and united in adherence to a simplistic, aberrant and brutal version of Islam. The most certain thing about al Qaeda, and its acolytes, is that they will attack again. So far, Canada is the only country on bin Laden's publicly aired hit list—for what that's worth—that has not yet been struck.

The difficulty lies in distinguishing real plotters from the mere victims of stupid, prejudiced, or even malicious, police or intelligence work. The problem is worse if the people you suspect are all members of one ethnic group, or of the same religion. All democracies face the same conundrum when threatened, or when they think they're threatened, by enemies inside: how to find the few bombers and killers while doing no harm to the mass of the innocent? How to maintain the ancient and hard-won rights and freedoms—due process, the presumption of innocence, the right to counsel, habeas corpus—while allowing police to head off the bomb in the bus or subway, the hijacked airplane?

Britain struggled for decades with how to deal with Irish Republican Army attacks in England—searching for the few dozen guerrillas embedded within the mass of Irish living there. There were terrible and gross miscarriages of justice: innocent men and women were tortured and spent years in jail before being cleared and released. Now, the British government and police face the same situation with Islamist thugs. As do all Western democracies.

Canada has no equivalent to the Guantánamo Bay detention camp, which held hundreds of "enemy combatants" without charge or trial. But a few Canadian residents have been held in prison under security certificates. These extraordinary legal devices authorize the government to detain and deport a foreign national or non-citizen living in Canada whom it suspects of violating human or international rights, or of membership in organized crime, or of being a threat to national security. In February 2007, the Supreme Court of Canada declared security certificates unconstitutional but gave the government a year to write a new law. The government responded with a new, watered-down mechanism that allows detainees limited legal representation and rights of appeal, and is modelled on similar British legislation (introduced after Britain's version of Guantánamo Bay had been ruled, by the House of Lords, as contrary to human rights).

The problem is: although the police often do get things right, they get them wrong often enough (in normal criminal proceedings, too) that it's difficult to trust what they say, or to accept without question their claims to have detained genuine al Qaeda terrorists.

In 2006, the eighteen Muslim men and teenagers, aged sixteen to forty-three, referred to by Patrick Buchanan, were arrested in Toronto by the integrated national security enforcement team made up of Mounties, CSIS agents, and Ontario Provincial Police on suspicion of planning terrorist attacks. However, Americans were not necessarily grateful for Canada's due diligence, nor for the fact that the "Toronto 18" were planning attacks only in Canada and not in the United States. True, then-secretary of state Condoleezza Rice made the pro forma public statement: the White House is satisfied that Canadian authorities have demonstrated that they are being duly vigilant against terrorism. Many Americans, however, were more prone to wonder what the hell these Islamist radicals were doing in Canada in the first place. Their arrest drew attention to their presence there, and the familiar distrust and fear bubbled up.

Congressman Peter King of New York, a ranking member of the Homeland Security Committee, and on record as claiming that some of the 9/11 attackers entered the United States from Canada, said: "There's a large al Qaeda presence in Canada . . . because of their very liberal immigration laws, because of how political asylum is granted so easily." Representative John Hostettler of Indiana (since defeated in the 2006 mid-term elections), chairman of the Judiciary Committee Subcommittee on Immigration, Border Security, and Claims, said: "South Toronto, like those parts of London that are host to the radical imams who influenced the 9/11 terrorists and the shoe bomber, has people who adhere to a militant understanding of Islam." Asked where "South Toronto" is, Hostettler replied, tautologically: "a location which I understand is the type of enclave that allows for this radical type of discussion to go on." In fact, there is no such area of Toronto.

King and Hostettler are, admittedly, closer to the edge than to the centre of opinion in the United States. Nevertheless, King's 9/11 prejudice is shared, in polls, by more than half of the American public.

On CNN, on June 6, 2006, three days after the Toronto arrests, two "security experts" appearing on *Anderson Cooper 360* agreed that Mexico was an economic threat to the United States, but that Canada was a terrorist threat. "Canada has always been a problem with extremists," said one guest. He cited the case of Ahmed Ressam. It seemed that, for many Americans, as one immigration commentator put it three years earlier, "the longest undefended border in the world now looks like a four thousand–mile-long portal for terrorists."

The border with the United States has always been of the utmost importance to Canadians. It is essential to our identity as "not-American." It has separated us, with tenuous success, from the political, military and cultural juggernaut next door. The 49th parallel is a symbol of all the complex, and contradictory, feelings that Canadians hold about the United States: fear, fascination, superiority, inferiority, admiration, contempt. Some of these emotions are the common response of any small nation-state to the imperial world power of the day. But for Canadians—close-by, both threatened and protected—America is an obsession.

There is no intellectual symmetry between the two countries' awareness of each other. Canadians (like Mexicans) have no alternative but to know a great deal about the United States. Americans could afford to know next to nothing about Canada—at least until now. One Canadian historian aphorized: "Americans are benignly ignorant of Canada. Canadians are malevolently well informed about the United States."

Now that imbalance is beginning to change. American administrations and politicians, consumed with security, are slowly giving up their indulgent indifference to Canada. If Canadians have always complained about American ignorance of their country, they may already regret the new closer attention being paid them.

The border divides the two biggest trading partners in the world, and the trading relationship demands the fast, easy flow of goods and services in both directions. Since the terrorist attacks of September 11, 2001, however, the United States has slowly and steadily choked the flux of trade both ways. The border is "thickening." Things are slowing down; "just-in-time" parts shipments are in jeopardy; trucks must wait for inspection and clearance; people must be questioned.

The border can't be both things: a goods-and-services conduit and a security perimeter. One form must trump the other, and there's little doubt that security will win out. The United States Department of Homeland Security will see to it. This will be the case in the near future, even if no terrorist attack on the United States originates in Canada. The idea of an open, and undefended, border will become a wistful memory.

Americans should pay more attention to their northern border. They need to know a great deal more about the neighbouring country in which at least eight hundred thousand Muslims live, their numbers growing fast. Security against a terrorist attack from Canada cannot be assured by sealing the border, or even by fortifying it with fences, virtual or otherwise, and with many armed guards. The border is just too long; it runs through country too wild and remote. It's impossible to secure the many river and Great Lakes boundaries. The potential strangulation of trade—or, at best, its reduction—would hurt all Canadians; it would also cause serious problems for Americans. The only way to get reasonable security against attack, while maintaining as open a border as possible, is through co-operation and agreement. The more sure Americans are about what Canadians are doing to interdict terrorists, the less reason they'll have to choke off the border.

So far, this doesn't seem to be where the zealots of Homeland Security are headed. And even the relatively moderate Napolitano, as one of her first acts as the new department head, ordered a review of northern border security.

The movement of illegal, or dangerous, human beings across the U.S.-Canadian border may soon go both ways. So far, the problem of illegal immigrants—*indocumentados*—has been an American problem, and it has involved only the southern border. Ten thousand illegals enter the United States from Canada each year, mostly from Asia, and only a handful enter Canada from the south. But this is likely a temporary condition, and Canadians should get ready for a new wave.

All borders are under pressure. Gary Williams in El Paso pointed out that what is happening around his city, and generally along the southern border, is part of a worldwide pattern. The poor want in—to Europe, to Australia, to North America. And there's a growing hierarchy of desirable borders in the developing world, too. Mexico, for example, has its own problem: economic refugees from Central (and, sometimes, South) America, crossing over its southern border. Some stay in Mexico; most are trying to get to the United States. In either case, they cause economic and social problems in Mexico.

The four-lane highway from Guaymas to Nogales, through Sonora, parallels the railroad line for part of the distance. Driving along it a few months ago, I passed several freight trains heading north. Men were sprinkled along the boxcar roofs, or peered out from their open doors. Some of them waved at me as I overtook them. A few miles on, there was a stopped train with a few dozen riders. I pulled off the highway, parked my vehicle, and walked over to the line. I asked one group of nine or ten men where they were from. Guatemala and Salvador, they said. The remainder were Mexican.

They were young, skinny and ragged; half of them looked Indian.

"Are the people on all the trains like that?" I asked.

"Si, claro," said one man.

"You are all going to the United States?"

They laughed. Of course; where else?

In the United States, Hispanic illegals used to be a serious problem mainly for the American border states, or the states immediately adjacent to them—in fact, the very territory taken from Mexico a century and a half ago. But the demand for cheap labour transcends state lines, and now the *indocumentados* are everywhere in the U.S. They are as likely to end up in Iowa, New York, or in Washington State as in Texas or California.

If they've already crossed one or two borders for work and hope, they may see no reason not to cross another for the same reasons. It may not be long before Canadian employers succumb to the temptations of cheap, compliant labour. If the supply is there, demand will grow; demand will encourage supply. Canadians may then begin to see a reason to guard the border on their side to head off the desperate people from the south who have nothing to lose.

Not long ago, I watched three men working in a boatyard in Anacortes, Washington, at the northern end of Puget Sound on the western maritime boundary with Canada, an hour's drive away from the border. They were removing old bottom paint from a boat, and applying new paint. It is filthy, toxic work. The men were Hispanic. I asked them where they were from. Mexico, they'd come up a while ago. They themselves were legal immigrants, they assured me, but they knew many Mexicans in Anacortes (the name itself a memento of an earlier Spanish presence on this coast) and elsewhere nearby—in Seattle, Tacoma, Bellingham—who were without documents.

"Would you think about going to Canada to work?" I asked.

"Si, por supuesto!—Of course!" they said. If there was work there, they would go. The weather couldn't be any worse than it was in Anacortes or Seattle.

"Would you cross without documents?"

"Por supuesto!" Documents meant nothing. If you needed to work and there was work, you went. Why not?

"Canada. La misma cosa, verdad?" said one man.

In Canada it's the same thing, isn't it?

CHAPTER 12

QUODDY HEAD

. . . A CITY UPON A HILL, THE EYES OF ALL PEOPLE
ARE UPON US.
—JOHN WINTHROP, 1630

A WAR WILL GIVE US COMMERCE AND CHARACTER.
—HENRY CLAY, 1811

I BEGIN IN COLD RAIN, wind and mist. Snow is falling a few kilometres away, farther inland. The temperature is above freezing, although not by much. Highway 1 to the border is slithery, and busy. I have to wipe my visor with my glove every ten seconds so that I can see. Even so, I know I'm missing a lot about the road and its traffic. I have some kind of flu bug; I'm achy and my throat is sore. This morning, I pulled on almost every layer of clothes and gear I had brought with me—long underwear, flannel shirt, fleece sweater, fleece underjacket, and my armoured riding pants, jacket and gloves—but after twenty minutes, I'm cold, though dry underneath. I'm riding from Saint John, New Brunswick, towards the border crossing at Calais, Maine. I'll enter the United States there, and follow the border from end to end. It is 6,400 kilometres long (not counting the

2,465 of the Alaska boundary), but I estimate I'll ride close to ten thousand kilometres before I'm done.

I feel all the complicated emotions the beginning of a hard trek engenders. I remember them well from my southern ride, not long ago. I'm a little apprehensive of the roads ahead, and their potential for breaking my bones, for rasping and gashing my skin and soft flesh. I'm wary of the pain and fatigue I know long hours and days in the saddle will produce. I feel uncertain about whether the whole trip is, in fact, worthwhile: a month or more of hard riding, talking to a few people here and there, absorbing how the country looks, and how the border winds its way across the continent. As I start out, I'm not sure I'll find the things I need to write the book I want to write. The Mexican border seems so different: an exotic borderlands of two cultures, rife with drugs, illegals, gunmen, crazies, cops and troopers, the strange topography and flora of the desert, the sense that a drama may unfold at any moment. But the northern border . . . separating my own beautiful, peaceful and sober (although fragile and complex) homeland from America? I'm just not sure.

As I ride, self-doubt, a writer's scourge, is hunkered down behind me on the pillion with my duffle bags. I've written a few books, and they turned out all right, but maybe, this time, that won't happen. These are burdens to bear while riding a dual-sport, heavily loaded thumper in cold rain, on a slick road with eighteen-wheeler grease and spume blasting you in the head, and ten thousand clicks to go.

It's not all bad, however. Far from it. For one thing, I am riding a motorcycle. Even in this rain and cold, on this road, with this virus, I feel the familiar surge of joy again. Cutting through the heavy air, everything around me direct, animate, vivid, I feel strong, and young (or younger, anyway). This is adventure, flush with risk and uncertainty, and I feel like a hero. I feel alive. I think of my lost friends. None of them would have liked this either, just at the soggy, freezing moment. But, as always, it doesn't matter why you're moving. For a while, the movement itself is everything, the antidote to despair, an inoculation against entropy. You may die while riding a motorcycle—by falling, or by impact with a four-wheeler, or an eighteen-wheeler, or with the ground, or with a utility pole. Somehow, that seems much better than the usual heart attack or tumour or bizarre spreading paralysis. You're not just waiting around for the slouching beast.

St. Stephen, on the Canadian side of the St. Croix River separating Maine and New Brunswick, is about an hour's ride away. Halfway there, the rain eases off, and then ceases. The mist fades and I see the flat, forested land around me. The traffic thins out, the bike hums along, and I feel myself settling in to the routine of the saddle with its familiar sensations: pressure points on my buttocks; wind noise and blast; an achy left wrist—as yet unused to squeezing the clutch; the sag of my right-hand palm against the rubber flap of the throttle rocker (a primitive cruise control); two fingers covering the front brake lever (in case I must stop in a hurry, I have an extra half-second in my favour); the rib of the pegs through my boot soles; the squeeze of Kevlar armour on my knees, shoulders and back.

I'm happily aware that this ride started out much, much better than my first effort in the south. I recall with rue and a shudder my near death on the freeway service road in San Antonio. This time around, I know exactly where to hang my bags, how to keep my gear-changing knee free, how to sling my camping gear duffle bag so I can butt my butt up against it. And, now, I don't ride like a greenhorn. I know much more clearly what to watch for, how not to put myself past that point of no return from which, for a rider, there is, literally, no return.

Yesterday, the man at the desk of my crummy motel in Saint John told me: "It takes longer to cross the border than to get there." But on this cold day in mid-May, there are only half a dozen vehicles ahead of me on the bridge waiting for U.S. Customs and Immigration. The affable guy in the booth asks me the routine questions. He's thorough, but it's obviously hard for either of us to imagine anyone bent on trouble crossing this narrow, homely bridge between two towns so much alike, between two long-amicable countries. He wishes me a good trip, and I ride, once again, into America.

Before I head west, I turn southeast. For symmetry's sake, I want to see the most easterly point of the United States and dip my hand into the Atlantic Ocean there. As I did in the south, I'll try to close the loop by doing the same thing on the Pacific coast—at Washington's Cape Flattery. These are unnecessary, symbolic acts, but I am compelled to carry them out. I'm traversing a continent, and tasting the salt of its two fringing oceans feels proportionate and fitting.

Different country, same highway. I take U.S. Route 1 through Calais towards the town of Lubec, and, a little beyond, the lighthouse on the rocky point at West Quoddy Head, on Passamaquoddy Bay. The road follows another river boundary—the St. Croix.

Because they move, rivers are often troublesome when they are used as borders: banks erode, oxbows gather, new channels invade one country or the other (like the Rio Grande cutting its wilful way through the soft, Chihuahuan desert). However, the St. Croix—like all the U.S.-Canadian border rivers—runs over more reliable rock and glacial till. It doesn't move around that much. Nevertheless, it has been a source of contention and confusion.

The St. Croix was one of the first borderlines invoked in the 1783 Treaty of Paris, when Great Britain gave up the Revolutionary War and acknowledged the independence of the United States. A British historian noted the imprecisions and omissions of the treaty, which made, "not a clean break, but a line of ragged connections" between the empire and its lost thirteen colonies. The St. Croix was a good example; no one knew quite which river it was in the unmapped north-eastern wilderness. It could have been the Magaguadavic River farther east in New Brunswick—the American choice— or what was then known as the Schoodic River, which is in fact the St. Croix. Border disputes were inevitable, and some of them were long-lived.

The St. Croix boundary itself (only a hundred kilometres long) was settled eleven years later in 1794 by Jay's Treaty, which embodied an American desire to get along better with Great Britain—although it was a temporary policy. The treaty also set a border line due north from the St. Croix River headwaters into the "Highlands" of northern Maine, leaving for a later time the delineation of where these were. In fact, it would take another forty-eight years, a war, various "alarums and excursions," and many negotiations, to settle the northern portion of the Maine-New Brunswick border.

As I ride towards Quoddy Head, cold and achy under a low, grey and drizzly sky, I consider that like almost all national boundaries, this is a border that was first established by war, although the exact location, extent and longevity of the line remained doubtful. It took a second war, the War of 1812— some historians have called it the "Second American Revolution"—to hammer out some clear understandings and demarcations. These included a more certain borderline—the 49th parallel made its first appearance, running west from Lake of the Woods to the Rocky Mountains—and a demili-tarization of the Great Lakes.

Canada was the pawn in the War of 1812 between the United States and Great Britain. It was the only part of the British Empire available to the Americans as a place to attack. They did not have the naval capacity to fight a full-scale war in the North Atlantic or to transport troops anywhere over-seas to fight the British. Canada became the victim by default, because it was there.

Although the United States began the war, it had reason to be angry and frustrated. Britain was engaged in its twenty-year-long struggle-to-the-death with Napoleonic France, and wasn't too particular about law or protocol when it interfered with American ships carrying trade goods through the Royal Navy's blockade of the European coasts. The British defini-tion of contraband was, understandably, wider than the American. And, as always, the Royal Navy was short of men. It took men off American ships whom it said were deserters, or British, even if they had become American citizens. The United States objected to the disruption of its trade as a neu-tral in the European war, and it regarded the illegal conscrip-tion of its seamen as a form of kidnapping.

At the same time, the United States was in the early stages of its westward-moving displacement—or mass killing—of native North Americans. At the Battle of Tippecanoe in the Indiana territory in 1811, the future president William Henry Harrison defeated an Indian force assembled by the charis-matic Shawnee, Tecumseh. Tecumseh was elsewhere seek-ing support for his Indian confederacy, and Harrison won the engagement (although not by much, and American casu-alties were higher). At that time, the government, and most Americans, regarded the Indian as a kind of aboriginal ter-rorist, and had long suspected that the British were arming them. As it happened, British weapons were discovered among the Indians at Tippecanoe.

Tecumseh would become a close ally of the British during the War of 1812 and was, arguably, the best general the British had. In fact, the War of 1812 was, in its western battlegrounds, a continuation of Tecumseh's War. When he was killed in 1813, at, or after, the Battle of the Thames, near Chatham,

Ontario, warriors carried his body away and disposed of their great chief in secret.

More important than its practical consequences for British-American relations, the War of 1812 consolidated, and added to, the stories each people was beginning to tell about itself. The political myths that the United States, and, much later and more gradually, Canada, created for themselves were begun during the American War of Independence and augmented by the War of 1812. For the new republic, that war became a gallant and glorious rebuff of British invasion, and a reaffirmation of the Revolution's necessity and rightness. It reaffirmed the American view of their Constitution as the sole source of legitimacy, and its mandate of light governance by the consent of fellow citizens, equal before the law. And there was a whole continent, or a good part of it, there for the taking.

Needless to say, the perspective north of the border was different. Canadians (or, more accurately, the English-speaking inhabitants of the remaining British North American colonies) thought that they were the ones who had repelled an invasion. They had a point. The conflict began with Madison's request to Congress, in June 1812, to declare war on Britain (in the days when presidents deigned to follow the Constitution with honesty on this point). It was American armies that repeatedly invaded Canadian territory, crossing the St. Clair, the Niagara, and the St. Lawrence rivers—and getting beaten back on each occasion. British ships did, indeed, sail up the Potomac (in a brilliant feat of seamanship) and bombard Washington, D.C., burning the White House and the Capitol, among other buildings. But this action came in indirect response to an attack on York (now Toronto), the capital of Upper Canada. American forces had captured the town and burned parts of it, including the parliament buildings. And U.S. state militias had destroyed many other towns and settlements as well, including Newark, now Niagara-on-the-Lake, chasing its inhabitants out into a freezing winter night. These tactics alienated the sympathy of many American-born settlers in the Canadian colonies for the American position, and they were, in fact, illustrative of the United States' clumsiness and ineptitude in its waging of the war.

In Canada, the war was fought mostly by British regulars, and by Indian allies (Tecumseh being the most prominent and effective) who, at this middle stage of their contact with whites, much preferred the treatment they got from the English king's redcoats and from Canadian settlers, to that of the American army, militias and frontiersmen. This native preference would persist along each country's westward-moving frontier. Canadian militias did take part in the battles—more and more as the war went on, and as American forces continued to invade Canadian territory. The experience of war in defence of home brought the Canadian colonists together, and gave them a sense of themselves as a people and potentially, as a nation—as wars fought by a nation's civilians tend to do.

Most important, Canada's defence of itself during the War of 1812 reaffirmed the position of the so-called United Empire Loyalists (known as Tories south of the border) and, through them, of the conservative, counter-revolutionary origin of Canada as a repudiation of revolution and republicanism.

The War of Independence had had the support of a minority of colonists. Perhaps a third were neutral, or disinterested, and another 20 to 30 per cent remained actively loyal to the Crown and the empire. When the war was over, the first great wave of American political refugees to Canada took place. Historians disagree on the number, but somewhere between sixty thousand and one hundred thousand loyalists felt strongly enough about opposition to the Revolution—or found it expedient to claim so—to give up everything they owned and had worked for. They moved north across the border, to the Maritimes, and to Lower and Upper Canada (now Quebec and Ontario).

They became refugees for many reasons. Some were civil servants who had worked for the Crown and didn't like their chances with its overthrow. Some businessmen, especially from the east coast, liked the idea of the British Empire's de facto common market. Opportunists saw the possibility of a fast social leg-up in the free land available in British North America. There were colonists whose mother tongue wasn't English, as well as pacifist Quakers, British-born settlers, Indians and blacks, including slaves, all of whom felt more comfortable in the polyglot and tolerant empire—which had abolished the slave trade in 1807, and would abolish slavery itself in 1834—than in the monolingual, zealous, slave-owning republic. There had, after all, been a long and violent revolution (although, it is notable that the new republican government did not engage in slaughter and pogrom, which are the aftermath of most revolutions.)

The United Empire Loyalists formed a critical mass of British subjects along the new border whom the British government would be obliged to defend against American incursion or invasion. The new settlers were numerous enough to form real colonies; both New Brunswick and Upper Canada were created to satisfy Loyalist aspirations. Maintaining the sovereignty of the colonies became a matter of imperial policy. Without the Loyalists, Americans from the border states would perhaps have drifted north and settled across the line in the fertile country of southern Ontario and the Eastern Townships of Quebec in the same way Americans moved across the southern border into the Mexican territory of Texas. Soon enough, these northern settlers might have made similar demands for independence, or for annexation to the United States, as had the Texians. Perhaps Mexico's fate—war, dismemberment, humiliation—would have become Canada's, too. The Loyalists forestalled this possibility; they were a British bulwark against America.

The Loyalists were also one of the main constructors of the Canadian character: conservative, gradualist in political orientation, anti-American, yet fascinated by, and obsessed with, life south of the border. They abhorred the republic—or, at least, had washed their hands of it—yet used it as the measure and judge of all they did at home.

When Congress declared war in 1812, the Madison administration thought that the large numbers of Americans in Canada would make victory quick and sweet. Thomas Jefferson said it would be "a mere matter of marching," a quote that rings a bell in connection with a more recent American war. In fact, the British North Americans (and the French of Quebec, too) feared tyranny from the south far more than from the imperial centre.

As with most wars, each side's version of what happened, and what it all meant, is mostly wrong. Neither side won. It was a bloody stalemate. No territory changed hands; the border stayed where it had been. And in the end, Canadians hadn't done much to protect themselves; they owed their non-American status to Britain, and to the Indians, who fought for their own reasons.

New England detested the war, while New York was indifferent, and their militias took no part in it. This was a serious problem for American strategy because the most vulnerable British territory lay along the St. Lawrence River; it was the logical place to attack with determination and force. The effective abstention of New York made such a course of action very difficult. Residents of New England along the border concluded private agreements with Canadian Maritimers and Quebecers that they would not fight each other, and would, in fact, continue to treat and trade. In Maine, for example, the residents of Eastport voted unanimously "to preserve a good understanding with the Inhabitants of New Brunswick and to discountenance all depredations upon the possessions of each other." British troops occupied, unresisted, the state east of the Penobscot, including Bangor and Belfast, and the country I was riding through now, along the beautiful and gentle St. Croix.

Nevertheless, myth trumps history. The War of 1812 produced "The Star-Spangled Banner," whose namesake flew over Fort McHenry in Baltimore and was still there at dawn, after a night of bombardment by British cannon. Flag and national anthem were immortalized, and sanctified, together. The United States was now truly a nation among nations, the "land of the free and the home of the brave." It had been successful in its underlying goal: to force the world empire of Great Britain to recognize, and to accept, the portentous advent of a new power in the western hemisphere. The 1823 Monroe doctrine was a continuation and elaboration of this American policy.

And when Canadians sing their national anthem, "O Canada," they have no doubt about the direction they're facing when they repeat its phrase: "we stand on guard for thee." The United States had attacked once; it might do so again. The close presence of this aggressive, acquisitive, restless people was, and is, a constant reminder of Canadian vulnerability. The loyalist British North Americans began to see their destiny: they would have to find a way to hold together in their northern land, squeezed between the warlike republic to the south, and the barren, wintry wilderness to the north. On this narrow ground, they would have to learn to survive.

The actual American nation, and the nascent Canadian nation, had different concepts of the border, of its function and of its meaning.

The Americans' view was that their borders (both southern and northern) were to be respected and honoured, of course, but they were ultimately provisional. Yes, the border was there and agreed upon, but perhaps, later, changed circumstances would nullify that agreement. Maybe it would become in the United States' best interests to cross the border, to challenge or ignore it. Or, some Americans might feel it was their God-given destiny to say: Damn the border; the land it denies us is ours nevertheless, or it should be, and the border will not stop us from taking it. And, if there were people, or conditions, on the other side that were a threat to the United States, then the border would not stand in the way of hot pursuit, or of a longer-term occupation or annexation of the land over the line.

These propositions were strengthened by the tenuous nature of America's neighbouring states after the War of 1812. British North America—a long way yet from becoming Canada—was an unorganized collection of British colonies clustered along the eastern border, and which petered out before the west really began. They had rejected annexation in 1812, but surely, thought the Americans, it was just good sense that they would join the new republic eventually. It was clearly in their best interests to do so.

Perhaps there is one source here for the enduring and peculiar attitude of Americans to Canada: the idea even now that Canada is really a kind of cold clone of the United States. Allan Gotlieb, a former Canadian ambassador to the United States, remarked in a 2008 interview: "We are definitely not Americans. But the nut of the problem is that they think we are."

This aperçu does sum up the American attitude towards Canada, an attitude composed of several strands. One is ignorance—in the sense of both ignoring and not knowing. Following from this is the assumption that Canada is, for all intents and purposes, just like the United States. Or, perhaps, it's the other way around: Because of the assumption that Canada is just like the United States, there's no reason not to ignore it, no good reason to learn much about it. Indeed, the conclusion is that if you know about the United States, you do, in fact, by definition, know about Canada, too.

American ignorance of Canada is oddly universal. One would expect Americans living near the border, or better-educated Americans, to know more about Canada than those living far to the south, or than the ill-educated. But surveys and anecdotal evidence both suggest that this particular lack of knowledge is not correlated to class, education, or even proximity to the border.

Many Americans believe that Canada may, perhaps, be somewhat misguided in its left-leaning, liberal politics, and in its tolerance of the intolerable: abortion, ethnic or religious fundraising organizations that may have terrorist links, same-sex marriage. On the positive side, maybe Canada is a little more sane than the United States: it has far fewer murders, for example, and takes a calmer approach to life in general. But these qualities could apply to Oregon, or to the New England states. None of them necessarily signify another country, distinct and separate. It's reasonable to assume as much variation within the regions of the United States, as between the States as a whole, and Canada. There is Quebec, of course, with its determined French speakers and intractable nationalists, forever threatening to break up the country. But even that has its analogues in the United States. After all, it fought a terrible civil war to prevent its own dissolution. Now, it is threatened by its own distinct society gathering itself together in the southwest, and spreading north and east: the Spanish, Catholic Hispanics, especially Mexicans, spilling across the southern border, taking back the land once taken from them.

The American view of Canadians has been remarkably consistent over time. If the Loyalists were American Tories who had moved north, the mere fact that they then lived on the other side of the pervious border did not make them any less American. The calculation by the Madison administration that the British North Americans would welcome U.S. troops as liberators in 1812 reflected that early misunderstanding: a wilful, condescending innocence about Canada. And it's bound to be a very tenacious attitude: If you don't know you don't know, or you assume you do know, then the issue of learning anything never arises. Nothing much has changed in nearly two hundred years.

Needless to say, Canadians (like the Mexicans) have had different ideas. The border was a defensive line. They had to watch it every moment. In a way, it defined them. From the beginning, the border meant that the people who lived north of it, whatever they were, were certainly not American, or rather—the terminology has always been cumbersome—they were non-American North Americans. The border symbolized rejection of the idea of a republic. And it stood for stability—it would never move south, nor could it be allowed to move north. Certainly, it could never disappear. The border was forever. Behind it, Canadians would watch and wait; they would monitor the threat from the south—military, political or cultural—and defend themselves against it.

One of the biggest impacts of the attacks of September 11, 2001, was to make a radical change in Americans' idea of their borders. One could say that 9/11 "Canadianized" their perception. Now, many Americans pay similar close attention to their nation's perimeter. Like Canadians, they believe it has to be secured, by a variety of means, against outside threats: in this case, the economic aggression of many illegal immigrants; the dislocating and costly intrusion of drugs; and, most important, potential attack by terrorists. For the United States to become Fortress America, the border must become a barrier, a defensive wall—literally, in the south, as the security fence is extended into the deep desert and along the River. Now, if you are an American, the Department of Homeland Security stands on guard for thee.

I ride into Lubec, the easternmost town in the United States. It has taken me longer than I'd anticipated to get here because long stretches of Route 1 are under construction, and I have travelled for miles through wet, sticky, red mud and gravel. It's the first day of this trip in mid-May, and the bike and I are already filthy. We look as if we've ridden off-road all morning. But it's raining again, and the mess is already washing off both of us. I ride through the little, frame-housed town to the hundred-yard-long FDR Memorial Bridge to Campobello Island. And, after an hour and a half in the United States, I cross the border back into Canada again. Campobello is one of the waifs left over from British-American disputes along the Maine border. Snugged up against the state as it is, the island, like Deer Island just to the north in the Bay of Fundy, remains Canadian territory.

The Customs and Immigration officer on the Canadian side is a beautiful, young, smiling, blond woman who asks me why I'm crossing over to Campobello. She doesn't ask for any ID. I tell her I want to see where Franklin Roosevelt spent his summers, and that's good enough for her. I'd like her to ask me more questions, but she's done. I ask her if the island is a security problem. She laughs.

"Not for us," she says, "but wait 'til you cross the bridge the other way."

"Are they very strict?" I ask. "Even if you've just been on the island an hour or so; that's all I'll be."

She's charming and breezy, and she laughs again. "You'll see. Sometimes, they're pretty paranoid."

"Are they concerned about smuggling, or other things?"

"Well," she says, "they're concerned about everything these days. There's some smuggling but it's done by boat; it's a lot easier."

"How about terrorists?" I ask.

The question prompts quite uproarious laughter from this representative of the government of Canada. "Right," she eventually manages to say—she does everything but choke, or snort coffee up her nose—"terrorists are going to cross into the States from Campobello Island and blow up Lubec."

She's still laughing as I ride off. I feel as if I've made her day.

The island, at the border's eastern extremity, can only be reached by land from Canada by travelling through the United States. In an odd, mirror-symmetry, Point Roberts, the tiny American peninsula at the extreme western end of the 49th parallel, can only be reached by land from Washington State by first travelling through Canada. Once endearing anomalies, these enclaves have become, for the United States, irritating little problems that have to be policed and guarded at disproportionate expense—although, they are no more vulnerable than the scheme of the wide-open northern border as a whole.

I park in the empty lot of Roosevelt Campobello International Park—it's operated jointly by the each country's parks service. Everything's closed, including the toilets, which are an object of some interest to me at this point on a cold day. I find a handy grove, and then clump down to the cottage in my boots, and padded and armoured riding gear. The rain falls heavily. I feel more and more achy and tired—my flu has been, understandably, exacerbated by riding a motorcycle in cold rain and wind. The cottage is actually a two-and-a-half-storey, thirty-four-room frame and shingle house. I read the plaques, look at the view of Passamaquoddy Bay, and try to imagine the scene during the president's idyllic boyhood summers. What innocence and peace must have prevailed here in those golden, opulent years before the brutal and terrible twentieth century had made its debut. What succour, perhaps leavened with childhood nostalgia, Franklin, the public man in that hard century, must have found in this refuge. That is, until the summer of 1921 on Campobello, when he caught the disease that paralyzed him—probably polio, although possibly Guillain-Barré syndrome.

I need to get warm, to eat, and to dry out a little. The restaurants are in Lubec. I mount up and ride back to the bridge. The beautiful Canadian customs officer's warning was prescient. The U.S. guy asks the usual questions, and then tells me to pull over to a curb for secondary inspection. Another officer comes out of the office pulling on latex gloves. He asks me what's in my bags. I go through the list: clothes, tools, spare parts, camping equipment, maps, camera and so on. Why do I have so much stuff? I'm riding all the way home to British Columbia, I tell him, right across the country. I'll be on the road for well over a month. He opens my bags methodically, one by one, and fingers through my possessions. I'm chilled and hungry; I feel as if I might faint. He notices me shivering.

"What's wrong with you?" he asks. He looks at me with hostility and suspicion. It's not just the fact that I feel like hell that is making me fancifully paranoid. He really is a son of a bitch.

"I'm cold, and I think I have the flu," I say.

He looks at me with distaste, as if I might infect him, and tells me to unstrap my duffle bags. He inserts his arm up to the armpit and pokes around my inflatable pillow, my sleeping bag and tent. He extracts my soap dish, and opens it up, picks up the soap, as yet unused, looks up at me quickly as if I might be showing fear that he's close to my stash—of whatever.

The officer in the booth had asked me why I wanted to go to the Roosevelt park when it was closed, and this guy asks me the same question—now he's manhandling my tape recorder, as if it's some alien artifact.

"I just wanted to see Roosevelt's cottage," I say.

"Why do you need a tape recorder?"

I tell him about my book, and how this trip is part of my research.

He asks for my passport, and goes back into the office. I wait, getting colder and shakier. I haven't yet realized that U.S. Customs and Immigration agents will google me. I time him. After six minutes and a few seconds, he comes back out and hands me my passport. He doesn't smile.

"Okay," he says, "have a nice day."

I eat a small part of an order of fish and chips, and drink a lot of hot coffee, at Uncle Kippy's Restaurant on the main road in Lubec. The sign outside says: "Stop in or we'll both starve." I linger to try to get less damp. Three guys in baseball caps and team jackets are eating at the next table. One of them asks me where I'm from. They haven't heard of British Columbia. I mention my unreasonable hassle coming back across the bridge. They laugh knowingly.

"They got fuck all to do this time of year," says the oldest man, late forties, with a greying beard. "In the summer, the cars are lined up, they just ask, 'Who the fuck are you?' and wave you on through."

"Yeah, come back in two months," says a second guy.

"Plus," says the older man, "you're riding a bike, right? They think it's like *Easy Rider*, you got cocaine in your gas tank."

"That's the only place he didn't look," I say.

"There ya go," says the second guy, as if that settles something.

"Is there any trouble with the border here—smuggling, or anything like that?" I ask.

They all laugh—knowingly once again.

"Oh yeah, there's always smuggling," one says. "It's kind of a tradition around here." They sound proud of it. I also get the impression that they, themselves, may well be acquainted with the activity.

"Any worries about terrorism?" I ask—the dogged reporter. I'm beginning to take notes in a small, damp spiral notebook.

To my surprise, they don't laugh. They shrug. "Who knows," the second man says.

"Do you believe that the 9/11 hijackers came into the U.S. from Canada?"

"Some of them did," says the third man, the first time he's spoken.

"What? Are you kiddin'?" The older guy turns to him. "They came from Saudi Arabia."

"No," I say, "I mean, some of them were from Saudi Arabia originally, but a lot of Americans seem to think they entered the U.S. from Canada."

"Right, yeah," says the older guy, "they did. You got all kinds of terrorists up there."

"They came from Canada?" I ask.

"You bet," he says. The other two nod agreement.

"Why do you think that?"

More shrugs. "Everyone knows it," says the second guy.

"But that's not so," I say. "They entered the U.S. directly from overseas, and they were all legal."

"No," says one guy.

"He's gonna say that, isn't he," says the older guy to the other two. "He's from Canada. What else is he gonna say?"

It's a short distance from Lubec to the West Quoddy Head lighthouse. No rain, now, but a cold, a bitter, wind off the sea. I park the bike beside the striped tower of the light, its Fresnel lens, a faceted insect's eye, glinting above me like a threat. The sea is tumultuous, rougher than even this strong wind should create. It must be blowing against the fast Fundy ebb tide, stacking up the slab-sided seas. I would not like to be out there in a boat. Over a few miles of the bay, I make out the low loom of Grand Manaan Island. With somewhat more logic than for Campobello, it, too, is part of New Brunswick. According to recent news reports about arson and gunfights, the island is a drug-runner's lair. The men in Uncle Kippy's were right about smuggling. It's the second oldest profession around here: George Washington commissioned the first revenue frigate in 1790, and its main area of operations was Lubec and the surrounding waters.

There is one car in the parking area, with a couple and a dog. They walk to and fro for a while, say hello, and then leave. I slide through a fence, slog across a small, sodden field, jump a narrow stream, and climb down the ragged black rocks until I'm close to the waves breaking hard and wild ashore. In a lull, I drop down, dip my hand into the North Atlantic Ocean, and leap up again to avoid the next comber rolling in. I lick the salt off my fingers.

Lubec may be the easternmost town in the United States, but West Quoddy Head—the very rock I'm standing on as best I can judge—is the easternmost point of unsubmerged land on the American part of the continent. It's an end and a beginning: the end of land, but the beginning of America. West Quoddy Head is the closest ground to the Old World, but it's also the start of the New World. From here, I'll go north to the farthest hollow of Maine, up against the Quebec and New Brunswick borders, which, for a while, people called the Republic of Madawaska. Then, I'll turn west. Like all arrivals in America, I must head west. That's the only way to follow the border, striking its way across the continent, etching the line between two similar countries divided by their essential differences.

I stand with my back to the sea, and to the hammer of the salt wind, on the edge of America. I look in towards its centre, its heart, and the line that separates it from my own country. I say to my lost friends Will, Chris and Mike: This will be for you, too. As it does for everyone who lands on its shore, America seems to promise me an adventure, something new and strange, an awakening or a confirmation—or, perhaps, a redemption.

CHAPTER 13

BORDERLANDS NATION

A NORTHERN FOREIGN POLICY? WE DON'T DO NORTH
IN OUR FOREIGN POLICY—UNLESS YOU'RE TALKING
ABOUT RELATIONS WITH THE POLAR BEARS,
WALRUS OR CARIBOU.
—UNATTRIBUTED FOREIGN POLICY ADVISOR TO
GEORGE W. BUSH

I HAD TAKEN IBUPROFEN FIRST THING in the morning, and my flu symptoms, at least, had diminished to a slight body ache. Sitting at the long counter of a greasy spoon in Van Buren, Maine, eating bacon and eggs, I'm trying to understand the odd French spoken by everyone around me. They are using English and French with promiscuous ease. It's quintessential franglais. An English sentence follows one in French, or the two languages flip back and forth in the same sentence: "Yeah, it's bon ça." I'm in the United States, but it sounds like Canada. This is the Republic of Madawaska. These people are Brayons. They are not Acadians—the original French settlers deported and displaced in the eighteenth century by their British conquerors across the continent as far away as Louisiana, where they became the Cajuns. Nor are they Quebecers drifted down from the north. The Brayons are a small, self-consciously distinct society, a symptomatic remnant of this region's tangled history. The border cuts through the heart of their territory.

The late-middle-aged man and woman behind the counter are tattooed, the blue pictographs cascading down their white arms, his lean and ropy, hers heavy with swaying flesh. The proprietor was born just across the river in Saint-Léonard, New Brunswick. I can see its buildings out the window of the back door. The river here is the Saint John, and it is the border in this northeastern angle of Maine. The man next to me at the counter joins in: he was born in the U.S., he says, but his two sisters are Canadian and live over the river; his family is half-and-half. The owner, too, has lots of family in Saint-Léonard, and elsewhere along the Canadian side. He's Canadian, but he has a permanent green card because his mother was born in the States. His grandparents were born here before the border between Canada and the U.S. was settled, he claims (he must be wrong unless they, and his parents, lived as long as Methuselah). There's lots of French here; everyone speaks it. Except the kids. They're not too interested in it any more. Everything's English for them.

All the people here are worried and angry about the new border document requirements the Department of Homeland Security is going to bring in. The families here are all big, he says. How can a family with five or six kids—some of them have eight or ten—and with lots of cousins, aunts and uncles, afford to get a passport for everyone at a hundred bucks a time? They won't do it. They'll just cross over the river by boat, which is what a lot of people do now, anyway, to visit family and friends on the other side.

Do they get across the border easily? I ask. Into Canada, yes, he says, but coming back into the States, the assholes ask you the same things over and over. They know you by your first name, and they know where you've been and what you've been doing—you know, shopping or visiting—but they ask you: "Citizenship? What was the purpose of your visit?" You say: "Come on, Bob, it's me, Josie," but they keep asking the questions anyway. He figures they have to because there are cameras, and the officers will get fired if they don't do it by the book.

Maybe the government will allow a better driver's licence instead of a passport, he says. The Border Patrol used to have its headquarters farther south in Houlton, but now they're building a big new HQ here in Van Buren. This shows how serious they are, he says. It's bullshit. The Mexican border is the dangerous one. That's where they should be building a wall. Doesn't he fear terrorists coming into the U.S. across this border, then? I ask. He laughs; he scoffs. The Mexican border—that's the dangerous one. Here, everyone on each side is the same.

I rode to Van Buren the day after Quoddy Head. It was an even colder May day, and the rain came down hard, relentless and constant. I followed Route 1 to the Chiputneticook Lakes where the St. Croix River begins. Then, I followed the line north, as the original treaty between Great Britain and the United States had stipulated, to the Maine "Highlands," and towards Van Buren in Aroostook County. The rain never ceased. Sometimes, it changed to sleet, and once or twice, briefly, to snow. I stopped from time to time to take a photograph or to record a note, and once to take more ibuprofen; but I had to quit because my hands got wet and very cold. I couldn't have kept going in these near-freezing temperatures without my heated handlebar grips. But when my gloves got wet through, the heat wasn't enough, and I could barely squeeze the clutch. When I stopped for lunch, I couldn't make my hands get a tight-enough grip on my riding jacket's stiff zipper to pull it down. I had to ask a man in the restaurant lobby to help.

An hour later, warmed up, although not dried out, I tried to leave. But this was a gas station and a truck stop, too. I stuffed in my earplugs and pulled them out, tugged on my helmet and yanked it off half a dozen times as man after man came up to start a conversation. Mostly truckers, they wanted to know why I was riding in this shit, whether I had ridden across the country from British Columbia (they knew where it was), where I was headed. Here in the north was the Anglo-America of easy conversation and innocent questions, of an amicable and presumed equality. No reserved, silent Hispanics—and *indocumentados*—culturally indisposed to chat with a gringo.

Earlier, I had passed the only other motorcycle I'd seen since I began this trip, heading in the opposite direction. It was a big Harley, or a clone, and its rider might have ignored me, as such riders tend to do. But he gave me a long, emphatic wave, which I returned. I thought to myself: What the hell is he doing out here on a day like this? He was probably thinking the same thing about me. Maybe he was researching a book, too.

I was also getting lots of practice riding in wet weather and on slick roads. The secret is to become conservative: be more upright, go slower, be deliberate—give up easy riding. You must husband the precious traction of the bike's contact patch on the road with even more care than usual. Good tires are essential, and I had bought new ones for this trip. I ride Route 1 with a thoughtful attention to the details of curves and camber, and to errant puddles or oil slicks.

The real problem is visibility. I don't have a fog mask in my helmet (I should, but they smell bad, and make me feel claustrophobic). I must control my breathing so that my breath doesn't mist up the inside of my visor: deep, slow exhalations. To maintain this rhythm, I must remain calm in the face of a tricky piece of road, or a dangerous four-wheeler (they're all dangerous). If I get angry or excited and my breathing speeds up, the visor fogs and I can't see. I have to crack it open slightly, letting in the noise, wet and cold. Breathing in and out, steady, calm and controlled: Zen and the art of motorcycle riding. Of course, rain and road spray builds up constantly on the outside of the visor. A short squeegee is built into the thumb of my riding glove, and I pass it across the plastic shield every twenty seconds or so, to scrape away the accumulating liquid.

In the motel in Van Buren, I conclude I'm truly hypothermic. Now, when I listen to my tape recordings made after I arrived, I sound as if I'd been drugged. I slur, and I can't seem to find the word I'm looking for. I forget which day of the week it is. My voice rasps and fades out, as if I'm ninety years old. I'm lucky the room has a new high-speed heater with a big fan. Much of my gear is wet, even—to my surprise—the stuff in my supposedly waterproof kayak duffle bags. I hang things up and spread them out until the room looks like a sodden junk shop. I realize I should have stopped hours ago. You can ride in rain, or in near-freezing cold, but not for long in both. In bed that night, I can't get warm for hours. Then, as if a switch has been flipped, I start to sweat. I doze and toss. Maybe it's a flu fever. It's close to morning before my internal thermostat seems to reacquire equilibrium.

The War of 1812 did not end the possibility of war between Great Britain and the United States, with Canada as the battleground. Indeed, the general assumption at the time was that the two countries would fight each other again. The idea of an undefended border remained, unimagined, in the future. For nearly sixty years, border disputes, the uneasy political evolution of the Canadian colonies, and a volatile America made for jumpy relations. The popular rebellions in Upper and Lower Canada in 1837, the American Civil War in the 1860s, and the intermittent cross-border raids by Irish Fenians around the same time all had their moments. But it was disagreements about the border that most nearly caused renewed war—and certainly brought the loudest threats of it. One of the most contentious of these was the boundary between northeast Maine and New Brunswick—the Madawaska country I'm riding through now.

During the 1820s and 1830s, more and more settlers from both sides moved into the fertile, and disputed, valleys of the Saint John and Aroostook rivers. But the issue became critical over the question of lumber: who got to cut down the trees? (As an example of the enduring nature of U.S.-Canadian trade arguments, softwood lumber is still one of the main annoyances between the two countries.)

In the winter of 1838–39, depending on whose version of history is believed, either: New Brunswick lumberjacks seized Maine's land agent who had been sent to expel them after they illegally cut down trees in the Aroostook area; or, New Brunswickers were obliged to arrest Maine lumberjacks who had illegally cut trees in the Aroostook. Maine, in full support of its lumber interests, mobilized its militia and began to move troops into the disputed territory. The U.S Congress, at Maine's insistence, authorized fifty thousand men and $10 million to fight the Aroostook War.

To the Canadian colonies, this looked like 1812 all over again. Some of the settlers in the Saint John River valley were veterans of that war, and had been given land for their service. The colony's lieutenant-governor, Sir John Harvey, had fought American troops many times. Much of New Brunswick's population was descended from the Loyalists who had run from the new independent republic in 1783.

Once again, British North Americans were obliged to respond to a U.S. threat of force, in the form of belligerent state militias who were threatening to invade across the border, or, at least, to resort to force to establish a border whose course had already been arbitrated. New Brunswick, supported by Nova Scotia, had no choice; it called up its own militia, and an edgy standoff began.

Since the conclusion of the Revolutionary War, Britain had been worried about American military action against its remaining colonies. It could not accept the Maine boundary claimed by the United States because it encompassed the upper Saint John River valley. British forces needed the valley as a military route in case they had to march east to defend the maritime colonies against the United States, and they wanted a road from the ice-free port of Saint John, New Brunswick, to Quebec City and Montreal to bypass the frozen St. Lawrence River in winter. (The present Trans-Canada Highway runs through the valley; it's the most logical east-west route.)

On the American side, the imperatives were strictly economic: lumber and the fertile soil of the river valleys. Then, as now, lobbying by self-interested businessmen and developers was quite capable of determining government (especially state government) policy. And baiting the hated Brits (anti-British feelings were strong in New England) and threatening war was, as always, a means of winning domestic battles and diverting attention from intractable local issues—Maine's politics were especially intense and vicious.

A belligerent, expansionist president might have used the boundary dispute as an excuse for all-out invasion of Canada. James Madison might well have done so. (James Polk would use the same excuse in 1846 to invade Mexico.) Unlike in 1812, however, President Martin Van Buren, the first president not to have personally experienced the revolution, sent one of his generals, Winfield Scott, to Maine to calm things down until a settlement could be negotiated. In the end, the federal government refused to allow one of the country's small border states to force it into open war with the British Empire. The Aroostook War remained shot-free and bloodless.

The U.S. secretary of state, Daniel Webster, and the British minister to Washington, Lord Ashburton, settled the issue in 1842. They gave the Aroostook valley to the United States, and Britain got its military route to the east along the upper Saint John. The federal government compensated grumpy Maine for the land it didn't get, and New Brunswick, which got more land than the King of the Netherlands had proposed in an initial arbitration attempt (the King had been agreed upon by both sides as a neutral party), was satisfied enough. In any case, it had no choice. Unlike Maine, which had clout with its central government, the colony had little influence on British imperial policy, of which the treaty was an example.

The losers in the boundary settlement were the Brayons, the French-speaking inhabitants of the region. They had dubbed themselves, half-seriously, the Republic of Madawaska. (The mayor of Edmundston, New Brunswick, is still, by tradition, the honorary president of the republic.) They had formed an integrated community across the entire region and didn't see the Aroostook or the Saint John as dividing them from anything. But this new border cut them in two. They had been consulted by no one. Like the Rio Grande dividing Hispanic communities when the Mexican state became the American state of Texas, the new Maine-New Brunswick border passed over the heads of half a population. The territories on each side of such a line are ready-made borderlands.

Whether a genuine borderlands—a species of third country— exists along the U.S.-Canadian line is a contentious question. If one exists, it's certainly a much different entity than the classic borderlands society of the U.S.-Mexico border. In the south, travelling along the Rio Grande, or skirting the fence in the New Mexico and Arizona deserts, or absorbing life in the many twin border towns and cities epitomizes immersion in a political and cultural stew distinct from either country's dominant society.

It bears repeating here that the term "borderlands" was first proposed in 1921 by historian Herbert Eugene Bolton (he used the expression "Spanish Borderlands"). The southern U.S. border is the prototypical borderlands, in that it meets perfectly the defining criteria: despite a separating political boundary, the people living there share common social characteristics; those characteristics make the people more like each other than they are to the general populations in their respective countries; and the very different cultures of the two adjacent countries blend in various ways within the borderlands.

It seems difficult to fit the U.S.-Canadian border regions as a whole into this classic definition. Some scholars and commentators claim that there is, in fact, no northern borderlands. Political scientist Ivo Duchacek writes that the term "borderlands" seems "misplaced when applied to the U.S.-Canadian border," and that it sounds "awkward, and few of us would use it." The argument goes that the cultures of the two countries are, on the surface, not very dissimilar, and it is hard to see how the populations along the border differ much, if at all, from their respective general populations. The northern border is too long, the country it runs through is too geographically varied, and people's affiliations tend to run north and south in various scattered regions across the continent, rather than east-west in any kind of uniform border society.

The most extreme expression of the irrelevance of North American borders in the face of economic and cultural similarities was articulated by Joel Garreau in *The Nine Nations of North America*. Garreau ignores national boundaries, and he divides the United States, Canada and Mexico into nine regions or "nations." For example, the country I'm riding through is part of New England, or Atlantica, and it is made up of the

New England states, the Canadian Atlantic provinces and Quebec's Gaspé Peninsula. Its capital is Boston. Other so-called nations include Ecotopia (the Pacific northwest from Alaska south to northern California and west of the mountains), the Empty Quarter, the Foundry, Dixie, Mexamerica, and so on. In the face of the natural and human integrity of these regions, Garreau argues, their political borders make no sense.

The Nine Nations idea was interesting, and provocative, when it was published in 1981, but its analytical power has diminished since 9/11 and the subsequent American obsession with border protection. Garreau's regions have real substance, but, where each one spills over an international boundary, its parts are becoming more divided, and increasingly isolated, from each other by the walls and barriers of the American security state.

From a distance, the Anglo societies of the United States and Canada can look too much alike to warrant making much distinction of any kind. When I spoke to historian Oscar Martínez at the University of Arizona at Tucson, he dismissed, with an indulgent smile, the notion that the U.S.-Canadian border constituted a borderlands in any sense, or that those two countries faced any real and enduring disagreements or conflicts. They are both Anglo countries with the same heritage, he said. They are pretty much the same culturally, and they are at almost identical levels of economic development. (Canada. La misma cosa, verdad?) There was no correspondence with the American-Mexican situation, with its language, racial, cultural and economic differences.

Martínez is right that there are large distinctions between the two borders, of course; but it seemed to me that he saw the blatant differences in the south while remaining blind to the subtle differences in the north. And, in any event, he equated the dimensions of dissimilarity with their importance: if people were very different, you could have a real problem; if they were only slightly different, what could go wrong?

I thought Martínez was mistaken. I recalled Freud's phrase, the "narcissism of small differences": the notion that we direct our most negative emotions—aggression, fear, hatred—against those who most resemble us, and we emphasize the small differences that distinguish us from them. It's easy to support this idea with contemporary examples: the Tamils and Singhalese of Sri Lanka; the Turks and Greeks of Cypress; the various ethnic nations of the Balkans. I wrote a book about the people among whom I was born: the Protestants and Catholics of Northern Ireland, who are, to an outsider, absolutely identical to each other, but who can distinguish among themselves with unerring and vicious ease. Any civil war supports Freud's view—the United States' very own conflict, for example.

Similarity, or apparent similarity, means nothing in deciding, or predicting, whether two groups will fall into conflict, or in foreseeing its intensity. Canada and the United States may have similar political and economic systems and cultures, but that's not the point. The fact that Canadians and Americans resemble each other in many ways is irrelevant to the scale or virulence of any arguments that might arise between them. Similarity is no barrier to conflict. On the contrary, Freud's phrase emphasizes that similarity can make any conflict more vicious.

Professor Martínez's view of the northern border surprised me, coming as it did from an academic who specializes in border issues. I had expected a more nuanced take on borders in general, and on the Canadian line in particular. But his attitude did confirm the proposition that Americans look at Canada in a more or less uniform way—regardless of class or education.

There are pockets along the border that can be described as borderlands in the sense that Bolton first described. The Madawaska country of the Brayons is the best example. In Van Buren or

Fort Kent, Maine, and in Edmundston, New Brunswick, the visitor has a clear view of a separate, and self-aware community that happens to straddle the international line.

Similar enclaves exist elsewhere along the U.S.-Canadian border, although they are much less clearly defined: the Acadian- and Québecois-Yankees of the Quebec–New Hampshire–Vermont borders; the communities along both shores of the St. Lawrence River between Montreal and Lake Ontario; some twin cities such as Windsor-Detroit, the two Niagara Falls and the two Sault Ste. Maries; the "empty quarter" of the prairies, the two sides united by topography, farming, ranching, mad cows and wind chill; the British Columbia–Washington border region west of the Rockies, sometimes referred to as "Cascadia," the province and the state both separated by the mountains from the rest of their countries, and thus, made a little eccentric. To the extent that these examples constitute kinds of borderlands (and they certainly stretch the standard definition), they are only scattered islands in an archipelago strung along the length of the long northern boundary.

There's no doubt that the Canadian-American examples are very different from the ambience of the "third-country" borderlands between the United States and Mexico. In the latter case, the co-existence of two very different cultures side by side necessitates a constant dynamic of interaction and negotiation. The two sides of the line are like Siamese twins in their intimate intertwining.

Perhaps, it is the main function of a borderlands to act as a mediating buffer between two unlike societies, especially when there are serious problems between the adjoining states—such as illegal immigration, drugs and the possibility of terrorist infiltration. And this even more so when one of the countries fears the territorial encroachment of the other—*la Reconquista* again. As we've seen, there have been wars and near-wars over boundary disputes along both borders, but in the south the bitter memories and guilty fears persist of American invasion and annexation of Mexican territory. There is the sense along the Mexican border that things haven't really been settled, that in the future, a version of "Greater Mexico" may well root itself on American soil—that maybe it ain't over.

There's nothing like that in the north; the border established after the War of Independence is still the same, with very minor adjustments, and with later negotiated extensions to the west, which both sides long ago accepted as reasonable. It may be that societies that are generally alike in their culture and economic status don't need what a borderlands provides: a place to mix and talk, to bargain over culture and political rights, and to defuse tension.

However, there is another perspective on the northern borderlands. Some historians (the American Robin Winks, for example) have argued that Canada itself—the whole country—is a borderlands society. Three-quarters of Canadians live within 160 kilometres of the U.S. border, and most of those live well south of the emblematic 49th parallel. (I'm typical: as I type these words at the relatively high latitude of 48 degrees, 51 minutes north, I can look out my window on my out-of-the-way island off the British Columbia coast and see the lights of Blaine, Washington, 55 kilometres away across the Strait of Georgia.) Geographically, therefore, the bulk of the Canadian population lives close enough to the border to qualify as residents of a true borderlands.

This southern tilt is a defining aspect of Canada: the concentration of people in the extreme south of a vast country. They have been forced there by climate, and by the availability of arable land. The north quickly becomes hostile, untenable: rock, boreal forest, then tundra and ice (all this is changing, of course, as the climate warms, but even that won't transmute the

Canadian Shield or tundra into tillable soil). Canada is the second-largest country in the world, behind Russia. But the Canada where almost all its people live consists of this narrow strip adjacent to the border. If Canada has one-tenth the population of the United States, and an economy roughly one-tenth as large, its viable, livable, workable territory (apart from resource-extracting operations like mining and forestry) is also a small fraction of that of the United States. What looks like a giant country is, in practical terms, a truncated domain whose people live in small population pockets spread out east to west, which are separated by long tracts of almost empty, or rural, land, or by the Great Lakes.

The great majority of Canadians have never travelled to the true north, and know as much about it as Americans know about Canada. "Up north" to a Torontonian means Muskoka or the Kawarthas—summer-cottage country, which, by any definition, is still in southern Ontario. The term has nothing to do with north of Superior, or Hudson Bay, let alone "North of 60" (degrees latitude) where the huge territories begin. The Yukon, the Northwest Territories, and Inuit-governed Nunavut extend far north, encompassing the islands of the Arctic Archipelago and reaching across what's left of the sea ice to the pole. Non-native Canadians cluster as far south as they can because that's where it's been easiest to survive. It was also, historically, where the means of transportation were: the rivers and lakes that penetrated halfway across the continent. But Canadians also live south because that's where the United States is.

Separated as they are by distance, mountains and Great Lakes into regional populations, Canadians have always found it easier to forge north-south relationships than east-west ones. The idea behind Garreau's Nine Nations—the existence of cross-border regions—is still relevant. Ontario is as linked to its adjacent border states through trade and a common culture as it is to Quebec. The Prairie provinces naturally look south to the familiar landscape and people of the Dakotas, Montana and Idaho, rather than east or west. The Maritime provinces have old connections with New England—and old quarrels, too—which forge their own bonds between people who must live side by side. Coastal British Columbians can see the United States to the south, but not Alberta across two mountain ranges, so south is where they more often travel and trade.

In the long aftermath of 9/11, these long-standing habits may be changing under the impact of American security measures along the border. As the south becomes more hostile, Canadians may draw together east and west in a way they have not had to before. Indeed, I believe that is happening already.

Canadian provinces are in the process of negotiating away trade and labour barriers within Canada. And, once again, the post-9/11 security regime in the United States, with its restrictive rules and regulations, makes transport of goods across the border progressively slower and more complicated, in spite of the Canada-U.S. Free Trade Agreement of 1988. Both developments will, in time, make east-west intra-Canadian trade easier and more extensive, even if American consumers remain the primary market.

Canadian economic interests have always dictated staying close to the border. It's where the economic action is. Until 2007, Canada was the biggest exporter to U.S. markets, having displaced Japan in 1991, although Canada has now been supplanted (likely for good) by China. During those years, the province of Ontario sold more to America than Japan did. No matter how it stands in relation to other countries' trade volumes, the United States will always be Canada's economic lynchpin. More than 80 per cent of Canadian exports go south, and, whatever happens to the actual dollar figures, that percentage is not likely to change. In fact, the huge reserves of oil-sands oil in Canada's west, and its cache of fresh water, will become more and more precious commodities. As they do, both the dollar value, and the percentage, of Canadian exports going to the United States will rise.

Canadians also look south because they know, or they believe, they live on the cold fringe of the continent, and that the centre lies over the border. The adolescent, or, from another perspective, the colonial, state of mind that has defined Canada from its beginning, persists. Canada has been doubly colonized. Even as it weaned itself—in slow, cautious, non-revolutionary steps—from the mother country, it fell into a similar political and cultural dependence on the United States. Canadians don't want to be like Americans (although at the same time, in some ways, they do). They don't want the American way of governing, or of conducting foreign policy (which so often takes the form of coercion, threat, bombing or invasion); nor do they want American social values like private health care (the devil take the poorest), or a gun in every pocket. But Canadians, like Iranians, say, or (secretly) the French—in fact, like most of the world—hunger for the cultural paraphernalia of America.

Being similar to Americans in so many ways, and living just next door, Canadians have, more than any other nation, a sometimes hopeful, often despairing, ambivalence about the United States. In recent times, American power has often exerted itself on the world in terrible ways. Its own existence is founded on the removal or elimination of native North Americans. (Although every state is conceived in killing and displacement, the American misfortune is that its sins are recent and documented.) Yet, the sense remains that America still has the ability to reinvent itself, and, perhaps, to get back closer to its founding, shining ideals. The idea of the city upon a hill has never quite disappeared.

The Democratic primary campaign involving Barack Obama and Hillary Clinton, and, above all, the nomination and election of Obama, was a reminder of this unique, long-lived capacity for renaissance. The president, in particular, seems to capture the old American theme: we can rid ourselves of history's baggage, and start again, making things new and better, and break with the deadly continuities of history.

The classic southern variety of borderlands may well be, as one commentator put it, "hybrid spaces . . . where binary distinctions falter and where new social realities flourish." Or, as another observer writes, the southern borderlands are "poetic kinds of places—inherently ambiguous and dual." In the north, however, the borderlands are an odd, one-sided, unbalanced phenomenon. They represent one nation's fear and fascination. And they reflect Canada's fate: to be compelled to know, and to understand, the United States, but to have to accept that Americans know nothing of this reflexive compulsion, and, therefore, of any necessity to reciprocate.

The next day, dried out and almost back to normal, I ride out of the Republic of Madawaska, and back into America.

In Van Buren, the morning is cold with a light rain. It takes me an hour to repack my clothes and gear, and load the bike. My flu symptoms have gone, except for a small headache—a minor wonder, I think, given yesterday's hypothermia. I check the tire pressure and oil the chain—the lubricating gunk needs replacing twice a day in this drenching weather. Once again, I put on almost all the clothes I have. Before I can leave, I start to sweat in the many layers; the cold wind is a relief when I do get under way.

I ride along the Saint John River in mist and mizzle turning to rain. Both banks are hilly, spring-greening farmland. I pass through Notre Dame, Lille, Frenchville. The churches and graveyards look just like those in New Brunswick and Quebec. Names on stores are mostly French. I stop in Fort Kent, the northern terminus of Route 1. Two-thirds of its people use every-day French, and many are dual citizens. It lies across the river-border from Clair and Saint-François de Madawaska. I walk around the Blockhouse, built in 1839 during the Aroostook War, although, of course, it was never fired from—or fired on. It's an historic site now, and I read the plaques about the old and toothless war. A few yards away, the Fish River is high, lead-coloured with runoff, and it rushes past towards the Saint John. There are no other vehicles in the large parking lot. The cold rain falls without let-up.

I mount up and head south on Route 11, the old Aroostook Road. I've made a long loop up into the northeast corner of Maine, and I have to get south again before I can make any westing. To the west, between Route 11 and the Quebec border, there are no roads through the Maine wilderness—little changed from the time the first, guessed-at border was agreed to in 1783.

I ride alongside the Fish River and past Eagle and Saint Froid Lakes. It's a good smooth road that rises, drops and twists in well cambered, gentle curves. There is almost no traffic. The country is rolling farmland, soon replaced by wooded hills. I stop in Portage to dry out a little and to drink a warming coffee. The waitress begins: "Yes, monsieur?" The whole area is French all the way down almost to Bangor, she says. She's a dual citizen, born in Edmundston, New Brunswick.

As I leave Portage, wondrous things happen. The rain slackens and stops; the clouds become lighter grey. The sun appears, misty and shrouded at first, then in intermittent full shine. There are patches of blue sky for the first time since I arrived in the east. As visibility grows, I see farther all around me the green hills of Maine, and, farther away, snow glinting higher up on its mountains. The road dries off.

Now I can ride.

The next six hours or so make up one of those days on a motorcycle that you always remember. They're what bring you back for more, no matter how cold, wet, saddle-sore or scared you get at other times. They are few enough, these instants of joy, of exultation, on a bike. They bring sailing to mind: most of the time, there's not enough wind, or there's too much, or it's too hot or cold, or the wind's blowing from the direction you want to go in, or things break, or, on the worst day, things go very wrong and you think you may die. Sometimes, however, everything is just right, and the boat hews her way through the sea in easy grace and gentle beauty, with a warm sun, or, if at night, under a bright, reflecting moon; or phosphorescence like all the jewels in the world bounces in your wake, and, perhaps, dolphins converge and "pahh" their companionable exhalations beside you. It's inconceivable to be bereft forever of those sensuous and intense moments. You return over and over again to plough your way through the shit that happens more often than not, hoping to stumble into that enchanted groove one more time.

The curves in the road come along one after the other. Approaching one going right, I ease off the throttle, maybe give the front brake a quick squeeze—I don't want to come in too hot—gear down one, maybe two, gears on this high-torque machine, look ahead into the curve, searching out its radius, waiting to see it open out again so I can judge how tight it is, looking where I'm heading. Coming in, I countersteer—the counterintuitive push on the right handlebar to destabilize the bike and put it into a lean to the right—heading for the left side of my lane to help me see what's ahead and get a better angle, keeping constant speed, countersteering both ways to keep my line. I see the radius open up, squeeze the throttle to settle the bike down harder on its contact patches to increase its traction, gear up again, more throttle as I come out of the curve, countersteering on the left handlebar to bring the bike upright again, accelerating hard out into the straightaway. I'm already sizing up the next curve ahead, maybe coming out of one and right into another, and then another, leaning side to side in slow undulations.

The rhythm is everything, and so is judging how fast to ride into each arc of the road. As always, I watch the surface: for loose stone or gravel spilled off the shoulder, or for greasy patches. This is moose country, too, and it's their season for ambling across highways more than usual. There are flashing lights on signs: "Danger: Moose Next 1,500 yards," or "Next 14 miles." In gas stations, men warn me about the big lunks. I hit one, I die. The country slides by in steady variety, but I see only quick flashes of it—trees, and the sudden long vistas of hills and distant mountains, the river rapids mile after mile gushing by on my left, and later, on my right. The road is everything. I must focus on its shape and texture, on the differential geometry of its bends and camber as if nothing else existed, like a hunter watching prey.

The ride becomes a kind of meditation. It takes me out of myself so that the speed, my shifting gaze ahead, and the mechanical functions of my hands and feet squeezing, pushing, lifting, twisting, become my universe. No other worries; no clutter, or disordered thoughts, in the mind; no tunes or music looping obsessively through it. I feel clean and centred. I'm at one with my quick, turning passage over the road.

At fifty or fifty-five miles an hour, I can't make a mistake. If I go off the high side of a curve, over the centre line, I'm in head-on collision territory (although this road is blessedly empty). If I misjudge a left-turning curve, I'm off into the unknown country of the shoulder, before a drop-off or a rock wall. I have to be right through each twisty. If I'm going to misjudge my velocity, I'd better go in too slow—speeding up again is easy. But then, too slow feels like a failure. Go in too hot just once, and I am in jeopardy. This constant rhythm of judgment and limits, of danger, and of the possibility of pain or death, draws out such strange and enigmatic joy. It hums through me like the flux of life.

CHAPTER 14

THE PARANOID STYLE

AMERICA OUR NATION HAS BEEN BEATEN BY
STRANGERS WHO HAVE TURNED OUR LANGUAGE
INSIDE OUT WHO HAVE TAKEN THE CLEAN WORDS OUR
FATHERS SPOKE AND MADE THEM SLIMY AND FOUL.
—JOHN DOS PASSOS, *USA*

IN ONE CORNER OF THE BIG, CLUTTERED ROOM, five or six rifles and pump-action shotguns lean up against the wall in a casual, offhand stack. I can't see any handguns, but I'm sure there are some about. Joseph Martin, the Minuteman, and I sit on the same side of a long wooden table. If it weren't for the view out the window, I'd feel I was back in the Arizona desert. Through the window, until night falls, I can see the fields and valley of the Androscoggin River, and rolling, wooded hills running to the north and east. Joe began building this house twelve years ago. It's across the road from the farm he was born on. His family has deep roots in this valley. His last name—originally Acadian—is scattered all through it.

Joe is a bull. He's in his early fifties, about five feet ten, muscular, big arms, a small gut growing. He has close-cut grey hair that comes to a peak low down on his forehead, and dark eyebrows. Chest and back hair billows out around his

T-shirt neck. He gives the impression of primitive power, of a strong-armed vigour. He does not appear to be the sort of man one wants to piss off.

Joe has prospected for gems and precious minerals all over Canada, and in twelve countries in Africa. Now, he is "prospecting" for renewable energy sites. His business card says: "Alternative Energy Procurement." Underneath that, a gentle lyricism seeps out in the words he has added: "Full Sun, Fairwinds and Falling Water." His other business card says, with the same poetic compression: "Maine Minutemen: Borders, Language, Culture," and, farther down, the uncompromising: "No illegal entry; No amnesty." Joe is the state director of the Maine chapter of the Minuteman Civil Defense Corps. You know where he stands.

Joe's wife, Cathy, is in the room, too. She works at a computer in one corner. She is pretty and quiet, says hardly a word. She is a pharmacist's assistant in town. She met Joe just after he got back from Africa. She hasn't travelled much, she says—just a small-town girl. For a woman in remote Rumford, Maine, a prospector's hard life in the bush of two continents must have seemed like exotic adventure. Joe strikes me as one of those men for whom there is no problem that cannot be solved. He can fix or build anything. The only thing that can defeat him is death. I've worked, and sailed, with men like this. They are the best of men with whom to face danger, or difficult times. They value honour, loyalty and honesty. But they can make hard enemies; they hold a grudge; they are capable of violence; they believe certain things about the world, and they are not prepared to concede a conflicting view.

I had called Joe, after my rapturous ride south out of the Madawaska, from a motel beside a covered wooden bridge on the Piscataquis River near Dover-Foxcroft. When I arrived in the late afternoon, the sun came out, and it actually got hot. I boiled and sweated in my many layers until I reached my room and could strip some off. After dinner, I went for a walk in shirt sleeves along the river and over—and under—the ingenious timbered web of the bridge. Maybe tomorrow would be warm and dry.

The evening's warmth and sunshine had been a teasing interlude. In the morning, it was cold and raining again. I rode over the Longfellow Mountains where, in the higher passes, the rain turned to sleet. For a while, I had to slow down to twenty miles an hour when freezing rain fell. I scraped ice off my visor. The bike skidded and slipped a little from time to time, but I was getting used to the existential hollowness of no-traction. If I went down at this speed, my crash bars and the bulk of my bags would cushion the bike's fall, and my bones and flesh felt secure enough in my bulletproof gear. It got cold, and when I stopped in a gas station store in Jackman, about fifteen miles south of the border, I hung about for a long time drinking coffee, and trying to warm up. A guy inside said to me: "Man, you are hard-core, riding that thing in this weather. You are really hard-core."

I thought, that's me: hard-core rider.

In a motel in Stratton that night, I recovered from my hypothermia by way of a long, hot shower and an hour in bed. My flu was gone—which amazed me given what I had been putting my aging body through. I felt I was toughening up, getting stronger. I was the only guest in the motel's twenty rooms. From my window, I looked out through the rain to a half-flooded field where seven ducks waddled and paddled. Low, wooded hills faded away into the mist.

It was a short ride to Rumford, close to where I would meet Joe that evening. And so, in the morning, I lingered over coffee, and bagels with cream cheese, which the motel provided. The elderly, garrulous owner told me at length about his own days many years ago riding around America on a Honda 90.

"It was slow going on that old boy, I'll tell you," he told me. "Now, a man wouldn't be caught dead on a little, tiny bastard like that."

The owner was typical of so many of the men I was running into, who had ridden bikes in the past, or who wanted to ride—just as soon as they could convince the damn wife to let them do it. They were all so wistful and admiring, although envious, too. Up here in northern Maine, there were lots of ATVs and pickups, men in hunting jackets, convenience stores with ammo and fishing rods for sale. A guy on a dual-sport thumper, loaded down and long-riding, was something they approved of.

I checked into the Blue Iris Motel just outside the village of Rumford Center, as one of two guests in its fourteen rooms. Joe Martin had recommended it. Out back, the Androscoggin River was in flood, and tongues of water had filled the gully between the riverbank and the buildings. Ducks and a muskrat mooched around below the room's rear deck. No nearby restaurants were open, and I didn't feel like doubling back to the town of Rumford, so I ate beef jerky, an apple and an orange for supper. Belatedly, I realized I could have set up my camp stove on the deck and boiled a pouch of expensive, high-tech camping grub—chicken stew or pad Thai—using my nifty compact pot, plate and cutlery. On the map, I could see all around me the jokey place nomenclature of this part of Maine: towns named after countries—China, Poland, Mexico, Sweden—and after cities—Naples, Berlin, Madrid, Moscow, Athens. At eight in the evening, I rode the six or seven miles to Joe's house.

My conversation with Joe is a reprise of my time with the southern Minutemen in the Arizona desert. There are the same elements of reasonableness, which abruptly disintegrate into fevered and fearful illogic. He is intelligent enough and articulate, but he is suspicious of other people's motives, and of the machinations of institutions and of governments. Sometimes he is paranoid. He doesn't quite understand how government and the legal system works, and he fills in the explanatory gap with sordid deals and conspiracies. In America, no one is supposed to lose. If you do, if things go badly for you, even though you're smart and work hard, then it must be someone else's fault. A conspiracy. Joe begins his analysis of America's problems in a reasonably calm and ordered, if idiosyncratic, manner. But very soon, his train of thought wobbles on its tracks; eventually it derails. And he proposes a solution that is both scary, and almost impossible to imagine actually happening. I am back, once again, in the America of pissed-off white men.

When Joe came back to the United States in the mid-1990s, after prospecting in Africa, he was shocked at how the country had changed. People were fatter and lazier. Many more of them were on welfare. They shopped at Walmart. Soon, he began to see a lot of illegal workers from Mexico arriving in Maine, and nothing happened to them. Maine is a "sanctuary state," says Joe. Illegals are protected here; they get driver's licences, medical care, welfare. The government estimates there are around five thousand *indocumentados* in the state. But, Joe says, there are at least twenty thousand, closer to thirty thousand during harvest season. Even though he lives close to the northern border, it's the Mexicans he's really concerned about, now that they've spread so far and wide. He thought he had to do something. He contacted the Minuteman headquarters, and got their permission to start a new chapter.

It's not like along the southern border, he says. There are only eight Minutemen in Maine. They include a lawyer, an ex-undersecretary of the navy, a press guy, a photographer. He's vetted more than fifty potential members to weed out the wackos and Rambos. They are not part of his view of the solution. Guys like that may be necessary in the south among the drug runners and gunmen. The southern border is a sieve. But the Canadian border is different. New England people have the same origins as Canadians, and relations are friendly. Maine especially: it's the only state with just one border with another state. The rest of its land boundary is with Canada.

Joe's not about to run campaigns along the line with night scopes and side arms (although other northern Minutemen have done just that). Instead, his group will make submissions to the legislature on existing and new legislation. They are in the process of informing sheriff's departments that they can get special policing training from ICE (Immigration and Customs Enforcement)—federal funding is available for that. If Joe hears about an employer hiring illegals, he'll tell the police. It's a low-key operation, he says.

Every Minuteman I've spoken to has said, sooner or later: I've got nothing against immigrants; we're all immigrants here; America is a country of immigrants. Now, Joe says exactly the same thing. His own grandfather—a McCafferty— was a recent immigrant from somewhere on the northwest coast of Ireland. It's the same in Canada, he says. But the problem is that these new immigrants—the illegals from Mexico and farther south—don't come here to join America, to be Americans. They stay in their own enclaves and speak Spanish. America has a culture, and immigrants have to "meld in." They must speak English.

Joe has become less wary of me. He is warming up, and I detect the early signs of confusion and disordered polemic. He says: Bush was a liberal who only ran as a conservative to get elected. He sat down with Kennedy, for God's sake. Almost all Republicans are liberals now, and the Democrats are social- ists. NAFTA has taken away the right of Americans to work in the United States; the jobs have all gone overseas. A lot of

Maine people are on welfare because of this. The government has taken complete control of our lives: regulations, taxes. It's all globalization and outsourcing.

Canada is even worse; it's entirely socialist, including its so-called Conservative Party. Nevertheless, if Canada becomes sensible, the northern border can be secured. A wall is probably not necessary, but many more Border Patrol agents are required, as is an equivalent force on the Canadian side. You also need electronic devices—cameras, motion sensors, drones. It's just a matter of enforcing the laws on each side, and of putting boots on the ground along the length of the line.

Just like the southern Minutemen, Joe is anxious to ask me what I think of him and his organization. And he is as eager to believe that his apprehension of the world is widely held. Isn't there a similar group in Vancouver, just like the Minutemen? he asks. Someone told him that. Because so many people are trying to get into Canada from the U.S. I haven't heard of any such group, I say, and, so far, the illegal traffic, such as it is, goes south across the border, not north—although that can always change.

Well, anyway, says Joe, Canada is nothing compared to Mexico. The Mexican government has conspired with the U.S. government, under the trade agreements, to send those twelve million illegal workers up here. The employers are all in on it, too. Business carries out lobbying in Washington to stop local sheriffs from getting rid of illegals. The sheriffs could do it if they weren't stymied by Washington. Wall Street is controlled by multinational interests, and it isn't American at all any more. The Bush administration's proposal for a solution to the southern border problem was amnesty, says Joe, and it only encouraged the continued flood of cheap, alien labour into America. It was no solution at all. The next administration can only be worse. He deeply fears for his kids and grandkids.

Here is Joe's prescription for the south: Build a wall along the southern border with double fences to back it up, creating a no man's zone. Build the wall with illegals you round up. When you catch an *indocumentado*, you give him and his family six months to pack up and leave. If they don't, they work for one year on the wall—no pay—and then you ship them back to Mexico. You give business a time limit, a short one, to get rid of illegal workers. If they don't do it, you nationalize the companies, seize their assets and sell them. Get the troops out of Iraq right now. Put all of them along the southern border. There are no legal problems with this because the army would be on the border and policing non-Americans. We know how to deal with traitors, and anyone objecting to the use of the army for this purpose, or to the wall, or to seizing private companies, is a traitor.

When Joe winds down and stops talking, there is a silence. Joe's wife, still sitting off to one side, watches her husband with a fond smile. I have heard this sort of preposterous bluster before, of course, but it still throws me. I can't shake the feeling that I am the butt of an elaborate joke, and that the speaker will suddenly break down in uncontrollable laughter at the idea I was beginning to take him seriously. Sucked the dumb Canuck right in. Joe's not laughing.

But, I say, what about the Constitution? Laws? Due process? Human rights? You can't use forced labour, or just grab a company and sell it whenever you feel like it. Joe amiably agrees. No, the will to implement this necessary solution is not there now. But Joe sees an economic crisis coming that will threaten to cripple America. Then, "some strong people" will get into politics, a "strong person" will become the country's leader (he doesn't say "president"), and things will happen. It's inevitable.

It's also late, and I must leave. Joe says that if I come by that way again, I should stay with them instead of in a motel.

They'd be glad to have me. We're neighbours, after all. He's genial and solicitous. Maybe I've been too polite, too goddamn Canadian—although he likes the fact that I arrived on a motorcycle and I'm humping it clear across the country. He warns me about the moose that come out of the forest for several miles along the road. Ride slow, he says, watch out for the big, mean bastards.

It is a very cold night, close to freezing, but clear, with an eighth moon. The indifferent constellations glitter across the arc of the sky. I ride down the winding, deserted road for about half a mile. I'm heading into a gentle left curve when all my lights cut out. I'm doing forty miles an hour, and I am utterly blind. The dark around me is absolute and uniform. It's like a soft, black wall I'm burrowing into. I try to follow what I remember of the curve, while I brake hard. I can feel the trees and ditches close by; I can smell the big, mean bastard moose. When I do halt, I'm still on the road, but I can't see a thing. I realize that my engine is still running, and now I see that my brake light and turn signals work. The bike has two light circuits. I must have blown a fuse in one, and the other is still intact.

I consider returning to Joe's place. But I'm reluctant to take him up on his hospitality—the offhand oddity and implied violence of his ideas. I decide that if I can see enough to go back, I can probably see enough to reach my motel. You might call this a temporary intensification of the adventure, I say to Will, Chris and Mike. I stand astraddle the bike and wait for my night vision to grow.

It does, and the moon fragment and starshine help. After a while, I can make out the shadowy line of the road, a faintly lighter path between the darker shadows of the trees. I move off in first gear. By moving my head from side to side, I can use that odd, human peripheral vision to catch the suggestion of where I need to point. Sometimes I have to stop and make sure where the road goes. If there's a moose out there, I'll hit it at only five miles an hour. If it doesn't stomp me to death afterwards, I should survive the impact. It takes me close to fifteen minutes to get to the main two-lane road. There's another two miles to the Blue Iris. I head down the shoulder. Five or six trucks come by in each direction. When they do, I pull over and stop with my brake light and turn signal on. The trucks destroy my night vision. I close my eyes, but even so, I have to wait a minute or so before I can see anything again. I make the motel in another fifteen minutes.

There, I read in my shop manual that one of the KLR's two circuits has a small capacity ten-amp fuse. I assume that this fuse blew because I had my handgrip warmers on high at the same time as the headlight was on high beam. A mechanic who didn't know Kawasakis had wired the warmers into the wrong circuit. It had taken this long for the problem to appear because it was the first time I'd ridden at night in the cold. I could have high-heat warm hands and low beams, or low heat and high beams, but not both.

I can't sleep, and I spend an hour making notes. I write more of my impressions of Joe the Minuteman: his strange, sad and muddled fears for America; his fierce, peremptory and absurd remedy. I reflect, as I so often do, on how his country got to this. It's still the city upon a hill, although down below, there are beasts and blood. But it's always been like that. In the very beginning, Englishmen in America preached the new Jerusalem in the New World. But they were the seed of Protestant fundamentalism with its intolerance and rejection of rationalism. They exalted their mission into the wilderness, but it would not be long before they began the slaughter and displacement of the people already here, for whom America was not a new world, but their world, the world itself. And the slaves: they, too, soon arrived. It was a new world of a different sort for them.

In 1782, Jean de Crèvecoeur asked: "What then is the American, this new man?" The French traveller predicted that "[his] labours and posterity will one day cause great changes in the world." He meant for the good. That's all Joe desires too. Perhaps most of the Minutemen have that same hunger. But they are trapped in their country's founding dichotomy. Even the best government is but "a necessary evil," wrote the Englishman Thomas Paine in the momentous year of 1776. The new republic's new men were imbued with a wary mistrust from the beginning. The generous impulse and the sour suspicion are the two warring faces of America.

CHAPTER 15

RIDING TO NIAGARA

IT WAS THE LAST NOSTALGIA:
THAT HE SHOULD UNDERSTAND
—WALLACE STEVENS, "ESTHÉTIQUE DU MAL"

THE TRAIL BEHIND GORDIE'S METALWORKING SHOP winds up the hill to where there's an old tractor parked, and then it peters out. From there, we walk a narrow path up through the trees until we reach what looks like the clear-cut marking the border between the United States and Canada. Gordie told us it was better not to cross the line. He thinks there are sensors in the ground, or maybe cameras stuck up in trees. The last time a guy he knew walked across the line there, the Border Patrol chopper was overhead in two minutes, and some witless fucker with a bullhorn was shouting down at the guy, telling him to report to the patrol post right fuckin' now, or he'd be subject to stiff, goddamn penalties under the law. What bullshit, says Gordie. The guy was heading over to visit a friend. He'd been doing it for years; he'd walk across into the States, have a few beers, and walk back. It was much easier than driving all the way around. Now, the fuckin' Border Patrol "buddies" (a local term expressing contempt) were all over it. Just bullshit. The guy's a dual citizen, for Chrissake, born in the USA.

I'm with my old friend John, who's from Ontario and has timed his stay with mine. We're both visiting our mutual friend Steve, who was born here, lived in Toronto for a few years, couldn't stomach city life, and came home again. Steve is Canadian, born in Sherbrooke, sixty-five kilometres to the north. But a cousin, who lives nearby, is a dual citizen. Like so many people here, he was born in Newport, just south of the border. Gordie is dual as well, born in Newport, which has the closest hospital.

John and I stand around for a while. This looks like the border, although it could also be just a nondescript clearing in the woods. We look for markers, cameras, for any signs of buried detectors but see nothing. We turn and head back down. When we tell Gordie where we got to, he says we didn't go far enough. We should have walked in another fifty metres or so to see the real clear-cut. It used to be you couldn't see a damn thing in there, he says, unless you fell over a marker. But now, they've hacked out the bush, and you can tell exactly where the line is. Our clearing had certainly looked to us as if it might be the border. We didn't want to go farther in case we, too, got shouted at by a chopper-borne witless fucker. So we missed seeing this small part of the line that cuts through the towns of Stanstead, Quebec, and Derby Line, Vermont, and through the lives of its people.

Such confusion is common along the northern border. A lot of security experts have pointed out the obvious: if you want to secure the border, first you've got to figure out just where it is. Both Canada and the United States are obliged, by treaty, to maintain a visible three-metre-wide slash through the trees and over the mountains and prairie. They must set up stone pylons marking the line so that everyone—whether honest travellers, drug runners, illegals, terrorists or dual citizens going for a beer—will always know when they've crossed over. However, in some places—like the dirt track I would later ride along, and then across, between Saskatchewan and North Dakota, the border is far from clear. It's at its worst in New England where the heavy bush grows fast. The clear-cut becomes indistinct, and, in a surprisingly short time, it disappears. Now, of course, there's a lot of work underway by the United States—and, under pressure, by Canada—to mark the border. That's a first step in installing electronic listeners and watchers, and in putting armed men on the ground.

Elsewhere in Stanstead, the border is always there, butting in, getting in the way. The town is an amalgamation of several smaller villages: Rock Island, Stanstead Plain and Beebe Plain. On the American side, the original, small, separated settlements were eventually brought together into the town of Derby Line. On both sides of the line, the founders were New Englanders from Massachusetts and Connecticut who arrived between 1776 and 1798. On the Canadian side, they may, or may not, have been United Empire Loyalists—as we've seen, Americans came to British North America after the Revolution for many reasons. It didn't really matter. Life was much the same on both sides—Heaven was high, and Washington and Montreal (and London) were far away.

The early settlers were attracted by the fast-flowing Tomifobia River (which marks the border in places), and they set up a sawmill and a corn mill, and they quarried granite. Quarrying became the main business in the area. During the war of 1812, the United States set up a garrison in Derby, mainly to try to stop the local inhabitants from trading and visiting with the Canadians—who were their friends and family—across the line. Later in the war, a force of Quebec militiamen burned down the garrison's fort with no loss of life on either side. It may have been a cross-border raid in furtherance of the war effort. More likely, it was an attempt to stop U.S. military interference with trade and neighbourly contact.

The border was meaningless from the beginning. The towns spilled over it both ways. Roads crossed it back and forth with their own commonsensical logic. Houses were built right on top of the border—a family might cook dinner in the United States and eat it in Canada. Some of the river mills straddled the line, so that people from both sides could use them. In 1904, Carlos Haskell, an American, and his Canadian wife built the Haskell Free Library and Opera House on the international boundary so that everyone could use that, too. The international line runs down the middle of the reading room. A whole tool-and-die factory was established with half the building in the United States and half in Canada. If you'd wanted to give future border security guards nightmares, the whole place couldn't have been set up any better.

Stanstead and Derby Line, and the surrounding smuggler's-paradise lake and countryside, constitute a classic borderlands, one of those islands in the borderlands archipelago that stretches along the northern boundary.

Walking or driving around Stanstead is a continuous mundane comedy. I feel as if I'm in a cartoon and the Border Patrol guys are Yosemite Sam, jumping up and down in impotent rage as sardonic critters go about their insouciant business, not worried at all, and only a little inconvenienced by the furious cowboy. They have their jolly lives to lead, and part of the fun is outwitting the pistol-packing ranter. Bugs Bunny is always daring Sam to "step across that line." Sam can never refuse the challenge, and, each time, he steps off a cliff or plummets down a mine shaft. Everything is set up against him. He can't win.

However, this vivid state of affairs is changing, as the Department of Homeland Security tightens its local noose. The old hello-and-a-wave across the border is long gone. New agents have gradually replaced many of the regulars, who had lived here for years and weren't prepared to treat Jim the plumber, or their third grade teacher, or Uncle Larry as if they were potential terrorists. Now, anyone can be searched, or scanned, for radioactive material, or taken aside for secondary questioning. They can also be harassed by armed guys shouting at them out of choppers with bullhorns. All this tends to make people resentful. The American government is saying it may block off the many side roads running across the border within the twin towns. That would really make people angry. (Security gates were installed on some unguarded roads in September 2009.) And the new passport requirement is making things even worse. Like the Brayons of Van Buren, Maine, the dual citizens of Stanstead and Derby Line deeply resent the expense and the necessity of a passport, and they may just decide to cross elsewhere, whenever and wherever they damn well feel like it.

The irony is that the Border Patrol is stretched very thin here. They should use the locals as their eyes and ears, as force multipliers. Instead, their heavy-handedness is just pissing people off. Now, say Steve and Gordie, people on both sides of the line are even more likely than they normally would be to look the other way when they get wind of smuggling, or of an illegal jumping the border. It sounds like a line in the old English smugglers' song: "Watch the wall, my darling, while the gentlemen go by."

To get into the front door of the public library, John and I walk past a border pylon plunked into the sidewalk, out of Canada and into the United States. Across the street, Yosem . . . er, a Border Patrol agent in a pickup watches us with no expression. A few strides and we turn left onto the library entrance path. We go into the reading room, past the reference desk, and, stepping across a thick black line painted on the floor, we walk out of the United States and back into Canada where the books are shelved. It's fun. We're filled with glee, as if we've broken a taboo and got clean away with it. The librarians, who have seen all of this many, many times before, watch us with surprising tolerance and good humour. They, too, seem happy with the small-scale anarchy. In the attached opera house, the performances take place in Canada while the audience sits in the United States. During the Vietnam War, young men who had fled to Canada to avoid the draft, or as deserters, would come to the library to visit their families. As long as they stayed on the Canadian side of the black line, their sanctuary was intact.

The back door opens into Canada. Now, it is kept locked on the Canadian side so that library visitors must use the front, although they can still exit at the rear. I ask the librarians if there have been any smuggling problems: people walking in the front door from the U.S. and out the back door into Canada. They laugh. Oh yes, there have been incidents, but they're not allowed to talk about them any more—gives people ideas.

We drive down to the river and the border-straddling tool-and-die factory. Only the U.S. side is operating now. At one point, a line of marker pylons crosses an open, grassed area. We park beside them. Steve warns us not to step over the line. We're certainly under surveillance—on camera, or in person—and it's a pain in the ass explaining things. At worst, we might be scooped up and arrested. One of the main official crossings is at an intersection. The American and Canadian customs buildings lie kitty-corner, twenty yards across from each other. Canusa (CANada-USA) Street branches off in-between, the houses on its two sides in different countries. Steve knows a guy on the Canadian side who is good friends with an American neighbour across the street. They used to cross over all the time to chat, or to borrow tools or a lawn-mower, or to have a beer together. They still do that, says Steve, except that now they do it after dark. They may have to stop, though. There's word that the Border Patrol is planning to scan the street with night-vision cameras or infrared detectors.

Steve lives out of town on the shore of Lake Memphremagog, which has always been a smuggler's delight. It's mostly in Canada, but its southern quarter is in the States. Steve stops near a hill overlooking the lake. From here, lookouts for booze- and drug-runners would scan the lake for cops. During Prohibition, the lake was a favourite conduit. A persistent local rumour says that some enterprising drug smugglers are using a mini submarine to run dope across the line—much like the ingenious subs freighting tons of drugs along the Pacific shore from Mexico. The Americans have, according to another local rumour, taken the suggestion seriously enough to equip their patrol boats with military-grade sonar.

Steve takes us to several spots along the border between his place and Stanstead where the border is a wire fence. You can cross over anywhere with ease. Steve's cousin, who lives in Newport, used to park his car on the American side, and hop over the fence to help his mother, who lived in Canada. Once, the Border Patrol happened to catch him doing it. This was before 9/11, so they just said, "Hello," and told him to use the official crossing next time. Now, says Steve, the Border Patrol would "line" him, that is, forbid him from crossing for years, and he would get a very big fine. If he wanted to cross the border again, he would have to get a lawyer and petition for a pardon.

Gordie takes us out onto Lake Memphremagog in his new inboard runabout. We head south and cut the engine close to the border, which is invisible. One tree-lined section of the shore looks the same as any other, the water an undifferenti- ated, rippled blue in the warm evening sun. Gordie knows where the boundary is, though. He points to the small island just ahead of us. There is definitely a U.S. Coast Guard boat hanging out behind it, he says.

"If we cross the line by a foot, they'll be on us like flies on shit."

We drift around for a while discussing the rumoured drug-running sub, the unreasonableness of the American authorities, how it doesn't matter a damn what they do: if you can't bring dope or whatever, or whomever, you want to bring across here, you can always bring it, or them, across somewhere. You can make it slightly more inconvenient, but there's no way you can stop it.

"They have to try, though, don't you think?" I say. "You can't just leave the border wide open."

Gordie laughs. "It's fuckin' wide open anyways," he says.

On my last evening in the Stanstead borderlands, Steve, John and I cross into the States to eat dinner at a lakeside restaurant in Newport. We leave early because, Steve says, you never know how long buddy will hold you up at the border. This time, however, it's easy. The U.S. guy asks us where we're going and if we're bringing anything in with us. He checks our documents (two driver's licences and my passport) with his computer, and says, "OK." Coming back, the Canadian guy, who has long hair tied up into a ponytail, says: "Hi Steve. Where've you been?" We tell him. "Enjoy the rest of your evening, gentlemen," he says. He doesn't check our documents. It seems that on the Canadian side the old ways of border officialdom persist after all.

By the time I ride out of Stanstead, it has become hot and humid. Now, my riding jacket is a heavy, sweaty encumbrance—just as it was down south. Again, however, I trade discomfort for protection. I open up all the jacket's vents, and that helps, as long as I'm moving. I soak my Gore-Tex bandana in cold water, and switch to my light riding gloves.

Crossing back into the United States at the little border post in the middle of town, beside Canusa Street, I get held up a long time—about fifteen minutes. No one searches me but the American agent asks many questions: Who was I visiting?

How long have I known Steve (whom the agent knows, and doesn't seem to like much)? What do I do for a living? Then, he goes inside with my passport for a long time. Steve had mentioned that the border guys googled you if you had any kind of public persona. For some reason, this hasn't occurred to me before. When the agent comes back out, I ask him, with a smile, if he's been googling me. I'm implying: that's okay with me; in fact, it makes perfect sense to do that. He doesn't smile back.

"We are not permitted to discuss operational details," he says.

I stand and sweat. It runs down my face and over most of my body. He asks more questions, but also makes odd comments. For example: Strange, isn't it, that you were born in Belfast, Northern Ireland, and Belfast, Maine, isn't far from here? It crosses my mind—far from the first or last time on my rides—that I may be dealing with an idiot. Or is this some sort of subtle security interrogation technique to trip up the doltish transgressor? If so, it's too subtle for me. Eventually, he hands back my passport and says, "Go ahead." In my rear-view mirror, I count nine cars lined up behind me, a traffic jam in this burg.

A few minutes later, I stop for gas in Newport. As I'm swinging off the bike, I catch my right foot on the gas pump curb and wrench my ankle. It's not bad, however, and I don't give it much thought. An hour later, I'm riding along Route 105, through the Cold Hollow Mountains, a mile or so south of the border. A white pickup truck pulls out of a side road right in front of me. I'm covering the front brake and paying attention, so I am able to stop hard, gearing down as I brake. I miss the pickup (or he misses me) by a few feet. I can't see the driver through the tinted windows. I curse the son of a bitch, who just keeps going. I've ended up on the soft, gravelly shoulder, which tilts sharply to the right. I put down my right foot to steady the bike. I've forgotten about my ankle, which, taking the sudden weight, gives a sharp shot of pain. On instinct, I ease up, and the bike begins to fall over. It weighs 450 pounds. Like a fool, I try to stop it. It drops anyway, of course, but on the way, it rips up my ankle, popping blood vessels, tearing ligaments. This is the injury that will plague the remainder of my northern ride.

I can't lift the bike myself with all my gear aboard, and a damaged ankle. Another fine mess I've gotten myself into boys, I say to my lost friends. I'm stripping my bags off the horizontal machine when another pickup cruises slowly by. The driver surveys my scene. I expect him to stop and so don't wave. But then he speeds up and disappears. I can't believe it; I must look as if I'm in distress. I try to muscle the bike upright using the single-handed method: you plant your feet with your back to the machine, and use your leg and gluteus muscles to lever it up. But I can't put enough weight on my ankle. After ten minutes or so, a delivery van stops, and then a sedan. The two drivers and I right the KLR with ease. I reload my gear, but I'm shaken up by all this: the near-miss collision, my inability now to get the bike upright again if I drop it, the pain, which is efflorescing. But I'm out in the boonies, and don't have a choice. I swallow some codeine and mount up.

In the Dreamland Motel in Malone, New York, that night, I get a bucket of ice from the sympathetic owner. I guess I can get my boot off, but I'm reasonably sure I wouldn't be able to get it back on again. I put my foot, ankle, sock and Triumph leather riding boot into the ice-filled pail, and soak the whole shebang. I can move, but only in a dead-slow hobble. I ride the half-mile into town and eat lousy chicken and a so-called Caesar salad at a restaurant in which I am the sole customer.

When I get back to the motel, the owner is speaking French to some guests. Later, he tells me he's from Quebec but that he's a dual citizen. He sounds perfectly bilingual; I'm still in the borderlands. Two guys are sitting outside the next room to mine, one short and skinny with an eastern

European accent, the other obese and florid with a southern accent. They are drinking non-alcoholic beer out of cans in the warm, humid evening. The big guy is from Tennessee, the other one is Polish, and they are New York hydro workers, surveying the lines along this part of the border area. They get up close to the boundary sometimes, says the big guy, but it's all heavy woods. They've never seen the clear-cut, but they've sure as hell seen the Border Patrol lately. Used to be they didn't know what the Patrol was, but now, they see a couple of vans and pickups every day.

"I guess they want to keep out all that Quebec bud," says the Polish guy, with a Mitteleuropa sneer.

"And terrorists?" I ask.

"Yeah, and all the Canadian terrorists, too," says the man from Tennessee, with a loud, snorting laugh. He laughs so much, he starts to choke on his ersatz suds.

That night, I lie in bed with the wet boot on. My ankle is very sore, and my iced-up foot feels frozen in the wet leather. By now, I don't think I can remove my right boot. I'd have to cut it off. Perhaps I'll cross the border tomorrow and see a doctor for free, courtesy of the socialized Canadian medical system. I manage only to doze a little now and then during the night.

The next morning, however, I soak my foot, ankle, sock and boot in ice water for twenty minutes, and I ride on west. What's a doctor going to tell me? Stop riding and rest my ankle until it stops hurting so much? I either keep going or I abandon the ride. In three more days, I'll cross the Niagara River to St. Catharines, Ontario, where my mother lives. I had intended to visit her anyway, and I can rest there.

St. Catharines is just fifteen kilometres from the border. It's where we settled in Canada as Irish immigrants. I went to junior high, and then high school—and lived there for a few scattered and turbulent years afterwards—in my very own United Empire Loyalist borderlands. If I have any kind of hometown in my peripatetic life, it's St. Catharines. My oldest, and best, friend, who died in an accident nearby when he was thirty-four, is buried there. My father suffered his years-long breakdown, and endured his unending depression, in St. Catharines. He died his easeful death, which he welcomed more than not, in one of the local hospitals. My mother scattered his ashes in some park woods where he loved to walk. I seldom go back, but when I'm in that town, I'm filled with sweet and bitter longings for home and youth, both long gone. If I have to quit my ride, that's the place to do it.

Later in the morning, in humid, building heat, smoggy haze, and a blasting headwind, I ride into the Mohawk Reserve of Saint Regis. Together with the Akwesasne Reserve on the Canadian side, the land of the Mohawk Nation bestrides the St. Lawrence River international boundary. Like the Tohono O'odham in Arizona, the Mohawk were there first, and then the border was plunked down without consideration, consultation or notice, cutting through their territory. That's one reason the Mohawk don't like the border. The other reason is their view of themselves as a sovereign nation; as a matter of international law and convention, it's a given that one nation can't lay down a border running through the territory of another sovereign nation. The Mohawk, like the Tohono O'odham, subvert the legal and political assumption upon which the idea of the contemporary border is based: that the line marks the clear end of the jurisdiction of one nation and the beginning of another's. Of course, the Mohawk know (as do the O'odham) that, in the last resort, their form of sovereignty is a limited and conditional one. Nevertheless, they believe it sufficient to justify special status for themselves where the boundary—with its myriad laws and regulations—is concerned.

I park beside the tribal government buildings, which are new and extensive. The lot is almost full of late-model, shiny vehicles. I've decided that I'm going to do my job in spite of my ankle, and I hobble, very slowly, over to the main office. A guy coming out to his pickup gives me a sympathetic smile. I'm beginning to notice that when I dismount from my bike and totter away with my obviously painful limp, I elicit interest and mixed reactions, which break down by gender. Men look at me with understanding, respect and compassion, as if I've been honourably wounded. Women look at me as if they're thinking I'm a damned fool who's old enough to know better.

I have no appointment here. I should have made one, and I curse myself again as a lousy journalist: disinclined to make cold telephone calls, and with a preference for solitary watching. But the people here are kind and helpful. Chaz, the public information officer for the tribal council, gives me an hour-long interview. He's in his thirties, a big man, tall and heavy. He is also intelligent and eloquent; I discover that he has two master's degrees. He obviously feels constrained by the requirements of his job, and his answers to some of my questions are often vague.

The aftermath of 9/11 has made a bad situation for the Mohawk much worse, says Chaz. The metastasis of Homeland Security's endless rules and requirements is making the people even angrier and more recalcitrant. The Mohawk have never accepted the legitimacy of any kind of hindrance or questions while crossing from one country to another. The border, having been laid down arbitrarily across their land, is the white man's problem, not theirs.

Since 9/11, the delays are much longer, and getting worse. It's most difficult getting into the United States, but the Canadians often give them a hard time, too. There are supposed to be Indian traffic lanes on the bridge, but lately these have been closed more often than not. The people can get Nexus cards (pre-approved security clearance by U.S. Customs and Border Protection and the Canada Border Services Agency), which make crossing faster, but there's a lot of rigmarole in applying for one, and the necessity rankles. The Mohawk reject completely the idea of getting a passport. That goes against the whole idea of the sovereignty of the Six Nations, of which the Mohawk are so prominent a part. People might go over the border several times a day to do work, visit family or friends, or to buy things. They never know when there will be a delay on the bridge, which makes it difficult to make plans, or to get anything done on time. Never mind the sheer irritation, and the sense of violation.

What the Mohawk really need is a bridge, or a ferry—for their own use only, says Chaz. They would exercise complete jurisdiction over it and would be responsible for security, with specialized police and sniffer dogs. Such a crossing would satisfy passport requirements and Mohawk sovereignty. It will never happen, though. Who would fund it? he asks. And what government, I add, would ever relinquish control over a major border crossing?

It strikes me how familiar all this sounds. Chaz could be talking for the Brayons of Maine and New Brunswick, or, like Gordie or Steve, complaining about the severing of neighbourly connections between Stanstead, Quebec, and Derby Line, Vermont. The people of the Mohawk reserve, and of the islands of the borderlands archipelago, have much in common.

Mohawk problems are exacerbated, says Chaz, by the many layers of police forces and government departments they must deal with. These groups have confusing and overlapping jurisdictions. In the U.S., the police forces alone include the Border Patrol, the State Police, local cops, Immigration and Customs Enforcement, the FBI. In Akwesasne on the Canadian side, there are the Mounties, the Quebec Sûreté, the Ontario Provincial Police, the Cornwall force. And in the

Mohawk view, these cops are, in any case, operating on Indian land, and therefore have tenuous legitimacy. Throw in two tribal councils in two different countries, funded by two different governments, and you've got an unholy mess. Not to mention the complicated structure of Mohawk society itself, with its clans—Turtle, Wolf and Bear—whose longhouses are now called "families." Families have declined in importance over the last fifteen years or so, but they are still important to many people. Overlying the traditional structures are the elected chiefs, sub-chiefs, and the tribal council with its bureaucracy. As they tend to be in all small communities, the politics are complicated, personal, down and dirty.

As I rode through the reserve, I noticed many small roadside stands and shacks with signs over them: "Cigarettes" or "Smokes." Cigarettes are shipped across the border in huge numbers. In the past, even big tobacco companies engaged in the trade with Mohawks, and with members of other Indian tribes along the border. I ask Chaz about smuggling. He is even more cautious on this topic. Smuggling is an old tradition here, he says. But that's the case all along the line; it wasn't only Indians who did it. Mohawks traded to help the British during the Revolutionary War, and they smuggled goods across the border during the War of 1812—once again to aid the enemies of the new republic. Al Capone ran booze across the border from Canada through Mohawk land. Now, the main illicit goods are cooking oil, gasoline and cigarettes. I ask about drugs and illegal immigrants, but Chaz sidesteps me. There are so many bad stereotypes involved in these issues, he says. He's bland and skilled and I can't pin him down.

I remark on all the new homes and the houses under construction, and on the unusual prosperity of this reserve. A lot of that is driven by well off ironworkers who are retiring and moving back with their families, or by retired military veterans, says Chaz. The population of Saint Regis has more than doubled in the last seven years. These older guys have been up in the high steel and out in the world for years. They are a small minority on the reserve, but they do provide something of a counterweight to the young men and women of the tribe who tend to be radical and militant about Mohawk rights. It's not just the radicals, says Chaz; mainstream activists on the reserve wear Che Guevara T-shirts.

Under the Great Law of Peace (which united the warring Iroquois tribes), all Mohawks, "Keepers of the Eastern Door" of the Iroquois Confederacy, are warriors, says Chaz. The radicals on the reserve take that literally. Hence, the Warrior Society and its prominent role in AIM (the American Indian Movement) and in various standoffs in Canada, such as at Oka, Quebec, and now in Caledonia, in Ontario. The occupation of Alcatraz Island was led by a Mohawk from Saint Regis. (The Mohawk have taken the initiative to establish links with the Tohono O'odham. At a meeting on the O'odham reservation, Mark Maracle assured the southern tribe that the Mohawk will support their campaign against "the militarization of their lands . . . by any means necessary. We are directed under our Law to go to the aid of others and not just sit back and watch the devastation," he said. The United States' fence through O'odham land "will disrupt nature and the natural order.")

Chaz remarks that I don't seem to have the usual agenda: Mohawks as bad-ass Indians running drugs, getting drunk, raising shit. It's true. I don't think they should be running drugs over the St. Lawrence, and they have to acknowledge the necessity of the border. But apart from that, I think they've got a strong case for a form of sovereignty, for a measure of autonomy, and for compensation for land taken from them, mostly by the Americans, but by the British and Canadians, too. I come from Northern Ireland, I say to Chaz. I was born among people who had been held down for a few centuries, and who only stopped killing each other in the aftermath a few years ago. I'm not over-simplifying—although it sounds like a cliché—when I say that I come from a people long oppressed and colonized (although the English-Irish relationship was an exceedingly complex one). When I think about the Mohawks, I think about the Irish, too—my own people.

Chaz has been generous with his time, but I've imposed long enough. I ask about a place to eat lunch, and, after some hesitation, he suggests the Sunflower, just down the road. It's an iron-workers' hangout, almost a shrine to the warriors of the high steel, and it should be interesting. As I'm leaving, Chaz says: It's okay to look around the restaurant—the walls are papered with photographs of Mohawk ironworkers—but probably better for a white man not to try to start a conversation with anyone. Unless they talk to me, keep to myself. It can be a tough place in the evenings, but it should be okay for lunch.

I ride up to the Sunflower. (They should have called it the Mayflower, I say to myself; that would have been funny.) It's just an average-looking restaurant. But outside, three young men stand and stare at me as I stop. They have long hair and one of them has braids. They are wearing beads and necklaces. One man has a headband with a single feather stuck in it cock-eyed. And yes, from thirty feet away, I can see that one of them is wearing a Che Guevara T-shirt. Maybe that means he's a mainstream activist. Maybe not; as I dismount, the three young men stiffen and glower. They look at me with contempt and dislike, as if they smell a stink. I'm a little intimidated, but not enough to ride away. I've had these sorts of stares before—along the southern border, from men who were openly armed, and in Northern Ireland, from hard men who shot and bombed people like me, someone from the "other side."

Besides, and more important, here in Saint Regis, it's noon and broad daylight beside a main road.

At the Sunflower, I'm saved by my ankle. It's as sore as ever in my still-damp boot (which helps keep me cool, at least), and I begin to limp very slowly, and in obvious pain, towards the warriors, and, I hope, a sandwich. Everything changes before I've taken four steps. The young men relax; their body language switches abruptly to concern and sympathy. One of them smiles.

"Had an accident, man?" a second one says.

"Oh . . . yeah," I say. I'm taken aback by the quick change of mood. "Yeah, I just about got wiped out by some guy in a pickup yesterday, and dropped the bike."

"I hear you, man," says the now completely amiable Mohawk, as his companions nod in brotherly compassion. "These fuckin' guys don't see you."

"Do you guys ride?" I ask. I'm more relieved than I realized.

They do ride: Harleys, of course. But they're politely interested in my homely thumper. We stand around the KLR for five minutes discussing its virtues, and ignoring its looks. They like the idea that I'm completely self-sufficient if I need to be, that I have strapped aboard everything I need. They think it's "pretty fuckin' neat" that I'm riding the border from end to end. I ask if they want to have some lunch with me, but they've eaten, and were just leaving when I arrived.

"Are you guys activists for the Mohawk cause?" I ask. It's a clumsy question, but I don't know how else to put it.

"Fuckin' right," says one guy.

"So you don't believe anyone should prevent you from crossing the border whenever you want?"

"It's your border, man, not ours," he says. "We believe that we have the same rights as the government in Washington. The border is a colonial imposition on us." This guy sounds like he's quoting from one of the many radical Mohawk websites I've looked at.

"This is the Mohawk Nation, man," says another.

"You guys were sure giving me the eye when I pulled up," I say.

All three laugh. "Yeah," says the guy with the braids, "sorry about that."

We shake hands biker-style.

"Be careful out there," says the man with the feather.

I go inside, and order an egg salad sandwich and some fries. On the walls are hundreds of photographs, and many paintings in a realist-heroic style. They depict Mohawk warriors in a score of big American and Canadian cities, perched on narrow girders, or strolling along them, hundreds of feet aloft, insouciant, working the high steel.

When I arrive home in British Columbia several weeks later, there's an email from Chaz. He says he googled me after our meeting (it seems everyone does it), and that he was "pleasantly surprised" by the other books I'd written, and especially by my book about Northern Ireland. He gives me his personal email address, and says he'd be happy to talk again in a personal, rather than an official, capacity. By the time I do have a chance to follow up with him by email, Chaz has left the Saint Regis Tribal Council and has become executive director of the Mohawk Chamber of Commerce at Akwesasne.

His comments are mainly elaborations on his earlier ones. Websites that, to an outsider, appear to be radical in their approach to Mohawk nationhood, are, from a Mohawk perspective, mainstream, Chaz writes. When I ask about radical activists, Chaz corrects me: they are "sovereignty activists." He abhors the "godawful awkwardness that is played out on the border, multiple times each day, when the uniformed government border control services insist on asking: 'What country are you a citizen of?' To Kanienkehaka [the 'people of the flint'], we are neither." The only reasonable answer is

"North American Iroquois." But that's not acceptable to either government.

It's always the same, Chaz says; governments divide and conquer. Everything the Canadian or American government does is a strategy towards the "endgame to see aboriginal sovereignty dissolved through assimilation and marginalization." Some tribal leaders go along with this in the name of pragmatism. But, to him, the word is merely "a buzzword for appeasement to the mainstream system." Such leaders constitute "Vichy councils."

The border crossing issue is an emotional powder keg for the Mohawks, Chaz says. The People of the Flint hold allodial (inalienable) title to Akwesasne—all of it, on both sides of the river. All Mohawks believe that. He himself tries to avoid crossing the border because getting stopped and questioned produces so visceral an anger. He will never forget "that day of infamy"—9/11—when Akwesasne was suspected to be an entrance point for the terrorists. That, too, played into the government's agenda: "to build up the bad guy so you can eventually take him down with a bigger thud."

I ride out of Mohawk land and follow the St. Lawrence River southwest—upstream—towards Lake Ontario. The day is sticky-hot. At times, I feel as if I'm riding one of the outer circles of the Inferno. I can almost convince myself that I miss the cold and rain of five days ago. But, now and then, when I swing close to the river, a cooling breeze that smells of fish and mud wafts from the Spring-cold sweet water.

The road follows the river and I need only look right to see Canada a few hundred yards away, its river-basin flat-land, farms and woods appearing identical to the country on the American side. Now, I'm entering the eastern edge of the real battlegrounds of the War of 1812. At scores of places along the river, the Americans crossed over in small raiding parties, or in full-scale army operations. Occasionally, the

British reciprocated. The United States' goal was to sever its enemy's supply lines between Upper Canada and the rest of the British North American colonies. If the United States had been able to do so, the war might have turned into a decisive victory for the adolescent republic. But the New York State militia's lack of enthusiasm—in fact, its near-hostile apathy—sabotaged a wholehearted American attack. As elsewhere along the boundary, the inhabitants of these borderlands thought the war an irritating disruption of their lives—and, in particular, of their trade and intercourse with their neighbours just across the big river. Thus, at Crysler's Farm, near Morrisburg, on the Canadian side, a force of four thousand American soldiers was turned back by eight hundred British regulars and Quebec militiamen, and their Mohawk allies. Fed up with the cross-river harassment, the British sent a force across the frozen river at Ogdensburg in the winter of 1813, and defeated the Americans there. Even after the British withdrew, the United States failed to re-establish its garrison in Ogdensburg. Amicable trade across the river resumed, and, in fact, the British forces bought most of their supplies from obliging New York merchants. It seemed that the United States river borderlands were rife with Tories, Americans who supported the British cause.

At the various American battleground sites, however, mythology is in full flower. The gist of the many plaques is that outnumbered American forces repelled what is always referred to as the "British invasion." As if the Brits started the fighting. There is far more historical sophistication, and truth, in the descriptions of events at sites along the southern border than here. Even at the Alamo, the mythic shrine of American nationhood, the Daughters of the Republic of Texas acknowledge nuance and historical controversy. Along the St. Lawrence, there are only certitudes of American virtue and courage standing against an alleged British-Canadian assault.

I had intended to walk the ground the war was fought on. But my throbbing ankle puts a quick end to that. I can limp thirty yards or so, and then I have to quit. I stop along the river near Morristown and soak foot, ankle, sock and boot in the cold water for half an hour. For the first time since I dropped the bike, I think I detect a slight decrease in the swelling.

A few miles southwest of Morristown, I encounter the scariest armed man I'll meet along this border. I'm riding at sixty miles an hour into a strong headwind. With my earplugs, I can't hear anything except wind noise, which is as loud as if I'm riding at ninety miles an hour. The road is almost clear of traffic. I don't see the state trooper coming up behind me with his lights flashing, and I certainly can't hear his siren.

He appears with a sudden shock on my left-hand side. I jump in the saddle, and swing to the right. There's no oncoming traffic and I haven't held him up. However, he gives me a glare as he easily passes me. I give an apologetic wave. He accelerates hard until he's out of sight over the road's gentle hills. I surmise I haven't checked my rear-view mirror for only about seven or eight seconds. The cop was moving so fast, that's all it took for him to take me by surprise. I wonder whom he's chasing, or what emergency he's running to.

A few minutes later, I see a police car on the road's shoulder. A trooper is standing behind it signalling for me to pull over. I come to a stop behind his car. It's the same cop, and he is obviously a very angry man. He walks towards me with his right hand on the butt of his side arm.

What does this fucker want?

"Do you know that you are supposed to pull over and let emergency vehicles pass?" says the cop. He grits out the words. He is so angry, his voice is shaking. He's beefy, with a gut, narrow eyes, shaved head, a high voice.

"I know," I say. "I'm really sorry, I just didn't hear you with the wind noise and my earplugs." I shut down my engine, and take off my helmet. He seems surprised to see my middle-aged face and grey hair. Maybe I'm not the punk he expected.

"That is a $120 ticket. You did not pull over out of my way. You did not get out of the way of an emergency vehicle."

Didn't he just say that? "I'm sorry," I say again. "I'm usually very good at watching my mirrors. I know it's really important to watch your mirrors if you really want to ride safe, but you came up on me so fast, I just didn't see you."

He appears to be disappointed by my abject apologies. He demands my licence. He takes it in his left hand and studies it. He seems perplexed by its nifty British Columbia hologram. His hand is shaking. He's sweating; the rivulets trickle down his cheeks. His right hand still grasps the butt of his pistol; the holster–restraining strap is unfastened. He seems barely under control.

"Is this licence valid?" he rasps. This is one seriously pissed-off human. The son of a bitch sounds as if he'd like to shoot someone.

I'm taken aback. "Yes, definitely." What else can I say? No, it's not, it's a fucking pretend licence from Canadian Tire?

He looks at it some more. He asks me where I'm coming from and going to. As we talk, I can see he's coming down from his testosterone frenzy. I'm relieved when—finally—he lets go of his goddamn gun. He's cooling out. But not completely. When he gets back into his cruiser, he peels away, spraying gravel back at me. Small stones chitter and ping off my gas tank and windshield. One hits me on the forehead right between the eyes. My hands shake a little as I pull on my helmet and gloves.

An hour later, I pull into a motel in Alexandria Bay on the Thousand Islands reach of the river. There are thunderstorm cumuli billowing up in the west, and the manager gives me a room with an overhang I can shelter the bike under. I eat fish and chips at the Admiral's Inn. A sign outside says: "We welcome our soldiers. Come home soon."

While I eat, a brief rain shower cools the air. Back in my room, I'm able to winkle my right foot out of my boot for the first time in almost two days. I make a poultice with ice and a towel, and I pack it around the grotesque, blue-black lump of my foot and ankle.

The next day, I begin a ride back into my past.

At Sackets Harbor, there's a Memorial Day parade, and the whole town is blocked off, cordoned and parcelled by yellow tape and signalling cops. I weave my way down to the waterfront, and gaze west out into the great inland sea of Lake Ontario. It has that freshwater smell I know so well: no tang of salt, but a fishy hint and a slight dankness—like the water in a deep cave, or a huge tank. It's as if the water has been enclosed here for so long—no renewing tides nor deep refreshing upwellings—that it's taken on the odour of its bland fish, sandy shores and muddy bottom.

I lived beside this stretch of water throughout my adolescence and early adulthood. I learned to sail on it, and my scores of days in various boats come back to me as I look out at the smooth, benign water of the great lake, a slight oily sheen glistening on its surface. I feel as if I'm working my way close to home, or, if not exactly home, then to the familiar comfort of a childhood place.

I extricate myself from Sackets Harbor, where, during the War of 1812, the Americans established a navy yard. Eventually three thousand men worked there, and built eleven warships and numerous lesser vessels. I ride on down the lake's shore through small towns including, strangely, the town of Texas, which lies on Mexico Bay. When I arrive at the small city of Oswego, I am truly on familiar ground. I park the bike and hobble—very slowly—the long way up to Fort Oswego. The plaques describe how, here too, Americans repulsed the British invasion. I'm truly offended by this consistent harping inaccuracy. Typical Canadian resentment bubbles up: Who started the damn war, for God's sake?

I spend that night in a small motel near Ontario, New York, just east of Rochester. It's strange but on this Saturday of a long weekend, I'm the only customer. The beautiful blond proprietress is grumpy, more interested in working on her impressive garden than in tending to travellers. She grudgingly gives me a bucket of ice for my ankle. As she hands it to me, I say: "Just the usual near-death experience on a motorcycle." She gives me a radiant smile, but says not a word. It is the only enigmatic motel I've ever stayed in. I'm not sure icing my ankle is useful at this stage but it does ease the pain.

I ride through Rochester early Sunday morning on deserted roads wet from the night's rain, although the sky is clearing, and the heat building. From Rochester, however, the lake lies a few hundred yards to no more than a mile away on my right, and its winter-cold water air-conditions my ride. I need my fleece underjacket and heavy gloves.

In the early afternoon, I come to yet another fort on this undefended border. Fort Niagara is on the American shore, in Youngstown, at the mouth of the Niagara River. Here, too, apparently, the British invasion was repulsed. It's an even harder fiction to maintain on this frontier. Just across the river is Niagara-on-the-Lake, which American militia burned to the ground one cold winter night. Close by on Canadian territory are the battlefields of Lundy's Lane (named after a divergent, early-immigrant branch of my family), Beaver Dams, Queenston Heights and Stoney Creek. A strange invasion of America, I think, when all the big battles were fought not in the United States, but in Canada, on Loyalist soil.

From this fort's ramparts, I look down on the river where I sailed my first boat, bought with paper-route money—a fifteen-foot wooden dinghy. Upstream, the big river's banks, and the Niagara escarpment in the distance, look like primeval forest. A few small buildings jut or peek out, but my impression, as it always was, is of an ancient and scarcely touched wilderness instead of this well-populated peninsula.

Everything looks the same as it did forty years ago: the lines of moored boats veined along the river's current; the big houses on the Canadian side which used to be owned by wealthy Americans; the Coast Guard station below the fort, now a front-line force against Canadian terrorists; the toppling waves on the river bar (to be avoided in a small open boat); the lake itself misty and pale blue under the heavy, humid late-Spring air. I feel overwhelmed by memory, and by the strange longing—like an unsatisfied thirst—for times past, hard and terrifying as they often were.

Soon, I mount up and ride seven miles upstream to Queenston and the bridge there. Away from the lake, the damp heat forces me to strip down to summer riding mode again. On the Canadian side, the statue of General Isaac Brock rises above the trees on its fifty-six-metre-high plinth atop the escarpment. He is one of the Canadian heroes of the border war. His British regulars and Indian allies defeated an invading American force at Queenston in 1812, early in the war. Brock died in the battle, depriving the British North Americans of their most capable general.

There are often long lineups at the multi-lane Queenston bridge, but today, I'm behind no more than seven or eight cars. The Canadian agent has only a couple of questions, and he doesn't ask for any identification. Perhaps he senses I'm home.

It only occurred to me, as I researched and thought about this book, that I grew up in a borderlands, as surely as if I were Steve in Stanstead, or a Brayon in Van Buren, or Wallace Stegner along his life-splitting 49th parallel, or, indeed, an inhabitant of the Valley of the Rio Grande, descended from generations living there long before the gringos stole the land and laid down their border. We never thought of the Niagara Peninsula as a borderlands, of course. We never even used the term "border"; we said we were going "over the river." That meant we were going to American Niagara Falls or to Buffalo to shop, or to see a movie, or, in our moments of aesthetic ambition, to visit the excellent Albright-Knox Art Gallery. Mainly, we went to drink.

In those days, Toronto seemed to be a cold, distant, cloddish, provincial burg. It just never occurred to us to drive there for any reason. The action was over the river. It seemed to us that all the glamour of the United States lay a few minutes drive away. We were mostly glad to be Canadian (and not to have to think about getting drafted), but we hankered after the idea of America: its jazzy, speedy danger. The drinking age was eighteen in New York when it was still twenty-one in Ontario. And in some notorious bars in Niagara Falls, if you were tall enough to see over the bar, they'd sell you a beer. Coming back across the border, sardonic or amused guards would wave through the carloads of dead-drunk Canadian kids. Or they would ask questions like: "Got any brassieres in there?"

When my parents and I went for the then-popular Sunday drive, we used to cross over into the States and amble along there, burning cheap gas. We went over to eat in American restaurants every weekend or so. I sailed my first couple of sailboats out of Niagara-on-the-Lake, and we often landed somewhere on the American shore of the river to have a picnic, or to walk down to one of the pubs in Clarkson or Youngstown. My friends and I were aware of breaking laws and rules, but I don't recall anyone worrying about it in the slightest. I crewed on a thirty-two-foot ketch that regularly cruised down the American shore of the lake to Wilson, or to Olcott, for the weekend. Sometimes, we'd call Customs by phone and report in, but mostly we didn't bother. No one seemed to care. For me, as for Mick in El Paso when he crossed the line to and from Juárez, the river was always "my fucking border."

When John F. Kennedy was assassinated, Canadians (like most of the rest of the world) wept and grieved with Americans, without restraint or self-consciousness. We felt as if it had been our young king laid low. We had loved Camelot, too, and had been as blind as Americans had been to its hypocrisies and inadequacies. In those years of the Cold War, America—which had saved Europe from Nazism, and then raised it up again—protected all of us against the evil empire of the Soviets.

Before Vietnam became a moral disaster, and before the civil rights movement ran into police dogs and burned churches, and ghettos and university campuses became battlegrounds patrolled by the National Guard—and even the army's tactical reserve unit, the 82nd Airborne—and before the assassinations of Robert Kennedy and Martin Luther King, and before drugs and sex and rock and roll, it was still possible to think of the United States as "America." It was imperfect, of course, but the Old World immigrant's selective vision still held me, and, I believe, most Canadians, too.

America was imperial, and overreaching and overbearing; some of it was racist; it was built on the bones of slaughtered Indians; it brimmed with hardcase fundamentalists and narrow paranoid certainties; it was strident, naive, rough and ready. But, nevertheless, somehow, it still seemed to contain that strange, almost joyous, possibility of becoming better, of fulfilling arrogant John Winthrop's prophecy: not a shining city, perhaps, but still something better than the rest.

When I thought of the United States and Canada then, the adjectives that came to mind were so different for each. America: expansive, dynamic, violent, cruel, exuberant, wide open; it was a field of dreams—which can, after all, be good

or bad. Canada: cramped, stingy, mean, sober, static, grudging, humane, law-abiding; it was an unrealized proposition
awaiting confirmation or falsification.

In 1775, Patrick Henry said: "Give me liberty or give me
death!" And he said: "If this be treason, make the most of it!"
In 1981, the Canadian government began its petition to
"repatriate" its constitution once and for all: "To the Queen's
Most Excellent Majesty: Most Gracious Sovereign: We, Your
Majesty's loyal subjects . . . respectfully approach Your Majesty,
requesting . . ." etc. The country of the revolution to the south,
and of the counter-revolution to the north.

In St. Catharines, I visit a medical clinic. The elderly doctor,
who has obviously seen it all many times over, is, nevertheless,
impressed by my ankle. This pleases me. Your ride's over, he
tells me. The X-rays show no broken bone, but the ligaments
are badly torn. I should rest it for at least two weeks. If anything happens on the bike and I have to put the joint to hard
use, I could damage it permanently. As it is, I'm almost a
candidate for surgery to repair the carnage. I usually follow
doctors' advice; unlike many men, I'm a good patient, and I
readily seek out medical attention for symptoms. But not this
time. I know good book material when I see it. Keeping
going on a wonky ankle will make me look good: courageous
and adventurous. It will add colour to my account of the
Canadian border, devoid as it is of the bandidos, assorted crazies and armed men of the south. I don't present this argument to the doctor, but say that I'm doing research and that I
have a living to make, a deadline to meet. Eventually, we
compromise: I'll rest the ankle for four days, and then ride
on. The doctor thinks I'm making a big mistake, but I can
see that he is also impressed by my apparent courage and for-
titude. This also pleases me. I'll go on in pain and finish my
ride. What a fine fellow I am.

CHAPTER 16

RIDING THE 49TH

CONQUER, OCCUPY AND POSSESS . . .
[ACQUIRE] DOMINION, TITLE AND JURISDICTION.
—HENRY VII TO JOHN CABOT, 1496

WHEN I LOOK BACK ON MY NORTHERN BORDER RIDE, it falls into four neat sections: the woods and rivers of the east; the Great Lakes; the prairie along the 49th parallel; the mountains and islands of the west. Of these, the prairies have stayed in my mind most vividly. Perhaps that's because they are, in many ways, so like the Chihuahuan and Sonoran deserts I rode through along the Mexican border. The northern high prairie, stretching from the Lake of the Woods to the abrupt rise of the Rocky Mountain foothills, has the same feel of light and space. The prairie and desert landforms share a vast, open geometry: a huge radius of sky and of long, unencumbered prospects. They free the breath and open the heart. They intimate existence without limits, and the exhilarating suggestion that the planet still has its unknown places, its frontiers and mysteries.

The 49th parallel is a symbol of the U.S.-Canadian border, and has long been a synecdoche—a part representing a whole—for everything lying on either side of it. People say, "south of the 49th," or north of it, to refer to an entire country or culture. The parallel's practical and symbolic pre-eminence for Canadians is clear. They hardly ever mention the arctic or ocean boundaries to the north, east and west, or pay much attention to them. (That's changing in the north with the retreat of arctic sea ice and the possibility of open sea transport through the Northwest Passage. Soon Canada may have a real sea border with Russia, and, in the form of Greenland, with Denmark.) The 49th is the border that matters. Yet, I'm almost halfway across the continent before I actually touch the iconic parallel. I ride from Minnesota into Manitoba at the Longworth border crossing a few miles west of Muskeg Bay on Lake of the Woods. I'm heading to Winnipeg to visit family there, and to get the KLR serviced. I also need to spend a few days resting my ankle again.

In a strange psychological illusion, I feel as if I have been struggling uphill to this point. It's an optical fancy as well. When I look at maps, I have the common, irrational sensation that heading north looks harder. It's as if I've been hacking my way up through the woods and hills of the northeastern states, and riding long, grinding miles to thread through the irregular contours of the Great Lakes, just to reach this real border, the one everyone talks about. Now, I can finally turn due west. I'll have to zigzag, of course, in order to stay as close to the line as I can, and to cross it from time to time. But, at the easternmost point of the 49th, I have the sensation of turning downhill. From here, it's an uncomplicated straight shot to home.

In a premonition of the open land to come—identical on both sides of the line—I break out of the eastern boreal forest a few kilometres north of the border, and I ride onto the preternatural, flat land of this part of the prairies. Until I reach the Rockies, trees will be sparse in the plane and undulating forms of the western croplands and grasslands.

Right away, however, I run into a familiar complication. Once out of the trees, the wind becomes stronger. As I ride past the Mennonite town of Steinbach, southeast of Winnipeg, the heading crosswind blows thirty or forty kilometres an hour. This, too, is just like the southern desert: I have no margin for error for road bends that break into the direction of the wind, but that's not much of a problem here because the road strikes like an infinite spear across the fertile bed of the old glacial lake. I push the handlebar grips, first one side, then the other, in a rhythm determined by how the wind's direction and velocity wobble and veer.

It's my fifth day out of St. Catharines. Just as the doctor had ordered, I propped my foot up on my mother's coffee table. Four perfect riding days slid by: dry, warm, windless, sunny. The forecast for my departure was for high, humid heat, wind and thunderstorms. I was behind schedule, and I would have to ride hard to cover the many remaining kilometres. I had intended to travel the American shores of all the Great Lakes to continue my policy of following the border as closely as possible, but now I would take the most direct route through to the west. The water boundary had never been part of my focus, in any event.

The Great Lakes present much the same set of problems— and opportunities—now as they always have: security and smuggling, but also joint agreements and action between the two countries to deal with water quality, pollution, shipping and so on. In a sense, the province of Ontario and the tier of American Great Lakes states constitute a loose kind of political-administrative borderlands: they have similar concerns about the condition of the huge but shrinking reservoir of fresh water; the province is by far the biggest trading partner of many of the states; and the clenching of the border by Homeland Security galls them all equally.

The Great Lakes have been demilitarized since the Rush-Bagot Agreement, which was reached in 1817. The United States Coast Guard has jurisdiction on the water, and, like the Border Patrol, it has beefed up its forces, increasing their numbers and firepower. Its plan to conduct live-ammunition, heavy–machine gun exercises on the lakes was aborted when both Americans and Canadians objected to the potential lead pollution, and the danger to small boats from stray bullets. But, as with the long, isolated sections of the land border, it is generally recognized that only so much can be done to secure these huge swaths of sweet water.

Crossing the main body of any one of them can be a daunting effort for a small boat—and terrorists, at least so far, are not renowned for their seamanship. But the Great Lakes are vulnerable to cross-border abuses along their narrow, connecting rivers—the Niagara between Lakes Erie and Ontario, the Detroit and St. Clair rivers between Erie and Huron, and the St. Marys between Huron and Superior—and at the lakes' crimped meeting places, where a fast boat trip along the shoreline will take you from one country to another. If bad guys want to cross the international boundary by water, they can cross. All the government can do is try to increase, slightly, the odds of catching them at it.

Between St. Catharines and the 49th parallel, I rode through humid heat, near-freezing cold, heavy rain, light rain, drizzle, mist, fog, dense fog, thunderstorms and wind, mostly on the nose (the prevailing wind up here is west, as it is down south). The weather changed every few hours, and with my proximity to the lakes. I put in long days—575 kilometres, 545, 600—so long that, at the end of them, my ass hurt as much as my ankle. These were long rides to make into headwinds on narrow back roads, which angled their way north and west. And I increased the distance even more by sticking as closely as I could to the ragged west shore of Lake Huron, and to the south shore of Superior from Sault Ste. Marie to Duluth.

As I rode, my main problem was that I kept dropping the bike.

Coming off the ferry across the St. Clair River from the Walpole Island Indian Reserve, on the Ontario side, into Algonac, Michigan, my injured ankle collapsed when I put my right foot down to steady myself—a most common manoeuvre—and I couldn't stop the KLR from falling over. The two U.S. Customs agents watched, without expression or any movement, from a few yards away as I struggled for several minutes to heave the heavily loaded thumper up again. Finally, a guy in a pickup coming off the ferry behind me stopped and helped me right the machine.

The agents had just completed a surly and thorough examination of every single bag, and had confiscated two oranges—which had been grown in California and shipped to Canada. Why was I carrying so much stuff? they asked with squinty-eyed suspicion. Their attitude might have had to do with all the smuggling across the river here. A friendly Walpole Island Indian (Canadian) on the ferry, who had a Harley in his garage, told me with a laugh that there was "a lotta smugglin' goin' on." Illegals and drugs of all kinds. The drug traffic goes both ways, he said. People around here had been doing it since forever, and they didn't see any reason to quit now just because the "fuckin' Americans got blown up real good" in New York. "No one around here gives a shit about the border, man," he said.

The next day, coming out of a restaurant parking lot, I dropped the bike again. I couldn't take the weight of the KLR as it leaned slightly to the right, and down it went. A guy with an eighteen-wheeler walked over right away and lent aid. I was feeling sorry for myself, and I feared the dirt and gravel roads farther west. If I went down on some deserted stretch, it might be a while before help happened along. Each time I had to struggle with the downed bike, my ankle swelled up again, and the augmented pain took hours to subside.

The long rides were beginning to bring out minor gear problems. The exhaust burned through one of my pannier bags and the bike's adjacent plastic cover panel. I'd fitted an aftermarket guard, but it left a small gap, and over time, the heat attacked the fabric bag. I repaired the panel and covered the gap with muffler tape and epoxy. One side of my helmet visor popped out at sixty-five miles an hour. The screws had come loose, and I spent an hour fiddling with the flimsy plastic gears. My gel saddle pad had begun to unravel on one side, and I had to patch it with tape.

The bridge across the Straits of Mackinac from Michigan's Lower Peninsula to the Upper Peninsula lay under thick, cold fog. I rode at ten miles an hour, aware of the long drop unseen over the railing I could barely make out a few yards away. About halfway across, a car came up behind me too fast and bumped my rear wheel. The impact wasn't hard, but the bridge surface was slick, and the KLR skidded sideways and my pannier bags glanced off the railing before the bike straightened out. I managed to keep it upright, but, in the adrenaline-saturated near-panic of the moment, I feared I might flip right over the railing, which didn't seem nearly high enough, fall off the bridge, and plunge down two hundred feet into the cold, black water I couldn't see. The car disappeared. I stopped and squeezed myself onto the side of the pavement for several minutes, but no traffic passed by. It was surreal in the muffled, opaque air. I could see maybe ten feet ahead. I thought it was too dangerous to stay where I was, and so eventually I rode very slowly off the bridge only to find, at the northern end, that it had been closed until the fog thinned out. I began to cultivate a muscle-contraction stress headache, which would last, off and on, for the next three days.

Along the Great Lakes shores of Michigan, Wisconsin and Minnesota, I rode each day until I couldn't ride farther, and the only motels were fleabags. They had smelly, smokers' rooms, and unknown insects scuttled by my bed in the dark. I ate chunks of unidentifiable meat smothered in thick, grey gravy, canned vegetables cooked to mush, salads of iceberg lettuce. I drank Budweiser beer, which helped me ignore my ankle and get some sleep. I talked to waitresses who said they couldn't understand my accent (very slight English), but who were friendly and chatty, and wanted to know the whole story of why I was limping. And just where the heck was British Columbia, anyway?

I've described earlier how the KLR broke down in International Falls, Minnesota, and Harry, the motel owner, and the town's bike guy got me going once again. Then how the bike refused to start for a while beside the Rainy River, where I saw the two men with backpacks and the rubber boat cross the river and drive away, and where I reported the incident to the Snickers-bar Border Patrol agent.

I passed a few other long riders on big bikes. In the rain and cold, or in the humid heat, or in the fog, they seemed inclined towards expressions of brotherhood. They all gave me emphatic, comforting waves.

In Winnipeg, I rest my ankle for two days with Greg and Debby, my kind and hospitable brother- and sister-in-law. I wait out a day of monsoon-like rain and storm-force wind—a prairie snorter. The Kawasaki dealer's mechanics check out my electrical system with multimeters, but can find no faults, no explanation for the bike's intermittent failure to start. It's fine, they say.

Two hours out of Winnipeg, just north of the Windygates border crossing from Manitoba into North Dakota, I stop to eat. Afterwards, the bike won't start. In the restaurant parking lot, I unload my bags, unroll my tools, take off the side panels and saddle, and check all the wires, fuses and connections I'd checked before. I call the Winnipeg dealer on my cellphone, and spend half an hour following his directions, taking off more pieces of the bike, reconnecting wires, trying this, trying that. Nothing works. He gives up; I give up. My cellphone battery gives up. I spend another hour fiddling with things, chatting with interested guys who saw me here two hours ago and wonder why I'm still here, sweating and hunkered down, or lying on my back, fucking around with my goddamn machine.

I've been there so long, I have to eat again. While munching a Kit Kat bar and speculating on how I might hunt down and kill the guys in Thailand who put this particular KLR together, I accidentally jiggle a connector adjacent to the fuse box. I've done the same thing before many times, but now, the ignition light flickers. I jiggle, and the light flickers. It takes me thirty seconds to tape the connection securely closed. The bike starts. I shut it down, take a deep breath, and turn the key. It starts again. I let it run for a while, and repeat. It starts. With all the starter relay switch analysis, multimeter tests, and mechanics' examinations, can that really have been the problem? As it turns out, yes. The KLR never falters again.

I cross into North Dakota at the village of Maida, where I have to open each of my bags for the border agent. I ride south a few miles and take the first available right, onto a gravel road. I stop for a few minutes to take a photograph, and to wipe dead bugs off my visor. The wind blows directly into my face at, I estimate, a sustained twenty-five or thirty miles an hour, gusting into gale force. The sun is out, and the heat is building in the early afternoon. I unzip the vents in my riding jacket. The flat, high prairie tableland stretches out ahead of me to the edge of vision, like a lumpy ocean in shades of green and brown. Now, I can see where I'm going; I can watch the weather systems, and local squalls, roll towards me, in their slow, inexorable grandeur. There is a blue horizon fifty miles away. I understand again why prairie boys do so well in the navy.

I take a swig of water, snap down my visor, pull on my gloves, and clunk the bike into gear. As I trundle down the hard dirt road (not a bad surface for once), the strong and stirring realization comes to me: this is the real frontier lying ahead, the mythic West.

The differences between Canada and the United States along their eastern border were defined in the past most vividly by revolution and by its refusal—by a renegade, radical individualism versus a sober, collective loyalism. Along the western border, the distinctions between the two societies were just as real and important, although not quite as much as Canadians like to believe.

The mythology of the American West is pervasive, and its colour and energy are overwhelming. The myth's components: wagon trains, cowpunchers, noble or evil Indians, Buffalo Bill, the O.K. Corral, Custer's Last Stand—the list goes on and on—have been promulgated through cheap novels and movies. They form a violent, intense tableau of America. In a way, these myths have become America. The men who populate them—the white men—are the beau ideal of American manhood: laconic, stoic loners skilled with the gun, who answer only to themselves and to the violent code of honour of the West. These ideal modes of action have their analogues in the periodic excesses of go-it-alone military adventurism by U.S. administrations, the younger Bush-Cheney episode being the latest, and one of the most notable, examples. Perhaps it's significant that each man comes from a western and frontier state: Texas and Wyoming.

The Canadian version of western mythology is, characteristically, a pale and anemic narrative by comparison, although for that reason it's somewhat closer to the truth. It has to do with intrepid French and Scottish explorers who befriended the Indians and learned from them—in fact, mixed with them to create the northern mestizos: the Métis—and of a handful of red-coated policemen who established law and order in the West through patient negotiation, reason, and the impact of their gorgeous uniforms as symbols of the Great White Queen, far away, yet genuinely solicitous of her red-brown children.

The 49th parallel soon became a "medicine line" for the Indians south of it. When the American blue-coated soldiers attacked them, or destroyed their food and villages, the Indians could always, if they were close enough to begin with, head for the line. Once the Sioux or the Blackfoot made it to Canada, the red-coated policemen offered them food, and the guarantee of safety—on the condition of good and peaceful behaviour in return. The bluecoats would not cross the line. The country was the same, the line invisible except, later on, for its few squat, plain marker posts. Yet one step across it could mean the difference between survival and slaughter.

These aboriginal refugees were part of the long tradition of Americans who fled to the inchoate British North American colonies, or, later, to the fragile country north of the line. The Loyalists were the first; more recently came Vietnam-era draft evaders who were, eventually, granted Canadian landed immigrant status right at the border, and the handful of deserters from the American imperial army in Iraq. Americans have long moved north for political reasons: to get away from what they see as a distastefully polarized and violent society—there are many on my British Columbia island. (When Canadians move south, it's always for economic reasons.) The medicine line is still there.

Perhaps the greatest distinction between the American and Canadian versions of western history is the fact that the United States had "the Frontier." That's not to say that Canada did not have a westward-moving thrust of European settlement and control that culminated in a single nation stretching to the Pacific Ocean. The Canadian frontier region was characterized by difficult physical conditions, uncertain jurisdiction, friction between white settlers and Indians, and among the settlers themselves, as they pursued different means of exploiting the land—farming versus ranching, for example. But to assert a Canadian frontier is merely to describe a set of temporary conditions as Europeans moved west across the country, displacing the Indians as they did so—although in a more or less peaceful manner. The American Frontier (the word must be capitalized in the American version), in contrast, represented, from its beginning, a bloody, desperate assault on the North American land and its indigenous peoples. It became a comprehensive symbol of the American experience in the New World, and of the nature of the new country itself.

One of the historical functions of the United States' border with Canada (and with Mexico) was to signify the division between different methods of appropriating the land of the New World, different modes of expansion and displacement, and of unique national narratives.

The "Frontier Thesis" is one of the major explanatory models of American development, society and character. It's also known as the "Turner Thesis," after the historian Frederick Jackson Turner. In 1893, Turner read a short paper titled "The Significance of the Frontier in American History" at the annual meeting of the American Historical Association in Chicago. In it, Turner purported to explain America and its exceptionalism, especially in comparison to Europe. His paper changed the study of history in North America, and elsewhere, too. Even though Turner's thesis has become an intellectual cliché, scholars of, and commentators on, U.S. history must still confront and deal with its century-old hypothesis. The paper is riddled with prejudice, inaccuracy, fuzzy language, ethnocentrism and downright untruths. (And Turner added to the confusion by tinkering with his ideas and their expression for the rest of his working life.) Turner's thesis encapsulates the mistaken assumptions of popular ideas of America's history. It also contains the particular lies that Americans tell themselves (every nation's people do this) about their history. In this way, they can avoid confronting what really happened; they can sidestep dealing with some of the real bleak and bitter strands of the story of themselves.

The Frontier hypothesis is compactly stated in Turner's sentence: "The existence of an area of free land, its continuous recession, and the advance of American settlement westward explain American development." Americans became the people they did, says Turner, because, in living along the expanding frontier, they had to confront the challenges of a harsh climate and difficult country—dense forest, vast plains, the successive lines of mountain barriers. They also had to face hostile Indians. As Americans dealt with these obstacles, which were so different from life in Europe, they became less European, and, through a series of necessary adaptations, forged themselves into Americans. The farther west they moved, the less European they became, and the more American—that is: more democratic, individualistic, egalitarian, violent and distrustful of authority.

Turner attempted to bring rigour to his analysis by defining "frontier" in terms of the recent national census. The Frontier divided territory with fewer than two European-Americans per square mile from that with more than two. In other words, the frontier was where white people were scarce, or, as one scholar puts it, "where white people got scared because they were scarce." A paragraph later in his paper, Turner writes: "The frontier is . . . the meeting point between savagery and civilization." These terms were, at the time, considered to be merely descriptive, and not prejudiced. Turner went on to state that the "American intellect owes its striking characteristics" to the frontier: "That coarseness and strength combined with acuteness and inquisitiveness; that practical, inventive turn of mind, quick to find expedients, that masterful grasp of material things, lacking in the artistic but powerful to effect great ends; that restless, nervous energy; that dominant individualism, working for good and for evil, and withal that buoyancy and exuberance which comes with freedom—these are traits of the frontier."

Finally, said Turner, what was most important in 1893, even as he spoke, was that the frontier was over, finished, closed. All the free land was gone. There was no more West to move towards. It was, therefore, a pivotal point in American history, and, in the future, whatever forces would operate to change the American character, they would have nothing to do with the frontier. Or, other frontiers would have to be found—a possibility taken up with enthusiasm by later American presidents (most notably by Theodore Roosevelt, and by John F. Kennedy, who adopted the election slogan, "The New Frontier," and who said, in 1960: "Our frontiers today are on every continent").

Turner's thesis has been the object of criticism ever since its promulgation. The land of the continent may have been free—in the sense that whites didn't have to pay for it—but it was not unoccupied. A corollary of taking it was that the Indians had to be driven off and herded into reservations on land unfit for European development. If necessary, they had to be killed. The Indian wars were the ironclad consequence of the westering European frontier. Turner's connections between democracy, character, individualism and the frontier were unproven assumptions. His work abounded in emotion, romance, symbolism and myth. He failed to define any of his terms. No single historical mechanism or phenomenon can be the cause of extremely complex effects (Turner acknowledged this point later in his life).

In spite of these objections, Turner's thesis had the power of all single-minded explanations: it commanded attention; it couldn't be ignored; it was a starting point for all other attempts to explain the American character and soul.

The "Frontier Thesis" had its successors, and each adopted at least some aspects of Turner's original proposition. In 1950, for example, historian David Potter acknowledged Turner's emphasis on land as the determinant of the American character. But for Potter, it was the sheer abundance of land that was significant. Neither land nor natural resources were ever in short supply. And, as the Indians knew all too well, there was also an abundance of white people to fill the land to two per square mile, and any number beyond that. With abundance came mobility: the American could pick up and move anytime. If his employer peeved him, if he grew to dislike his neighbour, if the grass looked greener, if he became bored, if he just damn well felt like it, he could load up and, like Huck Finn, light out for the territories. This notion of plenty, and of the constant possibility of movement created a new, and unique, kind of society.

In another Turnerian variation, in 1961, historian C. Vann Woodward stated his "free security" thesis: the amplitude of the frontier gave Americans free-of-charge security from outside threats. The United States didn't have to fear Mexico—it was, at best, a weak state, on the constant verge of failure. Canada? Not likely: it was the nation that should worry. And Great Britain's options against the republic were constrained by Canada's vulnerability to American military action. Canada was, in effect, a hostage. In the absence of external threat, the United States could concentrate all its resources on developing its industries, and its frontier.

Woodward's thesis did not deal with the actual security situation on the Frontier's ground, which was problematic until the end of the Indian Wars. One of the characteristics of the Frontier was that Americans there were engaged in constant, if sporadic, warfare with the Indians—freedom fighters, or insurgents, depending on one's point of view.

Woodward and Potter agreed with Turner that the frontier had closed. As a result, there was no more free land, no more natural abundance, no more free security. The disappearance of such a crucial, and long-standing, condition of American life was bound to create disquiet, uncertainty and nostalgia. The loss of security, in particular, was difficult to adjust to. The threat of missile strikes during the Cold War was a completely new fear for Americans, although, for Europeans, it was a new form of an old and familiar jeopardy. Nuclear war with the Soviet Union was a threat; the actual attacks of 9/11 completed the loss of a sense of security. Now, it's clear that any form of violent attack that can happen elsewhere in the world can happen in the United States. The borders with Mexico, and with Canada, have therefore assumed a new, and crucial, importance.

In the basement restaurant of the motel in Rolla, on the high, bare plains of North Dakota, as far from the sea as you can get on the continent, I eat fish and clam chowder. The cook is a sinewy guy, with a long, multi-tied ponytail, a baseball cap and many tattoos. The owner is a surly, abrupt man with an eastern European accent. I mention the wind. He scoffs. Today is nothing. It always blows up here, and it's usually much worse. Wait until tomorrow, he says happily, you'll get real wind tomorrow.

Two of the other patrons are my age, with grey ponytails. They wear leather jackets with the logo "Vietnam Veterans of America Motorcycle Club." I saw their bikes—the omnipresent Harleys—parked outside. I lean over and say I'm riding a bike too, and ask them where they're from.

"Fuckin' everywhere, man," says one guy.

The other stares at me without a word. I try again: I inform them I'm riding across the country from Maine to Washington on a Kawasaki thumper.

"Kawasakis are a piece of shit," says the same guy. His buddy stares at me as he lights up a cigarette in the no-smoking room.

"Well," I say, still hoping for a conversation, for something, "they're tough bikes and good on bad roads. I've been riding the dirt close to the border all afternoon."

"Yeah?" says the guy.

I ask him about the Vietnam Veterans club: how many members? Where's its headquarters?

"Where are you from?" he asks.

"I'm Canadian."

"Fuck," he says, and turns away.

The website for the Veterans of Vietnam International Motorcycle Club says, with emphatic redundancy, that they are "a fraternity of frothers." If you served in Vietnam between 1959 and 1975, were honourably discharged, and ride a bike bigger than 650 cc, you can join. "We are looking for brothers, not weekend warriors or patch collectors," writes the site's unknown essayist. "Our club colors are in honor of the Vietnam service ribbon. Ride free brothers." Like the Shakers, this group will not procreate; they'll cut it clean. "Ours is not a club that will be around forever," says the writer. When the brothers die off, the club dies, too.

Motorcycles and veterans have always been closely connected— veterans and motorcycle gangs even more so—at least in the popular mind. The Hells Angels are the Ur-gang. Their formation in Fontana, California, in 1948 has often been ascribed to blooded veterans of the war, adrenaline junkies unable to come down, and in endless need of the high of movement and danger. In one version of events, an ex–air force fighter pilot started the club, and suggested the name, reminiscent of the Flying Tigers and similar nicknames for fighter squadrons. Or, in another version, the club's founders were veterans of the 11th Airborne Division ("Death from Above"). The club's own history denies any of this, and there's no proof or documentation one way or the other. The original rules required club members to ride Harley-Davidsons, and that's what really began the public fascination with the bike: the bad-boy, romantic aura of the so-called one-percenters who rode it.

The weekend warrior—a nine-to-fiver during the week—who straps on his leather chaps and designer leather jacket, who straddles a big, low growler of a Harley, and rumbles and roars around the chic high spots for a few hours, is dipping into that reservoir of biker violence and alienation. And the biker image itself is quintessentially American: the lone rider, rebellious and refractory, resistant to authority, a laconic man of action; if he is answerable to anyone, it is to his brothers and to their code. These are the very qualities possessed by the American man of the fabled West on Turner's Frontier. This mythic man lives on astride a Harley, or, indeed, aboard any bike. I feel it myself as soon as I mount up. In fact, my westward rides along the border are, as I've admitted, a conscious effort, among other things, to appropriate the old and potent image of the lone rider heading west.

Rolla, North Dakota, is worth staying in only because it is close to the International Peace Garden. Like the Peace Bridge across the Niagara River between Buffalo and Fort Erie, like the joint-jurisdiction Roosevelt Campobello International Park or the Waterton-Glacier International Peace Park between Alberta and Montana, and like the Peace Arch Park at the Washington border south of Vancouver (with its "Children of a Common Mother" monument), the International Peace Garden is a relic of a time that has only just ended. These symbols of the long amity between Canada and the United States—no war since 1812; no threat of it since the 1870s—are now obsolete. And for the United States, the park and the gardens that straddle the border are no longer places for amiable mixing, but rather are holes in the country's security perimeter. They are as irritating as the trans-boundary Indian reserves, if somewhat easier to police. The Department of Homeland Security hasn't closed the International Peace Garden yet, but you know it would like to.

There are few other visitors when I enter the gardens' 2,339 acres of winding roads, natural wetlands and meadows, campgrounds, formal gardens and monuments. The entrance is in no man's land, the hundred-yard stretch between the Canadian and U.S. Customs posts. I spend a few hours in the pleasant, although well-fenced, grounds, riding the roads in one country, and then the other, and limping in the warm sun—although very strong, cool wind blows from the west. The unpleasant motel proprietor was right about the wind today.

The gardens are full of fraternal sentiments. One of the original cairns says: "To God in His glory / we two nations / dedicate this garden / and pledge ourselves / that as long as men / shall live, we will / not take up arms / against one another." This inscription moves me with its eloquence and innocence. But how sad that the pledge is obsolete. America is arming itself against my country once again. The United States could choose to keep the border open and to seek a common arrangement with Canada for hemispheric security based on mutual trust and confidence. But, instead, it is falling back into its old habits of isolationism and suspicion of outsiders. America's thickening of this border reflects its new perception that north of the line lie nothing but enemies and threats.

When I leave the International Peace Garden, I must go through a U.S. checkpoint, as if I had crossed the border. It is one of the most thorough examinations I've had—which is saying something. The agent is affable, but he pulls on his latex gloves and goes through everything on the bike with a truly dazzling attention. He opens my toiletry bag and I must explain my two prescription medications; I must disassemble my electric toothbrush; I must explain my vitamin pills and my Metamucil. I must tell him why I need a spare brake lever ("In case one on the bike breaks," I explain), why I have a camera, a tape recorder, ("To take photographs and to record my impressions," I assert), why I have a tent ("To camp in," I reply), why I have so many tools ("To fix the bike with," I say). As I have before in these circumstances, I wonder if there is idiocy afoot here, or a subtle technique I haven't yet grasped. I mention to the agent that he is being particularly thorough and ask if they have had smuggling problems here. Not really, he says, but "you can't be too careful." Yes, you can, I think. You really can be much too careful. The few cars behind me are pulled over for secondary examination, too, although they're released sooner than I am.

"It's kind of ironic, don't you think," I say to the still-friendly agent, "that you're doing all this outside the International Peace Garden?"

He pauses in his rubbery prodding of my underwear. "What do you mean?" he says. He's genuinely confused.

"Well," I say, "the garden is a symbol of friendship and trust between Canada and the U.S., but then there's all this heavy-duty inspection."

He opens my soap container, turns the soap over, closes the container again, and puts it back into my duffle bag.

"Yeah," he says, "I guess it is kinda weird."

The American Frontier thesis has hardly any relevance north of the Canadian border. The theory falters at the 49th parallel and so does the actual experience on the ground. A nation's mythology—the story it has decided to tell about itself—is an immensely powerful thing, but it can be stopped cold at an imaginary line across an undifferentiated terrain.

One might expect people of similar origins settling similar landscapes at roughly the same time in history and who were dealing with comparable problems—vast space, harsh weather, upset Indians—to arrive at more or less similar solutions. And one might also expect such people to have much the same view of the meaning of what they viewed as their civilizing enterprise into the wilderness. Americans, who assume that Canada is much like their own country, would be puzzled, if they were aware of it at all, by the abrupt end, at the border, of the consummate idea of America.

Turner's "Frontier Thesis" and its variants break down over a few simple Canadian facts. In Canada, there was no free land. Canada was a monarchy—in the sense that, even after Confederation, the head of state remained the British monarch—and that meant that land otherwise unoccupied or owned was Crown land (leaving aside Indian entitlement). Anyone who wanted to settle, even on a few isolated acres in, say, Saskatchewan, had to square it with "the Queen in Right of Canada," which meant, in reality, with the government. The Crown had also given control of huge tracts of territory to the semi-feudal Hudson's Bay Company early in Canadian history. For settlers, it made no difference. The Crown—and, therefore, the government—or the Company, controlled every square foot of land in the vast territories and colonies, and in the provinces after 1867, not already under private ownership.

When American settlers moved west, they felt as if they, themselves, were making things up as they went along, creating the structures and rules they would live within. Local government preceded the establishment of territorial government. As a result, Americans believed they were moving into true virgin land—a belief made easier by the prior decimation of Indian nations by disease, a process that had occurred across the continent. The settlers gave no credence to Indian claims of ownership of any land. The Supreme Court agreed. In 1823, ignoring legal precedent, Chief Justice John Marshall decided that even though Indians had a right to occupy their land, that right was conditional, and the government had title to it. The decision was a licence to steal.

Americans thought of the Frontier as a realm of boundless promise. The subjugation of the Frontier was a heroic venture that implied the virtue of the use of power. The transformation of the western lands from untouched prairie to cropland, or to fenced grazing, was obviously progress. White Americans thought that the Indians had moved over the land, had hunted on it, but had left no marks of possession (ignoring the tribes that were diligent and industrious farmers). The settlers dug deep into the surface, or delineated their interests in the land with long, straight fences and roads. Those were the marks of true ownership.

North of the border, westward-moving Canadians found territory already subject to English common law, and to whatever regulations the Hudson's Bay Company had established. Canadian settlers had to fit themselves into the legal and regulatory scheme they encountered, and which was already in place. Instead of cowboy, outlaw, Indian-fighter heroes, Canadians had policemen—the iconic Mounties—and the trans-Canada railroad, which was built in an anxious effort to hold together the tenuous new Dominion. As one historian has aphorized, Canadians were pioneers not in democracy, but in infrastructure. The seeds of dull, sober respectability, and of deference to authority, were sown early. Canadian attitudes to the law, to government, and to the nature and role of the state diverged from those of Americans from the beginning.

Settlers north of the 49th tended not to discard their old-world habits of deference and adherence to tradition. The presence of a large French-Canadian population, which feared the United States more than it resented the British Crown after the conquest of 1759, encouraged the status quo. If the amplitude of the West provided Americans with C. Vann Woodward's free security, the same space gave Canadians the annexation willies. The farther away Canadians settled from the country's centre of gravity in the east, the more vulnerable they felt to American expansion northwards. For Canadians, the western frontier was an additional source of anxiety, rather than of liberation.

The Canadian frontier was not continuous but interrupted by the Great Lakes, and by the southward thrust of the vast Laurentian Shield country, which was beautiful but inimical to settlement and agriculture. Canadians felt isolated and in danger in the West above the 49th parallel. This, too, encouraged an attitude of conservative social adhesion under the protection of the government, its police and its law. Finally, there was the nature of the landscape and the climate to contend with. The land was less fertile than in the United States and soon, to the north, gave way to the shield country, or to the tundra. The weather was correspondingly more harsh. The real Canadian frontier—the challenge to which Canada is still responding—lay more north than west.

The United States Army fought a continuous western war— often one of extermination—against the Indians from the end of the Civil War until the final massacre at Wounded Knee, South Dakota, in 1890. It is possible to use the word "genocide," writes Wallace Stegner. "Extermination was a doctrine accepted widely, both unofficially and officially, in the western United States after the Civil War."

The relative law-abiding peace of the Canadian frontier broke down on a large scale only twice, when the Métis, under Louis Riel, staged rebellions in 1869 and in 1885. Those were the two brief occasions in the long history of western expansion in Canada when the army was needed. For the rest of the time, the few hundred red-coated Mounties sufficed to maintain a reasonable degree of order across the immense sweep of the prairies.

No one can claim that Canadians treated Indians well. The process north of the 49th was the familiar one of racial prejudice, dispossession, broken promises and barren reserves. But, by and large, the Indians were able to stay close to the land upon which they had lived for centuries, or even continue to occupy and use it in their traditional ways. Stegner describes the western border, in particular, as a colour line: the blue of the U.S. Army "longknives" below; the red of Mountie uniforms above. Blue meant treachery, slaughter and broken promises; red meant protection, parleys and the straight tongue.

Riding towards the mountains across the prairie sea, beating hard into the gale-force west wind, I watch the weather roll towards me. There's lots of weather to watch. Nearing the border between North Dakota and Montana, in steady, light rain, not too cold, I look ahead to a dark, undulating curtain of roiling cloud. It stretches across my horizon. On this open grassland, I feel exposed, undefended.

I stop to oil my chain. A pickup, going in the other direction, pulls over. It's the first vehicle I've seen for half an hour.

"You doin' okay?" the driver asks.

"I'm fine, yeah, thanks," I say. "Just oiling up my chain."

"Okay then," says the middle-aged man. He's wearing a stained, white stetson, and there's a bale of hay in the back. "You take care."

For some reason—perhaps because I've been riding a long time and I'm tired, or because of the constant rain and wind, or because of this big, dirty cloud bearing down on me—this simple solicitude overwhelms me. I'm still not sure why; standing beside my bike on a straight and narrow North Dakota road, the rain falling over me, the wind fresh and fragrant of grass, I begin to cry. I'm not thinking of anything in particular. I don't feel wretched, or in despair. More than anything else, I realize, I feel serene. I'm ready to accept whatever's coming. This country is so beautiful. The weather rolling towards me is sublime in its majestic, unstoppable, uncontrollable power. I think of my friends again. Will, a boat builder and a sailor, would have loved this moment, too, the weather stirring the blood like a vast squall at sea, mixing together fear and elation. Mike and Chris? They were city boys: Let's for Christ's sake get in out of the goddamn rain, can we? I have a vision of stripping off my hampering riding gear under the approaching maelstrom, of running through tall grass in the blinding, purging rain. At that moment, my life feels precious beyond words, and fragile. Now, all I want to do is to mount up and ride hard, straight into the coming storm.

Like all such moments, this one passes. My fervent joy bleeds away in the hammering downpour. In the strong, slightly cross wind and scattered lightning, it's too dangerous to keep going. I pull over in the little town of Columbus, North Dakota, and spend an hour in a rundown cafe. I sit at the counter, drink a Pepsi, eat a muffin, shoot a solo game of pool, and chat to the middle-aged, grey-haired woman there. She's reserved at first, then flirty. It's a very small town, and out of the way.

She used to cross the border all the time, she says, to visit family in Bienfait and in Yorkton, Saskatchewan. Now, she seldom goes over. It's just too much of a hassle coming back in, she says. It's even harder for her Canadian relatives; they get searched every single time. Just because the border guards have a lot of time to kill—the border crossings out here are never busy. The guards are real assholes—"Pardon my French." And when they want a passport, that'll be it. She just won't go. It's stupid, she says. As if there's any danger from Canada. In the cities, maybe: all those Muslims. But out here . . .

As I sit, I think of the other Columbus down south in the hard light and arid heat of New Mexico, where I stayed in the adobe house with a beautiful artist and a handsome foreign correspondent, and walked in the abrupt desert-evening cold across the border to eat burritos and drink Dos Equis in a pink cantina in Mexico. This northern Columbus is grey and muted, cool and seedy. The Canadian border is five miles north, and no *indocumentados* try to run it, either way. The rain eases, and then stops. A sickly sun appears, but I'll take it. I ride on for an hour, until another storm cell massing ahead drives me into the only motel in Crosby, just east of the Montana line.

The next day is cool and cloudy. The wind is strong and promises even more heft later. I can see rain falling steadily across the horizon to the west. Outside a restaurant after breakfast, I'm pulling on my rain gear when a cowboy climbing into his pickup smiles and says, "That's quite a horse you got there."

At Opheim, Montana, instead of turning south to follow the paved road, I keep to the west, and take the gravel. It's not a smart thing to do because the weather has made a mush of the surface, and because my ankle stops me from standing on the footpegs in the best off-road riding stance. I stop, once again, to bleed pressure from my tires. The going is hard at first, and gets worse. There's nothing out here. Once or twice, I catch a glimpse of an isolated farm or ranch building far away. I ride for fifteen minutes or so, and then hit a slimy patch of mud and standing water. For the first time on my rides along either border, I drop the bike at speed.

I'm doing thirty miles an hour when I lose control, and close to that when I hit the ground. The bike flops onto its side and skids into a pool of mucky gloop. As it goes down—nothing is happening too fast at this speed—I push off, hit the ground on my side and slide on my back for ten or twelve yards. My riding jacket scoops mud off the surface, and forces it, ice-cold and gritty, down inside my padded pants, and then inside my jeans and underwear. When I stand up, I look like Mudman. But my armoured gear has just paid for itself. I walk over to the KLR and flick the kill switch to shut off the engine. The wind soughs through the prairie grass. It's raining, but lightly. Around me, from horizon to horizon, there is nothing. I undo my pants, and try to scoop the gelid muck out from underneath.

It takes three tries to get, and to keep, the bike upright. I am able to plant my feet and push with my back, but twice, the machine topples right over onto its other side before I can get into position to stop it. This ensures an even distribution of mud all over the bike. On the third try, I time it right. The effort makes my ankle very sore, and I take some codeine. As I load up, I think: now would be an appropriate time to discover that the electrical problem I thought I'd fixed hadn't been fixed. But it's all right. The sturdy thumper starts right away, and I head off into the mud once again.

It turns out—it's just as well—that that patch was the worst on the road. For the next sixty miles or so, I ride without a break at close to thirty miles an hour with only the occasional skid and slide on the gravelly dirt road. In a while, I find I can use my drugged-up ankle to stand up on the pegs in the bad stretches. It even becomes fun. Once you've gone down, I discover, the fear of crashing diminishes. The rain stops and the sun comes out. I pass Frenchman Reservoir, and then Whitewater, the only settlement on this road. I turn south to the paved 191, stop to re-inflate my tires, and ride on down into Malta for the night.

The motel is busy with railroad men—the line is just across the road—and half a dozen good ol' boys in pickups. The bike and I are filthy, encrusted with dried black and red mud, and we are the object of considerable interest. A dozen men gather round and look us over.

"Where the hell you been, son?" says a guy about my own age.

"I just rode across from Opheim," I say.

"Looks like you crawled across," says a second man.

"I dropped the bike; it's pretty muddy with all the rain."

"Well, hell, boy, you don't have to ride in that shit. There is a paved road, didn't anyone tell you?" says another guy.

"I know," I say, "but I wanted to ride close to the border."

"What the hell for?" says the first man. "There's fuck-all up there."

He's right.

The next day, I ride west into "Whoop-Up Country." It was a true borderlands during the last half of the nineteenth century. It got its name from the whisky traders who moved in and made sure the Indians, already beaten down, would also become pitiable, though violent, steady drunkards. These borderlands stretched across the semi-arid prairie grasslands from the Missouri River in Montana north to the Bow in Alberta, and from near the North Dakota line to the Rockies. The U.S.-Canadian border was an especially artificial intrusion here. Whoop-Up Country is part of one of Joel Garreau's nine nations of North America: the Empty Quarter, which paid no attention to the 49th parallel. Like all of Garreau's nations, the Empty Quarter embodied the logic of the huge continental land forms, including these identical American and Canadian prairies.

The Whoop-Up Trail, which ran mostly in the United States, from Fort Benton in northern Montana, 240 miles north to Fort Macleod in southern Alberta, was an ambiguous highway. It brought trade and white culture, ranchers and, later, farmers, to the high plains of both countries. The southern plains and deserts had been leapfrogged by settlers heading over the mountains to fabled California, but, after the

Civil War and into the 1870s and later, the northern Great Plains became known as "the last, best west." The Whoop-Up Trail was an avenue for development, and a main transportation thoroughfare into the heart of the west of both countries. It was also the conduit for whisky traders, wolfers, buffalo slaughterers, unscrupulous and crooked traders, land speculators, trappers, mule skinners, cowboys and Indians, cattle rustlers and horse thieves, assorted sociopaths and just plain, all-around bad guys.

The Americans, moving fast as usual, got to their western plains first; in Canada the pattern of movement and settlement, characteristically, always lagged a few decades behind that in the United States. When the Canadian settlers, the Mounties and the land grabbers did begin to open up the Canadian plains, the Americans were pleased. They thought that, in the future, the new country might just more properly belong to the U.S.

Inevitably, the opening up of this frontier meant much different things on each side of the border. For Americans, it was another chapter in the book of manifest destiny—a good and glorious thing. For Canadians, it was another occasion for anxiety and caution: the pressure of American population growth and economic activity was intense, almost overwhelming. Perhaps, the Whoop-Up Trail and the other cross-border trails and affiliations were a prelude to annexation.

The most notorious incident in the history of the Canadian west involved, among other things, the border and the question of sovereignty. In May 1873, a party of American wolfers, convinced that Indians had stolen some of their horses, tracked the presumed culprits north from Fort Benton. There was a culture gap over the issue of horse stealing. To the Indians, it was a kind of recreation, not to be taken too seriously. You retaliated, of course, but usually by stealing horses in return.

It was a sport; there were, after all, lots of horses on the plains. For the whites, horse theft was a capital crime. They lynched men who carried it out, white or red.

Like many men on this American frontier, the wolfers were veterans of the Civil War. It was the usual story: men who had endured the slaughter and brutalization of war, unable to become civilians again, restless, ruined, helpless to control the numbing rage. (In our time, they would have bought Harleys and formed a gang.) After the Civil War, such men could turn west and keep going. In those days, there was always the safety valve of a half-wild frontier.

The wolfers crossed the border, which meant nothing to them. They rode into the southwestern draws of the Cypress Hills and camped in the Battle Creek valley, near two Canadian branch-plant trading posts representing Fort Benton companies. Nearby, was an Assiniboine band of three hundred people or so, of whom about fifty were warriors.

Soon after their arrival, in the atmosphere of suspicion and prejudice, the, by-now drunken, wolfers opened fire on the Indian encampment. They killed at least twenty-three Assiniboine men, women and children, probably many more than that. The incident became known as the Cypress Hills Massacre.

In Fort Benton, the killers were heroes. Anyone who gunned down Indians was a hero—the more the better. In Canada, however, the reaction was different. Eastern newspaper editorials denounced the action, and its corollary, the violation of Canadian sovereignty. "Yankee desperadoes" (although at least four Canadians had participated) had crossed the border and had carried out a massacre on Canadian soil.

The lawlessness of Canadian Whoop-Up Country had concerned the government for years. Its previous plans to set up some kind of police force in the west had been set back by the Riel rebellion on the Red River in 1869–70. However, continuing violence provoked the government to finally pass a bill in 1873 authorizing the formation of the North-West Mounted Police (NWMP). It had received royal assent just a week before the Cypress Hills Massacre took place. The government feared that the sort of widespread and terrible warfare taking place south of the border might now break out in Canada's western territories. Or that there might be another Métis uprising.

By September of that year, the force began to be constituted. It marched west—in an epic story of folly, hardship and endurance all its own—the next year. The force was originally called the North-West Mounted Rifles, but the prime minister, John A. Macdonald, in a calculation that would remain a permanent part of Canadian policy making, substituted "police" for "rifles" to avoid alarming or provoking the Americans (or the Indians, for that matter). The force was modelled on the Royal Irish Constabulary, whose mandate had long involved a combination of police and army duties in order to keep the recalcitrant Irish in line. The NWMP was organized like a cavalry regiment but had the judicial powers of policemen as well. Its commissioner and superintendents could try, fine and jail suspects. There were 150 men in the initial NWMP unit. They would patrol an area of eight hundred thousand square kilometres. Their uniforms were red.

The mythology of the Canadian west is that the Mounties went in, caught the bad white men, reassured and pacified the Indians, with whom they developed close and good relationships, and, generally, avoided the violent excess of things south of the border. There's considerable truth in this. For example, after 1860, in a single region of Montana, more than thirty Indian massacres took place. Nothing remotely like that occurred in Canada. The Cypress Hills Massacre became notorious in Canada as the single worst atrocity against Indians. Nothing demonstrates better the general proposition of relative Canadian peaceability more than the singularity of Cypress Hills, and its effect on Canadian public opinion and government policy. In the United States, such killings were commonplace.

The Mounties' work was aided by several factors. Their commissioner, James McLeod, was a particularly intelligent, culturally sensitive and honest man. The Indians he dealt with believed his words and respected him. They found him worthy of his red coat. There were far fewer Indians, white settlers, cattle rustlers and outlaws north of the 49th parallel than south of it, and, therefore, fewer opportunities for conflict. The army made its two brief appearances to subdue the Métis rebellions, and, afterwards, it withdrew, leaving the Mounties as the sole face of official white power in the Canadian western territories.

Nevertheless, there are more similarities between the two countries' experiences on the northern plains than traditional historical accounts allow. There was more cattle rustling—a major source of conflict, and of cross-border tension—more small-scale conflict with Indians, more vigilantism, and more racial prejudice in Canada than is usually supposed. Of the Indians, one western Canadian editorialist wrote: "That a lot of dirty, thieving, lazy ruffians should be allowed to go where they will, carrying the latest improved weapons, when there is no game in the country, seems absurd."

In fact, there were far too few Mounties to handle the vast territory under their care. Cattle rustling and the liquor trade—an always-combustible element in white-Indian relations—continued. The Indians, at least, were driven to it by desperation. The buffalo disappeared in just a few years of slaughter, and with them, the entire framework of aboriginal life on the plains: the nomadic culture of buffalo, horse, and bow-and-arrow, or gun. Indians stole cattle to eat. Still, the Mounties did reduce the incidence of both rustling—which was frequently a cross-border enterprise—and liquor trading, and they helped tamp down their incendiary possibilities. Certainly, the Canadian police were a stark contrast to the American longknives, and to the posses and vigilantes of Montana. In 1884 alone, in one area of that state, at least twenty-one men were lynched at "neck-tie parties." Lynchings did take place in Canada, but they were rare.

The real importance of Cypress Hills is that it made the 49th-parallel border mean something. The massacre forced the Canadian government to act to establish a Canadian presence on the western plains. From then on, a few hundred redcoats managed to make it clear that there were, indeed, two separate countries out there, each contending with its problems in different ways. Never again would Americans cross the border at will—or at least not in force or unheedingly. After Cypress Hills, and the arrival of the Mounties, American posses or ranchers crossing the line in hot pursuit of cattle-rustling Indians or white varmints knew they were breaking a law. They knew they had left the United States and had entered Canada: the different country, with its other, alternative vision of the frontier, and of how life in North America might be lived.

The wind is my enemy all the next day. It blows at gale force, either on my nose, or across my heading, depending on how the road makes its long prairie curves. The rain has stopped and the sun beams down spring warm, interrupted half-a-dozen times during the day by short, cold rain squalls. I crouch as low as I can in the saddle, and deploy, yet again, my wind countermeasures. The wind on these empty plains is legendary. I remember again Stegner's observation that in this very region the wind "blows all the time in a way to stiffen your hair and rattle the eyes in your head." So much more the case, I think, when you're blasting into it at a sixty-five miles an hour; then it's hurricane strength. My hair stiffens and my eyes rattle.

Just before the town of Shelby, Montana, something momentous happens. In the distance, to the west, I catch the first, shadowy loom of big mountains—the Rockies. They are an intimation of home. I have a considerable way yet to go, but I feel as if I'm getting close.

The settlers in their labouring ox carts and wagon trains felt the same rush of expectation: after the endless march across the arid, Indiany plains, the mountains seemed like the end of their trek to the sea—a kind of anabasis. They were wrong. The worst often lay ahead: the high, cold passes through the Rocky peaks, the glacier-scored, ridged country beyond, and, most discouraging of all, the many more mountain ranges that lay between them and the valleys and fertile flatland of the coast. Wagons and carts could at least proceed across the high grasslands. The mountains were hell for them.

Times change. On my heavy-laden thumper, for me, the Rockies are truly a sign of the end. If I rode hard, I could get to my island's ferry in two days—if my saddle sores allowed. The machine diminishes the Earth, its amplitude and its perils. Just ride through the mountains, and down to the sea.

CHAPTER 17

A STRANGE LAND

. . . A SOMETHING POSSIBLE, A CHANCE, A DANCE
THAT IS NOT DANCED.
—PATRICK ANDERSON, "POEM ON CANADA"

I WAS ELEVEN YEARS OLD when my family immigrated to Canada. We were Irish—or at least as Irish as Ulster Protestants could be. We had been driven out of Ireland—as so many millions of Irish before us—by a milder form of the ancient national wants: we had food, but there were no houses to live in, and no jobs for my father to work at. First, when I was an infant, we crossed over to England. Eventually, that wasn't good enough for my father's modest ambitions. It was hard being a Paddy with little education—in spite of having a formidable intelligence—on that insular island. When he realized he had gone as far as an Irish ex-navy petty officer could go in the imperial centre, he took my mother and me to the New World.

In the inside covers of my *Schoolboy's Pocket Book*, the countries and territories of the British Commonwealth, which we schoolboys still thought of as a kind of Empire, were coloured the traditional red. The colour seemed to dominate the paler shades of everything else. Canada was, by far, the largest bright red blotch. On the Mercator-distorted map, the country seemed to overbear the entire western hemisphere. By some miracle of retention, I still have the small, slim book; its spine is taped, but otherwise it is intact. I look at the book now, and there it is: a vast, red, dominant Canada, with its major cities marked squatting on top of the paltry republic to the south. It is a flat-map-induced optical illusion.

Nevertheless, when I looked at my future home in my *Pocket Book*, its size and position atop the world seemed appropriate. I didn't then know "Canada" as the Nazi concentration-camp term for plenty, and therefore, for survival. But, a priori, I felt the same way about the place. Unlike postwar-straitened England, I thought Canada had everything: length, breadth, mountains, prairies, the North Pole, great lakes, minerals and wheat, cars, refrigerators and televisions. I studied our atlas, and I memorized where potash was produced, and which parts of the giant dominion held gold, or where people spoke French—an exotic ingredient. The photographs in books I took out of the library seemed filled with space: between houses, across the prairie and the northern ice, and in aerial photographs of the unbounded boreal forests. I foresaw milk-shakes, and blue jeans, and changing my accent to fit in—and to sound like my cowboy heroes. Canada wasn't America, but it would do as a decent alternative.

Looking back, I suppose I thought my new home would be like a halfway house between England and the USA. Like most English schoolboys (even from Ireland) in any century, I was a big supporter of the Empire. It was heroic and exciting, and it opened up the world beyond little England. I had no qualms about saying permanent goodbye to all my friends. Canada, like America, had the feel of a future. I thought my life would begin all over again when I arrived there.

As I write, that was fifty years ago. The Canadas of then and now are, in many ways, different countries. I have the sense that, as I grew up and matured, so did my country. Our coming of age coincided. At the same time, I believe that Canada has grown for itself a consistent, distinct, solid core. To most Canadians, that may seem like a reckless statement. Because we are not sure, it is our national pastime to try to make clear to ourselves who we are, and, most important to us, how we are different from America. Nevertheless, I have a very strong sense, a conviction—perhaps an immigrant's clarity of perspective—that my country is an authentic and definable place. Canada has a centre; it has a heart of its own. It has lately become, in recognizable ways, although by accident, an avatar of the world in the future. And I have no difficulty in distinguishing it from the United States across the border.

At the time my immigrant parents and I landed at Malton Airport outside Toronto, we discovered a country that largely fit my schoolboy image. Canada was mostly white and European. Its geography dwarfed the twelve million people strung along its southern border. It was a repository of natural resources—a hewer of wood and drawer of water—for the United States. Its culture seemed nondescript and hesitant, a self that barely dared to speak its name, either in writing or in art. It had always been caught between two empires—the imperial reach of the British, and the rising commercial power (an empire in all but name) of the United States. In the late 1950s, Canada was still trapped on this old, narrow political and cultural ground. It was still adolescent and subaltern.

To live in the country then was to feel overwhelmed, as Canadians always have been, by the immense, empty weight of its geography. The heavy Precambrian rock of the Canadian Shield, the sheer magnitude of the forest, the tundra, the eternal ice stretching to the pole, all seemed to lie heavy on the people, to push down on them—"the land God gave to Cain," as Jacques Cartier described it in 1534 (he was looking at the north shore of the Gulf of St. Lawrence). Huge as the country was, one could nevertheless be oppressed by its wilderness. It was easy to feel crammed into a small, habitable, safe, but always threatened, southern pale of settlement.

Like all European arrivals in the New World, we were ignorant of the aboriginal inhabitants, for whom the wilderness was a hard, but manageable, home, saturated with meaning, and with the means to live. And Canada was, as it had always been, a country of cold.

Canada, as it then was—rather than what it has since become—may come closer to the vague, benign notion many Americans have of the country: a cold, quiet, stable, boring, trustworthy, polite, peaceful place, Edmund Wilson's giant wildlife reserve next door, but with nice cities and a lot of French speakers. Perhaps part of the explanation for American opinions about Canada is that they are outdated. They are mostly wrong now, but, once upon a time, they were mostly right. Canada has changed mightily in half a century. The United States just hasn't noticed.

Of course, many Americans would now add to their view of Canada what they see as the less favourable characteristics I've noted: a carelessness with the border, a softness for radicals and terrorist fundraising fronts, a hypocritical free ride on defence against evil enemies, a fondness for letting just about anyone into the country to live, a propensity for socialist solutions to social problems—government-run, universal health care, for example.

In fact, there are now two mainstream perspectives on Canada in the United States, each inaccurate in its own way. These views can be broadly distinguished as: liberal, Democratic, blue-state versus conservative, Republican, red-state; or as the coasts versus the heartland. As a whole, Massachusetts and Oregon like Canada (although on a largely false basis); Texas and West Virginia do not (on equally mistaken grounds). Each narrative of Canada shares the defects of simplification and ignorance of complexity. The United States itself, like all large, heterogeneous societies, is an extraordinarily complicated place. So is Canada. Americans know this about themselves, but have difficulty acknowledging it anywhere else.

I ride a twisty, rolling road across the high plains of the Blackfeet Indian Reservation, the mountains a clear, jagged barrier to the west. There are few buildings on this back road, and no traffic. Angus cattle speckle the grasslands. The apparent wind, as I ride into it, or across it, varies between gale and hurricane force. I cross into Canada, once again, at Del Bonita—it's an odd, out-of-place Spanish name here on the Montana-Alberta line. On yet another slow day at an isolated border station, the young Canadian agent asks me lots of questions. He doesn't check my bags—no Canadian has. Then he talks on and on about my bike and my trip. It's something he's always wanted to do, as well, and, planted in his hut on the plains, he envies my animal-mobile liberty. I ask about smuggling and illegal border crossing. There's some of both, he says, but really, it's not a big concern around here. At least on the Canadian side.

"The Americans have got their balls in a twist, though," he says, with unexpected colloquial force. "If you were crossing the other way here, they'd take your bike apart."

"That's happened now and then," I say. "They're often very thorough."

"I shouldn't say this," says the agent of the Canadian government, "but, in my opinion, they don't know their ass from a hot rock. It just doesn't make sense to me to hold up the people who all live around here—or just plain tourists in the summer—and spend half an hour searching their pickups, or their RVs. It's just stupid, and it just makes people angry."

"They want to make the border a tough place to cross," I say.

"Well, after September 11th, they had to do some stuff, but this is just stupid. I mean, look around." His arm sweeps the horizon. "Why hold people up here for twenty minutes, when you can go twenty kilometres down the road and cross at trails and farm roads. There's nothing out there. Who is going to cross here with an intent to do harm?"

The next day turns bitterly cold, and light rain falls from a low sky, obscuring most of the mountains. It's full spring, but snow and washouts in the Rockies have blocked the road I want to ride through the Glacier National Park. The Going-to-the-Sun Road is closed. It peaks at Logan Pass over the Continental Divide and, up there, winter is in late, full bloom.

Like the International Peace Garden, the park is another creation of the time of optimistic brotherhood between Canada and the United States, a relic of the period of the undefended border. The park spills over from each country into the other, and the respective park services co-operate to manage Waterton-Glacier's plants and animals. The latter, as a brochure truly points out, "ignore political boundaries." I decide to follow the road that circles the fringe of the park the long way round instead, south and then west.

I begin to ride into the mountains. I'm always surprised by their abrupt rise out of the prairie, and I begin to climb right away. The cold rain becomes a sleety snow. Pavilions of soot-black clouds mass over the peaks ahead. The road is slick, and the KLR makes scary skips and short slides on the curves. My visor fogs up and I must control my breathing, or crack open the shield to the cold and strong west wind. Soon, katabatic gusts—williwaws—begin to sweep hard off the peaks broadside against me. One gust pushes me into the opposite lane and close to the drop-off there. It looks like a hundred yards or more down a steep slope of rock and scree. I skid to a stop on the shoulder, the machine not quite under control. My ripped-up right ankle gives way yet again on the uneven surface, and I can't stop the heavy bike from dropping onto its side.

There is no traffic, and snow is falling. I'm on a hill and close to the road's edge. I'm afraid that if I lever the KLR upright from where it lies, it might start to roll backwards, or that I might even lose it over the side and into the chasm below. I have to drag it on the cushion of its pannier bags out into the centre of the road and position it so that I'm pushing it upright towards the uphill slope. I unload the bags not pinned under the machine. My boots have little traction on the slick road surface. In the cold wind, I strain and sweat for fifteen minutes. My heart pounds much too fast. Sometimes, when sailing in remote parts of the world, and when things went wrong, I thought I might be pushing my aging body too hard, and that it might be my fate to die on some remote shore. I feel the same way now: "Middle-Aged Numbskull Found Dead on Road Beside Ugly Motorcycle."

Then I think: this is like being at sea; I'm alone and I must solve this problem. I notice a signpost near the road about fifty yards downhill. I haul and push the horizontal thumper down the slithery tarmac until it's beside the sign. I find some gravel, which I carry in handfuls and stomp down onto the surface for some traction. On the third try, I push the bike upright, my ankle swelling up again before my eyes, the pain keen and strong. The bike comes up against the post, and the handlebar hooks around it, under control at last. I hike back up the hill to retrieve my bags, and load up. I let air out of my tires, turn downhill, and ride—often slide—north, very slowly, out of the mountains until the snow changes to sleet and then to cold rain.

I ride through the Rockies in Canada by way of the Crowsnest Pass. At first, rain falls here, too. Signs warn of strong gusts, and they are right. The crosswind in the passes is ferocious. At times, I must slow right down and counter-steer hard. As soon as I cross the Continental Divide, however, and enter my home province—the divide forms the Alberta–British Columbia border here—everything improves. It's a kind of welcome home. The wind eases; the rain stops, and the sun returns. I shed my inner fleece. Codeine takes hold, and my re-swollen ankle becomes bearable again. My British Columbia licence plates are unremarkable now. I could be out for a few days' ride.

From Creston, I climb to nearly eighteen hundred metres over the Kootenay Pass through the Selkirk Mountains, the highest highway pass in Canada. Even though it's mid-June the snow is still thick on the ground here, and it is very cold, though sunny. I cross the border into Washington State, north of Metaline Falls in the beautiful, wooded, and warmer valley of the Pend Oreille River, a tributary of the great Columbia. The border guard performs the usual ritual: questions, passport inside (googles?), pokes through each of my bags, asks about my medication—what the hell's the reason for this obsession with prescriptions?—confiscates leftover Chinese food (or I can eat it on the spot, he tells me), confirms that my bag of beef jerky was made in the US of A, asks about the bike, what mileage it gets, my trip, the weather farther east, tells me he rides (a big Yamaha), wishes me good luck, says: Be careful out there.

I have ridden 360 miles, half of them on back roads and in odious weather, my second-longest day in the north. The Box Canyon Motel, just south of the town of Metaline, is quiet, and lies ten yards from the high river bank. I ice my sore ankle once again, and sit outside my room on a plastic chair. I am bushed, zonked, bagged. I watch the high, muddy water swirl by. Bald eagles patrol the far shore, and all around me, song birds sing.

I need to get home. For a long time now, I have had no doubt where that is. Canada has become my home in every sense of the word. I feel an emotion for the country that is, I suppose, a kind of love. It took me a long time to find this tenderness. For years after we arrived as immigrants, I was homesick for cosy England. Or, I was repelled and alienated by the school-boy violence directed my way in the small, southern Ontario village we settled in, which hadn't seen an immigrant in a couple of generations. I withdrew, and cherished my Anglo-Irish difference. For many years, in the schoolyard, Canada was like England had been for me. There, I had been harassed by bullies because I was an Irish boy; here, I was harassed because I was English. It was very confusing. But the result was the same: I had to fight my way to acceptance. Everyone gets bullied, of course (even the bullies at home), but it makes a difference why you're getting knocked around, why you have to plan your way home from school as if it was a fighting retreat. These things delay the development of a relationship; they thwart good feelings, and they certainly inhibit love.

Over time, I became more Canadian. I grudgingly gave up my accent and my sense of myself as an outsider, a temporary sojourner in a strange land. I ceased thinking of England as home—I'd never thought of Ireland that way—although it took a while longer to accept Canada as my place in the world. And as I reached chronological adulthood in the late 1960s and 1970s, Canada itself became a grown-up kind of country. It was less and less "the land of rye and caution," as Marshall McLuhan described it. During those, and the subsequent, decades, it grew more and more into a country easier to like and to value.

In fact, over the last five decades, Canada has undergone a renaissance. It has the cultural paraphernalia of a mature nation: musicians, artists and, especially, writers. Its economy is still primarily based on hacking stuff out of the generous ground—the oil sands are the latest example—but Canada has created a sophisticated manufacturing sector. The two free trade agreements with the United States, the second of which includes Mexico, have accelerated this development.

In 1965, Canada decided on a flag of its own: the maple leaf design (which Americans travelling outside North America sometimes use to forestall nasty treatment by people aggrieved with the imperial power) replaced the colonial symbol of a modified British Red Ensign. The new flag was intensely debated. To the old British of Canada, the symbolism was clear: the replacement of the established flag measured the degradation of the British and imperial (or Commonwealth) link. The traditionalists argued that it was the beginning of the end of British North America. They were right. But Canadian hunger for such an emblematic change was strong, and the maple leaf was fast accepted. You might view the new flag as a measure of the transition of Canadian dependence from one empire to another; but you can also see it as a sign of maturity.

Finally, during these years, Canada became completely independent. As the mother dominion in the British Empire and, later, the Commonwealth, Canada had been an essentially independent state since the Statute of Westminster of 1931. But one anomaly remained. To amend the Canadian constitution (the British North America Act) an act of the British parliament was required. In 1982, the Constitution Act came into effect in Canada. It repatriated the Canadian constitution, which also included the new Charter of Rights and Freedoms, a bill of rights similar to that of the United States constitution's various amendments. Instead of rubber-stamping the Canadian request, some British legislators, mostly in the House of Lords, had the astonishing arrogance to actually debate whether the proposed change was in Canada's best interests. The old imperial habits died hard.

Nothing demonstrates better the cautious, evolutionary, gradualist Canadian approach to its own constitutional and legal status as a state: the complete independence that was won by force of arms in the United States in 1783 was achieved in Canada by legislation two hundred years later. The juxtaposition of revolution and evolution, established during the War of Independence and reaffirmed by the War of 1812, remained intact. Even now, a confusing (for Canadians as well as Americans) residue of the British connection remains: the odd fact that the Canadian head of state is the British Queen, represented in Canada by a governor general. This, too, may be a transitory phase in the development of the Canadian nation. Sooner or later, this last relic of imperial subordination may disappear and a new republic constitute itself in North America. Or, Canadians, with their customary reticence and tolerance of anomaly, will keep the Queen's governor general. There are some advantages to having a head of state, with all its unifying symbolism, so dramatically divorced from the government's partisan and, often, sordid business—especially in a diverse and loose federation, ever-strained by language and ethnic differences.

From a Canadian perspective, it is astonishing that Americans are unaware of the immense changes in Canada over the past four or five decades. Canada's cultural renaissance and its constitutional (although not necessarily political) maturation have happened just next door, and right out in the open. If Americans have missed it, that's an indication of the deep insularity of the continental republic. The word "Canada" either puts Americans to sleep, or—as in the last few years, since 9/11—it appals them (unnecessarily) as a hole in America's antiterror armature. In either case, the view is one-dimensional. The disparity between image and reality is wide.

By any standard, Canada is a very complex society, and an extraordinarily complicated political entity. This complexity has many elements. First, and foremost, of course, there is the United States, the elephant next door, the overshadowing spectre in any Canadian government policy decision, at any level. It is the cause of a national approach-avoidance complex. The presence of the restless, magnetic imperial power saturates every aspect of Canadian public life.

While it balances its existence against the power of the United States, however, Canada must deal with its internal intricacies. These require further delicate compromises, compensations and offsets. Most important, of course, is Quebec, and the unending task of keeping the province enfolded within the federation. In 1995, Quebec sovereigntists came within less than one percentage point of winning a referendum that would have precipitated (we now know) a unilateral declaration of independence by the Parti Québécois. As I write, Quebec separatism is at one of its low points: a recent poll showed 36 per cent in favour of "sovereignty," the fudge word separatists use for independence. It's possible that Quebec separation has had its day. It's equally possible that it is in a hiatus and awaits another perceived insult from English Canada, or a charismatic leader to awaken the old dream of a French republic in North America—a fourth version of a North American nation (if one includes Mexico).

The need, since the conquest of 1763, to accommodate French Quebec and bind it into the Canadian Confederation, along with the necessity to balance French-English rights, has reinforced Canada's instinct to be a country of moderation and compromise. Many of the powers given to Quebec had to be extended to other provinces as well, creating the most decentralized federal state in the world. The provincial premiers are the barons at the court of the prime minister. Because language is at the heart of the debate about Quebec's status and role in Canada, words—in legislation, and in political and cultural discourse—must be calibrated and nuanced. They must be imprecise, and capable of differing interpretations to accommodate the incompatible, perhaps irreconcilable, requirements of English and French Canada. In such a political context, there must be fictions and allegories, an acceptance of anomaly and of paradox. Canadians are the masters of elision and of necessary ambiguity.

In the United States, liberals and conservatives shout at each other—especially conservatives at liberals. The radio talk show bellowing goes on incessantly. It is unpleasant and counterproductive; it polarizes further an already polarized country. But no one thinks that all the noise will lead to the disintegration of the United States. In Canada, public political discussion is, in comparison, quiet and polite. It has to be. American-style doctrinaire yelling could well be fatal to Canadian unity. Canadian politeness is real, but it is a necessary adaptation to the fragile state of the political union.

Politeness is an ambiguous quality in any event. It is equated with niceness, and that's wrong. Politeness is developed as a necessary means of defusing and sublimating internal enmities, and is not necessarily a manifestation of virtue. Canadian politeness masks, as politeness always does, a sense of superiority. And who else would Canadians feel superior to than Americans? It is the sense of greater worthiness of those in the ironic know over those who earnestly and naively labour under the unsophisticated impression that everything's okay.

The reality is that the most prevalent form of Canadian prejudice is anti-Americanism. My American friends living on my small island in British Columbia, lying within sight of the United States—and there are many Americans here—say that they often experience snide, reflexive discrimination by Canadians. Americans in Canada are not imagining things; bias and a subtle, veiled hostility are real.

However, even Americans living in Canada often have a problem of comprehension, which is a version of the failure of understanding about Canada common to virtually all Americans.

It boils down to this: when Americans think of Canada in benign and approving terms, they still have an idea of the country as a kind of extension of the United States, as an idealized model of the United States. In the mind, Canada becomes America as it should have been, the way the early promise could have been fulfilled, the real manifestation in modern times of John Winthrop's city upon a hill. The kindly views of Canada as more peaceful, much less aggressive, more caring, more moderate in its politics, slower—and polite (opinions that are not necessarily accurate) are often the reasons why Americans move north. Canada is boring, yes, but it is a sanctuary. Sanctuaries, by definition, are boring. Yet this approval is really of Canada as a farther periphery of America, as an extension of the United States into a nominally distinct territory, as a continuation, not of the United States itself, but of the idea of America, by other means.

Americans, even many Americans in Canada, cannot recognize Canada as a centre in its own right, with its innate, fundamental differences, which must be accepted and adjusted to. Canadians see this blindness, or they intuit it. They recognize the American inability to truly acknowledge—to see—an alternative political, cultural and social invention in North America.

The Canadian sense of ironic superiority—the reflexive mockery of the less powerful for the overlord—is endemic in Canadian life. The Irish used to feel this way about the English—some still do. In Canada, it's like an unspoken shorthand, and is present everywhere. A mundane example: some Canadian television commercials for beer appeal to Canadians on two levels: the overt claim that drinking Canadian beer is patriotic (besides the claim that it tastes better); and the subtle, shaded, implied message that sticks it to the Americans, who, poor saps, can't even recognize when they're getting insulted. A very popular Canadian television program, *Talking to Americans*, consisted of nothing but a Canadian comedian posing as a reporter, and asking Americans to comment on absolutely non-sensical statements about Canada. The genial, and, yes, polite, Americans (some of whom were, for example, students and professors at universities like Berkeley and Columbia) responded seriously by congratulating Canadians on finally outlawing the practice of setting elderly relatives adrift on icebergs to die, or on finally paving the Trans-Canada Highway. It was funny, but also vicious.

Irony is the refuge of the less powerful. It is a form of indirect communication and it depends on widespread awareness within a society of what might be called the terms of engagement with the superior power. Canadians stereotype Americans (as Americans do Canadians) as a necessary condition for ironic commentary on American ignorance of Canada. This might come across as anti-American, but in reality, the stereotype is largely true: the ignorance is real and virtually universal.

Canadian irony is a form of defence against an aggressive United States. From manifest destiny to the ominous border security measures of today, American threats against Canada have been real. These threats, and indeed, the entire Canadian enterprise in the shadow of America, were acknowledged in the winning phrase in a Canadian Broadcasting Corporation radio contest. Entrants had to complete the comparison: "As Canadian as ———" The sardonic winner was: "As Canadian as possible, under the circumstances."

Irony often manifests itself as smugness. Smug Canadians feel superior to Americans. It's an unpleasant characteristic. The Canadian actor/screenwriter Seth Rogen, commenting on the self-satisfied perspective a Canadian in the United States enjoys, told *The Guardian*: "When you watch the news, you don't think, 'Man, we're fucked!' You think, 'Man, they're fucked!' It's great, like there's an automatic, fake moral high ground that's just built into whichever situation you're in."

The American dream is composed of no limits, of indefinite expansion, of the frontier as an endless, universal zone, if it is pursued around the world and into the final frontier of space. This is a dangerous misapprehension of the natural world, and of the limits imposed by it, and by the competing, or contradictory, desires of other nations. Canadians believe, as one of Margaret Atwood's heroines says, that Americans have "turned against the gods." Cautious Canadians, once preoccupied with survival on their hard, cold ground, remain convinced of the existence of problems without solutions, fully aware of limits and the virtues of restraint.

The idea of the southern U.S. border as a permeable membrane, through which pass illegals—economic pilgrims—searching for a better life, has a northern variant. The Canadian border, too, allows for a flow of people, and for a much greater passage of ideas and culture (facilitated by a common language, and by the respective peoples' similar origins). But the border is also a sticky, metaphorical membrane. It's not really undefended. It is garrisoned by an ironic, rueful sense of self, and by an ingrained awareness of the limits of human endeavour.

Canada is unusual, perhaps unique, as a country that has got a lot of things right, but whose citizens either can't accept that proposition, or believe that their country has, in fact, got most things wrong. Many Canadians see the indeterminacy—some, the complete lack—of a distinct (meaning distinct from the United States) Canadian identity as a fatal flaw. The poet Earle Birney writes, "It's only by our lack of ghosts we're haunted."

The debate about what is a Canadian, what is Canada, seems endless. Americans might be able to understand the issue in the context of Henry James's obsession in the nineteenth century about how Americans (of a certain class and sensibility) could distinguish themselves from Europeans.

Many Canadians think that their country is not a proper country, or even that it is a failure, because they find it hard to define to themselves and to the world, and perhaps especially, to Americans, just who or what they are. No wonder Americans have a fuzzy and weird idea of the nature of Canada. Canadians can't even figure out the place. This has always been a problem. Susanna Moodie, who immigrated to Canada from England, and wrote about her new home in the early 1850s, describes an English friend's reaction to her stories of her new country: "Don't fill your letters to me with descriptions of Canada. Who, in England, thinks anything of Canada!" The United States has simply replaced Great Britain as an uncomprehending hegemonic presence.

However, perhaps Canada's assumed weaknesses are really its strength in the world as it's coming to be: globalized; interconnected through trade, travel and, most important, electronics; a world of multiple centres of economic and political-military power (the United States a short-lived hyper-power); a world of people moving and mixing, with immigrants and refugees flooding into the developed regions in an unstoppable torrent.

Canadians live in a "perpetual philosophic mood which nourishes flexibility in the absence of strong commitments or definite goals," writes Marshall McLuhan. Canada, in McLuhan's characteristic terminology, is cool—unlike the United States with its "heavy commitments and sharply defined objectives," which inhibit cool flexibility. For such a nation, its borders must also be sharply defined, guarded and defended; it may even be necessary to build a wall. The unitary mythologized culture within the United States' borders fears the complex, mongrelized reality outside them. For Canadians—perhaps dwellers in a nationwide borderlands—the border remains a line of demarcation between themselves and the United States, but they are better able to recognize the border's ambiguous, complex nature as a conduit and a bridge, as well as a barrier.

I have a dream: a musician friend on Salt Spring Island backs into my motorcycle with her beat-up car and knocks it over. She is very apologetic. There is a lot of damage: the front wheel is bent, the handlebars are crooked, and there are gouges all over the red and black paint. I'm surprisingly philosophical about it. I wonder how I'm going to get it fixed before I have to leave this morning. Maybe I'll have to store the bike here, and just go home. I begin to try to pound the steel wheel back into shape with my plastic-pipe, tent-peg hammer. I wake up.

Yesterday, in the wind, rain, snow and sleet, and when I was struggling to get the KLR upright on the greasy mountain road, I thought about Will, Mike and Chris. I thought: it doesn't matter what happens to me, or to the bike, on this mountain, and it's of absolutely no consequence that I'm freezing and wet and getting blown all over the damn road by williwaws. The simple consolation is that I'm alive. This morning, I wake from my trashed-bike dream with a bad headache—the inevitable hangover from a tough day—and I think the same thing. I'll ride a long way over yet more mountains with a sore, bum ankle, with an equally sore head, but none of it matters. I look forward to it, because it all signifies one fine fact: that I'm alive, and moving, and doing something, and whatever's wrong with me won't kill me.

I'm looking forward to getting home, but I see already the end of my simple and uncomplicated life over the previous four weeks: get up, check my gear, eat breakfast, load the bike, ride all day as far as I can, bear with cold, ice, rain, heat, wind and ankle, stay upright, unload, eat, sleep. Repeat. The rhythm and the routine are so familiar to me. I see their end coming, and I miss them already. I also know that after the riding comes the writing.

It's cold and cloudy, with more rain in the offing, as I ride south down the Pend Oreille River. At the town of Tiger, I turn west to climb over the Selkirk Mountains along the steep, twisty road. I follow the valley of the Colville River to Kettle Falls, where I turn north. It is wild, wooded country; the wind is cold on this mid-June day in the mountains, and I wear all my heavy riding gear. I follow the valley of the Kettle River and turn west again along the north fork of Boulder Creek. I'm heading for the port of entry at Ferry, where I'll pick up Highway 3 in British Columbia, ride to Osoyoos, and cross back into the United States. This is the last border crossing until Sumas, 160 miles west, near the Pacific coast. For almost that entire distance, the line runs through named mountain wildernesses—the Pasayten and Mount Baker— and through North Cascades National Park. The border is as good as impassable on the ground. It will be interesting to see what the Department of Homeland Security has in mind for this stretch of the 49th.

Somehow, I miss the side road to the border, and end up in a long, useless, semicircle detour over the Kettle River Range and through the Okanogan National Forest. There is heavy roadwork going on in this remote area, and the temporary surface is either soft sand, gravel, or ribbed tarmac waiting for repaving. Signs warn: "Surface extremely hazardous for motorcycles." Now that I've crashed at speed, I'm blasé about dropping the bike again—especially wearing all my armour. A few weeks ago, I would have pottered through here at ten miles an hour like an old geezer. Now, on the straightaways,

I blast through the soft, gravelly sand, and over the ribbed sections at thirty or forty miles an hour, the bike skipping and slipping from side to side in the grooves. I stand up on my pegs for miles, yahooing, exhilarated, like I'm crossing the Sahara in the Paris-Dakar Rally, until my thigh muscles, and my medicated ankle, can't take the strain any more. Even sitting in the saddle, I keep up my speed. I'm going like hell. This is crazy, but it is, without question, intoxicating. Construction crews beside the road wave and shout at me to slow down. To hell with them. Some of them wave and shout encouragement. One guy pumps his fist and yells something like, "Go for it, man!"

I get back to paved road, cross over the Wauconda Summit, and begin a long, twisty, sometimes switchback, descent into the desert valley of Osoyoos, Oroville and Tonasket along the Okanagan River. The temperature rises fifteen degrees in half an hour. This narrow strip of true Sonoran desert runs north into Canada, and it is a microclimatic anomaly of the lee side of the Cascade Range to the west. Coming down from the cold evergreens of the mountains, the traveller finds himself in what looks like southern California, an area of sandy, scrubby hills, irrigated orchards and vineyards.

In Tonasket, I strip off all my gear, except my riding jacket, and switch to my light gloves. I head south down Route 97 thirty miles, then turn west towards the Cascades, the last mountain barrier, rising steep and snowy ahead of me. It's an abrupt climb out of the desert valley in a fast-rising headwind. At the four thousand–foot Loup Loup Summit, I stop and put my sweater, fleece and heavy gear back on again, as the temperature drops and clouds mass on the peaks ahead. I ride into the faux–Wild West tourist trap of Winthrop, and check into an overpriced room on the bank of the high and fast Chewuch River.

The next day is sunny in Winthrop, although dark clouds hang over the mountains. The forecast says: "Snow and freezing rain at higher elevations." I couldn't care less. I've got some bit between my teeth. I'm running hard for the coast. I've ridden more than five thousand miles in most kinds of weather you can imagine. I've dropped the bike; I've crashed. I no longer fear it. I can get the bike up again by myself, banged-up ankle notwithstanding. I've figured out how to keep my thumper, heavy-loaded as it is, upright on icy roads, on sand, dirt and gravel. I'm aware that this may be dangerous overconfidence, but I don't care about that either. I just want to indulge myself in this short-lived paradox: keep this riding-high I've slipped into going for as long as possible; ride as fast as I can for the ocean; get home.

The road over the Cascades is marked: Closed in Winter. It's open in mid-June. I climb to Washington Pass at fifty-five hundred feet. Lost in heavy cloud to my left lie North Gardner and Silver Star Mountains, each close to nine thousand feet high. There's standing snow cover all around me. As I approach the pass, the light rain turns to snow, which keeps falling as I descend and then climb again to Rainy Pass. I'm mostly in the clouds up here; they are like fog. The wind is strong, and it swirls in all directions, sweeping off the jumble of surrounding peaks. At least, there are no williwaws. The traffic is very light, and I'm able to pick my speed on the tight curves. Finally, the road turns downwards along Granite Creek, and, soon, the snow becomes rain again. I'm grateful there is no interlude of freezing rain—tough riding when you have to use the brakes a lot. The road is slick but not too dangerous. It's a fast, and steep, descent out of the Cascades and into the narrow, flat, green valley of the Skagit River. Within another hour, the rain stops and the sun appears. Fifty miles to salt water.

Ten miles from Puget Sound, I stop beside a downed motorcycle. The passenger is lying flat on the road, tended to by a volunteer fire chief who was passing by. The injured woman's back and side are sore, she says, but otherwise she feels fine. An ambulance is on the way. The guy is standing astride his old Harley in the ditch. He has long grey, pony-tailed hair, a grey beard and fringed leathers. He seems okay, but he keeps repeating that he can't get the handlebars straight. He wrenches at them over and over again. I tell him it looks fixable, and that his friend is okay—that's the main thing. He gives me a thousand-yard stare, and goes back to hauling on his bars. He is in shock. I wait until the ambulance arrives, and say to the attendant that, besides the woman on the ground, her partner needs some help too. I go over and tell the rider I'm leaving. He shakes my hand and says, "Thanks for stopping, man." Tears overflow his eyes, and he starts to sob. I put my arm around his shoulders, and I keep it there until the medic comes over and leads the crying man away.

I ride on, crossing through Skagit County and over Fidalgo Island, and onto Whidbey Island. Riding south in warm sun, I note that the water to my right is the confluence of the Straits of Georgia and Juan de Fuca. Not quite the Pacific, but it's getting close. In the distance, I can see the mountains of Vancouver Island. As the crow flies, I'm fifty miles from my house. I join three other motorcycles on the ferry over to Port Townsend on the Olympic Peninsula. We disembark together, and, for the first time in close to ten thousand miles, I ride in formation with other bikes. I'm last in line, and it is an extremely odd sensation to watch the other machines lean one way and the other as they carve their way through the curves. I feel constrained, though, by their proximity, and the constant need to jiggle my speed to maintain formation. After twenty miles, they wave to me, and turn south, while I head west. I feel relieved; things are back to normal after a constricting interlude. Saddle- and ankle-sore, but relaxed, I ride the last thirty miles of this long, mountain-girdling day into Port Angeles, and a room for the night.

There is a ferry from Port Angeles to Victoria on Vancouver Island. I got home that way after my ride north from the

395 STRANGE LAND   395

Mexican border. Now, however, I'm heading on west to complete my trek from ocean to ocean. The border here is all maritime—straits, channels and passages between islands and the mainland. I don't really need to see the length of the wide Strait of Juan de Fuca, out to the Pacific, but I crave the symmetry of the line from Quoddy Head to Cape Flattery. Afterwards, I must double back to ride through the San Juan Islands on the American side of the boundary. They were the site of the last armed standoff between the United States and Great Britain, with Canada, as usual, the feeble pawn in-between.

The next day begins cold and drizzly, but, after I've been riding for half an hour, dries up and turns warm. I run the twisty road alongside the Strait. It's good riding except for logging trucks that crowd me, tailgate and cut me off. A pretty road, but the trucks make it one of the more dangerous ones I've encountered. I ride through the Makah Indian Reservation and its main town of Neah Bay. The last three miles or so run over a decent dirt road to a parking lot. From there, I limp half a mile to an overlook. Before me, under the mild sun and pale blue sky, the blue-green Pacific Ocean undulates in gentle, heaving rolls. Half a mile offshore is Tatoosh Island, which bears the Cape Flattery Lighthouse. It is the westernmost point of the mainland United States south of the 49th parallel. The cliffs here are high and steep. It's impossible to climb down to the water. I look out over the ocean for a while, take a few photographs, and peg leg it back to the KLR.

I ride to Neah Bay, park the bike, and walk over a soft-sand beach to the water. I dip my hands in the Strait of Juan de Fuca, splash some water on my face. It will have to do for the Pacific, of which, here, near its entrance, the strait is an indistinguishable part. Now, I feel as if I've completed my commitment at Quoddy Head, Maine: Atlantic to Pacific, cape to cape, lighthouse to lighthouse. The cold salt water feels and tastes the same.

I sit in the sun for a while, eat an orange, drink water and look across to Canada, eight miles away. I feel tired. I mount up, and begin to retrace my path: back to Anacortes on Puget Sound, and the ferry to the San Juans. As I ride, I realize that the wind has come up, and changed direction. I can't believe it. For the first time in almost five weeks and more than five thousand miles, I turn the bike east, and for virtually the only time in all those weeks, and over that whole distance, the wind is blowing from the east. I'm riding into a strong headwind, right on the goddamn nose.

Just before the outbreak of the American Civil War, in 1859, the United States and Great Britain almost went to war over a murdered pig. Nothing better illustrates the level of tension still remaining between the two powers. An American settler on San Juan Island shot a pig belonging to the Hudson's Bay Company, because it was rooting up his vegetables. The island, together with the other islands in the San Juan group, was disputed territory. Tension between Britain (as represented by the governor of the Vancouver Island colony, James Douglas) and the United States had been growing for some time, and the dead pig was the proverbial last straw. Each side sent forces, and then augmented them. Hotheaded American commanders threatened to fight. Eleven weeks later, on the small island, 460 American troops with fourteen cannons behind an earthen redoubt faced off against three British warships and 2,100 soldiers and marines. The British held off attacking with their superior force.

The crisis was a holdover from the 1843–46 Oregon Boundary dispute. The Treaty of 1818 had established the 49th parallel as the boundary between the United States and British North America, but only as far west as the Rocky Mountains. The so-called Oregon Country (the British knew it as the Columbia District, under the nominal control of the fur-trading Hudson's Bay Company), comprising today's Washington, Oregon, Idaho, parts of Wyoming and Montana, and British Columbia, was left wide open, its ownership (ignoring any prior claims by its aboriginal inhabitants) to be decided at some later date. In the meantime, the two countries agreed to a joint occupancy.

Various negotiations to settle ownership failed. The British (this was still prior to Canadian Confederation) claimed as far south as the Columbia River dividing present Washington and Oregon, but would have accepted a continuation of the 49th parallel. The influx of thousands of American settlers over the Oregon Trail began to tip the balance in favour of the United States—nothing worked like boots and spades on the ground. However, American expansionist sentiment was the main catalyst of crisis.

Following the 1844 election, the U.S. Democratic party under President James K. Polk asserted its aggressive agenda on two fronts: its claim to all of the Oregon Country up to 54 degrees, 40 minutes latitude, the southern limit of Russian claims in Alaska; and its annexation of the independent republic of Texas, an act that Mexico regarded as a most serious provocation. On the Oregon question, the slogan "Fifty-four forty, or fight!" defined the belligerent United States' position. And the newspaperman John L. O'Sullivan enunciated the imperial doctrine of manifest destiny, which applied without prejudice to both Canadian and Mexican territory.

Polk backed down. He decided he didn't want to fight the British Empire at the same time as he was invading Mexico. And that empire's preponderant navy was a prohibitive deterrent to any war the United States might consider starting. The Oregon Treaty of 1846 sensibly settled on the 49th parallel, but it fudged one small detail: it failed to specify which maritime channel it meant in deciding who got the San Juan Islands.

In late summer 1859, a British admiral arriving off San Juan Island with his flagship, HMS *Ganges* (for which the main village on Salt Spring Island is named), to take command of the British forces, made his views clear: he would not "involve two great nations in a war over a squabble about a pig." The American president, James Buchanan, felt the same way. He sent his cool troubleshooter, General Winfield Scott, to the scene. Scott, the "Grand Old Man of the Army," had successfully defused the equally ridiculous Aroostook War along the Maine–New Brunswick border twenty years earlier. Scott and Governor Douglas agreed to a compromise: each country would maintain a small force on San Juan Island in a joint military occupation until their governments could settle the issue.

The governments set up an English and an American camp at opposite ends of the island. Tensions dissipated. For the next twelve years, the two occupying forces lived in amicable proximity. They visited and entertained each other, played sports together, planted vegetables and made the best of things. For the first few years of this arrangement, the American troops counted themselves lucky. They were spared the killing fields of the Civil War. For the British, San Juan was just one more dull, remote posting in their worldwide imperial duties.

The Treaty of Washington of 1871 cleared up the few remaining irritants between Great Britain and the United States. These mostly involved the so-called Alabama Claims— monetary compensation from Britain for its covert support of the Confederate States during the Civil War—but the treaty also referred the San Juan boundary dispute to the Emperor of Germany for arbitration. The kaiser ruled in favour of the United States, and the pig war was over. From that time on, the U.S.-Canadian border was established (with a few very minor exceptions) and peaceful.

After the Treaty of Washington, the boundary, hitherto bristling with forts and garrisons, quickly subsided into the

famous undefended border. At least, until 9/11 and its aftermath of border restrictions and controls. The period between
1871 and 2001 may come to be seen as a discrete period in history which is now over—a 130-year-long hiatus, during which
both states found it possible to suspend the habitual armed
security along their border.

I spend a day taking ferries and riding the two main islands
of the San Juans. The island group is really the contiguous
southern portion of the Canadian Gulf Islands, of which my
home of Salt Spring is the main island. The idyllic topography
of hills, trees, meadows, peaceful winding roads, views of sea
and mountains, is all familiar to me as I ride to the partially
restored English and American Camps. On a warm and
mostly sunny day, I walk the green grasslands of this dry
island on the wet coast. The entire archipelago, on both sides
of the border, is in a rain shadow of the mountains of the
Olympic Peninsula, or those of Vancouver Island.

On the ferry back to the mainland, while I'm drinking
coffee in the boat's cafeteria, my KLR suffers its only substantial damage of both my border rides—while it's completely sta-
tionary. I hear an announcement for the "owner of a Canadian
motorcycle" to report to the car deck. I know immediately what
has happened. I had asked for blocks or tie-downs, but the ferry
crew assured me they weren't necessary, in fact, they have
none—in spite of the fact that they are required on the British
Columbia runs. Now, a sudden tidal surge has flung the bike
over onto its side against a steel bulkhead.

I'm very tired, and I lose it. On the car deck of the ferry, in
front of three crewmen and half a dozen car and truck drivers, I shout and curse. "I have ridden this fucking bike across
the fucking United States twice without a fucking bit of
damage (not true), and now, I'm a few fucking miles from
home, and you bastards manage to drop the fucking thing

into a fucking steel wall, and fucking wreck it." And so on. Or words to that effect, repeated often. I do everything but foam at the mouth. The crewmen, whom, in retrospect, I admire without reservation, nod with stoic sympathy until I run out of steam. The other passengers stare at me with alarm. I sound crazy, and maybe I'm even armed—they don't know. When I finally shut up, one of the crewmen says: "Let me help you get it up." He finds me a block. (*Now* he finds me a fucking block.) He gives me a compensation form to fill out and offers to buy me a coffee. He says he's sorry this happened and that he hopes my bike is okay. Now, I'm feeling guilty as hell. I decline the coffee, but I thank him, and the other men. They nod, still calm and non-judgmental. Where does the Washington State ferry system find these compassionate, patient employees?

Of course, the damage is actually minor. The heavy-duty handlebar guard, which I installed myself, has done its job. It has taken the full shock of the loaded bike's impact. The injury appears to be restricted to a jammed throttle. I take off the guard and the throttle works fine. (Later, at home, I'm able to straighten out the guard with a few sledgehammer blows.) My helmet, however, has been flung down and rolled around on the steel deck. It is badly scratched, as is my plastic visor. I resolve to sue the ferry company for a new one. Later, I realize getting compensation involves the usual cumbersome process of forms, affidavits, and expert evidence. It's not worth it for $250, and I give up.

The last day.

It produces a nice symmetry with my first day over a month ago: it is cold, and it rains hard and without let-up. I ride to the border north of Lynden, Washington, and south of Aldergrove, British Columbia. The port of entry here is one of only three (legal) crossings west of the mountains. It became famous a few years ago because a 110-metre-long tunnel was discovered running under the border. It was an excellent tunnel: one to three metres underground, reinforced with rebar and two-by-six wood supports. Its termini were in buildings on opposite sides of the line. The builders were a nicely multicultural Canadian crew with the last names Raj, Woo and Valenzuela. They were industriously lugging hockey bags (what else?) full of marijuana through the tunnel from Canada to the United States. Somehow, one of the many, many police forces and agencies on one side of the border or the other got wind of the project. They busted it in July 2005. It was the first, and, so far, the only, tunnel discovered under the Canadian-American line. Dozens—and counting—have been unearthed along the Mexican border.

Just before the checkpoint, I turn west and follow the U.S. border road to the west. It is dead straight through flat farm fields. It's June 17, but I am kitted out in my full riding gear, fleece and sweater, heavy gloves, handlebar grip heater on low. I cross into Canada at Blaine, Washington. It's a long line and takes a while, but the Canadian agent is typically brief. I'm through in twenty seconds. I ride, awash in heavy rain and vehicle spray, in a strong crosswind, on busy Highway 99—it's the main Vancouver-Seattle route. Remembering the weather that day, I realize it was atrocious. At the time, however, I ride with complete equanimity; travelling in heavy weather on a good paved road is easy.

I'm not celebrating yet, because I intend to cross the border twice more: in and out of Point Roberts. Campobello Island on the Maine–New Brunswick border, and Point Roberts bracket the border—the tiny, anomalous enclaves reachable by land only through the neighbouring country. There are two more such pieces of United States' territory: the Northwest Angle in Minnesota, and, to be consistent, the entire state of Alaska. Point Roberts, the 4.9-square-mile tip of the Canadian peninsula jutting into Boundary Bay, was cut off by the Oregon Treaty's establishment of the 49th parallel as the boundary line reaching to the coast. When the treaty was concluded, no one realized that the point would be isolated. British Boundary Commission surveyors realized the situation, and they requested that the tiny area be assigned to Britain. The border had already been bent well south of the 49th to give all of Vancouver Island to Canada. Somehow or other—perhaps the Americans never responded to this minor matter—nothing was done. In fact, because of a surveying error, the border here is 200 yards north of the 49th.

Point Roberts sees itself as the safest gated community in the United States. Half its property is owned by Canadians, who use it as a summering place. Its permanent American residents take the isolation in exchange for peace and security.

I am wearily fatalistic about crossing the border into the point. I've been searched and questioned at length so many times, and perhaps a border guard here will be suspicious of a loaded-down motorcycle making a run over the line on a cool, rainy Sunday. I inch up to the booth behind several cars; this agent is asking a lot of questions, and he's looking inside some trunks.

"How do you like the KLR?" are his first words.

"It's great," I say. "I like it a lot, it's a great machine."

He takes my passport but doesn't do anything with it.

"Are you going somewhere, or coming from?" he asks.

I tell him about my trip. He asks about the weather, and what changes I made to the bike. He tells me about his old 1996 KLR. We chat on and on, while a line of cars grows behind me. The guy doesn't give a damn. Eventually, he says, "Well, better get these four-wheelers moving." He hands back my passport, which he has held in his hand the whole time, and says, "Have fun."

I ride the quiet roads of the point; there are no strip malls, and just a few restaurants, gas stations, a general store and a marina. The landscape is flat and unremarkable, but on a clear day, you could see the mountains all around. I ride to Lighthouse Marine Park on the Strait of Georgia. I am the only vehicle in the parking lot, and there are no other human beings in sight.

The rain has faded to a drizzle under a low, dark overcast. From America, I look west towards Canada—Vancouver Island, and the Gulf Islands. I can just pick out my home island of Salt Spring—the steep jutting peak of Mount Maxwell. My house is six kilometres away from there. I make my last tape-recorder entry, which says: "Low cloud, south-west wind and faint drizzle. Might not be raining at all on Salt Spring."

I stand beside my motorcycle for ten minutes or so looking towards home. There is a lightening sky to the west, a glimmer of sun.

EPILOGUE

"CAN'T REPEAT THE PAST?" HE CRIED INCREDULOUSLY.
"WHY OF COURSE YOU CAN."
—F. SCOTT FITZGERALD, *The Great Gatsby*

AS I RODE THE EDGE OF AMERICA, the irreversible change underway along the United States' boundaries was made stark and
clear. The borders are regressing to a state of armed and suspicious vigilance.

Once upon a time, Americans saw their borders as barriers
against both Catholic mestizo Mexicans and counter-revolutionary British North Americans. Later, as Mexico settled
down and Canada confederated itself, the U.S. borders became
open and charitable, guarded in the north only by Winston
Churchill's "neighbourly respect and honourable obligations,"
and in the south by a river and a line in the sand that anyone
could cross more or less at will.

September 11, 2001, changed that irrevocably, and the past
became the future.

The Mexican borderlands, always uneasy and often violent, is a zone of danger and savagery once again. If illegal
migrants and drugs can flood over the border, a few terrorists would have no difficulty trickling across. The United
States will enlarge its new Iron Curtain and will maintain

its nervous watchfulness, as Mexico struggles to avoid collapse into a failed narco-state. Even supposed successes in President Calderón's war on the drug cartels spin their malevolent consequences. For example, the December 2009 killing by navy and army special forces of Arturo Beltrán Leyva, head of the eponymous cartel and one of the most-wanted men in Mexico, will not discourage or diminish the cartels. More likely, his death will add to the country's chaotic violence, as successors fight to replace him and competing cartels move in to grab his operations.

The Canadian border, innocuous and undefended, and therefore unique in the world for 130 years, was "the field where the battle did not happen, / where the unknown soldier did not die." Now the United States continues to turn the border into a monitored and guarded line across the continent. The Bush administration began this process, but nothing has changed under Obama. The new president is a pragmatic American to his core, and he has already made it clear that the United States, like any great power, has enduring interests but not necessarily abiding friends, even if they are its neighbours. "There can be no greater error than to expect or calculate upon real favors from nation to nation," said George Washington. Homeland Security secretary Janet Napolitano will intensify the American policy of treating the Mexican and Canadian borders as if they were the same.

In theory, there are alternatives. The United States could make policy to reflect the fact that Canada and Mexico are very different countries and cultures. For example, it's completely feasible for the United States to enter into a joint security arrangement with Canada, which has stability, internal control and an infrastructure comparable to that of the U.S., and is equal to the task of securing its own borders. Canada would find it difficult to raise its defences to the level the United States desires, but it could be done. Canadians would resent further American intrusion into their lives and government. However, even such a new and unwelcome level of integration between the two countries would be preferable to the slow, methodical strangulation of the U.S.-Canadian border.

The U.S. administration will not take this course of action towards Canada for two reasons: the administration fears a backlash from American Hispanics who see harshness towards Mexico and leniency with Canada as a racist distinction; and Homeland Security actually believes that Canada is a clear and present security threat that no degree of co-operation between the two countries can reduce. The escalation of the war in Afghanistan and its increasing extension into Pakistan may increase the chances of Islamist retaliation in the American homeland. If handfuls of the United States' own Muslims are plotting to carry out attacks on U.S. soil, or contriving to fight with al Qaeda–inspired groups against American soldiers abroad, many Americans believe they cannot trust Canada to uncover the plots inevitably conceived there.

The old saying, popular amongst terrorists of any kind, is that security forces have to be lucky every time, whereas terrorists have to be lucky only once. The odds are that, sooner or later, Islamist terrorists will get lucky and will pull off another mass-casualty attack in the United States. Even if the attackers do not enter the U.S. from the north, the 9/11 myth may well bring Canada under suspicion. If successful terrorists do enter the United States from Canada, Homeland Security will shut down the northern border. In the long run, the boundary will become as much of a fortified wall as the vast distances, dense forest and wild mountains will allow.

I rode the borders to see what they looked like, and for the adventure of it, and to cast out sorrow for my lost friends. I got what I wanted—more or less.

Over and over again along the U.S.-Mexican border, I met the armed men who sometimes held their guns on me, and I answered their questions and stood by while they searched my bags. At the end of scores of dirt roads and trails, I came down by the River, or looked over the straggly wire of the old border barrier, or bumped up against the new, yet already squalid, fence. I rode through a borderlands contaminated by murder, fear, greed and desperation.

In the north, I had the sense of the still-open and mostly unprotected Canadian border as a relic of a peaceful time that has ended. My ride along the northern boundary seemed to me in part an elegiac farewell to innocence. The United States is inserting into the beautiful space and tranquility of the northern borderlands its ever-stricter regulations, its arsenal of virtual surveillance and its augmented Border Patrol. Soon, it will be impossible to blithely dance back and forth across even the remote Saskatchewan–North Dakota prairie line. The Oscars will sense the vibrations of your happy jig, or the drones and cameras will watch your gleeful subversion. The witless fuckers with the bullhorns will be everywhere.

As I sat my thumper through long days in the borderlands, my friends—Will Walker, Mike Fitz-James and Chris Burke—were always in my mind. It had been hard to lose them so suddenly and terribly, and within so short a time. They were still young. They left behind nine children. And their deaths made those terrible, dark holes that appear when the universe of each human being ends.

Time helps, of course, although it's not the healer of all things it's supposed to be. Time is only a crude reconciler that makes losses come to seem a part of normal life. I had thought that being in motion might also help, and it did. The movement of my all-day, every-day passages to the west was a good thing. My rides had their mundane purpose of gathering information and impressions for a book, but they also gave me what I most needed: the assurance that life goes on; that, for now, my own life goes on.

AFTERWORD

NOT MUCH HAS CHANGED along the United States' borders since the hardcover edition of *Borderlands* was published in May 2010, but some things have.

In spite of objections from just about everybody along the Rio Grande—landowners, politicians, environmentalists—the 115-mile-long Texas portions of the Mexican border fence have been completed. Sometimes, the steel barrier hugs the bank of the river. Often, however, the stream's hairpin bends and lazy meanders have forced the fence into a straighter line inland several hundred yards, sometimes close to a mile. The fence isolates little pieces of the United States in a bizarre security no-man's land. For example, many farmers now have fields on both sides of the barrier, and the entire Fort Brown Memorial Golf Course in Brownsville is sandwiched between the fence and the river. As with the other sections of fencing along the entire southern border, the Texas wall is intermittent; it has ends and gaps. Its average cost (where it's pedestrian-proof) is $6.5 million a mile.

The Mexican drug wars are worse than ever. Their violence is savage and unrelenting, and they have spread throughout the northern border states and along a good part of Mexico's coasts. In 2010, there were more than eleven thousand confirmed drug-related murders, more than double the number in 2008. Today, I would not dare attempt some of the roads I travelled on my border research rides. They were hazardous enough then; they would be homicidal now. Ciudad Juárez is now one of the most dangerous cities in the world. It has lost almost 20 per cent of its population over the last four years—a majority of whom are men fleeing violence or migrating for work from the increasingly impoverished city.

President Calderón's war on the drug cartels is now almost five years old. It has failed to destroy them—it's impossible for the government's overstretched forces to do so. There have been some successes: major leaders killed or captured and their organizations effectively dismantled; cartel gunmen mowed down in vicious firefights; some progress in establishing a federal police force less corrupt than its predecessors. But overall, the government's campaign has made things worse in Mexico. Every police or military assault on the cartels and its leaders further destabilizes relations among the organizations. They fight each other for control of drug routes and territory with the same barbarism with which they resist the government. It could be that Calderón's best bet now is to back off from his war and allow the cartels to re-establish a balance of power. If he wants to get re-elected in the 2012 presidential election, he probably has no other option. If the cartels can carry on with business as usual rather than be forced to struggle for turf, or survival, the current levels of violence—which would be unendurable for any state—will decline. It's an undeniable victory for the bad guys.

The relationships among the cartels remain fluid and will no doubt have changed again by the time this paperback edition is published. What's certain is that there is no immediate prospect of a cessation of hostilities. And in fact, the cartels have escalated their violence in various ways: through augmented brutality (more civilian killings, for example, and more torture and beheadings); by killing

American citizens in Mexico and in the United States; by moving into new areas of operations such as migrant smuggling, oil theft, extortion and contract enforcement; by expanding their turf into other countries such as El Salvador, Guatemala, Belize and Honduras; and through the use of new weapons such as improvised explosive devices.

Arizona continues to be the hot spot for illegal immigration and to make draconian legislative attempts to deal with it. In 2010, the state enacted a law requiring police to check the immigration status of anyone they stopped whom they suspected might be an illegal migrant. A lower court judge suspended the main provisions of this legislation, Arizona appealed, and the case remains in the courts. The federal government is, in effect, suing Arizona for trespassing on its area of jurisdiction, which includes immigration. In February 2011, Jan Brewer, the governor of Arizona, announced that she would raise funds to counter-sue the federal government for failing to enforce immigration laws. The state will argue that it is being "invaded" by illegal immigrants from Mexico, and that the federal government has failed in its obligation to stop them.

Arizona has also proposed laws to eliminate "anchor babies" (the American-born children of illegals) by refusing them U.S. citizenship at birth; to prohibit migrants from driving; to limit their access to public colleges and other benefits; and to impose more severe punishment on employers who hire illegal workers. Other states have followed suit with similar legislation, much of which, like Arizona's, is tied up in the courts. Hispanic organizations, their influence expanding as the Hispanic voter base grows, are pushing back, but their power is still limited. In December 2010, a bill that sought to legalize the status of hundreds of thousands of illegal migrant college students was barely passed by the House but defeated in the Senate. Some of Arizona's punitive legislation has been softened under the influence of business groups, usually Republican in their political orientation, who, nevertheless, see these laws as bad for business.

The Minuteman Civil Defense Corps formally disbanded in March 2010, although the notice was surrounded by the organization's usual grandiloquent ambiguity and muddle-headedness. "The mental attitude of many Americans is turning meaner," said the group's president, Carmen Mercer. "You see aggression surfacing even at the Tea Party marches. We just did not want to deal with the liability anymore."

Mercer's profession of fear came only two weeks after she herself had made a particularly aggressive posting on the Minuteman website: "We return to the border locked, loaded and ready to stop each and every individual we encounter along the frontier that is now more dangerous than the frontier of Afghanistan. This operation will not be for the faint of heart." In light of this rhetoric, Mercer's announcement of the dissolution of the Corps was a surprise to most of the group's members. And the situation was confused further by her subsequent statement that, even if the national organization of the Minutemen was dissolved, local chapters could continue to patrol the border. But they should avoid the "lock and load" approach. Instead, said Mercer, they should follow the same rules of engagement as before: report suspicious border activity to law enforcement and avoid physical confrontation with illegal migrants.

As usual, the United States–Canada border is quiet in comparison with the rowdy and violent southern line. At times, Canada seems completely forgotten in the frenzy of news about the drug cartels, the border fence and the illegals. But there is always a sense of suspicion and foreboding in the United States about its northern boundary, with its opportunities for terrorism, which sometimes breaks out into public anxiety. In February 2011, for example, the U.S. Government Accountability Office (GAO) published a report which said that the threat of terrorism from Canada was much higher than from Mexico because most of the Canadian border remains unprotected. Out of 4,000 miles (excluding 1,500 miles between Alaska and Canada), only thirty-two miles have the necessary level of Border Patrol security to intercept and arrest malefactors, says the GAO. Echoing so many other American politicians, officials and commentators, the chairwoman of the hearings into the report said, "The northern border is essentially wide open."

In February 2011, President Obama and Prime Minister Stephen Harper met in Washington and made their "Beyond the Border" declaration on North American perimeter security and economic integration. Like all such announcements, it is made up of vague bromides, and is really an agreement to make a future agreement. Nevertheless, the declaration has potential for "un-thickening" the U.S.–Canada border, at least for trade, through, for example, integrated cargo and customs regulations and expanded "trusted shipper" procedures.

As for perimeter security, which in the U.S. view boils down to keeping out terrorists, the declaration refers only to increased cooperation in "air, land and maritime domains, as well as space and cyberspace." What this might mean in practice is anyone's guess, but many Canadians will see it as more of the same intrusion into their country's sovereignty through the large-scale exchange of detailed personal information on travellers, or an increased U.S. military presence around Canada's coasts—more American warships in the Northwest Passage, for example. And, in a kind of paranoid parallel, there is no shortage of Americans who view any such bilateral agreement with Canada, or with Mexico, as another cunning, veiled act in the conspiracy to create a North American political union which will destroy the independence of the United States.

All such putative agreements must overcome Americans' indifference to Canada (and paranoia about their own government's hidden agenda) and Canadians' fears for their fragile sovereignty. A similar initiative, the Security and Prosperity Partnership (which included Mexico), was brought out in 2005 with the same self-indulgent enthusiasm by then-leaders George W. Bush, Paul Martin and Vicente Fox. It died a quiet death when its three signatories left office. However, earlier comprehensive trade agreements did come to pass—the Free Trade Agreement between the United States and Canada in 1988, and the North American Free Trade Agreement, which included Mexico, in 1994. The "Beyond the Border" initiative may result in a freer flow of trade, and a level of security cooperation between the United States and Canada that's acceptable to most of each country's citizens. But it's just as possible that this agreement, too, will end up in limbo.

Derek Lundy
Salt Spring Island, B.C.
April 2011

ACKNOWLEDGEMENTS

This book would have been much diminished without the help of Jane Hickie on Salt Spring Island and in Austin, Texas. Her contacts and suggestions were invaluable. Many thanks also to Catherine Oborne, Tony McEwan and Liz Anderson on Salt Spring and to Barbara Chapman in Austin.

For their warm hospitality and kindness, I'm most grateful to Cleve and Rosemary Breedlove in Los Fresnos, Texas, Linda Lynch and Paul Salopek in Columbus, New Mexico, Steve Baker in Stanstead, Quebec, Mary Lundy in St. Catharines, Ontario, and Greg Mauro and Debby Cohen in Winnipeg.

For taking the time to talk to me, I'm indebted to Jesse Breedlove, Bob Armstrong, Linda Aaker, Billy Leo, Diana Natalicio, Gary Williams, Richard Dean, Ted White, Cecile Lumer, Oscar Martínez, Robert Williams and Ray Ibarra. My thanks also to Martha Smiley, Elizabeth Ann Gates, Glen Roney, Beto López, Harry Poster, Gord Gingles and Nose Ozykowski.

Mick Lynch and Jon Schwartz took me into Juárez, showed me a good time and brought me back alive; Jonathan Clark of the *Sierra Vista Herald/Bisbee Daily Review* and Susan Carroll of the *Arizona Republic* gave me crucial information; Susan Weisgram bought dinner and guided me around Bisbee; Charles Bowden was gracious and welcoming in Tucson when

I had Montezuma's revenge and was a mite grumpy; Gordie Douglas took me for a boat ride close to the border on Lake Memphremagog; Chaz Kader gave me time in Saint Regis/Akwesasne and corresponded with me later ("She:kon" from the Salish Sea); many members of the Minuteman Civil Defense Corps were hospitable and helpful in Arizona; Maine Minuteman Joseph Martin talked to me honestly and openly in Rumford; Brian Maracle taught me some Mohawk in Ohsweken on the Six Nations reserve; and John Murray was the old and good friend he's always been. My warmest thanks to them all.

I'm grateful to various members of the Canada Border Services Agency and, in the United States, to the many officers of Customs and Border Protection, the Border Patrol, BORTAC, sheriffs' departments, and State Police and Trooper detachments along the borders who talked to me and gave me information, or who didn't talk but gave me good book material nevertheless, or who looked out for my safety; and in particular I thank those who could have, but didn't, shoot.

My thanks to Nick Brune, Christine Mauro and Eric Wredenhagen who read the manuscript and made wise and helpful suggestions.

I am also grateful to the Canada Council for the Arts and the British Columbia Arts Council for their generous financial assistance during the writing of this book.

I'm indebted to all the people at Knopf and Vintage Canada who brought *Borderlands* to life. As always, my warmest thanks to Diane Martin for her editorial insights, intelligence and skill; to Jane McWhinney for her concise and measured copy-editing; to Amanda Betts and Marion Garner for their expertise and enthusiasm in producing the Vintage edition; to Deirdre Molina, Michelle MacAleese and Carla Kean for cracking the velvet whip of organization and production; and to Jennifer Lum for a dynamic, utterly fitting jacket design.

My thanks to Monica Pacheco at the Anne McDermid Agency, and my sincerest gratitude to Anne McDermid, who has provided unstinting support and encouragement, and has worked so hard on my behalf through these hard times for writers and publishers.

Finally, to my father-in-law, Arthur Mauro, my wife, Christine Mauro, and my daughter, Sarah Lundy, this is one more for you too.

BIBLIOGRAPHY

Bowden, Charles. *Down by the River: Drugs, Money, Murder, and Family*. New York: Simon & Schuster, 2002.

Crosthwaite, Luis Humberto, John William Byrd and Bobby Byrd, eds. *Puro Border: Dispatches, Snapshots & Graffiti from La Frontera*. El Paso: Cinco Puntos Press, 2002.

de Tocqueville, Alexis. *Democracy in America*. New York: Vintage, 1945.

Drache, Daniel. *Borders Matter: Homeland Security and the Search for North America*. Halifax: Fernwood Publishing, 2004.

Gibbins, Roger. *Canada as a Borderlands Society*. Orono: University of Maine, Canadian-American Center, 1989.

Gwyn, Richard. *The 49th Paradox: Canada in North America*. Toronto: Totem Books, 1986.

Lipset, Seymour Martin. *Continental Divide: The Values and Institutions of the United States and Canada*. New York: Routledge, 1990.

Martínez, Oscar J. *Troublesome Border*. Tucson: University of Arizona Press, 1988.

McKinsey, Laura, and Victor Konrad. *Borderlands Reflections: The United States and Canada*. Orono: University of Maine, Canadian-American Center, 1989.

Pastor, Robert A., and Jorge G. Castañeda. *Limits to Friendship: The United States and Mexico*. New York: Vintage, 1989.

Ruiz, Ramón Eduardo. *On the Rim of Mexico: Encounters of the Rich and Poor.* Boulder: Westview Press, 1998.

Urrea, Luis Alberto. *The Devil's Highway: A True Story.* New York: Little, Brown and Company, 2004.

Vázquez, Josefina Zoraida, and Lorenzo Meyer. *The United States and Mexico.* Chicago: University of Chicago Press, 1985.

Weisman, Alan, and Jay Dusard. *La Frontera: The United States Border With Mexico.* Tucson: University of Arizona Press, 1986.

PERMISSIONS

The author has made every effort to locate and contact all the holders of copyright to material reproduced in this book, and expresses grateful acknowledgement for permission to reprint excerpts from the following previously material:

Alurista, "A Child to be Born" in *Return: Poems Collected and New*, Bilingual Review Press, Ypsilanti, Michigan: 1982.

Anderson, Patrick, "Poem on Canada" from *Return to Canada*, McClelland & Stewart, Toronto: 1986.

Anzaldua, Gloria, from *Borderlands / La Frontera: The New Mestiza*, Spinsters / Aunt Lute, San Francisco: 1987. Copyright 1987, 1999, 2007 by Gloria Anzaldúa. Reprinted by permission of Aunt Lute Books. www.auntlute.com

Birney, Earle, "Can. Lit.," from *The Collected Poems of Earle Birney*, vol. 1, McClelland & Stewart, Toronto: 1975. Reprinted by permission of Madam Justice Wailan Low, literary executor for Earle Birney.

Frost, Robert, "Mending Wall," in *Robert Frost's Poems*, Washington Square Press, New York: 1964.

Derek Lundy is the bestselling author of *Godforsaken Sea: Racing The World's Most Dangerous Waters*, *The Way of a Ship: A Square-Rigger Voyage in the Last Days of Sail*, and *The Bloody Red Hand: A Journey Through Truth, Myth and Terror in Northern Ireland*. He lives and rides on Salt Spring Island, B.C.